W9-ATE-617

OUT OF WORK

OTHER INDEPENDENT INSTITUTE BOOKS

Out of Work

Unemployment and Government in Twentieth-Century America

Updated Edition

Richard K. Vedder and Lowell E. Gallaway

FOREWORD BY MARTIN BRONFENBRENNER

An Independent Institute Book

NEW YORK UNIVERSITY PRESS

New York and London

NEW YORK UNIVERSITY PRESS
New York and London

Library of Congress Cataloging-in-Publication Data
Vedder, Richard K.
Out of work : unemployment and government in twentieth-century
America / Richard K. Vedder and Lowell E. Gallaway ; with a foreword
by Martin Bronfenbrenner. — Updated ed.
p.   cm.
"An Independent Institute book."
Includes bibliographical references and index.
ISBN 0-8147-8792-4 (alk. paper)
1. Unemployment—United States—History—20th century.
2. Employment (Economic theory)   3. United States—Economic
conditions.   I. Gallaway, Lowell E. (Lowell Eugene), 1930–   .
II. Title.
HD7096.U5V43   1997
331.13'7973'0904—dc21   97-12516
                                    CIP

New York University Press books are printed on acid-free paper,
and their binding materials are chosen for strength and durability.

Manufactured in the United States of America

10   9   8   7   6   5   4   3   2   1

The **INDEPENDENT INSTITUTE**

The Independent Institute is a non-profit, non-partisan, scholarly research and educational organization that sponsors comprehensive studies on the political economy of critical social and economic problems.

The politicization of decision making in society has largely confined public debate to the narrow reconsideration of existing policies. Given the prevailing influence of partisan interests, little social innovation has occurred. In order to understand both the nature of and possible solutions to major public issues, the Independent Institute's program adheres to the highest standards of independent inquiry and is pursued regardless of prevailing political or social biases and conventions. The resulting studies are widely distributed as books and other publications, and publicly debated through numerous conference and media programs.

Through this uncommon independence, depth, and clarity, the Independent Institute pushes at the frontiers of our knowledge, redefines the debate over public issues, and fosters new and effective directions for government reform.

Contents

Foreword

Unemployment has been a principal preoccupation of critical economists, policymakers, and ordinary citizens in twentieth-century America. This volume combines economic theory and economic history to provide some provocative insights into how a "modern" approach to unemployment evolved, and why, in the authors' judgment, it ultimately failed.

The authors raise important issues: What has determined the volume of unemployment in America? Can the "macro" issues of full employment and output determination be explained in terms of a "micro" analysis of leading markets, particularly that for labor? Have revolutionary twentieth-century changes in economic thinking regarding unemployment policies served to befriend or harm workers and business interests? Have good intentions been overcome by unintended adverse consequences of policy actions?

In tackling these questions, this book uses empirical analysis and theoretical insight that are both instructive and illuminating. Vedder and Gallaway are not unique in suggesting that government unemployment policies have ultimately proven unsuccessful, but their blend of historical and theoretical insights makes the case in a more compelling and comprehensive fashion than other explorations into the unemployment problem. Combining the microeconomic theory of labor markets with some simple but powerful statistical analysis of twentieth-century American experience, they present a strong argument for the position that market adjustments explain cycles in employment activity and have outperformed nonmarket interventions as tools for achieving economic stability.

To be sure, the principal theses of Professors Vedder and Gallaway will doubtless impress some readers as distillations from "quaint and curious volumes of forgotten lore." To avoid or mitigate such reactions is, as I see it, the function of these introductory notes.

Our authors' principal, and admittedly heterodox theses are only two in number, the second thesis being a corollary of the first:

Their first thesis is a matter of theoretical economics. Unemployment is related directly to real-wage rates (adjusted over time for the "quality" and productivity of the labor involved). The British neoclassical economist Edwin Cannan put the point in one sentence in mid-Depression 1932: "General unemployment appears when asking too much is a general phenomenon."[1]

Vedder and Gallaway's second thesis is a matter of American economic history. They apply their first thesis to the American record in the twentieth century, claiming that the average or "natural" rate of unemployment[2] in the United States has in the last generation been rising, by reason of such governmental policies as minimum wages, social security, unemployment relief, affirmative action, and the encouragement of trade-union collective bargaining.

As recently as the first third of the present century, the first of the Vedder-Gallaway theses would not have deserved the title of "thesis." Rather, it was regarded by orthodox economists as a truism, too obvious to warrant either quantitative or historical investigation. Mere restatement sufficed, despite a significant volume of dissent from liberals, socialists, and underconsumptionists led by the economist John A. Hobson, the industrialist Henry Ford, and (as Vedder and Gallaway delight in reminding us) the public figure and eventual President Herbert Hoover.[3]

Now, of course, the shoe is on the other foot, and the Vedder-Gallaway sort of investigation remains under a cloud. It is no longer the truism it once was; instead, it has come to be regarded as something of a heresy. J. B. Say's complacent "economic law" about "aggregate supply being, or creating, its own demand" is largely replaced by "Keynes's Law"[4] about "aggregate demand creating its own supply" in the presence of significant unemployment. If aggregate demand is all that matters (in the presence of significant unemployment), concern with wages as costs of production and resistance to upward pressure on either money or real wages are wrong a priori.

Out of Work comprises fifteen chapters. The first three chapters, with the assistance of a technical appendix that contains a formal model of a macroeconomy, derive, compare, and examine direct econometric relations between measured unemployment rates (dependent variables) and real-wage levels adjusted for productivity changes and sometimes lagged over time (independent variables). For the quantitative economist as for the statistician, these constitute the case for the Vedder-Gallaway thesis. The last three chapters are the moral of the tale, which is that public policy has been systematically wrong-headed since approximately 1930, and that the role of market forces in labor relations should be restored to approximately its pre-1930 importance. The intervening nine chapters deal in chronological order with particular periods and incidents in twentieth-century American economic history, from the so-called "Golden Age" of the century's first generation (1900–30) through the so-called "Reagan Revolution" of the 1980s to the present. To the noneconomist, especially if brought up in the liberal or Keynesian environment of 1930–70, these are at once the most intelligible and the most challenging portions of the book as a whole.

Collectively, the contents of this book seem bound to inspire for many, if not most, readers a combination of surprises and questions. In my own case, for instance, my curiosity was continually piqued by such issues as:

- The underlying rationale for the change in adjusted real wage rates that drive the Vedder and Gallaway analysis.
- The role of public fiscal policies, public monetary policies, and public international-economic policies (not aimed primarily at labor-market developments) in influencing the behavior of the Vedder-Gallaway model.
- The importance of the embryonic or aborted "planned economy" of World War I as perhaps a dress rehearsal for the New Deal controls fifteen years later—with some of the same controllers not only involved, but elevated to higher positions with more authority.
- The impact of the sharp disinflation of 1920–22—the last "business cycle" of the nineteenth-century type—which aroused so much "compassionate" reflationary advocacy, so much wage-maintenance sentiment, and so many gloomy forecasts for the 1920s as it apparently did.
- How the Vedder-Gallaway conclusions fit with the argument offered by many Keynesians that if downward wage and price flexibility had continued after 1932, it would have led to "hyperdeflation"—an accelerated version of the 1865–96 deflation—rather than to economic recovery.
- The significance of the Vedder-Gallaway model for the role of monetarism in economic thinking.
- Their handling of the World War II (1940–46) era, when scarcities and black markets obscured the meaning of published consumer prices and real wages, and the composition of the national output changed in ways that cast doubt on the comparability of productivity estimates for those years with similar data for earlier and later periods. The easy and natural escape from these difficulties for many statistical analyses has been to omit some or all of these war years from their time-series regressions and correlations. Vedder and Gallaway, however, are bold enough to adjust them and include the war years, which indeed seem to fit quite well.

- The relationship between the Vedder-Gallaway model and what is called the "rational expectations" or the "new classical" approach to macroeconomic theory, a topic they confront directly in the technical appendix to the book.
- Why "Black Monday" (October 19, 1987), the Wall Street mini-crash, had few, if any, perceptible employment effects, contrary to the expectations of many contemporary "doomsters."
- How well the conclusion will stand the test of time. Will the Vedder-Gallaway estimating equations be accurate in future years? By the turn of the century we can anticipate an answer to that question.

In conclusion: Not only is this investigation completely "legitimate" on both economic and statistical fronts, but it is well worth repeating, possibly in modified form, for other market economies. Such repetition would test any hypothesis of American exceptionalism. At the same time, as already noted, another decade or two will test the robustness and stability of the authors' daring estimating equation for unemployment as a function of real-wage rates current and lagged, adjusted for productivity changes but independent of aggregate demand considerations.

In short, this book is both fascinating and insightful, and should be read by all who have an interest in the issue of unemployment.

MARTIN BRONFENBRENNER
Kenan Professor of Economics (Emeritus)
Duke University

NOTES

1. Edwin Cannan, "The Demand for Labour," *Economic Journal* 42 (1932): 367.

2. The meaning of this term is vague, perhaps necessarily so. I envisage it as a quasi-equilibrium rate of unemployment at which excess supply of labor in some trades or some regions is roughly "balanced" by excess demand for labor in other trades or regions—or would be so balanced if "job vacancy" statistics were fuller and more meaningful than they have yet become.

3. True confession: As a high-school and university student in metropolitan St. Louis (1928–34), I numbered myself among those dissidents who regarded wages as a source of purchasing power rather than a cost of production.

4. Lord Keynes himself neither stated nor supported "Keynes's Law." Rather, the "law" was devised by others as an implication of Keynes's underconsumptionist and oversaving views carried to their logical extreme.

Preface to the Updated Edition

In the foreword to the first edition of *Out of Work,* Martin Bronfenbrenner noted that "another decade or two will test the robustness and stability of the authors' daring estimating equation for unemployment as a function of real-wage rates." Although less than a decade has passed since that was written, we do believe that the experience of the 1990s strengthens the thesis of this book, namely that employers respond to the cost of labor in making their employment decisions, and that governmental policies have often inadvertently raised both these costs and unemployment. So in this new edition we add an afterword (chapter 16) that chronicles the experiences of the 1990s thus far. We find that the adjusted real wage explains unemployment trends in the last decade of the century as well as it did in the first nine.

We have also added a second appendix that deals with some of the issues raised either publicly or privately by colleagues in the economics profession. For researchers wishing to replicate our findings, we include some quarterly data for recent decades. We perform a number of statistical tests to deal with esoteric (to some readers) issues such as Granger causality, model specification, and heteroskedasticity. In doing this, we move somewhat away from the low-tech approach adopted in the first edition in order to increase confidence among professional economists in the power and validity of the basic theoretical framework. At the same time, we confine this material to the appendix so that the interested lay reader need not be burdened by excessive technical analysis. In the first edition, in two places we spoke briefly of geographic variations in unemployment; subsequently, we have done far more extensive work on this topic and present some of our findings here.

A plethora of studies have been produced since the first edition that relate to issues raised in this book. Although some of this research represents worthy scholarship, in our estimation nothing in it fundamentally challenges the approach used here in any convincing fashion, so we refrained from attempting to enumerate or comment comprehensively on the recent literature, although we do mention some of that work in the new material.

We thank the many persons who graciously commented favorably on the first edition and who have used the book in classrooms and elsewhere. We express our gratitude to New York University Press for its support in bringing out this new edition. Our colleagues Chulho Jung and Tony Caporale graciously assisted us on a number of technical and other issues, and their help is appreciated. Again, we wish to thank David Theroux of the Independent Institute for his entrepreneurial initiative and persistence, which led both to the initial publication of this book and to this subsequent revision.

RICHARD K. VEDDER
LOWELL E. GALLAWAY

Preface to the First Edition

Somewhere about one-third of the way through the twentieth century, the world abandoned an approach to business fluctuations and unemployment that had previously governed human behavior. In the world of economic ideas, the halfheartedly-believed theory that excessive wages were the root cause of unemployment was overthrown. The Keynesian Revolution led the economics profession down an unproductive, destructive path for decades. In our judgment, even today the corrosive impact of the intellectual ferment of the 1930s prevents most students of economic ideas from learning some simple but very powerful verities about the way things work. While the world has increasingly appreciated the power of markets in allocating goods and services, it has failed to grasp that the same market forces work equally well in providing jobs for those seeking them.

The Keynesian Revolution's influence, however, was not simply confined to misguiding a few academics. It provided the intellectual cornerstone for an alteration of the role of the state in modern society. It led to profound public-policy changes. It unleashed a world of unrelenting inflation, continuing budget deficits, and increased governmental intervention in previously private decisions involving resource allocation and income distribution. It inflamed a politics of envy and ultimately slowed the great economic engine that had propelled the American economy to becoming the mightiest in the world.

This book is about these intellectual and policy shifts as they relate to a great concern of citizens of the twentieth century, namely, unemployment. First and foremost, this book is a history of changing unemployment patterns in the United States, written from a labor-market perspective. Second, it is a critique of public-policy developments that have shaped that labor market and impacted on unemployment. It develops the thesis that the state has increased, not decreased, the magnitude of unemployment in this country, that macroeconomic manipulations of a monetary and fiscal nature have ultimately proved unsuccessful, and that the invisible hand of market forces has done a reasonably good job of providing jobs and incomes for Americans.

The research that led to this book began well over a decade ago. We wrote a little unpublished paper suggesting that unemployment variations in the United States could be nicely explained by using a neoclassical model stressing money wages, prices, and productivity. While we were given some early encouragement (most memorably by Martin Bronfenbrenner), the standard academic journals did not seem interested in our simple (too simple, in their opinion) yet powerful exposition of changing unemployment patterns over a large sweep of contemporary history. We presented the paper to various university audiences, at the Duke–North Carolina–NC State Research Triangle Economic History Workshop, Indiana University, the University of Chicago, and the University of Illinois, among others. The research was furthered by stints by both authors on the staff of the Joint Economic Committee of Congress, where, with the support of Bruce Bartlett and the late Charles Bradford (and indirectly Congressman Clarence Brown and Senator Roger Jepsen) we published (in late 1982) a paper on the "Natural Rate of Unemployment" that incorporated our unemployment model.

In 1983, while spending a delightful and highly productive summer in Palo Alto sponsored by the Institute for Humane Studies and funded by the Liberty Fund, we shared our findings with Murray Rothbard, who encouraged us to write a long paper for the inaugural issue of the *Review of Austrian Economics* (1987). That formed the nucleus of this book. Another paper (which is the basis for chapter 6), given in 1984 to what is now the Cliometrics Society, furthered our enthusiasm for the project; Donald McCloskey, then editing the *Journal of Economic History*, was particularly enthusiastic and supportive.

We then wrote a preliminary version of this work, but the pressure of other projects together with other difficulties delayed its publication. In the past year, however, we have returned to the project. The wage framework that is the centerpiece of this volume was used in writing a paper on the post–World War II transition to peace, which Murray Rothbard and Walter Block agreed to publish in the *Review of Austrian Economics*; Robert Higgs of Seattle University liked that paper, spurring us on further. We began in earnest a thorough revision of our earlier effort. David Theroux, president of the Independent Institute, helped enormously by offering to publish the manuscript.

As Roger Garrison of Auburn University pointed out in an extremely detailed and useful review of the manuscript, this book might be perceived as old-fashioned in many ways. Some will certainly say it is not on the cutting edge of modern economic theory: that the basic theory was espoused decades ago by Austrian economists such as Ludwig von Mises and English classical-neoclassical economists such as A. C. Pigou. For every 1990-era reference on efficiency wages, hysteresis, or real business cycles, there are probably two or three references to what most contemporary economists would consider obscure older works by such unknowns (to them) as W. H. Hutt, Benjamin Anderson, Murray Rothbard, Willford King, or Edwin Cannan.

The statistical analysis primarily uses ordinary least squares regression techniques, which modern econometricians regard as hopelessly primitive. There is no computable general equilibrium (CGE) model here, nor will one find Kalman filters or other such econometric nuances. Yet for other readers, including noneconomists and Austrian economists, there is probably a bit too much empirical emphasis and statistical testing. This is a distinctly low-tech manuscript that may well be scorned both by the devotees of high-tech empiricism, and by the philosophes and praxeologists who prefer a no-tech methodology. Yet we use the approach because it powerfully explains the way the world works in twentieth-century America and is relatively simple to understand, a quality that a majority of economists view with disdain but most Americans still applaud. Further, we feel that, properly interpreted, the arguments presented here are distinctly mainstream in nature and, in fact, represent a pushing back of the frontiers of economic knowledge by providing a broad-based explanation of how business cycles are generated in the United States.

We are indebted to a bevy of persons, including all those cited above. Several students, most recently Emily Stroud and Sam Chamberlin of Ohio University's Economics Department and David Broscious of its Contemporary History Institute, helped provide historical documentation. Judith Daso's staff in the government documents room of the Vernon Alden Library at Ohio University was always helpful; we were also assisted by staff at the Stanford University Library and the Library of Congress. John Gaddis has striven to provide a congenial working environment in the Contemporary History Institute. A variety of colleagues and graduate students have offered insight and suggestions over the years. At Ohio University, we have benefited from the comments of three Economics Department colleagues, David Klingaman, Douglas Adie, and the late John Peterson. Equally useful has been our Contemporary History Institute colleague (and distinguished Truman-era historian) Alonzo Hamby. Gene Smiley of Marquette University and Richard Timberlake of the University of Georgia have made insightful suggestions, as have Charles Baird of California State University at Hayward and Terry Anderson of Montana State University.

Other encouragement has come from Fred Glahe of the University of Colorado, Lawrence Kudlow of Bear Stearns, Joint Economic Committee economist Chris Frenze, and Steve Hanke of Johns Hopkins University.

Becky Huff and Angie Cook of the Economics Department at Ohio University provided invaluable secretarial help, as did Hallie Willard of the Contemporary History Institute. The Earhart Foundation indirectly helped with some needed financial assistance. Last, but never least, the project would never have reached fruition without the support of our wives, Karen Vedder and Gladys Gallaway.

We conclude this introduction on a sad note. The person who did the most to publicize our views on the labor market to a broader audience was the late Warren Brookes. Warren was a businessman who turned to journalism in midlife, writing an extraordinarily perceptive column dealing primarily with economic matters. He did as much to further the "supply-side" revolution in the late 1970s and early 1980s as any other person, and more recently he uncovered evidence that devastatingly exposed the true economic costs of new environmental laws and regulations. His untimely death has robbed the world of a great journalist, a superb economist, and, personally, a wonderful friend. We dedicate this book to Warren's memory.

RICHARD K. VEDDER
LOWELL E. GALLAWAY

1

The Unemployment Century

Of the five centuries during which the United States has been settled by Europeans, in only one, the twentieth century, has unemployment been a dominant political and economic issue. Whereas in nineteenth-century America passions erupted over inflation and deflation, tariffs and taxes, slavery, the disposition of public lands, central banking, and the regulation of monopolies, public debate about the "unemployment problem" was sporadic and localized. Indeed, the word "unemployment" did not even exist during most of the century, and when Alfred Marshall wrote the definitive nineteenth-century treatise on economics in 1890, he mentioned the word on but one page.[1]

By contrast, unemployment became the dominant economic issue of the twentieth century both within the academy and in the realm of public policy. During the 1890's, there were but two articles dealing with the issue in serious journals of economics and statistics; by the 1930s, scores of papers were published discussing the measurement, determinants, and effects of unemployment.[2] While in the last presidential election of the nineteenth century, that of 1896, the central economic issue was monetary policy and the gold standard, by 1932 unemployment had moved center stage.

Rising public concern over unemployment led to political pressure to "do something" about the unemployment problem. Even in the first decade of the new century, the unemployment arising out of the panic of 1907 led to cries to eliminate the root cause of financial instability. This, in turn, ultimately led to the Federal Reserve Act, the first major federal involvement in macroeconomic intervention. A few years later, during the 1920–22

1

economic downturn, a presidential commission on unemployment was created.

In the 1930s, a revolutionary activist approach to the unemployment problem was implemented as part of the New Deal. No longer was the government simply content to try to eliminate monetary instability or study the causes of unemployment. New legislation involved the government in labor markets in important new ways. Even before the New Deal, the Davis-Bacon Act got the federal government into the business of setting wage levels. The National Industrial Recovery Act, the Wagner Act, the Fair Labor Standards Act, and legislation creating the Civilian Conservation Corps and the Works Progress Administration are but a few examples of the burst of new federal government initiatives designed to bring about "relief, recovery, and reform"—and lower unemployment—during the New Deal.

The crowning manifestation of government activism was the Employment Act of 1946, which declared the eradication of unemployment a national priority. Public-policy efforts to end unemployment did not end with the Employment Act. Activism peaked in the 1960s and 1970s. Not only was further legislation passed emphasizing the importance of full employment as a national goal (e.g., the Humphrey-Hawkins Act), but numerous new institutions were created as an outgrowth of the War on Poverty (e.g., the Jobs Corps and the Office of Economic Opportunity). To deal with persistent unemployment, a variety of new public-assistance programs, such as Medicaid and food stamps, were created. While the Reagan era of the 1980s brought a stifling of new unemployment initiatives, little was done to dismantle the apparatus of federal programs, and the activist monetary and fiscal policies, that had been created over the previous decades. Just as earlier Republican presidents Eisenhower and Nixon had not attempted to dismantle the New Deal and the Great Society, so President Reagan, by far the most conservative modern American president, did relatively little to undo the "safety net." The legacy of macropolicy expansionism established in the New Deal era was left largely intact.

While interest in the unemployment problem tended to rise and fall with the business cycle, concern was not exclusively directed to cyclically related unemployment. Thus in the prosperous 1920s, there was mounting concern about technological unemployment. Likewise, the concept of what we now term "frictional unemployment" was developed.[3] Similarly, in the equally prosperous 1960s, structural unemployment was a concern—the mismatch of skills of those unemployed with the skills needed for jobs available.

In the 1970s, economists coined a term to refer to the noncyclical forms of unemployment: "the natural rate of unemployment." Much of the modern discussion about employment is related to the natural rate of unemployment and its determinants. Thus the twentieth-century discussion of the unemployment problem is partly a by-product of concerns over economic fluctuations, but also in part of concern over idleness that reflects other noncyclical factors.

Why the rise in interest in unemployment? To a large extent, the issue grew in importance with the urbanization of America. Before the Civil War, most Americans were engaged in farming. Most farmers, in turn, were either self-employed, or slaves who could not become unemployed almost by definition. After 1890 or 1900, cheap or free public land in the West was no longer readily available, and the proportion of Americans working for wages had grown strikingly with industrialization and urbanization. In the nineteenth century, the urbanized proportion of the American population rose from 6 to 40 percent of the total, and it became a majority by 1920.[4] Whereas no more than 5 percent of the labor force was engaged in manufacturing in 1800, by 1920 that proportion approached one-third.

The decline in the relative importance of self-employed individuals increased the vulnerability of workers to unemployment, and as a consequence the incidence of involuntary joblessness rose with the passage of time. Although good annual data are unavailable for almost all of the nineteenth century, it is unlikely that the nation suffered from a double-digit unemployment rate, at least on any sustained basis, until the 1890s. It was the Great Depression of the 1930s, however, with a full decade of double-digit unemployment, that led to the overwhelming preoccupation with the unemployment question.

Unemployment increasingly evoked both intense humanitarian concerns over the plight of individuals and broader concerns over the efficiency and effectiveness of the aggregate economy. Workers who lost their jobs "through no fault of their own" often found themselves with a dramatic drop in income and increasing financial pressures. They suffered dramatically, both economically, and also psychologically, as their self-esteem declined with each day of idleness. Nationally, the loss of 10 or more percent of the most productive resource meant a decline in total output, and a reduction in capital formation needed to augment longer-term increases in material well-being.

Variations in Unemployment over Time

The problem of unemployment was not merely that it was growing dramatically in size over time, but that its magnitude varied significantly over

TABLE 1.1

VARIATIONS IN UNEMPLOYMENT IN THE U.S., BY DECADES, 1900–1990

Decade	% Mean Rate	% Median Rate	Standard Deviation	Unemployment Rate Range	% of Years Less Than 5 Percent
1900–09	4.39	4.15	1.69	1.7–8.0	60
1910–19	5.04	4.85	2.38	1.4–8.5	50
1920–29	4.67	3.75	2.86	1.8–11.7	60
1930–39	18.23	18.10	4.76	8.7–24.9	0
1940–49	5.17	3.90	4.14	1.2–14.6	70
1950–59	4.51	4.35	1.26	2.9–6.8	60
1960–69	4.78	4.85	1.09	3.5–6.7	50
1970–79	6.21	5.85	1.19	4.9–8.5	20
1980–89	7.27	7.15	1.48	5.3–9.7	0

Source: U.S. Department of Commerce, Bureau of the Census, *Historical Statistics of the United States, Colonial Times to 1970* (Washington, D.C.: Government Printing Office, 1975), p. 135; *1990 Economic Report of the President* (Washington, D.C.: Government Printing Office, 1990), p. 330, and authors' calculations. The reported rates are for all civilian members of the labor force.

time and space, often striking individuals unexpectedly before they could prepare for it. Over the first nine decades of the twentieth century, the official annual unemployment rate averaged 6.6 percent, but varied between 1.2 percent and 24.9 percent.[5] Even if one looks at decade averages of unemployment (see table 1.1), the variation in rates is still huge. The 1930s stands out as an extraordinary aberration—mean unemployment rates well over double the next highest unemployment decade (the 1980s). Yet even the 1980s witnessed a mean decade unemployment rate over 50 percent higher than in four other decades (the 1900s, 1920s, 1950s, and 1960s.)

The bad news from table 1.1 is that the lowest mean unemployment rates tended to come early or in the middle of the century: the mean unemployment rate rose steadily by decade after the 1950s, and even the 1950s figure was higher than observed in the very first decade of the century. Whereas unemployment rates of 5 percent or less tended to be the rule rather than the exception in the period 1900–29 and also in the era from 1940 to 1969, by the 1980s unemployment rates that low simply did not occur.

The good news from table 1.1 is that the absolute variation around the mean or median unemployment rate was lower in the last half of the century than in the first half, reaching a nadir in the 1960s, when the highest unemployment rate for the decade was a mere 3.2 points above the lowest rate, and the standard deviation barely exceeded one. The good news with respect to unemployment variation is tempered, however, by the fact that moderate increases in fluctuations were observed after the 1960s.

Moreover, the official data for the first decades of the century were constructed from decennial census "benchmark" data, and are thus subject to considerable error. Christina Romer has made a compelling case that the variation in unemployment in the early decades of the twentieth century was much less than the official numbers indicate, and that the postwar unemployment instability is understated, suggesting that the observed reduction in unemployment instability shown in table 1.1 is in fact in large part a statistical artifact.[6]

It is tempting to try to draw broad-brush conclusions about trends in unemployment by comparing data for various subperiods in the twentieth century. The conclusion one reaches, however, is highly sensitive to the periods chosen. If one arbitrarily divides the ninety years of available data in half, the evidence shows that the mean unemployment rate in the first half, 1900–44 (7.9 percent), is considerably higher than in the last half, 1945–89 (5.49 percent). Moreover, unemployment variation (as measured by the standard deviation), is dramatically lower in the latter period. On the basis of this evidence, the inclination is to accept the conventional wisdom that the unemployment record has been clearly superior in the period of governmental activism that followed the Employment Act of 1946.

Yet one could just as rationally divide the twentieth century into three equal periods of thirty years each: 1900–29, 1930–59, and 1960–89. The first period is an era of very limited direct governmental involvement impacting on unemployment, the middle period is a transitional era where an interventionist policy came to be increasingly accepted, and the latter period is one of consistent governmental activism in the economy, albeit with increased skepticism about its effectiveness as the period unfolded.

The mean unemployment rate of 4.7 percent in the first (nonintervention) period was far lower than the 6.09 percent rate observed from 1960 to 1989, or the 9.3 percent average rate in the transitional era of 1930–59. While unemployment variation was somewhat lower in the 1960–89 period than in the early decades (standard deviation of 1.60 versus 2.29), Romer's insight suggests that this almost entirely reflects faulty data rather than a real phenomenon. Using this tripartite division, the evidence generally points to the conclusion that the unemployment situation was better in the relatively laissez-faire era before the Great Depression than in periods since.

Spatial Variations in Unemployment

In addition to substantial intertemporal variations in unemployment, interstate differentials in joblessness have been great throughout the period. Before 1960, good state unemployment data were not collected on an annual basis, although information was gathered as part of several of the

TABLE 1.2

INTERSTATE VARIATIONS IN UNEMPLOYMENT, VARIOUS YEARS, 1930–88[a]

Year	Mean Unemployment Rate		Standard Deviation	Unemployment Rate Range
	Weighted	Unweighted		
1930	6.13	5.40	1.99	1.8 – 10.8
1940	9.60[b]	8.79[b]	2.28	4.0 – 14.4
1950	4.80	4.69	1.51	1.8 – 8.8
1961	6.70	6.50	1.84	2.7 – 13.5
1964	5.20	4.95	1.21	2.5 – 8.8
1967	3.80	3.88	1.13	2.0 – 8.8
1970	4.90	4.80	1.39	2.6 – 10.3
1973	4.90	4.90	1.50	2.9 – 10.8
1976	7.70	7.15	1.92	3.3 – 10.4
1979	5.80	5.56	1.41	2.8 – 9.2
1982	9.70	9.26	2.27	5.5 – 16.5
1985	7.20	7.09	1.96	3.9 – 13.0
1988	5.50	5.48	1.91	2.4 – 10.9

[a]Data exclude Alaska and Hawaii prior to 1961.
[b]Numbers exclude governmental emergency workers from the ranks of the unemployed, unlike with the official data from the U.S. Department of Labor.

decennial population censuses.[7] In table 1.2, indicators of interstate variation in unemployment are presented for a number of years.

Note that throughout the period for which data are available, there are areas of the United States where the incidence of unemployment is three to four times that of other areas. Typically in recent years, there are states in which the unemployment rate is 10 percent or more, and other states where the rate is about 3 percent.

Do unemployment differentials between states tend to persist over time? The evidence suggests that in the very long run, there is no correlation between unemployment rates for different time periods. States that in one time period had high unemployment rates did not have a clear tendency to have relatively high rates in the later period. For example, the correlation between the unemployment rates for the forty-eight contiguous states and the District of Columbia in 1930 and 1988 is actually negative (− .13). Yet the "very long run" is actually quite long—perhaps forty or fifty years. There are relatively long periods in twentieth-century American history where unemployment variations have seemed to persist in something of a pattern. For example, the correlation between unemployment in 1961 and in 1988 for the forty-eight contiguous states and the District of Columbia is a fairly high .47. Between 1930 and 1950 it was even greater, .62.

Some states seem to have persistently high or low rates of unemployment. For example, for twelve of the thirteen years examined from 1930 through 1988, the unemployment rate in West Virginia exceeded or equaled the national average. By contrast, in every single year the unemployment rate in Nebraska and South Dakota was less than the national average. Thus it is clearly possible that there are some regional variations in the normal or natural rate of unemployment.

Demographic Variations in Unemployment

It is a well-established fact that in the late twentieth century unemployment rates tended to be dramatically higher for nonwhite than for white workers, and that younger workers have a much higher incidence of unemployment than is true among older persons in the labor force. On the other hand, gender differences in the incidence of unemployment are relatively small. Have these patterns persisted throughout the twentieth century?

RACIAL DIFFERENCES

The answer to that question, as table 1.3 suggests, is "no." Turning first to racial distinctions, note that the white-nonwhite unemployment rate differential widened dramatically in percentage terms as the twentieth century proceeded. The 1900 data are not comparable with other years, since they reflect unemployment *flows* over a twelve-month period, rather than the *stock* of unemployed as of a specific date. Data on the average duration of unemployment by race suggest that blacks and other nonwhites tended to be unemployed for shorter periods than whites in 1900. Some 55.4 percent of nonwhites were unemployed for three months or less, compared with 47.7 percent of whites.[8] The proportion of whites unemployed for seven or more months was nearly twice as high as for nonwhites.[9]

The effect of the differential duration is to bias the the reported race differential in the direction of overstating it. To illustrate, suppose that over a given year there were ten black workers, four of whom were each unemployed for three months, with each of their unemployment not overlapping with the others. Further assume there were ten whites, one of whom was unemployed for the entire year. The incidence of unemployment, twelve worker months, is the same for both groups. Yet the reported unemployment rate using the 1900 census procedure would have been 40 percent for nonwhites (four were unemployed out of ten), and 10 percent for whites. Using current measurement procedures, the reported rate for both racial groups would have been 10 percent.

Making a number of assumptions, it is possible to estimate a point-in-time unemployment rate for 1900 which is highly consistent with the official (Lebergott) annual data.[10] Doing so, we obtain a white unemployment

TABLE 1.3

AGE, RACE AND GENDER DIFFERENTIALS IN UNEMPLOYMENT RATES, 1900–88

Year	% Total Unemployment Rate	% White Unemployment Rate	% Nonwhite Unemployment Rate	% Teen-age Unemployment Rate	% Male Unemployment Rate	% Female Unemployment Rate
1900	22.25[a]	21.16[a]	28.78[a]	N.A.	22.01[a]	23.34[a]
1930	6.13[b]	6.19	5.17	7.42[b]	6.59	4.45
1940	9.65[c]	9.50	10.89	24.70	9.62	9.73
1950	5.30	4.90	9.00	12.20	5.10	5.70
1955	4.40	3.90	8.70	11.00	4.20	4.90
1960	5.50	5.00	10.20	14.70	5.40	5.90
1965	4.50	4.10	8.10	14.80	4.00	5.50
1970	4.90	4.50	8.20	15.30	4.40	5.90
1975	8.50	7.80	13.80	19.90	7.90	9.30
1980	7.10	6.30	13.10	17.80	6.90	7.40
1985	7.20	6.20	13.70	18.60	7.00	7.40
1989	5.30	4.50	10.00	15.00	5.20	5.40

[a] Not comparable to other years; see text.
[b] Based on the category A and category B unemployment numbers, which seem to resemble the closest contemporary unemployment definitions.
[c] Includes government-relief workers as employed.
Source: 1900, 1930, and 1940: Decennial censuses of population for given year; 1950 to present, 1990 Economic Report of the President, op. cit., p. 338.

rate of 6.47 percent and a nonwhite rate of 7.57 percent. The racial differential is about 17 percent, with the absolute differential being slightly more than one percentage point. The 1930 data suggest actually a slightly lower unemployment rate among nonwhites—5.17 percent—than among whites—6.19 percent. Assuming the 1900 and 1930 observations are reasonably representative of intervening years, it would seem reasonable to conclude that the white/nonwhite unemployment differential was of a negligible magnitude in the period from 1900 to 1930.

Further examination of the data suggests the large racial differential in unemployment rates had its genesis in the 1930s and 1940s, with an additional aggravation of that difference in the 1970s. While Americans often pride themselves on reducing racial economic distinctions over time, the evidence on unemployment is highly inconsistent with that sanguine interpretation. Other data on employment confirm the deterioration in black job opportunities.[11] It would appear that over time, racial variations in the natural rate of unemployment have grown very substantially.

GENDER DIFFERENCES

To a dramatically smaller extent, the same phenomenon exists with respect to male-female differentials. The 1900 data show a moderately higher female unemployment rate, but the 1930 numbers actually show women with a significantly lower incidence of unemployment, while in 1940 there was virtually no gender differential. Summarizing the data to 1940, it probably would be safe to conclude that gender differentials before 1940 were not systematic and minor in magnitude. By contrast, since 1950, female unemployment rates have tended to be consistently higher than male ones, especially in the 1960s and 1970s, although the differentials have narrowed significantly in recent years.

TEENAGE UNEMPLOYMENT

Teenage unemployment has consistently been higher than that for older Americans, although the differential reported in the 1930 census was very modest. Between 1930 and 1940, the teenage unemployment differential soared, then narrowed somewhat in the 1950s. On balance, the teenage differential has widened since 1950, as is demonstrated by comparing 1950 and 1989, years in which the aggregate unemployment rate was identical. In 1989, the teenage unemployment rate was 2.8 percentage points greater than in 1950.

The Importance of Unemployment

Why has unemployment become such a major policy issue as the United States has moved through the twentieth century? Why does it seem to dominate the nation's thinking whenever there is any significant rise in it, as occurred, for example, in the early 1990s? Possibly, this increased concern with the phenomenon can be traced to its present magnitude being appreciably higher than in the earlier part of the century. Perhaps unemployment is truly a more serious problem today than previously. However, the evidence in this respect is mixed. On the one hand, counterbalancing the higher absolute level of the unemployment rate, the variability of unemployment has possibly narrowed with the passage of time. At the same time, though, certain unemployment differentials, especially the racial one, appear to have widened. But in the other direction, what about the growth of public "social safety-net" programs designed to lessen the economic distress generated by unemployment? Do they, or do they not, make unemployment less of a problem?

There are, in fact, no clear answers as to why unemployment has increased in importance. Changes in its actual incidence do not seem to offer any clearcut clues. This may be due to unemployment being, more than anything else, a somewhat complex psychological problem. Today, data describing the actual unemployment rate are much more readily available than in the early part of this century. Every month, like clockwork, usually on the first Friday, the Bureau of Labor Statistics announces its estimate of the previous month's unemployment rate. Thus, there is much greater general knowledge of the volume of unemployment. In turn, what becomes important to people is the current level of unemployment *compared to the level that they anticipate*. If they are expecting double-digit levels for the unemployment rate, as existed in late 1982 and early 1983, single-digit levels seem wonderful. On the other hand, if they have become accustomed to low-level single-digit numbers, such as the 5.1 to 5.3 percent unemployment rates that marked 1989, an increase of as little as two percentage points can seem to represent a dramatic deterioration in the unemployment situation.

As a consequence, in combination with the greater knowledge of current levels of unemployment, the very existence of variability in its level, even though it be less than in earlier years, becomes the basis for the importance attached to unemployment in the arena of public policy. Changes in unemployment seem to have become at least as important, if not more so, than its actual level. Therefore, any understanding of the contemporary view of the unemployment problem requires insight into the sources of variation in the unemployment rate.

NOTES

1. The *Shorter Oxford English Dictionary* (Oxford: Clarendon Press, 1933), 2: 2296, dates the origin of the term "unemployment" to 1888. The term "unemployed" in the modern sense was used as early as 1667. Alfred Marshall uses the term twice on a single page of his *Principles of Economics*, 8th ed. (London: Macmillan, 1920), p. 710, but nowhere else, although he refers to "inconstancy" of employment in two places.

2. Using the American Economic Association's *Index of Economic Journals* (Homewood, Ill: Richard D. Irwin, 1961), we counted unemployment-related articles within the classifications 2.310, Income and Employment Theory—General; 2.311, Underemployment, Full Employment; and 19.202, Employment, Unemployment (counting, among the geographically oriented items, only those for the United States). For the 1890s, there were two articles on statistics of unemployment. In the 1930s, there were sixty articles listed in these classifications, plus numerous other articles in related classifications.

3. See A.C. Pigou, *Industrial Fluctuations* (London: Macmillan, 1927), p. 185, or his *Theory of Unemployment* (London: Macmillan, 1933), Part V.

4. For a table on urbanization by decade, see Richard K. Vedder, *The American Economy in Historical Perspective* (Belmont, Calif.: Wadsworth, 1976), p. 125.

5. See U.S. Department of Commerce, Bureau of the Census, *Historical Statistics of the United States, Colonial Times to 1970* (Washington, D.C.: Government Printing Office, 1975), p. 135, or Stanley Lebergott, *Manpower in Economic Growth: The American Record Since 1800* (New York: McGraw-Hill, 1964).

6. See Christina Romer, "Spurious Volatility in Historical Unemployment Data," *Journal of Political Economy* 94 (1986): 1–37. See also related papers, "Is the Stabilization of the Postwar Economy a Figment of the Data?" *American Economic Review* 76 (1986), 314–34, and "New Estimates of Prewar Gross National Product and Unemployment," *Journal of Economic History*, 46 (1986), 341–52. Romer's estimates suggest that the standard deviation on the unemployment rate was 1.23 from 1900 to 1929, compared with 2.29 using the official BLS data. For the 1950–79 period, the official estimates yield a standard deviation of 1.37, compared with over 2.00 using the Romer numbers. Romer's work has been criticized. See, for example, David R. Weir, "The Reliability of Historical Macroeconomic Data for Comparing Cyclical Stability," *Journal of Economic History* 46 (1986): 353–65.

7. An important step in filling this void has been provided by John J. Wallis in his "Employment in the Great Depression: New Data and Hypotheses," *Explorations in Economic History* 26 (1989): 45–72. Wallis reports employment (not unemployment) changes by state for the critical Depression decade.

8. See the U.S. Department of Commerce and Labor, Bureau of the Census, *Special Reports: Occupations at the Twelfth Census* (Washington, D.C.: Government Printing Office, 1904), p. ccxxxiv.

9. Ibid.

10. First, we calculated the average duration of unemployment during the previous year for the two racial groups, performing a linear interpolation within the

three categories of duration reported in the census. We then calculated the number of unemployed per worker-year of unemployment by dividing the number 12 (representing months) by the estimated mean unemployment duration. Next we divided the reported number of unemployed by the estimated number of unemployed per worker-year. For the entire population, the resulting unemployment rate of 5.68 percent is between the 6.5 percent rate reported by Lebergott for 1899 and the 5.0 percent rate for 1900—some of the unemployment measured in the census occurred in 1899, some in 1900. See *Historical Statistics of the United States,* p. 135.

11. For example, looking at males with less than an eighth-grade education, both whites and blacks had 84 percent of the work-age population employed in 1940. By 1985, the proportion for blacks had fallen dramatically, to 53 percent, while the decline for whites, to 76 percent, was much less substantial. See Gerald D. Jaynes, "The Labor Market Status of Black Americans: 1939–1985," *Journal of Economic Perspectives* 4 (1990): 16.

2

Unemployment in Theory

With the increased interest in unemployment came intense scholarly investigation into its causes. Whereas in the nineteenth century economists were concerned about the gains from trade, the determination of prices and quantities, and optimal production levels for firms in alternative market structures, over much of the twentieth century the dominant single interest in economics was the question of the determinants of unemployment. Indeed, a whole new branch of economics, "macroeconomics," developed.

Economists since John Maynard Keynes (who died in 1946) generally accept Keynes's interpretation of what he termed the "classical" economists' position on unemployment.[1] Actually, the use of the term "classical" is somewhat inappropriate, since the "classical" economists are generally considered to have written in the period from 1776 to about 1850 or 1860. A postclassical school, developing "neoclassical economics," began around 1870, dominated economic thinking to about 1930, and remains important today; and the unemployment theory that Keynes attacked was essentially a neoclassical theory. Roughly simultaneously with the neoclassical developments, a second school of economists, the Austrians, was developing on the European continent. While the Austrian position on business cycles differed from neoclassical thinking, the Austrians reached many similar conclusions with respect to unemployment determination. Thus we can talk of a "neoclassical-Austrian" perspective on unemployment.

13

Wage-Based Perspectives on Unemployment

At the outset, it should be stated emphatically that in his *General Theory* Keynes created a straw man, a caricature of true thinking by the orthodox neoclassical and Austrian writers of his time. Keynes implied that these economists had a well-developed and articulated theory of unemployment that was virtually universally accepted as part of orthodox economic doctrine. That assertion is somewhat dubious. To be sure, the accepted price theory carried with it an implicit explanation of unemployment. As mentioned in the previous chapter, however, there was very little explicit scholarly writing about unemployment before 1930, and textbooks of the era generally gave scant attention to the subject. Moreover, when the Great Depression began and businesses, under government prodding, began to follow policies antithetical to those that the theory of orthodox economists suggested, there was little outcry from that group. This was in marked contrast to their behavior with respect to the increased tariffs passed as part of the Smoot-Hawley Act.[2] While there was an orthodox economic explanation of unemployment, a majority of economists did not believe it with the great conviction they felt about other parts of conventional economic doctrine.

With this caveat in mind, what was the predominant view of the causes of unemployment during the first three decades of the century? In short, the important determinant of unemployment is the wage rate. Unemployment is created when existing wage rates exceed the level necessary to "clear" the labor market. Just as a surplus of wheat exists if the prevailing price is above the equilibrium level that equates the quantity supplied and the quantity demanded, so there is a surplus of labor—unemployment— when the prevailing price, or wage, of labor exceeds the equilibrium level that eliminates unemployment.

Figure 2.1 can help further elucidate the theory. The quantity demanded of labor varies inversely with its price. At lower wages, the quantity demanded is greater, because the additional revenue a worker brings to a firm, or marginal revenue product, is lower the greater the quantity of labor.[3] Put differently, lowering the wage makes it profitable to hire some workers whom it would be unprofitable to hire at a higher wage.

It is generally acknowledged, as figure 2.1 depicts, that the quantity of labor supplied varies directly with its price.[4] As employers raise wages, some persons are willing to work who would forego the opportunity at a lower wage.

Suppose that initially the wage rate is OW, and the demand for labor is denoted by curve D. Note that at wage OW the quantity of labor supplied exceeds the quantity of labor demanded; there is unemployment in the

FIGURE 2.1

WAGES AND THE DETERMINATION OF UNEMPLOYMENT

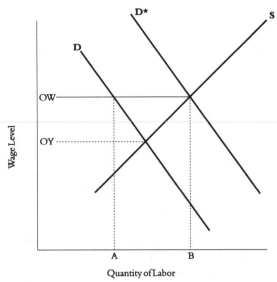

Quantity of Labor

amount AB. The basic price theory suggests that there are four ways in which the unemployment might be eliminated:

1) a reduction in the existing money wage from level OW to OY;
2) an increase in labor demand (e.g., to curve D*) from higher prices on goods that workers produce; this raises the money value of the marginal revenue product of labor;
3) an increase in the demand for labor arising from an increase in labor productivity, reflecting technological advances, increased capital availability, etc;
4) a decrease in the supply of labor, denoted by an upward movement in the supply curve (not shown in figure 2.1).

A decrease in money wages would reduce unemployment both by decreasing the quantity of labor supplied and by increasing the quantity of labor demanded. Increases in the prices of goods or services produced by labor raise dollar revenues attributable to any given amount of labor, thus increasing the amount employers would be willing to pay to obtain any given number of workers. Also, higher prices mean that a given money wage has less purchasing power, so an increase in prices means a reduction in real wages. Higher productivity means higher physical product per worker which, in turn, means higher revenues per worker, similarly increasing demand. Finally, a shift to the left in the labor supply curve reduces the gap between the quantity of labor demanded and supplied.

If labor supply is highly inelastic (relatively nonresponsive to wage changes) and if it moves over time slowly and predictably with demographic and other trends, then the theorizing above would suggest that short-term variations in unemployment are determined by changes in money wages, prices, or the productivity of labor.[5] As indicated, the money wage divided by the price level is the real wage. The real wage per unit of physical output is simply the real wage divided by the productivity of workers, or what we might call the "adjusted real wage" or "real unit-labor costs." The bulk of the remainder of this volume will be devoted to testing the validity of the proposition that unemployment in the United States has been systematically positively related to the adjusted real wage: higher adjusted real wages mean higher unemployment.

There is another way of expressing the basic hypothesis that unemployment is positively related to the adjusted real wage. Real wages are equal to money wages (W) divided by some price index (P), or W/P. Similarly labor productivity equals money output per hour (O) divided by a price index (P), or O/P. Assuming the same price index in both calculations, dividing real wages, W/P, by labor productivity, O/P, gives W/O. The latter expression is simply labor compensation as a proportion of total output (GNP, or using distributive-shares data, national or personal income). Thus the adjusted real wage can be measured by looking at labor's share of personal income. If that share rises, the adjusted real wage is rising and, the theory predicts, unemployment should rise as well.[6]

While the theory as expressed above was not often or well articulated by the bulk of economists living in the first third of the twentieth century, few would disagree with it. At least one, A. C. Pigou, laid the theory out very explicitly and at great length.[7] One obvious problem with the theory is that, at any given moment of time, there always was some unemployment, and the wage mechanism was never fully successful in completely clearing the labor market—unemployment never fell to zero.

Pigou recognized this, and considered "frictional unemployment" explicitly. At any given time, a certain number of workers would be temporarily between jobs; when one loses one's job, it is unusual for the unemployed worker instantly to obtain new employment. Learning about job opportunities takes time and effort, and the fact that labor-market information is not costless and instantly available means that some unemployment is inevitable, as unemployment is traditionally defined.

Later economists, particularly in the 1960s, introduced the concept of structural unemployment, arguing that often there is a mismatch between the skills of those out of work and the skills needed for available jobs. Unskilled, unemployed construction workers cannot fill vacant positions for computer programmers.

The labor force can be defined to exclude those temporarily idle individuals currently between jobs (the frictionally unemployed); some economists consider these workers voluntarily unemployed and thus not part of the involuntary jobless.[8] It might be defined also to exclude those whose inappropriate skill levels make them de facto not "able" to work at jobs that are available—the so-called structurally unemployed. So defined, a full-employment (no-unemployment) level occurs where the quantity of labor demanded equals the quantity of labor supplied.

Less than full employment, or what economists generally call "cyclical unemployment," exists when wages exceed the market-clearing equilibrium wage. It is possible also to have, temporarily, a below-equilibrium wage where there are, in the context of figure 2.1, labor shortages, or, to use conventional contemporary terminology, negative cyclical unemployment—people are working who would not normally work at the prevailing wage. They work because they are temporarily misinformed as to their true wage since they suffer from "money illusion," or perhaps because labor contracts require them to do so even though they would not choose to do so if the legal obligation were not present.

Normally, however, the theory suggests that wages will tend to move toward equilibrium. Using our restricted labor-force definition, unemployment is zero at that equilibrium. Using the official unemployment definition, there is frictional and structural unemployment. Officially defined unemployment at the equilibrium wage equals what is now often called the natural rate of unemployment.

While most of the remainder of this book attempts to use the simple wages model discussed above to explain variations in cyclical unemployment in the United States in the twentieth century, in chapters 13 and 14 historical dimensions of frictional and structural unemployment are discussed, both in general and with respect to demographic (race, gender, and age) and geographic variations in the natural rate of unemployment.

AUSTRIAN PERSPECTIVES ON UNEMPLOYMENT

No school of economic thought has placed a greater emphasis on the importance of markets in coordinating economic activity than the Austrian school. With respect to unemployment, Austrians accept the view that unemployment reflects discoordination and disequilibrium in the labor market, or, more simply, excessive wage levels.[9] As the late Friedrich von Hayek put it, "The cause of unemployment . . . is a deviation from the equilibrium prices and wages which would establish themselves with a free market and stable money."[10] Recently, scholars have supported this view empirically.[11]

Recognizing that, however, the Austrians generally believe that the disequilibrium in the labor market often may be a by-product or consequence of human-caused disturbances in other markets. In particular, increases in the stock of money induced by monetary policies of the central bank (Federal Reserve Bank in the United States) change the purchasing power of the circulating medium. Such a move tends to push interest rates in a downward direction not justified by true human time preferences. The price of capital resources falls relative to the price of labor services. This, in turn, leads to a distortion in resource allocation toward capital-intensive ventures and away from labor-intensive ones.

A Digression on Unemployment Statistics

In the discussion above, we suggested that the labor force could be defined to exclude workers who are conventionally classified as frictionally or structurally unemployed. That may seem artificial and arbitrary. It is important to realize, however, that the official unemployment definition is inherently arbitrary in several ways. For example, at the present time no one under the age of sixteen is included in the labor force, even though there are some child entertainers whose work earns them seven-digit annual incomes. There are millions of housewives and househusbands who "work around the house" doing economically productive activity. Yet they are excluded from the labor force since they do not sell their services in a market. A person working in a child-care facility is "employed", while a mother who takes care of her own four children at home is "not employed" (as distinct from "unemployed") even though she probably provides as many (and as high-quality) child care services as the person selling her services in the labor market.

Another problem comes from the fact that many of those persons classified as unemployed in fact have opportunities to work and have chosen not to exercise them. They choose to be unemployed. Suppose an aerospace engineer with graduate degrees is dismissed from his $60,000-a-year job with a defense contractor because of defense cutbacks. Suppose he stops into a local fast-food restaurant after his last day of work and starts talking

FIGURE 2.2

THE DURATION OF UNEMPLOYMENT

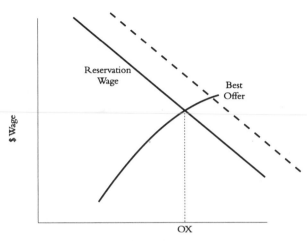

Duration of Unemployment

with his friend, the owner of the restaurant. Suppose further that the friend offers the engineer a job as restaurant manager at a salary of $500 a week ($26,000 a year.) Suppose also that the engineer turns him down. Is the engineer unemployed? Yes, as far as the Bureau of Labor Statistics is concerned, as long as he continues to search for a job similar to his previous one. Clearly, such a definition of "unemployed" fails adequately to convey voluntarily foregone job prospects. Consider figure 2.2. Unemployed individuals have a *reservation wage*—a minimum wage that they will take as a condition for accepting a new job. A freshly unemployed person may have high aspirations with respect to a new job, expecting a relatively high wage. The longer he or she is unemployed, however, the more likely the worker is to lower the reservation wage, as the reality of job opportunities and the financial pressure of unemployment impact on decisions. Similarly, the longer one searches for a job, the better the job that the unemployed individual is likely to find (although there is an obvious limit to the gains in wages obtainable from more thorough searching.)

In figure 2.2, the individual chooses to take a new job when the best offered position equals (or exceeds) the reservation wage. It is optimal for the individual to remain unemployed for a duration of OX weeks. Government policies might change the reservation wage. For example, if the unemployed receives generous unemployment benefits, he or she may be more choosy about taking a new job. In the context of figure 2.2, unemployment compensation raises the reservation wage to the dotted line, leading to the optimal employment occurring after a longer duration of unemployment. This raises the reported unemployment rate, as well as the natural rate of unemployment.[12]

There are still other difficulties with the unemployment definition. Some persons become discouraged after long unemployment spells and stop looking for jobs, even though they certainly would like one. They are dropped from the labor force and no longer classified as unemployed, even though in a meaningful sense they are in fact unemployed. Still other problems deal with part-time work, workers in the "underground economy" not included in the government statistics, and with some welfare recipients in workfare programs.[13]

Some economists believe that the employment-population ratio is a better measure of job opportunities. Over time, that ratio has tended to rise with increased female labor-force participation. For example, in both 1960 and 1988, the civilian unemployment rate was 5.5 percent. Yet 62.6 percent of the noninstutionalized population over sixteen worked in 1988, compared with but 56.8 percent in 1960. By the unemployment measure, job opportunities were similar in both years, but the employment-population ratio tells a different story.

While the imperfections of the unemployment statistics are numerous, to some extent they cancel each other out. While the fact that some people temporarily choose to be unemployed leads to some inflation in the unemployment numbers, so the discouraged-worker effect causes some understatement of the problem. In any case, changes in the unemployment rate from year to year should be a pretty good indicator of changes in employment opportunity, even if the exact magnitude of the statistics is incorrect.

Underconsumptionist and Income-Expenditure Approaches

The demand for labor services is ultimately derived from the demand for goods and services: labor markets are impacted by product markets. At the same time that modern neoclassical and Austrian economics was evolving at the turn of the century and beyond, a different explanation of business fluctuations and unemployment was put forward. The alternative theory placed most of the blame for declines in business activity on inadequate spending, either consumption or investment. Until the 1930s, these theories were generally dismissed by neoclassical economists as being superficial and mistaken. With John Maynard Keynes's *General Theory of Employment,*

Interest and Money (1936), however, the underconsumptionist approach rose to a position of dominance among economists.

Among the pre-Keynesian writers, John Hobson and, at a more popular level, William T. Foster and Waddill Catchings emphasized the importance of demand for products in the maintenance of prosperity.[14] This, in turn, implied that adequate purchasing power was necessary to sustain production and full employment. Implicitly, these writers rejected the classical/ neoclassical propositions of Jean Baptiste Say that "supply creates its own demand."[15]

In his *General Theory*, Keynes did not actually reject the appropriateness of the simple wage theory as outlined in figure 2.1, but he did reject the notion that reductions in money wages were likely to succeed in restoring full employment. He pointed out that money wages were often rigid, set by contracts, making rapid wage adjustments infeasible. However, even if money wages were somehow reduced, the marginal cost of producing goods would decline, increasing product supply and lowering the prices of goods. Thus, as wages fell prices would likewise fall, causing the demand-for-labor curve to shift to the left, and leaving real wages essentially unchanged. Thus a policy of wage reduction was not likely to be effective in restoring a full employment equilibrium.

Keynes argued that unemployment can be reduced, however, by stimulating the aggregate demand for goods and services. If, at existing income levels, people increase the amount they wish to spend, this will lead to both increased output of goods and an increased demand for labor. In the context of figure 2.1, the demand-for-labor curve can be shifted rightward by increased demand for goods and services.

How does one stimulate aggregate demand? By engaging in such fiscal policy actions as increasing levels of government spending or by increasing people's disposable (after-tax) income by simply lowering taxes. Either increased government expenditures or reduced taxation serves to increase the budget deficit of the government. Thus deficit government financing will stimulate aggregate demand (consumption, investment, government, and net export spending), thus increasing the demand for labor, reducing unemployment.

In classical and neoclassical economics, saving was viewed as a positive economic act, since the act of saving ultimately stimulated investment by lowering interest rates, and thus enhanced capital formation, productivity, and real output. In Keynesian economics, however, saving took on a negative connotation. Higher saving meant a reduced "propensity to consume," and with that, a reduced aggregate demand for goods and thus a reduced demand for labor. Surges in consumer saving meant sudden reductions in the aggregate demand for goods, with the initial decrease in consumption (arising from more saving out of a given income) getting multiplied several times as the chain reaction impact of reduced spending spread throughout the economy.

The stimulus to aggregate demand from deficit-financed government fiscal actions would directly raise the demand for labor, the Keynesians believed. In addition, increased demand for goods would lead to increased prices, particularly in sectors where the economy was already operating near capacity. Higher prices, in turn, other things equal, meant lower real wages. Thus inflation, previously viewed as an evil that reduced the efficiency of the price mechanism as an allocative device, was somewhat virtuous. A generation after Keynes, A. W. Phillips developed the famous Phillips curve which, as modified by others, stated that higher rates of inflation are associated with reduced rates of unemployment.[16]

While Keynes very explicitly discussed the neoclassical approach to unemployment, he nonetheless believed that cyclical fluctuations were largely related to financial and capital markets, not the labor market. Neoclassical economists argued that another key price—the interest rate—could adjust to resolve problems arising from sudden reductions in consumer or investment spending. If people tried to save (not spend) more than businesses wanted to invest for new plant and equipment, a reduction in economic activity would be thwarted by falling interest rates. Keynes argued that was not necessarily so, introducing the concept of the "liquidity trap" where interest rates would not fall beyond a certain point. Moreover, lowering interest rates was of limited effectiveness in increasing aggregate demand, since investment spending was not all that sensitive to interest rates anyhow.

The classical or neoclassical economic models argue that Keynesian views that government-induced increases in economic activity can stimulate aggregate demand are wrong. Suppose the government increases its spending, financed by borrowing. Increased demand for loanable funds would raise interest rates, lowering investment spending. Higher interest rates would also increase savings, lowering consumption. Increases in government spending would be offset by declines in investment and consumption spending, leaving aggregate demand unchanged. Thus demand-side intervention is inherently ineffective.[17]

Returning to a comparison of the Keynesian and neoclassical perspectives, Keynes never went so far as to say "wages do not matter," but he implied there was little one could do about wage levels in a policy sense. Later Keynesians increasingly ignored wages or even implied that unemployment was negatively related to wage levels.[18] Generally, in the 1950s and 1960s, the subject of wages was seldom even mentioned in discussing the issue of unemployment. Essentially the view had become, "Wages don't matter," almost in direct contrast to the neoclassical position that almost said "Wages alone matter."

Late Twentieth-Century Perspectives on Unemployment

By the middle part of the twentieth century, Keynesian economics was the new orthodoxy, and the wages approach to unemployment determination was all but completely abandoned. As Richard Nixon, a moderately conservative Republican president, is alleged to have said around 1970, "we are all Keynesians now." Yet beginning in the 1960s a challenge to the Keynesian approach arose as to the cause of economic fluctuations and, by inference, the causes of unemployment.

MONETARISM

Even before the twentieth century, economists were aware that the amount of circulating medium—money—was a factor in determining the level of prices, interest rates, and possibly other important economic phenomena. Roughly simultaneously with the development of both the neoclassical and pre-Keynesian underconsumptionist (demand-oriented) theories of unemployment, the quantity theory of money was more systematically elucidated.[19] A more sophisticated and appealing version of the theory gained increasing acceptance in the 1960s and 1970s, largely because of the work of Milton Friedman.[20] Adherents of the modern version of the quantity theory were called "monetarists."

Monetarists believe that the primary cause of economic fluctuations is variations in the supply of money. Over time, they suggest, there is a strong statistical correlation between changes in the stock of money and changes in prices and, when monetary changes are unanticipated, real output. Out of monetarist thinking came still another school of economics in the 1970s, the New Classical school, discussed below.

In some respects, there are similarities between the neoclassicals, the Austrians, and the monetarists. All of them have considerable faith in the ability of markets to correct imbalances. All three groups tend to be skeptical of governmental intervention to right macroeconomic wrongs.

Monetarists, however, like most Keynesians, tend to speak little about labor markets, and usually give little emphasis to the role of wages in unemployment determination. Most monetarists seem to believe that any unemployment-creating wage imbalance likely has its origin in monetary disturbances. For example, a decrease in the supply of money would lower prices and, money wages unchanged, raise real wages, thus aggravating unemployment. Commodity prices are greatly influenced by the supply of money and, other things the same, changing commodity prices mean changing real wages.

EXPECTATIONS AND THE NEW CLASSICAL ECONOMICS

Around 1970, some respected economists, notably Milton Friedman and Edmund Phelps, started to sharply question the long-run efficacy of the prevailing Keynesian/underconsumptionist theory.[21] They questioned whether demand stimulus could maintain sustained high-employment levels. They intimated that the negative inflation–unemployment relationship suggested by the Phillips curve was unstable in the short run and non-existent in the long run.

The evidence from the 1970s supported these and other critics, and a new group of younger economists—the New Classical school—formulated innovative theories that put greater emphasis than previously on the role of expectations. The thrust of these arguments was that government policies designed to stimulate demand would induce behavioral changes among individuals in the private sector, changes that would render the policies ineffective.[22]

For example, suppose the government announced big spending increases to stimulate aggregate demand or, alternatively, that the Federal Reserve took steps to increase the money supply by creating new bank reserves. Individuals and businesses, sensing the inflationary potential of such policies, would alter their behavior in several ways. Banks would become more concerned about getting paid back their loans in dollars of depreciated purchasing power, and would demand higher interest rates. Thus deficit-financed new government spending would, indirectly, "crowd out" private spending that is sensitive to interest rates. While some proponents of rational expectations disagree with this conclusion, they nonetheless agree that deficit financing would not stimulate aggregate demand because of increased private savings that would mean a lower propensity to consume goods and services by the private sector.[23]

Also, expansionary federal fiscal (or monetary) policies would lead labor unions to become more militant, demanding larger wage increases. Higher wages, other things equal, would reduce employment (figure 2.1). The demand and employment stimulus of governmental policy, then, if anticipated, would be offset by behavioral modification among the populace. Only if the population were deceived would the policies work.[24]

In the most extreme form, the new theoretical perspectives evolving in the 1970s and 1980s implied both that cyclical unemployment would not exist for any length of time, and that governmental policies could almost never be effective, even in the short run. Regarding the first point, at least one advocate of the new theoretical approach, in all seriousness, explained away the unemployment of the 1930s as a spontaneous surge in the demand for leisure—involuntary unemployment simply could not exist.[25] As Franco Modigliani characterized this interpretation, "What happened to the United States in the 1930s was a severe attack of contagious laziness."[26]

It should be pointed out that some of the New Classical economists have exhibited views on the unemployment-wage relationship that is the opposite of that of the original neoclassical/Austrian perspective. For example, when low wages occur, some New Classical economists have argued that workers find leisure less costly in terms of wages foregone, leading them to withdraw from the labor force until wages improve. If actual real wages are less than expected wages, this can lead to labor-force withdrawal. Thus while the New Classical economists are similar to the earlier neoclassical and the Austrian economists in believing that "wages do matter," they do not adopt the simple view that unemployment is primarily the result of an increase in the relative price of labor.

Other New Classical economists have used other arguments to try to explain unemployment and business cycles. Some have rediscovered Joseph Schumpeter, who argued that fluctuations in the rate of innovation and technological change largely determined business cycles.[27] Others have emphasized the unemployment effects of costs associated with sectoral shifts in employment.[28]

So-called New Keynesian economists turned to microeconomic analysis to question some of the New Classical postulates. Some emphasized wage rigidity.[29] Some studies have rediscovered another old hypothesis, namely that firms can maintain labor productivity at high levels by keeping wages high during periods of unemployment; this is the so-called "efficiency wage" argument.[30] Others have discussed the stickiness of prices.[31] Still others have argued that even with wage and price flexibility, you do not necessarily get economic stability.[32]

We should note that European economists have struck something of a "middle road" by formulating complex models in which excessive real wages are sometimes the explanation for so-called "classical unemployment," while at the same time price rigidities in goods markets are permitted to create "Keynesian unemployment."[33] This is consistent with the general trend of theoretical developments of the past two decades: an increasing tendency to look more closely at the microeconomic foundations of unemployment, even to the extent, on occasion, of analyzing unemployment in terms of real wages and other phenomena.

To recapitulate, while economists were generally indifferent to unemployment during the first third of the century, they tended to blame the phenomenon largely on wages in excess of an equilibrium market-clearing level. In the second third of the century, underconsumptionist thinking came to dominate in the form of Keynesianism. Unemployment was largely attributed to insufficient aggregate demand for goods and services. Unlike the previous orthodoxy, Keynesian theory supported activist macroeconomic government policies. The last third of the century has been characterized by a variety of theories competing for dominance. Keynesianism and underconsumptionism have been in at least partial retreat, while theories denying the effectiveness of policy actions have dominated, along with some renewed attention to the role of wages in explaining unemployment. Nevertheless, the ghosts of Keynesianism and underconsumptionism are still with us in many ways.

The remainder of this book explores the historical record of unemployment in the United States. In particular, we will examine the original neoclassical wage-oriented theory and its effectiveness in explaining observed variations in unemployment. A number of questions will be explored, such as: Was the neoclassical theory really ever a dominant orthodoxy in the United States? Was its almost total passage from the intellectual scene in the 1930s justified on the basis of historical experience? Does the Keynesian (or other) explanation fit the experience better? Was the great governmental involvement in the macroeconomy that followed from the Keynesian revolution a success or failure? What seems to have caused the rise in noncyclical unemployment? Why is it that the incidence of unemployment has varied so dramatically with age, sex, and race in recent decades, but not earlier? These are but a few of the issues with which we will deal.

NOTES

1. See John Maynard Keynes, *The General Theory of Employment, Interest and Money* (New York: Harcourt Brace, 1936).

2. On the behavior of economists of the late neoclassical era, see William J. Barber, *From New Era to New Deal* (Cambridge: Cambridge University Press, 1985).

3. This is so in part because of the famous law of diminishing returns. Also, where there is imperfect competition in product markets, firms must lower prices to sell increased output, lowering the dollar revenue received per unit of increased

production. Profit maximizing firms will hire workers up to the point where the marginal cost of the labor is equal to the marginal revenue product of the labor.

4. There is some evidence supporting the view that occasionally a backward-bending supply curve exists (the elasticity of labor supply with respect to wages is negative.) For a discussion of labor-supply elasticity that incorporates some empirical results showing negative elasticities, see Mark R. Killingsworth, *Labor Supply* (Cambridge: Cambridge University Press, 1983).

5. The elasticity of labor supply is usually estimated to be .20 or lower. For a rigorous discussion of the estimation issues, with citations to several studies, see Thomas E. MacCurdy, "Interpreting Empirical Models of Labor Supply in an Intertemporal Framework with Uncertainty," *Longitudinal Analysis of Labor Market Data*, ed. James J. Heckman and Burton Singer (Cambridge: Cambridge University Press, 1985), chap. 7.

6. A number of modern economists have empirically observed the relationship posited by the wages hypothesis. For a recent example, see Stephen J. Nickell and James Symons, "The Real Wage–Employment Relationship in the United States," *Journal of Labor Economics* 8 (1990): 1–15.

7. See his *The Theory of Unemployment* (London: Macmillan, 1933); *Industrial Fluctuations* (London: Macmillan, 1927); and "Wage Policy and Unemployment," *Economic Journal* 37 (1927): 355–68. Well-known later papers include "Real and Money Wage Rates in Relation to Unemployment, ibid., 47 (1937): 405–22, and "Money Wages in Relation to Unemployment," ibid., 48 (1938): 134–48. Other writers espousing similar views include Jacob Viner, *Balanced Deflation, Inflation or More Depression* (Minneapolis: University of Minnesota Press, 1933), especially pp. 12–13; William H. Beveridge, *Causes and Cures of Unemployment* (London: Longman, Green and Co., 1930), chap. XVI; Willford I. King, *The Causes of Economic Fluctuations* (New York: Ronald Press, 1938), chap. 8; and Lionel Robbins, *The Great Depression* (London: Macmillan, 1934).

8. See Ludwig von Mises, *Human Action*, 3d rev. ed. (Chicago: Henry Regnery, 1966), pp. 600, 770.

9. See F. A. Hayek, *Monetary Theory and the Trade Cycle* (New York: Augustus Kelley, 1966). On the Austrian position as it relates to the Great Depression, see Murray Rothbard, *America's Great Depression* (Kansas City: Sheed & Ward, 1963.)

10. Chiaki Nishiyama and Kurt R. Leube, eds., *The Essence of Hayek* (Stanford: Hoover Institution Press, 1984), p. 7. Hayek, however, believes that "we are . . . unable to demonstrate a statistical correlation between the distortion of relative prices and the volume of unemployment" (ibid.). This volume in fact does provide evidence of such a statistical relationship.

11. See, for example, Richard J. Jensen, "The Causes and Cures of Unemployment in the Great Depression," *Journal of Interdisciplinary History* 19 (1989): 553–83, T. J. Hatton, "A Quarterly Model of the Labour Market in Interwar Britain," *Oxford Bulletin of Economics and Statistics* 50 (1988): 1–23, and Michael Beenstock and Peter Warburton, "Wages and Unemployment in Interwar Britain," *Explorations in Economic History* 23 (1986): 153–72.

12. For further discussion of the natural rate of unemployment, see below, chapter 13.

13. Specifically, in some states able-bodied recipients of public assistance must register with unemployment offices in order to receive welfare benefits. In some cases, these individuals are not truly looking for employment.

14. See John A. Hobson, *The Economics of Unemployment* (London: George Allen & Unwin, 1922); W. T. Foster and W. Catchings, *Profits* (Boston: Houghton Mifflin, 1925); Foster and Catchings, *Business Without a Buyer* (Boston: Houghton Mifflin, 1927); see also C. H. Douglas, *Credit-Power and Democracy* (London: C. Palmer, 1920).

15. Actually, Say's contribution was more than simply "supply creates its own demand." For an extended discussion, see Thomas Sowell, *Say's Law: An Historical Analysis* (Princeton, N.J.: Princeton University Press, 1972.)

16. See A. W. Phillips, "The Relation Between Unemployment and the Rate of Change of Money Wage Rates in the United Kingdom, 1861–1957," *Economica* 25 (1958): 283–99. As the title indicates, Phillips's original paper examined the wage-unemployment relationship. However, the emphasis soon shifted to the price-unemployment relationship. See Paul A. Samuelson and Robert M. Solow, "Analytical Aspects of Anti-Inflation Policy," *American Economic Review* 50 (1960): 177–94, and Richard G. Lipsey, "The Relation Between Unemployment and the Rate of Change of Money Wage Rates in the United Kingdom, 1862–1957: A Further Analysis," *Economica* 27 (1960): 1–31.

17. An excellent treatment of the classical versus the Keynesian perspective at a moderately rigorous level is found in Richard T. Froyen, *Macroeconomics: Theories and Policies* (New York; Macmillan, 1990.)

18. See Phillips, "Unemployment and the Rate of Change."

19. Irving Fisher popularized the "equation of exchange" and other concepts used by quantity theorists. See, for example his "'The Equation of Exchange' 1896–1910," *American Economic Review* 1 (1911): 296–305, for a typical study. The preeminent quantity theorist between Irving Fisher and Milton Friedman was Clark Warburton. See, for example, his "The Volume of Money and the Price Level Between the World Wars," *Journal of Political Economy* 53 (1945): 150–63, or "The Misplaced Emphasis in Contemporary Business-Fluctuation Theory," *Journal of Business* 19 (1946): 199–220.

20. The classic empirical study supporting monetarist views is Milton Friedman and Anna J. Schwartz, *A Monetary History of the United States, 1867–1960* (Princeton, N.J.: Princeton University Press for the National Bureau of Economic Research, 1963). See also their *Monetary Trends in the United States and the United Kingdom* (Chicago: University of Chicago Press for the National Bureau of Economic Research, 1982).

21. See Milton Friedman, "The Role of Monetary Policy," *American Economic Review* 58 (1968): 136–49, and Edmund S. Phelps, *Microeconomic Foundations of Employment and Inflation Theory* (New York: W. W. Norton, 1970). While Friedman's critique dealt with monetary policy, it was clear that he likewise questioned the efficacy of fiscal policy. The Friedman-Phelps concerns were not new. See, for

example, the preface to Ludwig von Mises, *The Theory of Money and Credit*, new ed. (New Haven, Conn.: Yale University Press, 1953.)

22.   An early application of rational expectations was Thomas Sargent and Neil Wallace, "Rational Expectations, the Optimal Monetary Instrument, and the Optimal Money Supply Rule," *Journal of Political Economy* 83 (1975): 241–54.

23.   In a classic paper, Robert Barro has argued that when the government runs a budget deficit, individuals and businesses regard the deficit as a future tax obligation; to avoid future adverse financial consequences of this obligation, taxpayers increase their current savings out of income. Thus the impact of using deficit rather than tax financing is simply to substitute voluntary saving for involuntary saving (taxation). The interest-rate effects of deficits are zero. See Barro's "Are Government Bonds Net Wealth?" *Journal of Political Economy* 82 (1974): 1095–1117. Empirical evidence on Barro's hypothesis is mixed, although Paul Evans has garnered impressive support. See his "Do Large Deficits Produce High Interest Rates?" *American Economic Review* 75 (1985): 68–87, or "Do Budget Deficits Raise Nominal Interest Rates? Evidence from Six Countries," *Journal of Monetary Economics* 20 (1987): 281–300.

24.   It has been suggested that the role of unanticipated inflation in business cycles has recently received less interest by macroeconomic theorists. See N. Gregory Mankiw, "A Quick Refresher Course in Macroeconomics," *Journal of Economic Literature* 28 (1990): 1652.

25.   For an excellent summary of the New Classical position, see Eric Kades, "New Classical and New Keynesian Models of Business Cycles," *Economic Review, Federal Reserve Bank of Cleveland* 4 (1985): 30. The increased leisure argument is used by Lucas and Rapping in their important paper. See Robert E. Lucas, Jr., and Leonard A. Rapping, "Real Wages, Employment, and Inflation," *Journal of Political Economy* 77 (1969): 721–54.

26.   Franco Modigliani, "The Monetarist Controversy, or Should We Foresake Stabilization Policies?" *American Economic Review* 67 (1977): 6.

27.   See Joseph A. Schumpeter, *The Theory of Economic Development* (Cambridge, Mass.: Harvard University Press, 1949), chap. 2; John B. Long, Jr. and Charles I. Plosser, "Real Business Cycles," *Journal of Political Economy* 91 (1983): 39–69; Edward C. Prescott, "Theory Ahead of Business Cycle Measurement," *Carnegie-Rochester Conference Series on Public Policy* 25 (1986): 11–44.

28.   Fischer Black, *Business Cycles and Equilibrium* (New York: Basil Blackwell, 1987.)

29.   Stanley Fischer, "Long-Term Contracts, Rational Expectations, and the Optimal Money Supply Rule," *Journal of Political Economy* 85 (1977): 191–205; John B. Taylor, "Aggregate Dynamics and Staggered Contracts," ibid., 88 (1980): 1–23. For an extended study of modern thinking about labor markets, see Thomas J. Kniesner and Arthur H. Goldsmith, "A Survey of Alternative Models of the Aggregate U.S. Labor Market," *Journal of Economic Literature* 25 (1987): 1241–80.

30.   Joseph E. Stiglitz, "Theories of Wage Rigidity," *Keynes' Economic Legacy: Contemporary Economic Theories*, ed. James L. Butkiewicz, Kenneth J. Koford, and Jeffrey B. Miller (New York: Praeger, 1986), p. 30. The increased leisure argument

is also used by Lucas and Rapping, "Real Wages, Employment and Inflation." For an older perspective supporting this approach, see, for example, Selig Perlman, *A Theory of the Labor Movement* (New York, 1928), pp. 212–14.

31.   George A. Akerlof and Janet L. Yellen, "A Near-Rational Model of the Business Cycle, with Wage and Price Inertia," *Quarterly Journal of Economics*, Supplement, 100 (1985): 823–38; Michael Parkin, "The Output-Inflation Tradeoff When Prices Are Costly to Change," *Journal of Political Economy* 94 (1986): 200–224; Laurence Ball, N. Gregory Mankiw, and David Romer, "The New Keynesian Economics and the Output-Inflation Tradeoff," *Brookings Papers on Economic Activity* 1 (1988): 1–65. Robert J. Gordon asserts that New Keynesians stress product-market (price)-induced rigidities more than labor-market ones. See his "What Is the New-Keynesian Economics?" *Journal of Economic Literature* 28 (1990): 1115–71.

32.   J. Bradford De Long and Lawrence H. Summers, "Is Increased Price Flexibility Stabilizing?" *American Economic Review* 76 (1986): 1031–44.

33.   The pioneering study is Edmond Malinvaud, *The Theory of Unemployment Reconsidered* (Oxford: Basil Blackwell, 1977.)

3

The Neoclassical/Austrian Approach: An Overview

In the previous chapter, it was suggested that neoclassical and Austrian economists essentially believed that unemployment varies directly with what was termed "the adjusted real wage." Increases in the adjusted real wage, other things equal, price some labor out of a job, increasing unemployment. It was further suggested that changes in any of the components of the adjusted real wage could change unemployment. Specifically, unemployment grows with increased money wages, but decreases with increased prices or productivity growth. We now proceed to examine the general validity of this neoclassical/Austrian perspective, and then comment on some general criticisms of the approach. In future chapters, we will analyze more closely the historical experiences that unfolded during the century.

Testing the Basic Model

In its simplest form, the hypothesized model is:

$$(1) \qquad\qquad U = a + b \ W,$$

where U stands for the unemployment rate, W for the adjusted real wage (real wages divided by labor productivity), a is a constant term, and b is a coefficient measuring the degree to which unemployment changes with changes in the adjusted real wage.

From information on unemployment and the variables comprising the adjusted real wage, it is possible to perform a statistical evaluation of the neoclassical position. Generally accepted data on the aggregate unemployment rate are available from 1890 to the present.[1] Money-wage data are available in abundance, although there is less consensus on which series is appropriate. From 1947, the widely cited official Bureau of Labor Statistics data on money compensation per hour in the business sector are used.[2]

There is a problem with wage data for the period before 1947. Ideally, wages should be related to a specific period of work effort, so hourly wage data are most desirable. Unfortunately, hourly data are available only for some specific classes of workers, not the economy as a whole. Annual earnings data are available that are much more comprehensive in their coverage, although they suffer the drawback of representing varying amounts of time worked. The solution we arrived at was to combine the comprehensive Department of Commerce annual wage data with other estimates of the average work week to obtain estimated hourly wages for the entire work population.[3]

Productivity (output per hour) data are readily available; we employ the estimates in *Historical Statistics of the United States* for the years to 1946.[4] These widely accepted data were originally derived by John Kendrick.[5] Beginning with 1947, the standard Bureau of Labor Statistics data are our choice.[6] For prices, we use the consumer price index.[7] Dividing the hourly wage by the price index gives us a measure of real wages. Dividing real wages by productivity produces the adjusted real wage.

We can employ ordinary least squares regression procedures to examine the relationship between the adjusted real wage W and the unemployment rate U for the ninety years from 1900 through 1989. Doing so, we obtain the following results:

(2) $U = -24.658 + 0.315\ W, \quad \overline{R}^2 = .836,\ D-W = 1.920,$
       $\quad\ (3.891)\quad (5.067)$

where the numbers in parentheses are t-values.

The results suggest that there is a positive relationship that is highly significant in a statistical sense between the adjusted real wage and the unemployment rate. Moreover, variations in the adjusted real wage alone can explain about five-sixths (83 percent) of the observed variation in the unemployment rate over time.[8] The results are highly consistent with the neoclassical/Austrian view that unemployment is largely determined by adjusted real wages in excess of equilibrium (market-clearing) levels.

In the typical (median) year, the adjusted real wage moved by 1.85 points (ignoring the direction of the change). Thus the results suggest that in a typical year, the unemployment rate moves about 0.6 percentage points (say, from 5.0 to 5.6 percent) as a consequence of fluctuations in the adjusted real wage.[9] Not all years are typical, of course. Indeed, in some twelve of the ninety years, the adjusted real wage rose or fell by more than five points, implying an unemployment-rate change of at least 1.6 percentage points (e.g., from 4.5 percent to 6.1 percent.) Thus fairly frequent relatively major changes in unemployment seem to be attributable to changes in the adjusted real wage.

The results reported in (2) are very supportive of the basic neoclassical/Austrian perspective, but they fail to fully describe the relationship between unemployment and changes in the various components making up the adjusted real wage—money wages, prices, and productivity. Also, it is possible that unemployment responds, at least in part, in a lagged fashion to changes in the adjusted real wage. This year's increase in unemployment may partly have resulted from last year's increase in the adjusted real wage.

To provide greater detail and to allow for some lag in the unemployment response to wage changes, we can expand the model:[10]

$$(3) \qquad U = a + b\,W_{t-1} + c\dot{W}_m - d\dot{P} - e\dot{O},$$

where W^{t-1} represents the adjusted real wage one year earlier, ... $\dot{W}_m$, $\dot{P}$, and $\dot{O}$ denote the change in percentage terms in money wages, consumer prices, and output per hour worked, respectively, over the past year, a is the constant term, and b, c, d, and e are coefficients measuring the extent to which the explanatory variables impact on unemployment. We can submit the expanded model to regression analysis:[11]

$$(4) \qquad U = -31.137 + 0.390\,W_{t-1} + 0.172\,\dot{W} - 0.437\,\dot{P}$$
$$ (4.163) \quad (5.288) \qquad (2.835) \qquad (6.891)$$

$$-0.302\,\dot{O}, \quad \overline{R}^2 = .899, \quad D-W = 2.001.$$
$$(5.858)$$

The model confirms even more strongly the neoclassical/Austrian position. Every variable has the expected sign and is significant at the 99 percent level of confidence. Higher adjusted real wages last year are associated with more unemployment this year. Rising money wages in the past year are associated with more unemployment, while rising prices and productivity (both lowering the adjusted real wage) are associated with lower unemployment. The model explains an impressive 90 percent of the variation in unemployment over time.

It is interesting to see how the model performs in explaining the major cyclical episodes in modern American unemployment history. Figure 3.1 shows the actual and predicted unemployment rates by year from 1900 to 1989. The two lines in general move closely together, and there is not a single major downturn or upturn in unemployment that is not captured, albeit sometimes imperfectly, by the adjusted real wage model.

Because of the large amount of detail included in the small space of figure 3.1, it is difficult to ascertain with any precision the differences between the actual unemployment rate and the unemployment rate predicted by (4). In figure 3.2, the 90-year period is divided into approximately equal quartiles of 22–23 years each to allow a better look at the model's forecasting ability. The model underpredicts the rise in unemployment at the beginning of World War I somewhat, but rather accurately forecasts the dramatic increase in unemployment in 1921. It does even better in predicting the Great Depression in the early 1930s. In the postwar era, the model accurately forecasts major upswings in unemployment (e.g., 1958, 1975, 1982), but often a year later than they actually occurred. Thus the lag between real-wage changes and unemployment may have changed over time. Later in the book, we will deal with this problem by using quarterly data that are available for the postwar period.

In summary, variations in unemployment throughout the century are well explained by changes in the adjusted real wage. How sensitive is unemployment to changes in the components of the adjusted real wage? In the typical year, money wages changed by 5.4 percent (median change, ignoring the direction of the change.) Multiplying that "typical" change by the coefficient from (4), 0.172, we see the effects of a typical year's money-wage increase is to change the unemployment rate by about 0.9 percentage points (e.g., raising it from 5.5 to 6.4 percent.) Similarly, a typical productivity change of 2.88 percentage points (median change, ignoring signs) also had the impact of changing the unemployment rate by about 0.9 percentage points (2.88 × .302 = 0.870.)

The median price change was 3.26 percent (ignoring the direction of the change.) Multiplying that by the coefficient from (4), we observe that unemployment typically was changed by about 1.4 percentage points (3.26 times 0.437) because of changing price levels (e.g., from 5.5 to 6.9 percent.) All three components seem to have measurable impacts on unemployment, with the price variable being moderately greater than the money-wage or productivity factors in relative importance. In addition, of course, each

FIGURE 3.1

ACTUAL VS. PREDICTED UNEMPLOYMENT, 1900–1990

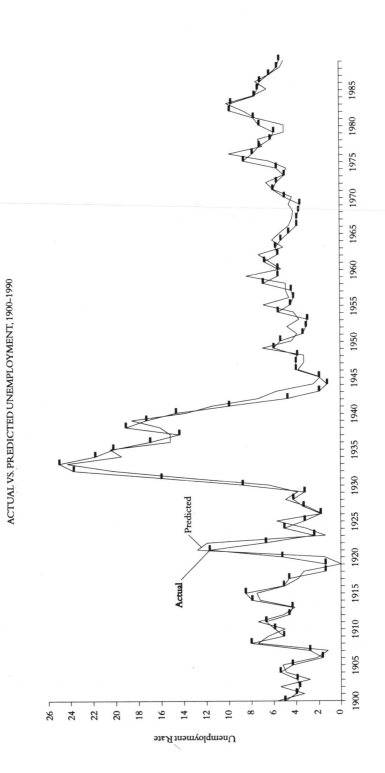

FIGURE 3.2

A CLOSER LOOK AT ACTUAL VS. PREDICTED UNEMPLOYMENT

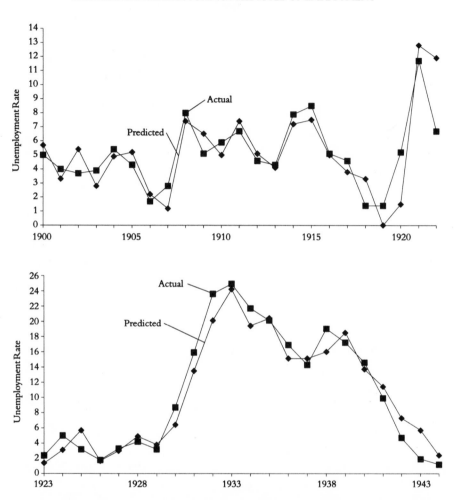

component enters into the determination of the adjusted real wage, which, in lagged form, is also included in the regression equation. Therefore, the total impact of, for example, a 5.4 percent money–wage increase is greater than indicated above.

The Changing Flexibility of Wages, Prices, and Productivity

From the model, it would appear that the degree to which wages, prices, and productivity fluctuate in their movement over time is an important

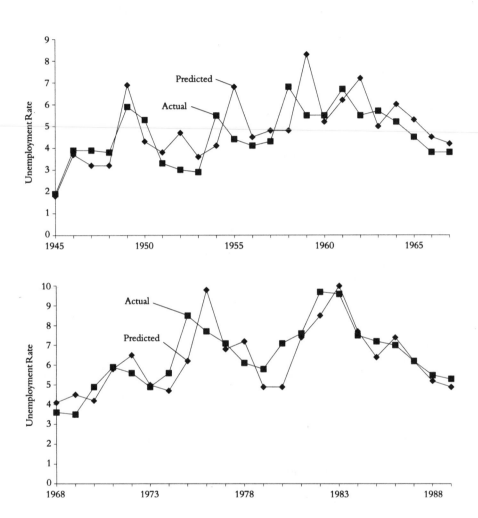

determinant of variations in unemployment. Table 3.1 shows movements in the adjusted real wage, unadjusted real wages, money wages, prices, and labor productivity for a variety of time periods in the twentieth century.

Looking at the first three periods, note that the standard deviation of the adjusted real wage variable is about the same from 1960 to 1990 as it was in 1900–1929; the fluctuations in both periods were much lower than from 1930 to 1959, when that variable seemed to bounce around more. Note also that the absolute mean value of the adjusted real wage was highest

TABLE 3.1

CHANGES IN THE COMPONENTS OF THE ADJUSTED REAL WAGE, 1900–1989

Variable	Statistic	Period: 1900–29	1930–59	1960–89	1947–68	1969–89
Adjusted Real Wage	Mean	93.47	104.64	101.03	101.90	100.22
Adjusted Real Wage	Standard Deviation	3.92	5.64	3.94	2.35	4.43
Change, Adjusted Real Wage[a]	Mean	0.46	0.39	-0.41	-0.39	-0.52
Change, Adjusted Real Wage[a]	Standard Deviation	3.74	4.60	1.26	2.42	1.39
Change, Money Wage[a]	Mean	5.07	4.78	6.49	5.47	7.04
Change, Money Wage[a]	Standard Deviation	6.19	5.66	2.29	2.03	2.38
Change, Prices[a]	Mean	2.61	1.91	5.00	2.72	6.28
Change, Prices[a]	Standard Deviation	6.42	5.14	3.32	3.43	3.12
Change, Productivity[a]	Mean	2.11	2.54	1.87	3.15	1.29
Change, Productivity[a]	Standard Deviation	4.09	3.24	1.55	1.69	1.42
Change, Real Wage[ab]	Mean	2.46	2.86	1.46	2.75	0.75
Change, Real Wage[ab]	Standard Deviation	3.03	3.86	1.76	2.79	1.61
Unemployment Rate	Mean	4.70	9.30	6.09	4.68	6.59
Unemployment Rate	Standard Deviation	2.29	7.36	1.60	1.13	1.55

[a]Annual percent changes.
[b]Unadjusted (money wages divided by prices). For more on definition of variables, see text.
Source: Authors' calculations; see text.

from 1930 to 1959, and lowest from 1900 to 1929. It is not surprising, then, that unemployment was also highest on average from 1930 to 1959, and lowest, on average, from 1900 to 1929. Also the variability in unemployment was greatest when the standard deviation of the adjusted real wage was greatest.

Although the standard deviation of the adjusted real wage variable is a measure of variation in the adjusted real wage over each time period examined (usually thirty years), short-run fluctuations in that variable are better measured by the standard deviation of annual percent changes. On that score, fluctuations in the adjusted real wage were markedly lower in the 1960–90 period than in the earlier eras.

Not only has the instability in the adjusted real wage declined since the era of the Great Depression, but there has been a pronounced diminution in the fluctuations in the components making up that wage. Productivity, price, and money-wage changes tended to vary far less from year to year in the latter decades than early in the century. Even unadjusted real-wage growth tended to bounce around less in the more recent decades.

The evidence from table 3.1 seems to be consistent with what some economists view as a decline in the downward flexibility of wages over time. According to this view, markets cannot function to eliminate unemployment because of wage rigidity. It is true, for example, that in nine of the first forty years observed (1900–1939), money wages actually fell, whereas in none of the past forty years have money wages risen less than 3 percent.

From the standpoint of real wages, however, there is a different pattern. In ten of the first forty years in the century, they fell. Yet, in six of the past twenty years (1970–89), real wages also have declined, a slightly higher proportion of years. Early in the century, falling real wages were brought about in some years by downward wage adjustments, in other years by upward price adjustments, and in some years by both factors; late in the century, however, decreases in real wages have come about exclusively through upward adjustments in prices.

Put differently, early in the century, private decision-making in the private sector in response to market conditions seemed to initiate downward real-wage adjustments in several years; in modern times, downward real-wage adjustments seem to have resulted from price increases that may be largely initiated by macroeconomic policy. Also, in the early part of the century, downward real-wage adjustments may have come quicker than in recent years. For example, real wages fell some 11 percent between 1979 and 1989—but in no single year did they fall as much as 2.7 percent. Real wages were quite flexible downward—but it took time for the full adjustment to occur. By contrast, on eight different occasions before America's entry into World War II, real wages fell more than 3 percent in a single year.

It may be, however, that the observed decline in the variability of wages has been exaggerated by biases arising from splicing together sets of wage data for different periods computed using different methodologies. Steven Allen has replicated methods used to calculate wages in the prewar era for postwar data, concluding that money-wage volatility has not fallen—the observed decline is a statistically created illusion.[12]

Nonetheless, the prevailing wisdom still is that real-wage flexibility has diminished. The reasons for this will be explored in greater detail in coming chapters. We would observe here that two constraints on wage flexibility are found today that did not exist to a major extent in the first decades of this century. First, in the earlier years, relatively few employees worked under contracts. The growth in collective bargaining brought about more wage rigidity. Workers usually work under multiyear contracts; cost-of-living adjustment clauses in some contracts make it difficult to reduce real wages in the short run. Also, the growth in the relative importance of government employment has increased the "wage inflexibility" problem since government compensation has historically been notoriously slow to respond to changing market conditions.

A second problem has been the growth in direct government intervention in labor markets. With the Fair Labor Standards Act of 1938, the federal government imposed minimum-wage requirements that have materially altered the market for relatively unskilled labor. Other legislation (e.g., the 1931 Davis–Bacon Act and similar state laws) even impacted on compensation for skilled labor. More recently, civil-rights legislation and perhaps even the Medicare program have affected the ability of employers to pay market-determined wages. Further substantial effects on employee compensation patterns have come from governmentally mandated fringe benefits, such as the social security program.

The decline in wage flexibility has been interpreted by some as a sign that market adjustments will be inadequate to deal with substantial unemployment, and that governmental macroeconomic intervention is desirable. We are skeptical of that conclusion for at least three reasons. First, if indeed wages are less flexible than previously, the solution to that is to restore wage flexibility by removing obstacles to that flexibility, not to consider self-correcting market adjustments as an inadequate policy tool, particularly given the strong evidence in (4) that unemployment is closely associated with movements in the adjusted real wage. Second, there is some question as to the degree to which relative wage-price flexibility has truly declined, given the nature of some of the data available. Errors in early data collection and presentation may well serve to distort early wage patterns. More recently, the consumer price index has come under a good deal of criticism for overstating the inflation of the 1970s and early 1980s. Third and perhaps most important, it appears that a reduction in volatility in the adjusted real wage and its components has contributed to reduced unemployment volatility. If wages are somewhat less flexible on the down side, they also have tended to increase in a predictable and not very volatile fashion in recent years. There has not been a single increase in real wages in excess of 4 percent in any of the past thirty years, for example, a factor contributing to the relatively few observed surges in unemployment in that era.

Criticisms of the Model

The model presented in (4) above is very unfashionable these days. To most contemporary mainstream economists, it is naively low tech, a simple single equation. Allegedly, far more complex models are capable of dealing with the material of the simple model while also offering more profound insight. The model here is appropriate for 1950 or possibly even 1970, but not 1990 or beyond, since econometric knowledge has expanded in the past generation. Also, it focuses directly on the labor market, whereas most economists of the mid- and late twentieth centuries have tended to explain unemployment indirectly by looking at other markets, in particular money markets. The model does not talk about consumption or investment or the stock of money or interest rates or any of the other things that economists usually bring up in discussing unemployment.

The approach here is even subject to criticism by the one group of economists that in general solidly agrees with the conclusions, the Austrian school. Austrian economics, which has had a healthy resurgence in recent years, tends to be highly skeptical of econometric and mathematical work.[13] The Austrians tend to reject the modern scientific perspective that there is no a priori knowledge. Also, they question the aggregation used in constructing data series. For example, there are very serious conceptual problems in the construction of price indices, not to mention practical difficulties. Thus the approach used by us is criticized by one group of economists as being insufficiently empirical and by another group as being excessively empirical and quantitative.

Regarding the mainstream criticism, it is our goal to communicate our ideas to an audience of intelligent laypersons as well as to professional economists, and highly complex econometric models are beyond the understanding of much of our audience. Great economists from Smith to Keynes wrote books that the intelligent layperson could largely understand; current economic analysis is beyond the comprehension of that audience, and we view that as unfortunate. Later, we will deal with some of the specific objections to the model, but would note here that it seems to work well in describing the realities of twentieth-century unemployment variations. Moreover, the most straightforward way to look at unemployment is to look directly at labor markets, rather than indirectly at other markets that might have an impact on labor demand and supply.

As to the Austrian critique, we are increasingly sympathetic to some of the criticisms of the quantitative approach, a criticism that has spread to some of the leading econometricians themselves.[14] Still, to convince the unconverted in modern times that one's theory is valid, one must present some empirical evidence. To win consideration of one's views, one has to use the appropriate rhetoric. The current "rhetoric of economics," to borrow from Donald McCloskey, is econometrics.[15] Hopefully, the empirical approach used here is quantitative enough to command attention of academic economists, but descriptive enough to command the attention of the public, even if the rhetorical approach is not perceived as ideal by either group.

Furthermore, the overwhelming majority of economists (including ourselves) reject the Hayekian view that the Austrian approach is inherently untestable. While quantitative economics is not infallible, we believe there is overwhelming solid evidence that the use of statistical method strengthens our knowledge of economic theory and our understanding of institutional arrangements. While economic propositions cannot be proven with absolute certainty, econometrics can strongly demonstrate their real-world insight in a convincing manner. Virtually every economist, for example, accepts empirically verified propositions that the quantity of almost any good demanded varies inversely with its price, or that increases in the quantity of money are associated with increases in prices. The validity of hypotheses about human economic behavior has been successfully demonstrated on countless occasions by the use of techniques similar to those used in this book.

DATA PROBLEMS

Turning to some specific potential problems in the previous statistical analysis, there are legitimate concerns about the quality of the data used. Questions have been raised about the basic accuracy of the government unemployment-rate data; the wage series used is subject to an unknown but potentially considerable amount of error, particularly before 1947; and the consumer price index has been considerably maligned by economists and others for years.

To deal with these difficulties, we reexamined the basic model outlined in equation (4), substituting alternative data sources. We used the unemployment-rate estimates for most of the period developed by Christina Romer, along with Michael Darby's calculations for the 1930–43 period.[16] We are not certain that these estimates are correct; we merely wish to see if the statistical estimation reported above is highly sensitive to which data are used.[17]

Regarding wages, we developed two alternative wage series. The wage information used so far derives hourly earnings by dividing annual earnings data by an estimate of average annual hours worked. The estimate of hours worked is based on a subset of the employed population, and thus may be in error. As a first alternative, we selected the wage series developed by Paul David and Peter Solar for hourly earnings for lower-skilled workers.[18] The David-Solar estimates might be viewed as inferior as they relate only to one subset of the working population, unskilled workers. On the other hand, that category is particularly vulnerable historically to unemployment. Moreover, the accuracy of the data is believed to be relatively high. After 1974, we spliced hourly wage data for production workers in manufacturing to the David-Solar series. Those workers are not all unskilled, but a large proportion are.[19]

One might argue that the David-Solar data are a useful measure before 1947 (a period for which the data on hours worked are somewhat suspect), but that after that date the widely used BLS employee compensation data for the business sector are more appropriate, since they cover much more of the labor force and incorporate fringe benefits, not included in the David-Solar measure. Thus, a second alternative wage measure incorporates the David-Solar data up to 1947, and the BLS data subsequent to that date.

From the standpoint of the supply of labor (workers), the relevant price variable is the consumer price index or some other measure of consumer prices. Real wages are money wages related to consumer prices. Yet from the standpoint of the demand for labor (employers), the relevant price variable is some measure of producer or wholesale prices, since the marginal revenue product of labor depends in part on the selling price of goods. One could maintain, therefore, that wholesale prices should be used in calculating the adjusted real wage and as our price variable in (4). Accordingly, as an alternative price measure, we used the Bureau of Labor Statistics component of the wholesale (later, producer) price index for "finished goods."[20]

With two different unemployment measures, three indicators of wage payments, and two price indices, we have twelve different possible variants on (4). Performing regression analysis on the data as before, we obtain interesting results (table 3.2). In general, the findings are relatively robust, with the explanatory power of the model varying between 78 and over 90 percent. The critically important lagged adjusted real wage variable always has the expected positive sign, and in most (nine out of twelve) cases is statistically significant at the 1 percent level (and in eleven of twelve instances, at the 10 percent level.) The model does not appear fragile with respect to the critical variable—one can alter the data in a variety of ways and still obtain results consistent with the major hypothesis that increased adjusted real wages are associated with higher unemployment.

Moreover, we consistently obtain the expected negative sign on the productivity and price change variables, with the results again being highly significant in most cases (at the 1 percent level in nine of twelve cases for the productivity variable, and in eight of twelve instances for the price variable.) Indeed, in every instance the productivity-change variable is significant at the 5 percent level.

The one factor that does not perform as well when subjected to sensitivity analysis is the change-in-money-wage variable. In only six of twelve instances does the variable have the expected sign; in only three of twelve cases are the results statistically significant. Where negative signs are obtained, however, the results are extremely weak and never different from zero in a statistical sense. It should be stressed that money wages also impact importantly on the lagged-adjusted-wage term, which is robustly and positively related to unemployment.

This exercise in sensitivity analysis confirms our faith in the basic model's validity. In general, the results are not sensitive to definitional changes

TABLE 3.2

TWELVE VARIANTS OF THE BASIC UNEMPLOYMENT RATE DETERMINATION MODEL 1900-89[a]

Form of Variable Used:[a]

Wage	Price	Unemployment	Adjusted Real Wage (-1)[b]	Change in Wages[b]	Change in Productivity[b]	Change in Prices[b]	$\bar{R}^2$	D-W
Com/BLS	CPI	BLS	.390[c]	.172[c]	-.302[c]	-.437[c]	.899	2.001
Com/BLS	CPI	Romer-Darby	.397[c]	.158[c]	-.244[c]	-.305[c]	.814	2.051
Dav-Sol/Manufacturing	CPI	BLS	.191[c]	.011	-.240[c]	-.313[c]	.895	1.969
Dav-Sol./Manufacturing	CPI	Romer-Darby	.052	-.045	-.108[d]	-.109	.784	1.990
Dav-Sol/BLS	CPI	BLS	.317[c]	.046	-.264	-.351	.904	1.999
Dav-Sol/BLS	CPI	Romer-Darby	.133[e]	-.033	-.129[d]	-.123[e]	.792	1.995
Com/BLS	WPI	BLS	.181[c]	.052	-.230[c]	-.190[c]	.880	2.001
Com/BLS	WPI	Romer-Darby	.190[c]	.079[e]	-.180[c]	-.124[c]	.796	1.999
Dav-Sol/Manufacturing	WPI	BLS	.190[c]	-.003	-.227[c]	-.167[e]	.891	2.000
Dav-Sol/Manufacturing	WPI	Romer-Darby	.127[c]	-.023	-.135[c]	-.077[e]	.790	2.000
Dav-Sol/BLS	WPI	BLS	.203[c]	-.027	-.208[c]	-.197[c]	.890	2.001
Dav-Sol/BLS	WPI	Romer-Darby	.132[d]	-.052	-.109[d]	-.057	.794	1.994

[a]For full definition of variables see text.
[b]Numbers represent regression coefficients.
[c]Significant at the 1 percent level.
[d]Significant at the 5 percent level.
[e]Significant at the 10 percent level.
Source: Authors' calculations; see text

TABLE 3.3

THE DETERMINANTS OF UNEMPLOYMENT: AN EXPANDED ADJUSTED REAL WAGE
MODEL

Statistic or Variable	Lag	Coefficient	T-Value
Constant	N.A.	-69.612	3.999
Adjusted Real Wage	7 Years	0.801	4.699
% Change, Consumer Prices	None	-0.461	6.615
% Change, Consumer Prices	1 Year	-0.214	2.270
% Change, Consumer Prices	2 Years	-0.581	5.073
% Change, Consumer Prices	3 Years	-0.539	4.179
% Change, Consumer Prices	4 Years	-0.568	3.854
% Change, Consumer Prices	5 Years	-0.665	4.311
% Change, Consumer Prices	6 Years	-0.674	4.145
% Change, Labor Productivity	None	-0.484	6.894
% Change, Labor Productivity	1 Year	-0.588	6.141
% Change, Labor Productivity	2 Years	-0.748	6.220
% Change, Labor Productivity	3 Years	-0.773	5.762
% Change, Labor Productivity	4 Years	-0.741	5.167
% Change, Labor Productivity	5 Years	-0.764	4.853
% Change, Labor Productivity	6 Years	-0.663	4.235
% Change, Money Wages	None	0.159	2.350
% Change, Money Wages	1 Year	0.312	3.339
% Change, Money Wages	2 Years	0.546	4.668
% Change, Money Wages	3 Years	0.508	3.821
% Change, Money Wages	4 Years	0.639	4.398
% Change, Money Wages	5 years	0.592	3.871
% Change, Money Wages	6 Years	0.606	3.772
R^2		0.940	
$\overline{R}^2$		0.917	
F-Statistic		40.386	
D-W		1.995	

Source: See text.

in variables. There is little doubt in our mind that unemployment varies importantly with changes in real wages adjusted for productivity change.

EXPANDED LAG STRUCTURE

In the process of performing sensitivity analysis such as reported in table 3.2, we experimented with models incorporating more extensive lags than indicated in (4). Perhaps unemployment responds to changes in the components of the adjusted real wage over several years. That indeed is the case. In table 3.3, we report the results of a variant on the original model with some twenty-two explanatory variables. The adjusted real wage variable is lagged some seven years behind the unemployment rate (e.g., unemployment in 1987 is related to the adjusted real wage in 1980.) The relationship between the unemployment rate and the percent change in prices is exam-

TABLE 3.4

TIMING OF UNEMPLOYMENT EFFECTS OF CHANGING WAGES, PRICES AND
PRODUCTIVITY

Variable	Lag	Percent of Unemployment Effect Realized by Date in Question
% Change in Money Wages	None	24.9
% Change in Money Wages	1 Year	48.8
% Change in Money Wages	2 Years	85.4
% Change in Money Wages	3 Years	79.4
% Change in Money Wages	4 Years	100.0
% Change in Consumer Prices	None	68.3
% Change in Consumer Prices	1 Year	31.8
% Change in Consumer Prices	2 Years	86.1
% Change in Consumer Prices	3 Years	79.9
% Change in Consumer Prices	4 Years	84.3
% Change in Consumer Prices	5 Years	98.6
% Change in Consumer Prices	6 Years	100.0
% Change in Productivity	None	62.6
% Change in Productivity	1 Year	76.1
% Change in Productivity	2 Years	96.7
% Change in Productivity	3 Years	100.0

Source: Authors' calculations from regression coefficients in Table 3–3.

ined for the current year, and each of the past six years. The same is true
of the percent change in labor productivity and percent change in the
money wage rate.

The findings are truly extraordinary. The model explains some 94 percent of the variation in the unemployment rate over time. Of the twenty-
two explanatory variables, twenty were statistically significant at the 1
percent level with the expected sign, and the other two, also with the
expected sign, were significant at the 2 percent level. In fifty-four of ninety
years, the actual unemployment rate was within one percentage point of
what the model predicted. Only in one year (1931) did the actual rate
deviate from the predicted rate by as much as three percentage points. The
model is equally good at predicting at the beginning and at the end of the
century. Indeed, the two decades in which the model predicted unemployment within one-half of one percentage point of the actual rate in six or
more years were the 1900s and the 1980s.

The results suggest that some of the impact of changing wages, prices,
and productivity on unemployment comes long after those variables
change, although there is a short-run impact as well. Table 3.4 indicates
the proportion of the ultimate effect of changing money wages, prices, and
productivity that is observed immediately, after one year, two years, etc.
Starting with money-wage changes, the findings suggest that in a year
when money wages rise by 1 percent, unemployment rises by 0.16 percent
as a consequence. Four years later, this year's 1 percent wage increase will

have an impact on unemployment in that year of 0.64 percentage point. Thus only about 25 percent of the effect of the wage increase is what might be termed "short-run" or immediate, with the remainder coming over time. Note the full (maximum) impact is reached after four years—after that the lagged wage–unemployment relation weakens somewhat.

With productivity change, however, more of the impact comes immediately. A 1 percent productivity increase per worker this year will lower unemployment by 0.48 percentage points. The maximum cumulative impact is reached after three years, 0.77 percentage points. Thus over 60 percent of the productivity-change impact is felt in the year that it occurs. With price changes, the findings are similar. The immediate impact of a 1 percent increase in prices is a fall in the unemployment rate by 0.48 percentage points; the maximum long-term impact, after six years, is 0.67 percentage points, suggesting that about 70 percent of the impact comes immediately.

With all three components of the adjusted real wage, the impact of a change is mostly (85 percent or more of the maximum observed impact) seen within two years. The long-term effect as measured by the maximum regression coefficient runs from a .64 percentage point impact for a 1 percent change in money wages to a .77 percentage point movement for a 1 percent change in labor productivity. The three variables are approximately equal in potency, with the long-term impact somewhat greater than indicated in (4) above, especially for money-wage changes.

ISSUES OF CAUSALITY

Just demonstrating that a statistical relationship exists between two or more variables does not, of course, prove causality. Going back to our simplest expression of the neoclassical/Austrian perspective in (1), it is at least theoretically possible that instead of rising adjusted real wages causing higher unemployment, higher unemployment causes higher adjusted real wages. Yet such a conclusion is implausible. One might dismiss that possibility on the basis of economic theory or logic. It makes sense that higher wages would price workers out of the market causing increased unemployment, but makes no sense that higher unemployment would cause wages to rise (if anything, higher unemployment might induce wage-cutting.)

However, critics of the model above would argue that only the proximate causes of unemployment are examined, not the underlying factors. For example, the unemployment-price change relationship observed in (4) and table 3.3 above ignores the causes of price changes. Similarly, the underlying causes of changes in the money-wage variable are not made explicit. These criticisms have some validity, and as the discussion unfolds in the next several chapters we will look at some of the deeper causes of changing prices and wages.

The most criticism, however, relates to productivity change. Keynesians would argue that productivity change is highly procyclical, responding to fluctuations in aggregate demand. For example, they might make the point that if aggregate demand declines, businesses face a decline in the demand for labor (the demand curve in figure 2.1 shifts downward and to the left). At least initially, businesses do not reduce staff proportionally with reduced production, leading to a decline in output per worker. If true, changes in the adjusted real wage are at least partly determined by Keynesian-style aggregate-demand shifts, making the statistical results cited above far less unambiguously supportive of Austrian or neoclassical perspectives on the determinants of unemployment.

It is true that there is a positive statistical association in the twentieth century between short-term fluctuations in economic activity and changes in the productivity of labor. Running a regression between the percent annual change in labor productivity and the percent growth in real GNP (the best measure of economic activity), we find that for the ninety-year period, about one-third of the annual variation in labor productivity growth is explainable by fluctuations in the level of economic activity.[21] Moreover, the observed relationship is highly significant in a statistical sense. Over some subsets of the century, the proportion of productivity variation explained by changing real GNP is slightly higher, although never as much as half.

We could call productivity change induced by cyclical shifts in aggregate demand "Keynesian productivity change." Yet a large majority (about two-thirds) of the observed variation in labor productivity is not of this nature. Thus, the claim that the productivity variable's behavior is largely determined by shifts in aggregate demand seems questionable.

Moreover, in any given year, the growth in real GNP reflects not only cyclical forces (such as changing aggregate demand), but also the long-term growth in real output, influenced by such things as the formation of productive inputs, especially capital, and the resultant increase in the capital-labor ratio. This is the type of productivity advance talked about by Adam Smith in *The Wealth of Nations*, and can be termed "Smithian productivity change."[22] Moreover, even with respect to cyclical fluctuations, it may be true that spurts and lapses in technological progress and innovation may themselves cause business cycles and also explain variations in productivity growth over time: this was the argument of Joseph Schumpeter, and consequently, we might speak of "Schumpeterian productivity change."[23]

In short, the cyclical component of real-output change may be caused by multiple factors.

One final test of the role of productivity change was performed. Keynesians have often argued that shifts in human behavior regarding one of the key components of aggregate demand have been a decisive factor in explaining cyclical activity. For example, the Great Depression has been explained in large part by downward shifts in the investment and/or consumption components of aggregate demand.[24] Out of any given income in 1930, people spent less than what historical experience would have predicted, thus triggering a depression (helped by a "multiplier effect"). In the lingo of economists, "autonomous consumption fell." Similar demand shifts have allegedly explained both the onset of the World War II boom (increase in autonomous government spending) and the lack of a depression at the end of the war (increased autonomous consumption and investment).[25]

The relevant question here is, to what extent have shifts in one of the key components of aggregate demand impacted on labor productivity, the adjusted real wage, and thus unemployment? The proposition that fluctuations in labor productivity are partly induced by Keynesian-style shifts in one of the components of aggregate demand is subject to empirical analysis. We performed a two-stage regression procedure. First, we identified shifts in autonomous consumption or investment spending that potentially could cause a shift in aggregate demand. This involved, in the case of consumption, estimating a consumption function where consumption is related to disposable income.[26] Similar investment and government-spending functions were estimated. The discrepancy between actual spending (say, for consumption) and predicted spending is an indication of the extent that spending in a given year deviated from the normal long-run trend consistent with that income or output level. It provides a means of measuring changes in autonomous consumption (or other components of spending). Second, we related the year-to-year changes in autonomous spending to observed productivity change using a simple bivariate regression. In every case (consumption spending, gross private domestic investment spending, government purchases of goods and services, and net exports), we found no statistically significant relationship, even at the 10 percent level using a one-tailed test. Indeed, a majority of the results had a negative sign, not the relationship predicted by Keynesian analysis. On the basis of this, we believe that the proposition that shifts in components of total spending are an important determinant of productivity change is not defensible. At the same time, however, it is true, over all, that the business cycle is related to productivity changes to a moderate extent. Cycles in innovation and capital formation may impact simultaneously on productivity (Schumpeterian and Smithian changes) and output growth. This in no way detracts from the usefulness of the adjusted real wage model in analyzing the proximate determinants of unemployment variations.

There is very strong statistical evidence of a relationship between the adjusted real wage and unemployment. Higher adjusted real wages, other things equal, mean higher unemployment. The three factors determining the adjusted real wage—money-wage levels, price levels, and labor productivity—are of roughly equal importance in their unemployment impact. There is some evidence that unemployment reacts to changes in the adjusted real wage almost immediately, with the bulk of the impact felt within two years. At the same time, there is some lingering effect felt even after that lag. The productivity variable has a cyclical component to it, but the empirical evidence suggests that shifts in the aggregate demand for goods and services play no significant role in explaining this component of the adjusted real wage.

   In brief, the neoclassical and Austrian view of the determinants of unemployment seems to have a great deal of validity. We now turn to a closer look at the changes in unemployment in American history, with this theory in mind, hoping to ascertain in greater detail the underlying factors that have generated both changes in the adjusted real wage and variations in unemployment.

NOTES

   1.   Data before 1947 were originally compiled by Stanley Lebergott. See, for example, his *Manpower in Economic Growth: The American Record Since 1800* (New York: McGraw-Hill, 1964.) The Lebergott estimates, slightly modified, serve as the basis of the official Bureau of Labor Statistics data. See U.S. Department of Commerce, Bureau of the Census, *Historical Statistics of the United States, Colonial Times to 1970* (Washington, D.C.: Government Printing Office, 1975), p. 135. For recent unemployment statistics, see the *Economic Report of the President 1991* (Washington, D.C.: Government Printing Office, 1991), p. 330.
   2.   See ibid., p. 346. In the postwar period, the growth of fringe benefits has led to a growing divergence between money-wage growth and the growth in total money compensation costs. The latter concept is used here, as fringe benefits are part of the true compensation package. Also, businesses presumably consider their total compensation costs in making employment decisions.
   3.   The critical wage series used in calculating our wage measure is found in *Historical Statistics of the United States*, Series D-724. They were calculated by the U.S. Office of Business Economics as a by-product of calculating the national income and product accounts. Because of lags in the model, data for the 1890s were

needed. Data for that decade, obtained from Series D-735, ibid., were spliced to the data series for 1900 to 1946. The 1890s data were originally estimated by Lebergott, *Manower in Economic Growth*. The 1890–1946 data, in turn, were spliced to the data for the post-1947 era and turned to index number form, with 1982 = 100. Annual hours worked were obtained by using weekly hours data and multiplying by 50. The hours data for the 1890–1918 period came from *Historical Statistics of the United States*, Series D-767; for 1919–1946, the data are from Series D-803. The 1890–1918 data were originally compiled by Paul H. Douglas in his *Real Wages in the United States* (New York: Houghton Mifflin, 1930).

4. Series D-683.

5. John W. Kendrick, *Productivity Trends in the United States* (Princeton, N. J.: Princeton University Press for the National Bureau of Economic Research, 1961).

6. As reported annually in the *Economic Report of the President* (on p. 346 of the 1990 edition), and monthly in *Economic Indicators* (on p. 16.)

7. As reported in *Historical Statistics of the United States*, pp. 211–12, and in the *Economic Report of the President 1990*, p. 359. The pre-1946 data were spliced to the post-1946 data using the 1982–84 base years = 100.

8. The regression reported included two ARIMA adjustment terms, not reported, so as to deal with the existence of serial correlation. The reported results have no significant evidence of serial correlation. The unreported F-statistic is healthily large (over 114).

9. The 0.6 figure is derived by multiplying the regression coefficient, .315, by the median change (ignoring signs) in the adjusted real wage, 1.85, obtaining 0.583.

10. A detailed theoretical derivation of this form of the model is presented in the appendix.

11. Three ARIMA terms created to eliminate autocorrelation are not indicated. The results are not significantly impacted by the nature of the adjustments made to deal with the serial correlation issue.

12. "Changes in the Cyclical Sensitivity of Wages in the United States, 1891–1987," *American Economic Review* 82 (1992): 122–40.

13. See Ludwig von Mises, *Human Action*, 3d rev. ed. (Chicago: Henry Regnery Company, 1966), pp. 350–57 for a flavor of the philosophical objections that the Austrians have to the empirical approach. Friedrich von Hayek said similar things. Speaking of the Austrian theory, he said that it "cannot *by its very nature* be tested by statistics." See Chiaki Nishiyama and Kurt R. Leube, *The Essence of Hayek* (Stanford: Hoover Institution Press, 1984), p. 7.

14. Our favorite is Lawrence Leamer, "Let's Take the Con Out of Econometrics," *American Economic Review* 73 (1983): 31–43.

15. See his "The Rhetoric of Economics," *Journal of Economic Literature* 21 (1983): 481–517. For a more extended treatment see McCloskey's *The Rhetoric of Economics* (Madison: University of Wisconsin Press, 1985).

16. Christina Romer, "Spurious Volatility in Historical Unemployment Data," *Journal of Political Economy* 94 (1986): 1–37; Michael Darby, "Three-and-a-Half Million U.S. Employees Have Been Mislaid: Or, an Explanation of Unemployment, 1934–41," *Journal of Political Economy* 84 (1976): 1–15.

17.   Reviewing several attempts to estimate unemployment rates for the critical decades of the 1920s and 1930s, Gene Smiley seems to conclude that Lebergott's approach was quite valid. The Smiley evaluation was written before the Romer estimates were compiled. See Gene Smiley, "Recent Unemployment Rate Estimates for the 1920s and 1930s," *Journal of Economic History* 43 (1983): 487–493.

18.   Paul A. David and Peter Solar, "A Bicentenary Contribution to the History of the Cost of Living in America," in *Research in Economic History*, Paul Uselding, ed., vol. 2 (Greenwich, Conn.: JAI Press, 1977), pp. 1–80.

19.   The data, originally compiled by the U.S. Department of Labor, come from the *Economic Report of the President 1990*, p. 344. The David-Solar and Labor Department data were spliced together and indexed, with 1982 = 100.

20.   Actually, for years to 1912, the BLS "manufactured commodity" index is used. See *Historical Statistics of the United States*, Series E-89. From 1913–46, data come from the same source, Series E-84. From 1947, the data are derived from the *Economic Report of the President 1990*, p. 365. Again, the series are spliced together and indexed with 1982 = 100.

21.   The adjusted R^2, after inclusion of autoregressive terms, was .3243.

22.   Adam Smith, *An Inquiry into the Nature and Causes of the Wealth of Nations* (Oxford: Oxford University Press, 1976), book I, chap. 1, especially p. 17.

23.   Joseph A. Schumpeter, *The Theory of Economic Development* (Cambridge, Mass.: Harvard University Press, 1949).

24.   See, for example, Peter Temin, *Did Monetary Forces Cause the Great Depression?* (New York; W. W. Norton, 1976), chap. 3, or his *Lessons from the Great Depression* (Cambridge, Mass.: MIT. Press, 1989), pp. 43, 105–6. Temin seems somewhat more sympathetic to the "wages" approach used here in his 1989 book than he did in 1976, perhaps because of a spate of studies supporting that approach to explaining Depression-era conditions. For an earlier account with some Keynesian flavor, see John Kenneth Galbraith, *The Great Crash, 1929* (Boston: Houghton Mifflin, 1955).

25.   This subject is explored in detail in chapter 8.

26.   Data on the components of GNP are consistently available only from 1929, so the estimated consumption function regressed consumption against disposable income for the period 1929 to 1989. The residuals from that regression represented deviations of the consumption-income relationship from its long-term norm. Changes in those residuals represented changes in autonomous consumption—that component of consumer spending not directly related to income. The residuals from the consumption function were then regressed against changes in labor productivity to see if a significant positive relationship existed. Similarly, functions were created where gross private domestic investment, net exports, and government purchases spending were regressed against GNP.

4

The Gilded Age

In many respects, the first three decades of the twentieth century were the golden age of the American economy. Despite the absence of national income statistics, it became very apparent during this period that America was the world's premier economic power. The economic performance of the nation from 1900 to 1929 clearly established that this was "the American century" as far as economic growth was concerned.

Not only did real output expand at a very respectable 3.4 percent annual rate, but the growth far outdistanced that of older economies in Europe. It has been estimated that real output rose only 1.8 percent annually in the area constituting today's European Economic Community (Common Market).[1] There is some dispute as to how the fruits of this considerable economic progress were distributed.[2] Yet there is no denying that the typical American family in 1929 owned a car, went to talking movies, listened to the radio, and owned a telephone—none of which was true in 1900. While his framework may be flawed, Walt Rostow makes a valid point in arguing the United States entered an "age of mass consumption" during this era.[3]

By the standard macroeconomic indicators of today, the first three decades of the century were highly successful. The inflation rate was 2.5 percent per annum, considered high by contemporaries but extremely low by present-day standards. Moreover, most of the inflation occurred in a few years during and immediately following World War I; during peacetime, prices were about as likely to fall in any given year as to rise.

Unemployment, as measured by the official Lebergott/BLS data, averaged only 4.67 percent for the thirty years 1900 through 1929, with the median unemployment rate being 4.30 percent. In only one year, 1921, did the unemployment rate average in double digits, and unemployment was under 3 percent more often (six versus four years) than it was above 7 percent.

Before extending our analysis of unemployment, it is very interesting to note that this era of prosperity and stability occurred during a period of relatively little government involvement in the economy. To be sure, there was an increase in some forms of regulation (passage and enforcement of antitrust laws, and railroad rate and food and drug regulation), the passage of a federal income tax amendment to the Constitution, and the beginning of institutional macroeconomic intervention with the creation of the Federal Reserve system. Collectively these factors led one distinguished economic historian to term the era 1897–1917 "the decline of laissez-faire."[4]

Yet by modern-day standards, there was still a good bit of laissez-faire left in the American economy. Government purchases of goods and services absorbed only 8.2 percent of gross national product in 1929, and some 85 percent of that was carried on at the state and local level. After a high level of both spending and regulation during World War I, government involvement decreased during the 1920s, albeit to not quite as low levels as before the war.[5] While it is true that total governmental expenditures rose from 7.7 percent of GNP in 1902 to 11.8 percent in 1929, the latter figure is only one-third the proportion of recent times; most of the growth in expenditures reflected high income elasticity of demand for goods and services traditionally provided by government, such as highways and education, rather than bold new forms of government involvement. The era was characterized by both relatively low levels of unemployment and relatively little state involvement in the economy.

The Unemployment Experience, 1900–1929

Moving to a less aggregated view of the period, table 4.1 shows the unemployment experience, by individual year, for the first three decades of the century. Only in 1921 did the unemployment rate average more than 8.5 percent for a single year. The notion that very high unemployment levels were commonplace in the era before major macroeconomic policy intervention by government does not seem to be supported by the empirical evidence. In 80 percent of the years, the unemployment rate averaged less than 6 percent for the year, a rate that today is considered fairly low.

When relatively high unemployment developed during recessionary periods, it did not tend to persist.[6] There were three episodes (about one a

TABLE 4.1

UNEMPLOYMENT IN THE UNITED STATES, 1900–1929

Year	% Unemployment Rate
1900	5.0
1901	4.0
1902	3.7
1903	3.9
1904	5.4
1905	4.3
1906	1.7
1907	2.8
1908	8.0
1909	5.1
1910	5.9
1911	6.7
1912	4.6
1913	4.3
1914	7.9
1915	8.5
1916	5.1
1917	4.6
1918	1.4
1919	1.4
1920	5.2
1921	11.7
1922	6.7
1923	2.4
1924	5.0
1925	3.2
1926	1.8
1927	3.3
1928	4.2
1929	3.2

Source: U.S. Bureau of the Census, *Historical Statistics*, p.135.

decade) in which unemployment rose above 8 percent. In none of those instances did unemployment remain at an 8 percent or higher average for two consecutive years. After peaking at 8 percent in 1908, unemployment dropped sharply to slightly over 5 percent the following year. After peaking in 1915 at 8.5 percent, the unemployment rate plunged 40 percent in 1916 to a near normal 5.1 percent rate. Even in 1921, when the unemployment rate soared to 11.7 percent, recovery came quickly, with the unemployment rate falling 43 percent in the following year to under 7 percent.

A similar flexibility in the unemployment rate occurred when low unemployment existed. Only once, in 1918 and 1919, was one year of very low unemployment (2.5 percent or less) followed by a second year of similar very low joblessness. Generally unemployment tended to gravitate fairly quickly back to something approximating its natural rate. Only once, from

1906 to 1908, was the unemployment rate outside the 3 to 6 percent range (annual average) for three consecutive years, and even in 1906–8, the rate went *through* the natural rate range, going from below 3 percent in 1906 and 1907 to above 6 percent in 1908.

There is some dispute about the unemployment statistics as they relate to this period. As previously indicated, Christina Romer believes that in general unemployment rates fluctuated less than the Lebergott/BLS statistics show.[7] Regarding the 1920s, R. M. Coen has argued that the rates for most of that decade tend to be understated.[8] After 1922, for which he records a 7.3 percent unemployment rate, Coen finds annual unemployment rates for the rest of the decade ranged between 4 and 6 percent in every single year. Although his average rate is higher than the BLS estimates, even Coen finds rates that tended to cluster between 3 and 6 percent.

In chapter 3, we argued that variations in unemployment in the twentieth century are largely explainable in terms of changes in "the adjusted real wage," or the compensation of workers in terms of purchasing power related to their productivity or output. Unemployment will tend to rise with increases in the adjusted real wage, which in turn can reflect rising money-wage rates, falling prices, or falling productivity of labor. Similarly, a fall in the adjusted real wage tends to reduce unemployment, *ceteris paribus*. Falling adjusted real wages can result from one or a combination of three factors: falling money wages, rising prices, or rising labor productivity. Several variants of the basic model were developed, and the one used here is taken from table 3.3, which suggests unemployment in this year depends on changes in the components of the real wage over the past six years, plus the adjusted real wage itself lagged seven years.

Table 4.2 indicates the actual unemployment rate by year for the 1900–1929 period, as well as the unemployment rate predicted by our adjusted real wage model. The model does reasonably well in forecasting major shifts in the unemployment rate. In no year did the actual unemployment rate deviate from the rate predicted by our model by more than three percentage points (e. g., 7.0 percent vs. 4.0 percent.) In 70 percent of the years, the deviation of the predicted unemployment rate from the actual rate was less than one percentage point. The model does a remarkably good job of predicting major increases in unemployment. The first major episode of moderately high unemployment comes after the panic of 1907. Unemployment rose from 2.8 to 8.0 percent, while the adjusted real wage model predicts a rise from about 0.5 to over 7.7 percent. Similarly, in 1914 and 1915, unemployment again rose to the 8 percent range for two years, up from the 4.3 percent level prevailing in 1913. Our model predicts a rise to a peak rate slightly over 8.8 percent in 1915, very near the actual rate.

TABLE 4.2

ACTUAL VS. PREDICTED UNEMPLOYMENT RATES FOR THE U.S. 1900–1929

Year	Actual Rate	Predicted Rate	Difference in Rates
1900	5.00	4.40	+0.60
1901	4.00	3.53	+0.47
1902	3.70	4.66	-0.96
1903	3.90	4.61	-0.71
1904	5.40	5.26	+0.14
1905	4.30	3.90	+0.40
1906	1.70	2.09	-0.39
1907	2.80	0.46	+2.34
1908	8.00	7.74	+0.26
1909	5.10	5.10	-0.00
1910	5.90	6.85	-0.95
1911	6.70	7.33	-0.63
1912	4.60	4.24	+0.36
1913	4.30	5.66	-1.36
1914	7.90	6.70	+1.20
1915	8.50	8.05	+0.45
1916	5.10	4.20	+0.90
1917	4.60	5.34	-0.74
1918	1.40	1.90	-0.50
1919	1.40	-1.08	+2.48
1920	5.20	2.34	+2.86
1921	11.70	12.13	-0.43
1922	6.70	8.60	-1.90
1923	2.40	2.14	+0.26
1924	5.00	3.46	+1.54
1925	3.20	3.72	-0.52
1926	1.80	2.94	-1.14
1927	3.30	3.89	-0.59
1928	4.20	4.29	-0.09
1929	3.20	3.37	-0.17

Source: U.S. Bureau of Commerce, authors' calculations.

The major downturn of the first three decades was the 1920–21 depression. Unemployment was abnormally low in 1919, 1.4 percent, rising to 5.2 percent in 1920 and 11.7 percent in 1921 before falling to 6.7 percent in 1922 and 2.4 percent in 1923. The wage model actually predicted negative unemployment in 1919. In the most important forecasting error for this era, the model predicts a rise in unemployment in 1920, but to only slightly over 2.3 percent. Yet the model accurately explains the huge rise in unemployment in 1921 (predicting a 12.1 percent rate), and a significant decline in unemployment in 1922 and 1923 (the model shows unemployment rates of 8.6 and 2.1 percent, respectively, for these years).

In the halcyon days from 1923 through 1929, unemployment varied modestly, ranging between 1.8 and 5.0 percent; our statistical explanation indicates values between 2.1 and 4.3 percent, not a very large discrepancy. In short, variations in unemployment during the Gilded Age are well explained by movements in money wages, prices, and labor productivity.

Interpreting the Unemployment Experience, 1900–1919

Before 1913, price data are very crude, with the consumer price index reported only to the nearest whole number. Thus, our interpretation of the proximate determinants of the first major episode of rising unemployment in 1908 must be somewhat cautious owing to data limitations. The evidence is, however, that a combination of price deflation and a fairly sharp productivity decline led to a rise in the adjusted real wage, more than offsetting a modest (1.1 percent) decline in money wages. Real wages rose in a period of falling labor productivity, pushing the adjusted real wage up fairly sharply. This, in turn, led to a near tripling in the unemployment rate.

The unemployment rate returned fairly quickly to a range near equilibrium in 1909. The real wage–enhancing deflation ended. More importantly, labor productivity rose over 7 percent, more than the rise in money wages, leading to a decline in the adjusted real wage.

The 1907–8 surge in unemployment triggered by rising adjusted real wages was unquestionably in large part a result of the shock to prices. Our regression estimates suggest that they had the direct effect of raising the unemployment rate by about two percentage points, approximately 40 percent of the observed increase. The evidence on wholesale prices suggests that the true decline in prices was in fact probably greater than our inadequate consumer price data indicate, so the role of price shocks may be even greater. The more than 8 percent drop in the stock of money from May 1907 to February 1908 resulted at first from gold outflows but after October 1907 reflected the banking panic that developed in New York, with the resultant rise in depositor fear and a shift from deposits to currency. Between May 1907 and February 1908, bank deposits declined nearly 10 percent while currency holdings rose almost 6 percent.[9]

The story of rising unemployment in 1908 is highly consistent with the standard neoclassical, the Austrian, and also the monetarist interpretations of the period. Austrians emphasize the discoordinating effects of price shocks, the monetarists the link between money changes and prices, and the neoclassical economists the importance of relative prices. While there are differences in perspectives on some issues among these groups, all provide useful insights into the developing disequilibrium in the labor market and its solution.

While there may have been economists who believed that the unemployment of the era would be solved in time by price and wage adjustments, they were certainly not outspoken in expressing themselves. By contrast, a number of prominent Americans with an activist, Keynesian-style economic philosophy spoke up forcefully. In a speech at Cooper Union, William Jennings Bryan implied that the government should serve as the "employer of last resort," guaranteeing jobs to those needing one.[10] Even Theodore Roosevelt, in speeches made during the 1908 presidential campaign, seemed to lend his support to the principle of "maintaining the prosperity scale of wages in hard times."[11]

Still, the prevailing atmosphere was not one of clamor for government intervention. For example, the *Nation*, even then a liberal periodical, showed some skepticism about expanding public-works employment: "there lies the ever-present danger in 'making work.' The work is badly and expensively done, and what is really 'made' is an addition to the ranks of the unemployed."[12]

The 1914–15 downturn usually gets less attention among economic historians, but from an unemployment perspective it was a more significant episode than that arising from the panic of 1907. In terms of the components of the adjusted real wage, the 1914–15 downturn resulted almost entirely from a sharp productivity shock. Money wages moved very little in either year; the same is true of prices, which rose very slightly; thus, real wages changed very little. A massive productivity shock, however, led to a very severe decline in output per worker in 1914. Output per man hour fell by 6.5 percent in 1914, the largest productivity decline observed in the twentieth century. The cause of the decline is something of a mystery, although conventional wisdom probably would attribute it at least in part to the outbreak of war. It is not clear, however, how the war specifically impacted on productivity, particularly since it only started in August. The productivity decline almost certainly does not reflect changing capital stock per worker ("Smithian" productivity change), as the evidence does not show a decline in the capital-labor ratio, although good annual data on this score are not available for this period.

Was the decline the result of "Keynesian" productivity movements? Specifically, did a decline in autonomous spending lead to falling output, while the number of workers did not fall as much? To examine that possibility with respect to the most important component of aggregate demand, consumption spending, we estimated a simple Keynesian consumption function for the period 1901 to 1928. The statistical fit was very good, with the coefficient of multiple determination (R^2) approaching .98.

Deviations of actual consumption spending from what the consumption function relationship predicts are a measure of shifts in the propensity to consume from the long-run trend. Examination of those deviations ("residuals" to econometricians) shows that consumption in 1914 rose substantially *above* the predicted amount; there was an increase, not a decrease, in autonomous consumption. Indeed, the "overconsumption" (relative to the long-run trend) in 1914 was the greatest for any year in the entire 1901–1928 period. Consumption remained above trend (although less so) in 1915. Accordingly, the productivity drop cannot be attributed to underconsumption. As mentioned in chapter 3, based on longer-term evidence, there is no basis to believe that shifts in aggregate demand are systematically related to changes in labor productivity.

Much of the productivity decline may well represent what we previously termed "Schumpeterian" productivity change—exogenous, random occurrences that are reflected in rises and falls in the rate of innovative activity. This is also consistent with much of the new classical literature on the real business cycle. Of course, 1914 was the beginning of World War I, and some structural shifts in output probably were beginning to occur, shifts that may have rendered some of the capital stock less useful and contributed to the productivity decline.

Policymakers did relatively little to respond to the mounting unemployment in 1914–15; whatever progressivism Woodrow Wilson possessed did not translate into economic activism to deal with the problem. In his major message in December 1914, he did not even mention unemployment.[13] Some talk was given to making it easier for the unemployed to go into farming; the Labor Department held a conference to promote intergovernmental cooperation to deal with the issue.[14] But the problem seemed to solve itself before governmental efforts came to anything.

To be sure, there were some relatively isolated cries for more forceful governmental intervention. In a remarkable editorial that espoused a Keynesian approach some two decades before Keynes himself did, the *New Republic* proposed "to enrich the future through the transmuting of waste labor into permanent improvements and valuable stocks. . . . The only real obstacle to effective action . . . is a short-sighted reluctance on the part of the government to increase the national debt. . . ."[15] This call for what later was termed countercyclical fiscal policy was ignored.

Following 1915, unemployment fell back to near-normal or equilibrium levels in 1916 and 1917, and then declined to 1.4 percent, well below the equilibrium level, in 1918 and 1919. Our analysis of that decline is somewhat handicapped by sharp movements in wages and prices, making the measurement of changes in real wages a somewhat hazardous process. Any inadequacies in the consumer price index were probably magnified during this period of intense inflation. One thing is clear: labor productivity rose sharply in the 1918–19 period (8 percent in 1918, 6.7 percent in 1919), and hence was the leading force in the fall in the adjusted real wage.

Despite the data problems, the model still does reasonably well in accounting for the unemployment decline. It indicates 1.9 percent unemployment for 1918, well below the normal rate although somewhat above the actual rate of 1.4 percent. As to 1919, the model dramatically underpredicts (a negative rate versus the actual rate of 1.4 percent), but captures the essential low-unemployment situation prevailing during that era.

The 1920–1922 Depression

THE EMPIRICAL EVIDENCE

By far the most important business cycle development of the first three decades of the twentieth century was the very sharp economic downturn of 1920 and 1921. Unemployment rose to the double-digit level in 1921. Since the annual rate of unemployment reached 11.7 percent, some months within that year witnessed even higher unemployment—possibly as much as 15 percent.

While the magnitude of the 1920–22 downturn was severe (and indeed exceeded that for the Great Depression of the following decade for several quarters), its duration was not. By 1922 recovery was already underway, and in the following year unemployment was actually less than its normal long-run rate. Despite movements in major components in the demand for labor, including sharp increases and then decreases in prices and money wages, the labor market adjusted reasonably quickly to disequilibrium conditions, in marked contrast to the 1929 downturn discussed in the next chapter.

The standard model with multiple lagged variables using annual data correctly predicts the rise and subsequent decline in unemployment. The model understates unemployment in 1920 rather considerably, but at least indicates a fairly sizable increase for the year (the actual unemployment rate rose 3.8 points.) Yet the model predicts very accurately the dramatic upsurge in unemployment in 1921 (calling for 12.1 percent instead of the actual rate of 11.7 percent), and the subsequent drop in 1922 and 1923 (the model somewhat underpredicts the magnitude of the decline, showing, for example, 8.6 percent unemployment for 1922 instead of the actual 6.7 percent).

Analysis of the 1920–22 downturn requires use of more detailed data than that employed in the basic model. While unemployment data are not

available on a monthly or quarterly basis, factory employment data are, as
are factory payroll, industrial production and wholesale price data. From
these sources it is possible to discern changes in productivity in manufacturing by dividing industrial production by factory employment. This provides a measure of output per worker. To the extent that employers
shortened the workweek in response to declining output, this productivity
measure may misstate changing hourly output per worker. Fortunately,
however, the evidence is that hourly output per worker fell only modestly
in manufacturing. Data collected by the Bureau of the Census, and analyzed
by pioneering statistician Willford I. King, reveal that the workweek, from
peak to trough, declined slightly less than 4 percent.[16] Accordingly, any
bias introduced by the use of this productivity measure is relatively small.

Similarly, wages per worker are derived by dividing factory payrolls by
the number of employees. Again, the relatively modest nature of changes in
the workweek over time suggests that this very crude measure of employee
compensation in fact is not too bad in this particular instance. For purposes
of our analysis here, we averaged monthly figures to obtain quarterly estimates of the relevant variables.[17]

Table 4.3 reveals the trends in the major variables. Factory employment
from the beginning of 1920 to the trough in the third quarter of 1921 fell
slightly more than 30 percent on a seasonally adjusted basis, a sharp drop
by any standard.[18] Similarly, industrial production fell by a like proportion.
An even steeper decline occurred with respect to wholesale prices. Between
the second quarter of 1920, when they peaked, to the third quarter of 1921,
a period of slightly over one year, wholesale prices fell nearly 44 percent,
one of the steepest decreases recorded in American history.

The substantial fall in prices greatly exceeded the drop in money wages,
so real wages rose markedly until the third quarter of 1921. It would be an
overstatement, however, to characterize money wages as rigid. After all,
they did fall over 19 percent from the summer of 1920 to the end of 1921.
It is more accurate to say that wages proved less flexible than prices.

In no sense can the business cycle downturn of 1920–21 be attributed to
a productivity decline. Only in two quarters did average output per worker
fall below that at the beginning of 1920, and given the small reduction in
the workweek that occurred, hourly productivity probably did not fall at
all. At the low point in factory employment in the summer of 1921, output
per worker was somewhat higher than when the downturn began in early
1920. Indeed, productivity was remarkably stable during the downturn,
only to rise robustly during the recovery that began in the fall of 1921.

The fall in employment and the corresponding rise in unemployment is
well explained by the sharp rise in the adjusted real wage, which in turn
was entirely a consequence of the price deflation. As figure 4.1 illustrates,

TABLE 4.3

QUARTERLY EMPLOYMENT AND LABOR MARKET INDICATORS, U.S. 1920–1923

Quarter	Factory Jobs	Industrial Output	Wholesale Prices	Money Wages	Real Wages	Output/Worker	Adjusted Real Wage
1920							
I	100.0	100.0	100.0	100.0	100.0	100.0	100.0
II	95.2	95.2	106.2	106.4	100.2	100.0	100.2
III	90.5	93.0	104.5	106.7	102.1	102.8	99.3
IV	82.0	82.0	90.3	105.7	117.0	100.0	117.0
1921							
I	71.0	69.6	73.1	99.1	135.6	98.0	138.4
II	71.1	69.6	65.4	92.5	141.5	97.9	144.5
III	69.9	71.0	59.7	88.1	147.6	101.6	145.3
IV	71.6	74.9	62.5	86.4	138.2	104.6	132.1
1922							
I	73.5	80.3	61.0	87.1	142.8	109.3	130.6
II	76.2	86.7	64.0	86.9	135.8	113.8	119.3
III	79.8	91.3	66.0	90.0	136.3	114.4	119.1
IV	84.3	102.3	65.2	92.1	141.3	121.4	116.4
1923							
I	89.0	105.4	67.4	96.7	143.4	118.4	121.1
II	91.4	111.7	66.6	99.1	148.8	122.2	121.1

Sources: Federal Reserve Bulletin; see text. 1920–I=100.

63

FIGURE 4.1

EMPLOYMENT AND THE ADJUSTED REAL WAGE, QUARTERLY DATA, 1920-23

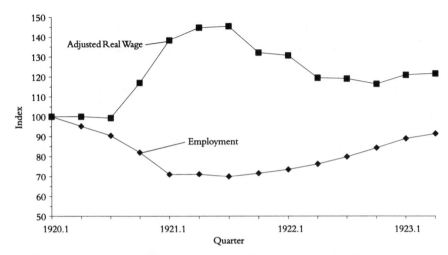

the adjusted real wage peaked in precisely the quarter when employment reached its lowest point. Note that the adjusted real wage never returned to the level prevailing at the beginning of 1920—but neither did factory employment.

A statistical examination of data similar to that in table 4.3 reveals what the figure tells us visually, namely that there is a striking and statistically significant negative correlation between the adjusted real wage and factory employment. A model regressing wholesale prices, money wages, and productivity (output per worker) against factory employment shows an expected positive relationship between price and productivity movements and employment, and a negative relationship between money-wage changes and employment. Moreover, the relationships are statistically significant and the overall explanatory power of the model is high ($R^2 = .86$).

As already noted, the root cause of the rising real wage and accompanying fall in employment was the acute price deflation. Changes in monetary variables fit the price history of the downturn reasonably well. According to Friedman and Schwartz, the money stock peaked in May 1920 at $30.3 billion (the same quarter in which prices peaked), falling by 8.9 percent to $27.8 billion by the third quarter of 1921, the same quarter in which prices reached a low point. Over the next year, prices increased by about 10 percent.[19]

At the same time, a monetarist explanation does not tell the entire story. The stock of money in the third quarter of 1920 was actually greater than in the first quarter, yet over 30 percent of the observed decline in factory employment had already occurred. Rising money wages in the first months of 1920 rather than falling prices seems to explain the initial employment downturn.

The decline in prices was so substantial-about as great as in the Great Depression that followed—that it seems difficult to attribute it solely to an 8 percent fall in the money stock. There was, by any measurement, a sharp decrease in the velocity of money. The American experience was similar to that in most other countries, and indeed the Federal Reserve Board actually attributed the American price decline to falling prices overseas.[20] Certainly the Federal Reserve's raising discount rates twice in 1920—to a record of 7 percent that stood for over half a century—contributed to the decline in borrowings from the Federal Reserve that led to a sizable decrease in the monetary base. Unlike after 1929, there was no decline in depositor confidence, as the deposit-currency ratio actually increased. This was not sufficient, however, to offset the impact of a highly contractionary monetary policy. The Federal Reserve seemed to have failed in its first peacetime attempt at monetary and price stabilization.

The fall in the income velocity of money that accompanied this monetary policy is not too surprising in light of contemporary experience. When inflationary expectations increase, as they did during World War I and 1919, the opportunity cost of holding cash balances rises and people conserve on those balances, maintaining relatively small amounts of cash (money) for any given income. When prices fall, after having risen for many years, inflationary expectations are shattered, particularly when the long-run historical trend was for prices to remain roughly stable. Accordingly, the perceived opportunity cost of holding cash falls, and people start to increase their cash balances. Since demand deposits paid interest, and since prices in any case were falling, the real rate of return on cash balances in 1920 and 1921 was actually very high—those balances were getting more valuable daily as prices fell. Thus the deflationary impact of a decline in the stock of money was furthered by the resulting fall in velocity associated with changing expectations.

EVIDENCE FROM THE IRON AND STEEL INDUSTRY

Readers of the last chapter and the discussion above might be dubious of our statistical evidence on the relationship between real wages and unemployment on the grounds that we are dealing with highly aggregative data for the whole economy. Do our findings hold if we reduce the analysis to the level of the individual industry? Is there some sort of "aggregation bias" that gives a false wage–employment relationship that falls apart when individual industry wage, price, and productivity data are used?

Fortunately, data exist to examine the relationship between factory employment and money wages, prices, and labor productivity on a quarterly basis for 1919 through the second quarter of 1923 for the iron and steel industry, one of the nation's largest.[21] That industry underwent wrenching changes in the period, with steel output in the third quarter of 1921 being two-thirds less than in the first quarter of the previous year.

The findings tend to confirm the wages hypothesis. A regression model explaining iron and steel employment in terms of metal prices (largely iron and steel), money wages in the steel industry, and output per worker in that industry, using quarterly data, works well, explaining nearly 93 percent of the variation in steel industry employment over that period. That variation was extraordinary, with employment dropping almost precisely 50 percent between the first quarter of 1920 and the third quarter of 1921. The expected positive relationship between prices, productivity, and employment is observed, statistically significant at the 1 percent level. The expected negative relationship between money wages and employment is not obtained; there is evidence, however, of multicolinearity (strong intercorrelation among the variables in the model.)

To deal with this, we eliminated one variable by using a model regressing real wages and productivity against employment; it works in the expected fashion:

(1) STELEMP = 187.604 − 1.425 RLWAG + 0.622 PRDTY,
         (10.591)   (8.003)   (5.984)

$\overline{R}^2$ = .817,   DW = 1.987,   F Statistic = 26.306

where *STELEMP* is employment of production workers in the iron and steel industry; *RLWAG* is the real wage, unadjusted for productivity change; *PRDTY* is productivity per worker, and numbers in parentheses are standard errors; an autoregressive adjustment term is omitted. All variables are indexed with the first quarter of 1919 equal to 100.

The model works as predicted. Increases in real wages are associated with reduced employment (increased unemployment), while productivity and employment are positively related. Both variables are significant at the 1 percent level, and the model explains over four-fifths of the considerable variation in employment over the four-and-a-half-year period.

CONTEMPORARY ANALYSIS OF THE 1921 DEPRESSION

Our explanation of unemployment in 1920–22 is not new, but rather is a reaffirmation and rediscovery of what several economists observed during and shortly after that downturn. Both Paul Douglas and Alvin Hansen noted the sharp rise in real wages occurring during the period.[22] Hansen attributed the rise in unemployment to the fact that wages were "much higher than the industrial situation warranted."[23] Downward wage adjustments to deal with the economic situation had been endorsed as early as 1919 by the *New York Times*.[24]

Nonetheless, remember that the classical/neoclassical interpretation of unemployment was not a major preoccupation of most academic economists or policymakers of the era. Economics textbooks barely mentioned the subject. Indeed, the idea that excessive real wages contributed to the unemployment surge in 1920 and 1921 was more widely espoused by businessmen than by professional economists.[25]

The notion that the market mechanism would correct for imbalances between the quantity of labor supplied and the quantity demanded was explicitly rejected by many prominent Americans. Henry Ford and Thomas Edison wanted to ease the downturn by creating fiat money on a large scale.[26] The activist new secretary of commerce, Herbert Hoover, who assumed office under Warren Harding in January 1921, convinced President Harding that the unemployment problem needed attention. At his instigation, a President's Conference on Unemployment was called. Hoover controlled the participants and to a considerable extent the agenda, and saw to it that the laissez-faire view that unemployment was a problem that the market would cure was not allowed to become widely accepted.[27] He also promoted a proto-Keynesian policy of pressuring governors to speed up the awarding of road-building contracts.[28]

Many Americans, including some highly conservative ones, instinctively reached for solutions more consistent with underconsumptionist or Keynesian thinking than with the neoclassical position. In 1919, two prominent governors who later became even better known, Calvin Coolidge and Al Smith, both promoted public-works spending as a means of relieving unemployment.[29] Church groups called for high wages to maintain purchasing power.[30]

Labor leaders, who had previously proclaimed their faith in a high-wage policy as a means of stimulating consumption, added new wrinkles, promoting shorter workweeks to "spread the work" and restrictions on immigration to prevent job displacement of native-born Americans.[31]

Many of the participants in the Unemployment Conference were of the view that unemployment was a result of inadequate spending. They favored high wages as a means of providing purchasing power and dealing with underconsumption. At least one interpretation of the conference was that the goal was to raise the adjusted real wage: "if it really succeeds in its commendable attempt to stimulate buying by forcing manufacturers, middlemen and merchants to accept lower profits, it will have done better than could have been expected."[32] Most emphatically, the conference rejected the view that adjustments in relative prices (especially downward adjustment in wages) could solve any severe unemployment problem without government intervention. The leading proponent of that position within government, Hoover, said in 1923: "We are constantly reminded . . . that there is an ebb and flow in the demand for commodities that cannot . . . be regulated. I have great doubts whether there is a real foundation for this view."[33]

The Unemployment Conference, which met intermittently until February 1929, accepted the notion of countercyclical public-works spending to stimulate demand, speaking of the "multiplying effect of successive use of funds in circulation."[34] It spoke of the need for business-government cooperation, the need for better economic statistics, etc., but not of the ability of the market system to alleviate problems of unemployment. The report sounded more Keynesian or post-Keynesian than neoclassical in its approach to the problem.

In short, while there was some awareness of the role that wages might have played in explaining the 1920–22 business fluctuations, the idea that excessive real wages were the culprit was very far from universally held. Moreover, the people who most strongly rejected the neoclassical approach, especially Hoover, were destined to assume greater importance in the decision-making process within a few years, a development that had tragic results.

The New Era, 1922–1929

The seven years from the autumn of 1922 to the autumn of 1929 were arguably the brightest period in the economic history of the United States. Virtually all the measures of economic well-being suggested that the economy had reached new heights in terms of prosperity and the achievement of improvements in human welfare. Real gross national product increased every year, consumer prices were stable (as measured by the consumer price index), real wages rose as a consequence of productivity advance, stock prices tripled. Automobile production in 1929 was almost precisely double the level of 1922.[35] It was in the twenties that Americans bought their first car, their first radio, made their first long-distance telephone call, took their first out-of-state vacation. As noted earlier, this was the decade when America entered "the age of mass consumption."[36]

THE EMPIRICAL RECORD AND THE WAGES HYPOTHESIS

As indicated above, our adjusted real wage model does an excellent job of predicting the strong labor market of this period. Our mean annual estimate of unemployment over the period of 3.4 percent is only very slightly different from the actual rate of 3.3 percent.

The only year which can even remotely resemble a high unemployment year was 1924, when unemployment reached 5 percent. The modest increase in unemployment that year reflected a large increase (5.6 percent) in hourly wages. The adjustment mechanism, however, worked well. Hourly wages stopped rising the following year. Productivity fell very slightly, but this in turn was more than offset by some increase in prices. The adjusted real wage accordingly fell in 1925, and with it, the unemployment rate.

THE GENESIS OF THE IMPENDING CRISIS

While there is no dispute that the twenties were a period of great prosperity and little unemployment, it can be argued that the seeds of the economic debacle that followed were being sown during the New Era. There was a tremendous growth in the popularity of an underconsumptionist line of reasoning that rejected the classical doctrine of nonintervention in market processes. In addition, monetary intervention in the form of "fine-tuning" was beginning to be practiced, and this created a tradition of intervention that was to prove devastating a few years later.

The evidence regarding the first point is strong. There was growing respect for what William J. Barber calls the "high-wage policy" from three quarters: businessmen, writers, and government officials.[37] High wages meant greater purchasing power and, to some, better worker morale and thus productivity. While Henry Ford popularized the high-wage policy with his five-dollar-a-day wage in the previous decade, others took up the cause. The very highly regarded Boston retailer Edward Filene (patron of the Twentieth Century Fund) wrote in defense of minimum-wage laws and other wage-enhancing measures.[38]

The view that business downturns and unemployment reflected inadequate purchasing power (what Keynesian economists later called "insufficient aggregate demand") was popularized by two amateur economists whose books were widely read, William Trufant Foster and Waddill Catchings.[39] Some writers, like Stuart Chase and Rexford Tugwell, believed that cyclical fluctuations required governmental planning and intervention.[40]

The strongest opponent of a noninterventionist, laissez-faire philosophy within government was Secretary of Commerce Hoover. Hoover's initial appointment to President Harding's cabinet was strongly opposed by old guard Republicans on the grounds that Hoover was "too liberal, too internationally minded, too popular, and too ambitious."[41] Hoover was sometimes called the Secretary of Commerce and "assistant secretary of everything else."[42]

Involved in virtually everything, Hoover believed that the government could enhance efficiency by working with trade associations, by, for example, promoting standardization of measurements and parts among competing firms. A believer in what later was called indicative planning, Hoover took actions to increase economic information (such as initiating the *Survey of Current Business*) in the hope that it would permit reductions in business cycle activity. He favored strict immigration restrictions and high tariffs as a means of stimulating wages and purchasing power.

Some Austrian economists have suggested that emerging inflationary tendencies in the Twenties contributed to the problems that were to follow.[43] To non–Austrian economists, a cursory inspection of the price indices of the period makes one skeptical of this argument, since the consumer price index in 1929 was only 0.4 percent higher than in 1923, while the wholesale price index had declined about 5 percent, and the GNP price deflator also showed a small decline.

At the same time, however, there is some basis for the Austrian position. Typically (for example, after the Civil War), prices fell after wars to levels not too different from those that prevailed before then. Yet, in 1929 consumer prices were higher than at the end of the war, and substantially higher than at the beginning. The money supply (M2) was almost 30 percent higher at the beginning of 1929 than six years earlier, an annual average increase of more than 4.4 percent, and the ratio of reserves to deposits fell significantly while the ratio of deposits to currency rose.[44] Between 1923 and 1928, Federal Reserve loan and security assets, reflecting open-market operations and loans to banks, rose a robust 47 percent, signaling an extremely expansionary monetary policy. Nominal interest rates on bonds fell twenty to over one hundred basis points from 1923 to 1928.[45]

The new central bank undoubtedly contributed to greater monetary expansion than would have existed in its absence, contributing perhaps to the boom in the twenties (by keeping real wages and real interest rates lower than otherwise) and to the subsequent decline, which was aggravated by a retreat from the overexpansionary policy after 1928. According to the

Austrian view, a "discoordination" of relative factor prices resulting from the expansionary monetary policy sowed the seeds for the depression that followed. This, of course, assumes that the public's expectations in this era were slow to react to policy changes (e.g., that money wages were not dramatically impacted by the substantial monetary expansion).

As the Gilded Age wound down, unemployment tended to be low and quickly returned to a normal or natural rate after short-lived increases. By all standards, the years after 1922 were especially successful. Yet, beneath the surface of that prosperity, the basis for future problems was being laid, as a new interventionist philosophy on the part of popularizers of economics, "progressive" businessmen, government officials, and monetary authorities was gradually winning favor, even taking credit for the extraordinary advances that occurred. Increasingly, the view that unemployment fluctuations reflected temporary market disequilibrium was de-emphasized and a new, more interventionist approach was gaining respectability. This development would soon contribute in an important fashion to the policy mistakes that would produce the greatest economic downturn ever observed in this country.

NOTES

1. Paul Bairoch, "Europe's Gross National Product: 1800–1975," *Journal of European Economic History* 5 (1975): 273–340. Unless otherwise indicated, all macroeconomic statistics on the American economy in this chapter are from U.S. Department of Commerce, *Historical Statistics of the United States, Colonial Times to 1970* (Washington, D.C.: Government Printing Office, 1975).

2. The debate is particularly pronounced as to whether lower-income groups shared in the prosperity of the 1920s. The conventional view is that they did only to a very limited extent. See, for example, John Kenneth Galbraith, *The Great Crash* (Boston: Houghton Mifflin, 1961), p. 182. Empirical support for this view is found in Charles Holt, "Who Profited from the Prosperity of the Twenties?" *Explorations in Economic History* 4 (1977): 277–289. In our judgment, however, Gene Smiley has effectively destroyed this argument. See Gene Smiley, "Did Incomes for Most of the Population Fall from 1923 to 1929?" *Journal of Economic History* 43 (1983): 209–16.

3. W. W. Rostow, *The Stages of Economic Growth* (Cambridge: Cambridge University Press, 1959), pp. 10–11.

4. Harold U. Faulkner, *The Decline of Laissez Faire, 1897-1917* (New York: Rinehart & Co., Inc., 1951).

5. On this point, see Robert Higgs, *Crisis and Leviathan: Critical Episodes in the Growth of American Government* (New York: Oxford University Press, 1987), especially chaps. 6 and 7.

6.   The implication is, of course, that there was a great deal of real-wage flexibility in this period. This conclusion has been challenged somewhat by William A. Sundstrom in his "Was There a Golden Age of Flexible Wages? Evidence from Ohio Manufacturing, 1892–1910," *Journal of Economic History* 50 (1990): 309–20.

7.   Christina Romer, "Spurious Volatility in Historical Unemployment Data," *Journal of Political Economy*, 94 (1986): 1–37.

8.   R. M. Coen, "Labor Force and Unemployment in the 1920s and 1930s," *Review of Economics and Statistics* 55 (1973): 46–55.

9.   The definitive study, of course, is Milton Friedman and Anna J. Schwartz, *A Monetary History of the United States, 1867–1960* (Princeton, N.J.: Princeton University Press for the National Bureau of Economic Research, 1963), pp. 156–168. For money stock data, see ibid., p. 706.

10.   *New York Times*, April 22, 1908, p. 3.

11.   Ibid., December 17, 1908, p. 8.

12.   *The Nation*, November 5, 1908, pp. 429–30.

13.   *New Republic*, December 19, 1914, p. 4.

14.   *New York Times*, July 7, 1915, p. 9; August 7, 1915, p. 14.

15.   *New Republic*, April 10, 1915, pp. 250–51.

16.   Willford I. King, *Employment, Hours and Earnings in Prosperity and Depression*, 2d. ed. (New York: National Bureau of Economic Research, 1923), p. 87. This volume is an invaluable source for persons interested in labor-market developments during the 1920–22 downturn.

17.   The data used in the analysis of the 1920–22 downturn were obtained from the *Federal Reserve Bulletin* for various issues between 1921 and 1925.

18.   The factory employment data and price data can be found in an enormously useful volume, Geoffrey H. Moore, ed., *Business Cycle Indicators*, 2 vols. (Princeton, N.J.: Princeton University Press for the National Bureau of Economic Research, 1961), 2: 118.

19.   See Friedman and Schwartz, *Monetary History*, p. 710. See also their discussion on pp. 231–39.

20.   Ibid., p. 237.

21.   The data were obtained from various issues of the *Federal Reserve Bulletin* for the years 1920 to 1923.

22.   Paul H. Douglas, "The Movement of Real Wages and Its Economic Significance," *American Economic Review Supplement* 16 (1926): 17–53, and Alvin H. Hansen, "Factors Affecting the Trend in Real Wages," *American Economic Review* 15 (1925): 27–42.

23.   Alvin H. Hansen, "The Outlook for Wages and Employment," *American Economic Review Supplement* 13 (1923): 37. Hansen's views on the wage-unemployment relationship changed dramatically in the late 1930s. For an excellent analysis of economic thought during this period, see William J. Barber, *From New Era to New Deal* (Cambridge: Cambridge University Press, 1985), especially the first two chapters.

24.   *New York Times*, February 2, 1919, section 3, p. 1.

25. On this point, see Joseph Dorfman, *The Economic Mind in American Civilization*, 5 vols. (New York: The Viking Press, 1946–59), vol. 4, chap. 2.

26. Ibid., pp. 33–34.

27. The anti-interventionist nature of the Unemployment Conference and Hoover's dominant role in its creation and operation have been extensively documented. See, for example, Barber, *From New Era to New Deal*, pp. 27–28.

28. *New York Times*, July 29, 1921, p. 2.

29. Ibid., April 25, 1919, p. 24; May 14, 1919, p. 12.

30. The Federal Council of the Churches of Christ in America promoted high wages in a platform document. Ibid., July 14, 1919, p. 11.

31. Ibid., February 7, 1921, p. 2; August 31, 1921, p. 6; November 18, 1920, p. 1; April 25, 1921, p. 15.

32. *The Nation*, October 12, 1921, p. 389.

33. Herbert Hoover, introduction to Lionel D. Edie, ed., *The Stabilization of Business* (New York: Macmillan, 1923), p. v. See also Barber, *From New Era to New Deal*, p. 15.

34. *Report of the President's Conference on Unemployment* (Washington: Government Printing Office, 1921), p. 103.

35. For a convenient summary of major economic statistics of this period, see Richard K. Vedder, *The American Economy in Historical Perspective* (Belmont, Calif.: Wadsworth, 1976), p. 367.

36. Rostow, *Stages of Economic Growth*, pp. 10–11.

37. See Barber, *From New Era to New Deal*, especially pp. 27–30.

38. Edward A. Filene, "The American Wage and Efficiency," *American Economic Review* 13 (1923): 411–15.

39. See William T. Foster and Waddill Catchings, *The Road to Plenty* (Boston: Houghton Mifflin, 1928) or their *Business Without A Buyer*, 2d ed. (Boston: Houghton Mifflin, 1928.) Foster was a forensics expert and college president, Catchings a highly successful Wall Street investment banker.

40. See Stuart Chase, *The Tragedy of Waste* (New York: Macmillan, 1925), or Rexford Guy Tugwell, *Industry's Coming of Age* (New York: Harcourt, Brace, 1927). See also Barber, *From New Era to New Deal*, chap. 2.

41. Robert K. Murray, *The Harding Era: Warren G. Harding and His Administration* (Minneapolis: University of Minnesota Press, 1969), p. 98. Harding appointed Andrew Mellon as secretary of the treasury to mollify the old guard with respect to the Hoover appointment.

42. Ibid., p. 193.

43. The standard Austrian interpretation is found in Murray Rothbard, *America's Great Depression* (Kansas City: Sheed and Ward, 1963). Professor Rothbard's encouragement of our research was a major factor in the completion of this book.

44. For details, see Friedman and Schwartz, *Monetary History*, appendix A.

45. *Historical Statistics of the United States*, p. 1003.

5

From New Era to New Deal

The four years from 1929 to 1933 were a watershed in the economic history of the United States. The old order that had existed in some sense from the beginning of the republic began to crumble, and a peaceful but real revolution overtook the polity, bringing with it a dramatic change in the role of the state in American life.

The peaceful revolution that led to the New Deal in 1933 was the lasting consequence of the greatest economic downturn the nation ever witnessed. Hence it is essential to examine the Great Depression from the perspective of unemployment and the labor market. We begin by reviewing the decline in economic conditions and the rise in unemployment between 1929 and 1933. In the following chapters, we show that the banking crisis closely associated with the downturn owed its existence to the labor-market disequilibrium that evolved out of inappropriate public policies, and that the same disequilibrium explains why the recovery from the Depression was so long and anemic.

Economic Decline: 1929–1933

By any meaningful measure, the economic decline from 1929 to 1933 was the greatest in American history, usually by a wide margin. Using annual data and comparing 1929 with 1933, money gross national product fell by an extraordinary 46.4 percent. There is no other four-year period since

1900 (not including any year from 1930 to 1933) where there is any decline in GNP, much less one of 46 percent. From 1892 to 1896, GNP fell by 7 percent, a trivial decrease compared with that of the Great Depression.

Prices fell by anywhere from 22 to 31 percent, depending on the price index used. That decline is smaller than the abrupt drop in prices observed in 1921, but it is still substantial. Real output per capita decreased by 31 percent, far outdistancing any other decrease. Auto production in 1932 was fully 75 percent below the 1929 peak, and similar sharp reductions in output occurred for virtually every major consumer durable good.[1]

Unemployment broke all records. Of the seventeen years of double-digit unemployment in the one hundred years for which data are available, ten were during the Great Depression. Prior to the Great Depression, the peak unemployment rate was 18.4 percent in 1894. During the thirties, that record was exceeded in five years; for four consecutive years, the unemployment rate was above 20 percent, and for ten consecutive years, it was greater than 10 percent.

Even these statistics do not fully portray the incidence of unemployment. Annual average statistics disguise periods of unemployment in excess of those averages, as will be demonstrated shortly. Beyond that, however, the burden of unemployment varied considerably between various demographic groups and geographic areas. For example, it has been estimated that unemployment among female blacks in the city of Detroit in January 1931 was around 75 percent, at a time when the national rate was probably about 14 percent. Similarly, teenage unemployment in 1937 was estimated at 36.5 percent, more than double the national rate. Moreover, the average duration of unemployment was substantial. For example, of unemployed men in Massachusetts at the beginning of 1934, a large majority (62 percent) had been unemployed for one year or more.[2]

The misery created by the Depression was so substantial that it is hard for Americans under the age of sixty to imagine. With the absence of a comprehensive governmentally provided safety net, it is undeniable that millions of Americans suffered a great deal. At the same time, however, the distribution of the burden of the Depression was very unequal, and millions of Americans lived normal, even prosperous lives. Sales of cars in 1937 were the second highest in history, and more radios and refrigerators were sold in 1935 than in 1929.[3] The tragedy of the Great Depression derived as much from the distribution of the fall in income as the size of the decline itself. While the decrease in agricultural income is one reason for the unevenness of the distribution of the misery, the single most important problem was unemployment. Many Americans suffered little or no income loss, while others had their income fall drastically to near-starvation levels.

Monthly Estimates of Unemployment Rates

The annual data on unemployment disguise important intrayear variations in the incidence of joblessness, and fail to give us details on the timing of the downturn and subsequent recovery. Unfortunately, monthly or quarterly data were not collected until the Depression was nearly over.

To deal with this data inadequacy, we have developed monthly estimates of unemployment, which are presented in table 5.1.[4] The procedure for constructing the estimates is straightforward. First, we formed a regression model of the annual unemployment rate for the 1923–37 era, utilizing as explanatory variables manufacturing employment, an index of help-wanted advertising (a proxy for job vacancies), freight carloadings, and the Babson index of business activity. The model's explanatory power was quite high ($R^2 = .9947$).

Monthly values of the various explanatory variables were then used with the regression results derived from annual data to calculate monthly estimates for the unemployment rate. We altered the results in two ways. First, we corrected the estimates for the deviation of the predicted annual estimate (from the regression discussed above) from the official BLS estimates. Second, we used the Department of Commerce's X-11 seasonal adjustment procedure to correct for seasonal variations in the data.

In addition to the table, figure 5.1 shows the unemployment variations visually and relates them to some of the major happenings of the Depression era. What do the results indicate? The unemployment rate before the beginning of the Depression was very low, below 2.5 percent.[5] The unemployment rate at the bottom of the Depression, in March 1933, was 28.3 percent, suggesting that unemployment rose by about 26 percentage points from 1929 to the 1933 trough. The increase in unemployment came in four phases separated by periods of stable or even falling unemployment.

About one-fourth of the increase in unemployment came with a rush, in the last quarter of 1929. The December 1929 increase was the second largest recorded during the Depression decade. The first effects were substantial, more than some symbolic beginning.[6]

The initial increase in unemployment was followed by a long period of stable or even falling unemployment, lasting through the first ten months of 1930. Suppose that the natural rate of unemployment in 1929 or 1930 was around 4 percent. The decline in unemployment from 9 percent in December 1929 to about 7 percent in the third quarter of 1930 meant that unemployment had recovered about 40 percent of the way back to the natural or normal unemployment rate.

The second phase in the development of the Great Depression was short, lasting but two months, but it witnessed an increase in unemployment that

TABLE 5.1

ESTIMATED MONTHLY UNEMPLOYMENT RATES, NOVEMBER 1929-DECEMBER 1939

Year	January	February	March	April	May	June	July	August	September	October	November	December
1929	–	–	–	–	–	–	–	–	–	–	5.0	9.0
1930	8.3	7.6	7.6	6.6	6.8	6.3	7.8	6.4	7.0	6.1	11.6	14.4
1931	13.8	14.7	14.5	14.0	14.9	15.0	15.5	16.0	17.4	16.7	18.6	19.8
1932	19.7	20.4	21.1	21.7	23.7	25.8	25.8	26.4	27.9	25.6	23.2	22.3
1933	25.9	26.1	28.3	27.3	27.3	24.9	23.3	23.4	23.9	22.9	23.2	22.4
1934	21.2	20.3	20.0	21.4	21.0	20.7	21.8	22.3	23.5	23.5	23.2	21.6
1935	19.3	18.6	18.5	18.7	20.1	19.4	21.3	20.0	19.6	21.9	21.8	20.2
1936	18.7	18.0	19.4	18.4	17.5	16.9	16.0	16.1	15.0	17.7	13.9	15.3
1937	15.1	15.1	13.5	13.2	12.3	13.6	13.7	13.5	12.5	13.3	17.1	18.9
1938	17.4	18.8	19.2	20.1	20.1	20.6	19.9	20.2	19.5	17.1	17.7	17.5
1939	18.7	19.3	19.3	20.7	19.9	18.5	18.3	17.6	14.3	11.6	13.9	14.4

Source: See text.

FIGURE 5.1

UNEMPLOYMENT AND MAJOR EVENTS DURING THE GREAT DEPRESSION

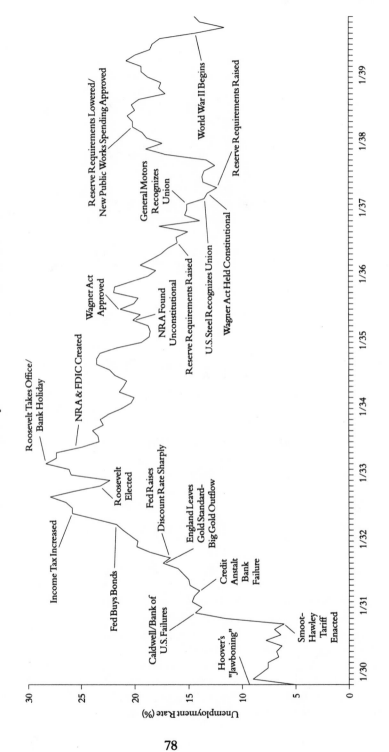

exceeded the initial shock following the stock-market crash in October 1929. The rise in unemployment in November 1930 is almost certainly the largest single monthly increase in unemployment in the history of the nation. That surge in unemployment turned a recession into a depression. Thus, explaining the fall 1930 phase is important in explaining why the Great Depression developed.

After four months of relative stability in early 1931, the third phase of the downturn began. Unlike the earlier periods, the 1931–32 episode was a long, continuous decline rather than a short sharp movement. In fourteen of the seventeen months from April 1931 to September 1932, unemployment increased. The accumulated effect was to double the unemployment rate, accounting for fully half of the increase in unemployment observed from peak to trough. The third phase was the biggest, the longest, and the one that made *a* depression into *the Great* Depression.

The 1931–32 slide began rather slowly and then accelerated. If our estimates are correct, unemployment rose by an average of .51 percentage points per month from April to August 1931, but at a brisker 0.95-point rate from August to December 1931. After some slowdown in the rate of decline (but not a reversal) in the first quarter of 1932, unemployment rose at an extraordinary 1.13 percentage points per month from March to September 1932.

The fourth quarter of 1932 saw still another reversal, with a significant reduction in unemployment being recorded. Conditions deteriorated again in the final phase of the downturn during the first quarter of 1933, with unemployment peaking in March at a slightly higher level than observed the previous September.

While the post-1933 recovery is taken up in detail in chapter 7, it is striking to note that a fairly brisk recovery seemed to be under way in the summer and early fall of 1933, but that it simply died after October of that year, not to resume with any real vigor until 1936, the first full year of really sustained recovery. An important question is: why did the upsurge of 1933 stop for more than two years?

Unemployment and the Adjusted Real Wage, 1929–1933

The adjusted real wage model developed in chapter 3 does an excellent job of explaining the 1929–33 rise in unemployment. We recognize, of course, that there is some dispute regarding the magnitude of unemployment during this era. Both the Coen and the Darby estimates place unemployment at lower levels in the early thirties than the official Bureau of Labor Statistics estimate derived by Stanley Lebergott.[7] We are inclined to agree with Gene

TABLE 5.2

UNEMPLOYMENT RATES, ACTUAL AND PREDICTED, 3 DATA SOURCES, 1929–1933

Unemployment Rate Data	1929	1930	1931	1932	1933
Lebergott/BLS					
Actual Unemployment Rate	3.2	8.7	15.9	23.6	24.9
Estimated Unemployment Rate	3.4	7.6	12.8	21.6	25.7
Error (Residual)	-0.2	1.1	3.1	2.0	-0.8
Michael Darby					
Actual Unemployment Rate	3.2	8.7	15.3	22.5	20.6
Estimated Unemployment Rate	3.4	8.2	13.0	19.7	22.0
Error (Residual)	-0.2	0.5	2.3	2.8	-1.4
R.M. Coen					
Actual Unemployment Rate	5.5	9.1	13.8	18.8	19.8
Estimated Unemployment Rate	4.6	8.9	12.1	17.9	20.5
Error (Residual)	0.9	0.2	1.7	0.9	-0.7

Source: See Text.

Smiley that the Lebergott/BLS estimates are probably as good as any.[8] Most of our analysis, including our monthly estimates presented above, is centered around the BLS numbers, although we also performed some additional sensitivity analysis, using the alternative estimates, to ascertain whether our basic wages model is sensitive to differences in data sources.

Table 5.2 summarizes the actual unemployment rates for the years 1929 through 1933 using the BLS, Darby, and Coen data, and also gives the statistically estimated rate obtained using the expanded basic adjusted real wage regression model outlined in chapter 3 relating unemployment to changes in prices, money wages, and productivity over the past six years, as well as the lagged adjusted real wage. The results are based on the 1900–1989 period. In addition, we used a somewhat different model with the Darby data, utilizing some wage and productivity data compiled by Darby.[9] The alternative Darby model, not reported here, behaved less well than the results reported, although the essential rise in unemployment was captured.

With all three data sets reported, the predicted unemployment rate rises, correctly, as the downturn proceeds. All models do a superb job of predicting the unemployment peak in 1933; all do less well in predicting the 1931 unemployment rate, although all the models predicted large (but not large enough) unemployment increases for that year. The most striking thing about the results is the fact that the adjusted real wage model does an excellent job of explaining the rise in unemployment with all three, quite disparate, data sources.

In 1930, money wages fell only slightly (a little over 2 percent). Consumer prices, however, fell at least as much (2.5 percent), so real wages remained unchanged or even slightly increased during the first year of the Depression. At the same time, however, a moderately severe productivity shock led to lower output per worker (almost 4 percent.) The impact of that, of course, was to raise the real wage, adjusted for productivity, fairly substantially in 1930. Thus the initial unemployment surge can be explained by a productivity decline not offset by a corresponding reduction in real wages. Alternative data sources, using different wage and productivity measures, tell about the same story.

While the initial increase in unemployment can be largely explained by the productivity shock, the very sharp rise in unemployment in 1931 was not related to further declines in output per worker. Productivity per worker changed little, actually rising somewhat (0.9 percent) by the measure used here (an alternative productivity measure shows a 0.5 percent decline.) It is probably close to correct to state that labor productivity essentially was unchanged in 1931. Money wages fell, but rather anemically. Whereas in the 1920–22 depression a roughly 20 percent fall in money wages was observed in one year, the 1931 decline was less than 3 percent. By contrast, prices fell more substantially, 8.8 percent, so real wages actually rose significantly in 1931, and were higher in that year than in 1929, despite lower output per worker. The 1931 price shocks, accompanied by a failure of money wages to adjust to either it or the previous year's productivity decline, seemed to be the root cause of the rise in unemployment to over 15 percent in 1931. Alternative data sources show a somewhat greater decline in money wages in 1931 (in the 4–5 percent range), but all data sources suggest that real wages actually rose fairly noticeably in 1931.

The rigidity in money wages prevalent in 1930 and 1931 (as distinct from 1921) broke down somewhat in 1932, when money wages fell more than 7 percent. Still, the decline, occurring amidst 20 percent unemployment rates, was anemic compared with the 1921 experience (when unemployment was lower). Prices declined by 10.3 percent, so real wages actually continued to increase.

Other (but, in our judgment, inferior) data sources show a rather different story, but the main conclusion is the same. Some data series suggest that money wages fell as much as 12 percent or so in 1932, implying a very small real-wage decline. Even with the modest decline, real wages on an hourly basis were higher in 1932 than in 1929, and they were approximately the same using annual wage data.

The probable continued rise in real wages in 1932 was not the sole explanation for worsening employment opportunities. Output per worker fell 3.8 percent. The net effect of the wage, price, and productivity changes was to again increase the adjusted real wage, by a substantial amount (7.7 percent). Other data sources suggest a smaller rise in the adjusted real wage, with real wages falling slightly and productivity falling perhaps 5 percent.

Money wages continued to fall some in 1933 (7.9 percent). With the fall in prices slowing (to 5.1 percent), real wages actually fell for the first time during the downturn, albeit not dramatically. A continued decline in productivity, however, (about 2.0 percent), prevented adjusted real wages from showing any meaningful change.

While alternative data sources tell roughly similar stories for 1930, 1931, and 1932, that is not the case for 1933. Some hourly wage data suggest an actual increase in 1933 (using the David-Solar wage index). Moreover, output per worker on an hourly basis declined another 2 percent, adding even more upward pressure on the adjusted real wage.

Money wages were particularly robust among unskilled laborers (the group represented by the David-Solar wage index), a sector where the incidence of unemployment was particularly high. The data hint that in some sectors of the economy, wages fell as predicted by the neoclassical theory, but in others they remained rigid despite record unemployment.

At the depth of the Great Depression in 1933, the real hourly wage of workers was some 12.5 percent higher than in 1929, despite the fact that fully one-fourth of the labor force was unemployed. Money wages had fallen less than 15 percent, a smaller decline than had occurred in the much shorter 1921 downturn. Hourly productivity per worker had fallen by 8.5 percent. While the productivity shock is significant, most of the 22.8 percent increase in the adjusted real wage from 1929 to 1933 is attributed to the real-wage increase, reflecting a stickiness in money wages.

In the four years of the worst downturn the nation had ever known, real wages had risen at a compounded annual rate of 3.0 percent a year. By contrast, in the most prosperous period in American history, 1923 to 1929, real wages had risen less, only 2.3 percent a year. While other data sources do show some real-wage decline, it is small and far more than offset by falling productivity. Thus the wage mechanism did not adjust in the manner discussed by such neoclassical theorists as A. C. Pigou.[10] It is the failure of this adjustment to occur that, in our judgment, is the root cause for the extraordinary increase in unemployment in the years following the stock-market crash.

Alternative Statistical Estimation with Quarterly Data

Before discussing reasons for the failure of the adjusted real wage to respond to the rise in unemployment, it is interesting to note that the basic model was estimated employing some data sources that provide quarterly (as opposed to annual) data. For example, for one test we took the National Industrial Conference Board index of money wages for twenty-five industries on a quarterly basis, divided by the consumer price index to get real wages, and then divided by a labor productivity index derived from the Federal Reserve index of industrial production and an index of factory employment.[11] For unemployment, we simply used the average of monthly estimates presented in table 5.1 to obtain quarterly unemployment rates. Regressing the unemployment rate against the real wage and productivity change lagged two quarters, for the period from the second quarter of 1929 through the first quarter of 1933, we obtain a statistically significant (at the 1 percent level) positive relationship between the unemployment rate and real wages, with an equally significant negative relationship between unemployment and productivity change:

(1) UNEMPL = -1.195 + 0.906 REALWAGE(-2) $-$ 0.830 CHPRTY(-2),
     (0.044) (5.563)   (5.984)

    $\overline{R}^2$ = .928, F = Stat.: 71.991,

where *UNEMPL* is the estimated quarterly unemployment rate, *REAL-WAGE* is the money wage divided by consumer prices, *CHPRTY* is the percent change in labor productivity, and the numbers in parentheses are t-statistics. The wage and productivity variables are indexed, with the fourth quarter of 1929 equal to 100. Because of the limited number of observations and some multicolinearity problems, the real-wage variable was used rather than separate money-wage and price variables.

The alternative quarterly data are highly consistent with the annual data over the ninety-year period 1900–1989. The worsening unemployment situation was tied closely (albeit with a few months' lag) to sticky, even rising real wages, and falling labor productivity.

The actual and predicted unemployment rates from the lagged model using quarterly data are presented in table 5.3, along with the data for the variables included in the adjusted real wage. The model does a good job of accounting for the behavior of unemployment, catching the major increase in unemployment from spring 1931 to fall 1932 particularly well. The model fails to detect the fall in unemployment in the fourth quarter of 1932 or the rise in early 1933, suggesting that the two-quarter lag structure may have changed late in the downturn. Still, for a model based on a unicausal explanatory framework, it does extremely well.

Money wages held remarkably constant in the early phases of the downturn, moving virtually not at all until the fourth quarter of 1930, when the unemployment rate averaged 11.7 percent (the same as the 1921 average). While money wages began to deteriorate beginning in late 1930, the initial decline was not momentous, being barely 5 percent on an annual basis, far

TABLE 5.3

UNEMPLOYMENT, WAGES, PRICES AND PRODUCTIVITY, U.S., 1929–1933

Quarter	Actual Unemployment[a]	Predicted Unemployment[a]	Money Wages	Consumer Prices	Real Wages	Labor Productivity	Adjusted Real Wage
1929							
IV	5.7	N.A.	100.0	100.0	100.0	100.0	100.0
1930							
I	7.8	N.A.	100.0	98.5	102.2	99.5	102.7
II	6.6	6.3	100.0	96.5	103.6	99.9	103.7
III	7.1	8.1	99.7	94.4	105.5	96.4	109.5
IV	10.7	9.7	98.3	93.0	105.7	94.3	112.0
1931							
I	14.3	14.4	97.1	89.3	108.8	97.1	112.0
II	14.6	16.2	96.5	86.4	111.6	98.6	113.3
III	16.3	16.7	95.5	85.2	112.0	95.1	117.8
IV	18.4	18.1	92.1	83.4	110.4	92.5	119.3
1932							
I	20.4	21.4	89.5	79.8	112.1	89.9	124.8
II	23.7	22.0	85.3	77.5	110.1	85.9	128.2
III	26.7	25.7	81.9	76.3	107.4	87.3	123.0
IV	23.7	27.2	79.4	74.9	106.0	90.2	117.5
1933							
I	26.8	23.5	78.0	72.0	108.4	90.6	119.6

[a]Unemployment rate; predicted rate is from regression model; see text.
Source: See text.

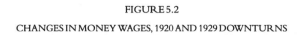

FIGURE 5.2

CHANGES IN MONEY WAGES, 1920 AND 1929 DOWNTURNS

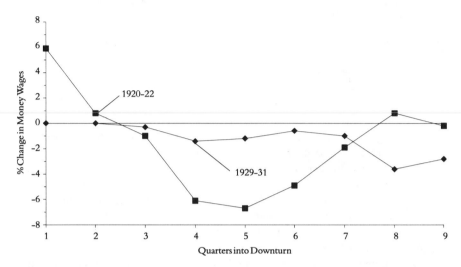

less than the money-wage decreases observed in 1920. Figure 5.2 shows the percent change in money wages from the previous quarter for the downturns beginning in 1920 and 1929. Significant wage cuts in the 1929 downturn begin only in the eighth quarter of the downturn, whereas in the 1920–22 depression, major wage reductions occur as early as the fourth quarter of the cycle. Moreover, money-wage reductions in any quarter of the 1929 downturn never reached the percentage magnitudes achieved during the 1920–22 depression.

Turning to the details of table 5.3, the rise in the adjusted real wage in the first half of 1930 was almost entirely a consequence of price deflation, as both money wages and productivity moved little (wages, in fact, were perfectly constant). The sharp rise in the adjusted real wage beginning in the third quarter of 1930 reflected in part the continued rise in real wages as money wages fell less rapidly than prices, but to a larger extent resulted from a major drop in labor productivity. The combination of deflation and productivity decline in 1930 led the adjusted real wage to rise by 12 percent from the last quarter of 1929 to the last quarter of 1930—over 40 percent of the increase observed during the downturn.

Productivity rose in the first two quarters of 1931, and even after a decline in the third quarter it was still higher than in the fourth quarter of 1930. Yet the adjusted real wage rose, since the very modest decrease in money wages was more than offset by falling prices. A major decline in

TABLE 5.4

PREDICTED UNEMPLOYMENT IN 1932 III, UNDER ALTERNATIVE ASSUMPTIONS[a]

Assumed Circumstance	% Predicted Unemployment Rate
Money Wages and Prices Fell Equally, 1929–IV to 1932–I[b]	14.7
No Price Deflation, 1929–IV to 1932–I[b]	5.2
No Productivity Decline, 1929–IV to 1932–I[b]	17.3
No Real Wage or Productivity Decline, 1929–IV to 1932–I	6.3
Actual Predicted Rate	25.7

[a]The actual rate was 26.7 percent.
[b]And everything else occurs as it actually happened.
Source: Calculated from regression equation; see text.

money wages began only in the fourth quarter of 1931, when unemployment already averaged more than 18 percent.

The rise in the adjusted real wage in the first half of 1932 to the highest level recorded in the downturn was largely a consequence of falling labor productivity, as unadjusted real wages at last stopped rising. Still, prices were falling almost as fast as wages, so the real wage in the second quarter of 1932 remained more than 10 percent above the level prevailing in the closing months of 1929.

The adjusted real wage began to fall in the last half of 1932, contributing to the 1933 recovery. The decline resulted from a continued decrease in money wages which, at last, exceeded the decline in prices (pushing real wages down), and also from an increase in labor productivity.

Looking at the entire downturn, it is true that the decline in productivity was an important factor—at one point output per worker was 14 percent below levels prevailing in late 1929. Yet the extraordinary thing was that wages did not adjust adequately to take account of the productivity decline or price deflation. In every quarter from the beginning of the decline, real wages were higher than at the end of 1929. Real wages rose faster during this period of massive unemployment than in the high-employment twenties.

Table 5.4 presents estimates, derived from the unemployment-rate regression equation using quarterly data incorporating a two-quarter lagged adjusted real wage, of what unemployment might have been in the third quarter of 1932 under different circumstances. The third quarter of 1932 is used as our reference point because unemployment very nearly peaked in that quarter; the first quarter 1933 high only slightly exceeds the early one, and only because of a big run-up in unemployment in the single month of March.

Had money wages fallen as fast as prices from the fall of 1929 to the first quarter of 1932 (real wages remained unchanged), we estimate that unemployment in the third quarter of 1932 would have been 14.7 percent—

twelve points less than actually recorded. The increase in real wages, then, is estimated to explain over 60 percent of the rise in unemployment rates from the 7 percent rate already existing in the fourth quarter of 1929 to the nearly 27 percent level prevailing in the summer of 1932.

A somewhat less important factor was the productivity decline. Had it not occurred but everything else remained the same, it is estimated that unemployment in the third quarter of 1932 would have been 17.3 percent. Had either the real-wage increase or the productivity decline not taken place, unemployment would not have risen to the levels recorded in the 1893 depression, and the depression following 1929 would have been severe, but not "the Great Depression." Had neither of these things occurred, a normal very mild recession would have evolved and the course of history would have been dramatically altered.

During the Depression, many despaired about the fall in prices. The unanticipated decline in prices pushed up the adjusted real wage and contributed enormously to the disequilibrium in labor markets that occurred. If prices had not fallen after 1929 but everything else, including money-wage rates, had followed their actual course, we estimate that unemployment in the summer of 1932 would have been only 5.2 percent. Of course, in the absence of deflation it is possible that the money-wage reductions that were obtained would not have been fully forthcoming, so the actual impact of deflation may be less than indicated, but surely the deflation turned what might have been a severe recession (with perhaps 10 percent unemployment) into an unprecedented depression. At the same time, however, we have reason to believe that the falling level of prices occurred partly as a consequence of the rigidity of money wages, so the overall effect of relative rigidity in money wages was probably more than the twelve percentage point impact on unemployment indicated in table 5.3. The arguments and evidence backing up this assertion are reserved for chapter 6.

With respect to the productivity decline that was an important secondary factor in the rise of unemployment, we should note that it came in two phases. The first big drop in productivity occurred in the last half of 1930, while the second drop is in the last half of 1931 and the first half of 1932. The larger of these two declines was the second, taking place in late 1931 and early 1932.

Recall that productivity change may take three forms: "Smithian," reflecting variations in the capital stock; "Schumpeterian," involving innovative activity and the dissemination of invention; and "Keynesian," reflecting the impact of shifting aggregate-demand schedules on output per worker.

A very strong case can be made that the 1931–32 productivity drop was Smithian in character. Investment expenditures fell dramatically beginning in 1930. While net investment was positive in 1930, even in that year the real value of equipment in industry declined.[12] The deterioration in the real capital stock accelerated in 1931 and 1932 as net investment turned negative. The real stock of equipment in "all industries" fell 13.5 percent from 1929 to 1932.[13]

The sharp decline in the capital stock from 1931 to 1933 contributed to a leftward shift in the demand-for-labor curve and a subsequent rise in unemployment. Given that (1) the real wage remained virtually constant between those two years, and (2) the capital stock declined, it is possible, using a Cobb-Douglas production function framework, to predict the unemployment effects of that decline. Starting with 1931 as our base, we estimated that unemployment would have risen to 24.3 percent in 1933 because of the roughly 10 percent observed decline in the capital stock.[14] That is quite close to the actual rate of 24.9 percent.

While a Smithian explanation of the productivity decline following mid-1931 is very much in order, the capital stock explanation would not appear to be valid in explaining the decline in productivity observed in 1930, since the capital stock as a whole modestly increased in that year. That leaves a Keynesian or Schumpeterian explanation. It is interesting that in the most comprehensive Keynesian explanation of the downturn after 1929, Peter Temin ignores the productivity decline of 1930 completely.[15] Either he views it as irrelevant or he has no explanation for it.

Actually, earlier in his volume, Temin suggests that a decline in autonomous consumption and, to a lesser extent, exports, led to a fall in aggregate demand that brought on the Great Depression. Statistically estimating a consumption function using annual data for the period 1919 to 1941, Temin notes that consumption in 1930 was slightly less than the predicted value, whereas in the 1921 and 1938 downturns, consumption was considerably greater than the predicted values. Assuming that the 1921 and 1938 experiences were normal, he argues that the difference between his residual value for 1930 and the average of that for 1921 and 1938 represents a shift in autonomous consumption. Consumption is estimated to have been about $5 billion below normal in 1930 given the income and wealth levels prevailing in that year.[16] Temin finds it hard to explain exactly why consumption fell, although he rejects the view that it largely reflected declining wealth. However, Mishkin has demonstrated that the deterioration in the household balance sheet was sufficiently large to explain a large decline in consumption.[17] Hyman Minsky argues along similar lines.[18]

The Temin findings of an autonomous downward shift in consumption have been attacked, rightly in our view, on several grounds. First, Thomas Mayer has pointed out that Temin's model suggests that underconsumption (as defined by Temin) was much greater in some years of prosperity, notably 1925, than in 1930.[19] In their own consumption function analysis,

Gandolfi and Lothian find little evidence of unusual underconsumption in 1930.[20] Our own limited testing likewise shows no substantial indications of massive underconsumption, that is, a downward shift in the consumption schedule. More importantly, we reiterate the point made in the previous chapter: there is no evidence that downward shifts in consumption were associated with negative movements in labor productivity during the early decades of the twentieth century. In conclusion, it is doubtful that there was a large decline in consumption in 1930 relative to typical behavioral patterns, and even if there were, there is no evidence that it would be associated with declining labor productivity.

An alternative explanation of the declining productivity after 1930 is suggested by Austrian economic theory.[21] In the Austrian view, new money creation, permitted by Federal Reserve monetary policies in the late 1920s, lowered the loan rate of interest and tilted the investment/consumption expenditure mix from its natural rate dictated by the true rate of time preference. Unless the Fed maintained an increasing rate of growth in the money stock, the level of investment arising in the late 1920s was not sustainable. There was malinvestment in the late 1920s due to the discoordination of market prices (interest rates) by public (Federal Reserve) intervention. This set the stage for a reduction in investment expenditures after 1929 and the resultant decline in the capital stock, with its associated impact on productivity. Entrepreneurial reaction to the monetary excesses of the twenties, in this view, was normal and to be expected. While this may not explain the initial decline in productivity in 1930, it is certainly consistent with the later and far more severe reduction in the capital stock and labor productivity.[22]

Unemployment and the "New Economics" of Herbert Hoover

The most critical difference between the 1920 and 1929 downturns was the failure of wages to adjust to changes in the labor market. Figure 5.3 shows the relationship between the adjusted real wage and factory employment in the two downturns. In the 1920–22 downturn, six quarters into the cycle the adjusted real wage turns downward, whereas in the 1929 cycle, the rise in the adjusted real wage continues for several more quarters. As figure 5.3 shows, money-wage adjustments in the 1929 downturn tended to be smaller and come later than in the earlier depression. Understanding the reasons for this change in the adjustment process is the key to explaining the rise in unemployment to unprecedented levels in the Great Depression.

Analysis of the literature and the empirical evidence leads to an inescapable conclusion: the failure of money wages to fall in the downturn begin-

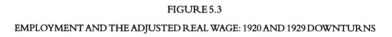

FIGURE 5.3

EMPLOYMENT AND THE ADJUSTED REAL WAGE: 1920 AND 1929 DOWNTURNS

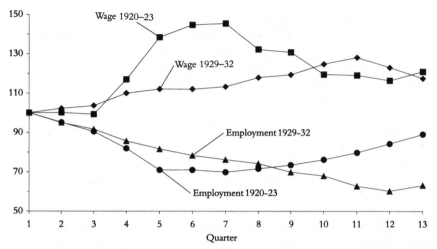

ning in the fall of 1929 was largely a consequence of public-policy intervention by President Hoover and his political allies. As a consequence of this intervention, real wages rose rather than fell, and unemployment increased to previously unattained levels. The Great Depression was not a tragic example of market failure as is conventionally believed, but rather was an example of government failure. It can be argued that the failure of the academic community, government policymakers, and the general public to realize this has been one of America's greatest mistakes during the twentieth century.

We have identified two major reasons why money wages were maintained at high levels after 1929. First, President Hoover and other government and business leaders exhorted companies to maintain high wages in order to preserve purchasing power. Second, Hoover supported a high-tariff policy to enhance buying power in agriculture and in industry. Hoover correctly believed that high tariffs would stimulate wages and help retard any normal tendency for wages to decline.

As indicated earlier, Hoover was rightly considered a progressive, interventionist politician by his contemporaries in the twenties. The image of Hoover as the last laissez-faire president was popular in the fifties and sixties and probably reflected his fairly cautious stance on public-works expenditures and deficit spending late in his administration, and his preference for economic decisions to be carried out by the private sector, even though they may have been made essentially by government.

Hoover has been described as cold, aloof, given to formality, insensitive, and uncomprehending of the real world. He was certainly formal and rather aloof: what other president would wear formal clothes to dinner even when dining alone at the White House? Yet as to his sensitivity and astuteness, Hoover has been misrepresented. Schlesinger noted that Hoover, speaking of jobs in the Depression, said that "many persons left their jobs for the more profitable one of selling apples," saying this "epitomized the presidential incredulity."[23] Yet that quote is taken entirely out of context.[24] Indeed, it might be argued that Hoover, the architect of Belgian relief after World War I, was hypersensitive to human suffering. Seeing starving people in Europe, he never wanted to see that again. Indeed, it was this specter of deprivation that drove him to promote consumption as desirable, and high wages as a means of attaining high consumption.

An early believer in what later became called indicative planning, Hoover had a paternalistic view that government leaders had a selfless and accurate perception of the public interest, and should pressure the private sector to act in accord with their conception of the world. Hoover's attitudes in this regard were shared by many intellectuals and members of the business community who were profoundly influenced by the role government played during and immediately after World War I. During that war, the government made fundamental allocation decisions in a manner unprecedented in modern American history, even nationalizing the nation's most important single industry, the railroads. Because of this experience, many of the nation's leaders developed the view that a beneficent central government could positively alter the actions of the market in order to promote the public good. This view was popular not only with some of the intellectuals who went to Washington in 1917, but also with some major names in American business, including Henry Ford, Thomas A. Edison, Edward Filene, and Gerard Swope of General Electric.

So vivid was the war experience that Hoover and his leading subordinates increasingly drew an analogy between the emerging depression and war. As one leading historian of this period has put it, "Hoover resorted constantly to the imagery of war to describe the depression."[25] The president's exhortations were not merely timid forms of moral suasion, but rather were forceful appeals to the patriotism and civic duty of our nation's business leaders. Given Hoover's enormous popularity and prestige, at least in the early days of the downturn, it was very hard to ignore an extraordinary request from the president, almost unique in American peacetime history to that time. The nation was already stunned by the stock-market crash of October 1929, and its business leadership was looking for guidance as to how to proceed. The president was one of their own, a successful entrepreneur, a millionaire, one of the nation's leading engineers. He was, in a sense, our first "scientific" president, in an age when science commanded much respect. To rebuke him was nearly unthinkable, at least in the critical early months of the downturn.

IMPLEMENTING THE HIGH-WAGE POLICY

It was scarcely three weeks after the stock-market crash when Hoover began to push actively his high-wage policy to maintain purchasing power. Meeting with many of the nation's business leaders (including, for example, a Ford, Mellon, and du Pont) at the White House in late November, the president received wholehearted cooperation from business leaders. The press release that was issued summarized the conclusions reached at the conference:[26]

> The President was authorized by the employers who were present at this morning's conference to state on their individual behalf that they will not initiate any movement for wage reductions, and it was their strong recommendation that this attitude should be pursued by the society as a whole.
>
> They considered that, aside from the human considerations involved, the consuming power of the country will thereby be maintained.

Henry Ford left the meeting with Hoover announcing plans to increase wages to stimulate the economy. He went on by giving a classic statement of the underconsumptionist, high-wage view:[27]

> Nearly everything in this country is too high priced. The only thing that should be high priced in this country is the man that works. Wages must not come down, they must not even stay on their present level; they must go up.
>
> And even that is not sufficient of itself—we must see to it that the increased wages are not taken away from the people by increased prices that do not represent increased values.

In other words, Ford was saying that not only must money wages rise, but real wages must rise as well. Coming from a man of legendary accomplishments, this statement inevitably added to the resolve of other businessmen to follow the wishes of the president they had so strongly supported only the previous November in his landslide election. One of the participants at the conference, Julius Rosenwald of Sears Roebuck, apparently thought the policy would be so successful that the nation would face a labor shortage.[28]

Contemporary observers noted how the high-wage program was being followed obediently by the nation's businessmen. As early as its first issue of 1930, the fledgling business weekly news magazine *Business Week* noted in the title to a story, "This Time They Did Not Cut Wages."[29] That, of course, was only a few weeks after Hoover enunciated the high-wage policy approach. Did contemporaries believe that the policy was being followed months or even a year later? The answer is clearly yes, as remarks at the American Economic Association meeting in December 1930 indicated. Commenting on a paper by Joseph Schumpeter in which Schumpeter observed that wages were proving quite inflexible, Carter Goodrich remarked: "It seems highly probable that the year 1930 . . . will also show an increase rather than a decrease in the rates of real wages. So far, at least, the patient does not seem to have swallowed the prescribed medicine."[30]

Labor economists and other students of wage behavior observed the unusual wage rigidity. Leo Wolman, writing in 1931, said: "It is indeed impossible to recall any past depression of similar intensity and duration in which the wages of prosperity were sustained as long as they have been during the depression of 1930–1931."[31]

Goodrich and Schumpeter were not alone in noting the rigidity in wages. The Alexander Hamilton Institute, perceptively in our view, noted in early 1931 that "It is becoming increasingly clear that the efforts to maintain wage scales have been an important factor in prolonging the business depression."[32]

In the standard history of American labor, written during this era by John R. Commons and several associates, Don Lescohier contrasted the wage behavior in the 1920–22 and 1929–31 downturns:

> In 1921 wage cuts were advocated early in the depression to liquidate labor costs. In 1930–31 they were opposed both by the government and by leading employers, in the hope that the maintenance of wage earners' incomes would furnish a market for products and help business recovery. In 1921 they were inaugurated long before business had reached a dangerous position; in 1931 they became common only after a larger number of businesses had taken heavy losses. Realization of the reluctance of a large number of employers to cut wages caused wage earners and the public to accept them calmly when they did come, perhaps too calmly.[33]

Not only academics and businessmen concluded that the Hoover high-wage policy was a big success. The secretary of labor, James Davis, later a senator and coauthor of the Davis-Bacon Act, speaking to the Advertising Federation of America in May 1930, said:

> There never has been a crisis such as we have had as the stock market crash that threw . . . millions out of employment that there wasn't a wholesale reduction in wages. . . . If Hoover accomplishes nothing more in all of his

service to the government, that one outstanding thing of his administration—
no reduction in wages—will be a credit that will be forever remembered not
by the working classes alone but by business men as well, because without
money in the pay envelope business is the first to suffer.[34]

There is even at least one statistical assessment consistent with the view that
the adjusted real wage was rising. *Business Week* in early 1932 reported that
"labor's share of business income is now going up."[35] That is the equivalent
of saying that real unit-labor costs or the adjusted real wage were rising.

The no-wage-cut policy, then, was followed not only by a few eccentric
businessmen like Henry Ford. Even in 1931, the president of U.S. Steel,
James A. Farrell, proclaimed that "those who advocate wage reductions have
not stopped to weigh the implications."[36] Several months later, operating at
32 percent of capacity, that corporation reluctantly changed its policy, and
reduced wages. For that, William Randolph Hearst blasted them: by wage-
slashing, he said, corporations "have contributed their utmost toward the aggravation of the depression. . . ."[37] Hoover's spokesman weighed in with the
assurance that "Mr. Hoover's anxiety for the maintenance of the standard of
living in this country has been consistent, and is unaltered."[38]

In a survey of business leaders in mid-1930 by *Printer's Ink* magazine, corporate executives were near-unanimous in their support of the high-wage
policy coming out of the November 1929 conference at the White House.
Howard Heinz, the ketchup maker, said: "In this enlightened age, large
manufacturers . . . will maintain wages . . . as being the far-sighted and . . .
the constructive thing to do." Carleton Palmer, president of E. R. Squibb
& Son, advocated increasing hourly wages by reducing the workweek and
maintaining weekly wages constant. William Wrigley, the gum magnate,
said he would not reduce wages, while Charles C. Small, president of the
American Ice Co., said he believed in "good wages to aid purchasing
power."[39] George F. Johnson, president of Endicott Johnson Corp., echoed
that sentiment, declaring that "reducing income of labor is not a remedy for
business depression; it is a direct and contributing cause."[40]

Big business felt it had a duty to carry through the high-wage policy.
As an observer of International Harvester put it, "big industries like International Harvester behaved during the economic collapse after 1929 as if
they were carrying the economic system on their shoulders."[41] But they
were acting out of more than patriotic duty. Anthony O'Brien makes an
excellent case that business leaders who had lost heavily in the 1920–22
downturn wanted to do things differently after 1929, believing that wage
maintenance would also maintain sales.[42]

The use of public pressure to "jawbone" business leaders into maintaining high wages was supplemented by private talks that Hoover regu-

larly had with them, in which he stressed that he "would need their cooperation—especially by maintaining wage rates and accelerating or increasing construction projects."[43] But Hoover had a second weapon to promote the high-wage policy—protective tariffs. Tariffs insulate the owners of both labor and capital resources from foreign competition, allowing them higher prices for their output and, in the case of labor, higher wages. Hoover saw that one advantage of the tariff was its usefulness in promoting high wages.

Hoover had spoken positively about tariff relief in his campaign in 1928, but had not endorsed a comprehensive bill similar to Smoot-Hawley. However, the Smoot-Hawley bill was the leading legislative event of 1929, passing the House of Representatives in May. As Charles Kindleberger has noted, "the course of the legislation through Congress had been followed with close attention."[44] According to Joseph Jones, many foreign governments enacted retaliatory tariffs in early 1930 in anticipation of passage.[45] Hoover himself apparently had some misgivings about the tariff, but later argued that it was an insignificant factor in the whole Depression story.[46]

A number of writers have argued that the Smoot-Hawley Tariff was a major cause of the Great Depression. Jude Wanniski makes a good argument that the anticipation of congressional approval led to the stock-market debacle of October 1929.[47] Christian Saint-Etienne is typical of economists who assign an important role in the 1930–31 worldwide economic decline to the tariff.[48] But none of the writers stress a point that Hoover himself believed, that the tariff was a weapon to be used in enforcing the high-wage policy.

Evaluating the Success of the High-Wage Policy Empirically

Was the verbal support for the Hoover high-wage policy matched by deeds? How different was the wage behavior of firms in 1930 and 1931 in the aftermath of the stock-market crash? To get at answers to these questions, we devised a simple econometric model explaining wage rates during the period 1900 to 1929. The wages equation produced the following results:

$$(2) \quad \text{WAGES} = -3.486 + 0.225 \text{ CPI} + 0.145 \text{ PRDTY}$$
$$\phantom{(2) \quad \text{WAGES} = } (20.485) \ (16.650) (13.797)$$

$$+ \ 0.008 \text{ TARIFF} - 0.014 \text{ IMM/POP},$$
$$ (2.614) \phantom{\text{ TARIFF} -} (0.224)$$

$$\overline{R}^2 = .9964, \ D-W = 1.978, \ F = \text{Stat.: } 1585.358,$$

where *WAGES* is the comprehensive measure of hourly wages used previously in our empirical analysis; *CPI* is the consumer price index; *PRDTY* is the measure of output per hour used previously; *TARIFF* is the average percent tariff imposed on dutiable items; *IMM/POP* is the percent of the population that had arrived as immigrants over the past year (with a six-month lag); and the numbers in parentheses are t-statistics; an autoregressive adjustment term is unreported.[49]

The model does an extraordinarily good job of explaining wage variations over time. Inserting post-1929 values of *CPI, PRDTY, TARIFF,* and *IMM/POP,* we can obtain predicted wage levels for 1930 (and beyond), and compare that with the actual levels to get some indication of the impact of the high-wage policy. The results are as follows.

1) Wages in 1930 were some 8.3 percent higher than predicted; in 1931, they were an extraordinary 10.5 percent more than predicted; in no year from 1900 to 1929 was a deviation as large as 10 percent recorded;

2) The sharp rise in tariffs from 1929 to 1931 had the impact of raising wages about 2 percent, about 20 percent of the estimated excessive wage arising from the high-wage policy; the Smoot-Hawley tariff, then, was a moderately important secondary factor in the labor-market discoordination;

3) Under reasonable assumptions, the high-wage policy, including the Smoot-Hawley tariff, raised the unemployment rate by 9.8 percentage points from 1929 to 1931, or some 77 percent of the observed increase;

4) Immigration had no significant impact on wages.

The third point requires some elaboration. The deviation of actual wages from predicted wages in the 1900–1929 period might be viewed as a measure of "shocks" that take wages away from their normal equilibrium level determined by price, productivity, and other conditions. When wages go below the normal or "natural" level, unemployment tends to fall below its normal or natural rate. We regressed the wage shocks, estimated from (2), against the actual unemployment rate for the 1900–1941 period (the shocks for 1930 to 1941 were estimated based on the 1900–1929 experience.) The highly significant results explained 77 percent of the variation in unemployment. That model (implicitly a two-stage regression model) suggested that a 9.8 percentage point rise occurred in the unemployment rate by 1931 because of the deviation of wages from their normal pattern. Use of alternative data sources for wages produces very similar results.[50]

Using the 8.3 percent estimate of a positive wage shock arising from the high-wage policy for 1930, the wage bill for those working was about $3.5

billion more than "normal," in an economy with a personal income of only $75.4 billion. This $3.5 billion wage overhang precisely accounts for the drop in corporate profits (before inventory valuation adjustments) from 1929 to 1930.[51] As we shall see in the next chapter, that fall in profits played an important role in the banking crisis of late 1930 and the subsequent price shock that helped keep real wages from falling in 1931 and 1932.

The Unemployment Effects of Smoot-Hawley

While we will argue in the next chapter that the wage policy–induced banking crisis served to increase the wage shock, and thus unemployment, in 1931 and 1932, it should be noted that Smoot-Hawley's negative effects were not fully felt until the latter year. Between 1929 and 1932, the average duty on dutiable goods rose from 40.10 to 59.06 percent.[52] From (2), we estimate that by 1932 the tariff had raised wages by about 3 percent on average. Our simple wage-shock regression suggests that, without Smoot-Hawley–induced tariff increases, the unemployment rate would have been 3.8 points lower in 1932 than it was. Since the unemployment rate had risen slightly over twenty points since 1929, the analysis suggests that nearly 20 percent of the massive rise in unemployment was tariff-related.

It is worth noting that many nations enacted retaliatory tariffs, not reflected in the above estimates, that tended to reduce the demand for American labor and thus add to the unemployment problem. Therefore, the impact of the tariff, on balance, was possibly significantly more negative than the calculations cited above indicate. It is clearly an exaggeration to blame the Depression on the tariff alone, but it nonetheless played an important role in the debacle that occurred during the first third of the thirties.[53]

The Economics Profession and the High-Wage Policy

CONTEMPORARY REACTIONS

How did the economics profession react to the high-wage policy? While there appeared to be some concern among a few economists about its inappropriateness, by and large the profession remained silent. This is not because academic economists of the era were timid, or had an aversion to expressing themselves on issues of policy. On the Smoot-Hawley Tariff, economists were furiously indignant. More than a thousand of them from

179 colleges and universities in forty-six states protested vehemently in a statement made public on May 4, 1930.[54]

By contrast, the economists were either silent or approving of the high-wage policy. According to Irving Fisher, "Fulfillment of the pledges by the nation's business leaders . . . that wages will not be reduced . . . should suffice to bridge across the business recession that slightly antedated and accompanied the crash."[55] Another prominent economist, John Maurice Clark, said in December 1929 that Hoover's actions were "a great experiment in constructive industrial statesmanship of a promising and novel sort."[56] Debating with socialists before four thousand people on the virtue of capitalism in February 1930, Clark's colleague at Columbia, Professor Edwin Seligman, used the unemployment conference as evidence of the potential for a more compassionate, cooperative capitalist spirit, a "kinder and gentler" capitalism.[57]

As indicated earlier, the contemporary view is that economists before the Keynesian Revolution of the 1930s tended to believe that unemployment would not persist for long and would be cured by wage adjustments. There is some truth in this assertion, but it also conveys a misleading perception. By and large, economists largely ignored the issue of unemployment. Moreover, many of the writers on the topic acknowledged the existence of market imperfections that prevented the wage-adjustment mechanism from working fully. In short, the notion that a self-correcting wage mechanism would solve the problem of unemployment was not part of the central core of economic theory that almost every economist uncritically accepted.

To be sure, most writers of elementary economics textbooks during the twenties suggested that wage adjustments would tend to relieve unemployment. As Frank Taussig put it, "A steady supply of unemployed laborers tends to bring its own remedies. . . . It brings . . . a readjustment of terms between employers and employees."[58] Yet the whole topic of unemployment absorbed less than five pages of a book over one thousand pages long. Irving Fisher barely mentioned the topic, saying that "unemployment tends to correct itself," but also that "in practice this equalization of supply and demand works itself out slowly and imperfectly."[59] Thomas Carver ignored unemployment completely.[60]

Not all textbooks were devoid of coverage of the unemployment issue, though. Fairchild, Furniss, and Buck, in their two-volume, twelve-hundred-page work, devoted a whole chapter (twenty-five pages) to the topic.[61] They noted that the "relative rigidity of the wage rate as compared with other prices," along with the immobility of labor, prevented a full employment equilibrium.[62] To deal with such market imperfections, they spoke positively of countercyclical public-works schemes, hardly the classical position as it is usually portrayed.[63]

The notion that economists of the 1920s were all classical theorists who advocated wage cuts to eliminate unemployment is without foundation. The commitment to a theory that stressed unemployment being rooted in inappropriate relative prices (in this case wages) was quite weak. That became more apparent as the Depression unfolded. The signers of a 1930 petition to Congress supporting the Wagner bill to increase public-works spending included such illustrious names as John Bates Clark, John Maurice Clark, Davis R. Dewey, Paul H. Douglas, Frank A. Fetter, Irving Fisher, Edwin W. Kemmerer, and Frank Taussig.[64]

The economics faculty at the University of Chicago took a leading role in articulating support for a countercyclical fiscal policy, arguing that market adjustments would not be adequate to do the job. Particularly vocal was Jacob Viner, an economist who so epitomized the neoclassical tradition that Joseph Dorfman called him "the twentieth-century Ricardian."[65] Generally supportive of the Viner position were other Chicago economists, including noted free-market advocate Henry Simons. Rather than criticizing Hoover for promoting high wages, the Chicago economists joined others in promoting Keynesian-like policies designed to stimulate aggregate demand.

The classical tradition that emphasized the importance of relative prices and the market mechanism was far more entrenched in Europe than in the United States. In Britain, prominent economists like A. C. Pigou, Henry Clay, Edwin Cannan, W. H. Beveridge, and Lionel Robbins all stressed the importance of high wages in explaining unemployment.[66] On the continent, the Austrian economists, led by Ludwig von Mises, argued strongly that unemployment reflected a discoordination of markets.[67]

THE IDEAS OF LATER ECONOMISTS

To be sure, some American economists were aware of the importance of wages. Despite his advocacy of public-works spending, Viner recognized the disequilibrium in wages, as did Willford I. King.[68] In the midst of a high tide of Keynesianism in the forties through the sixties, several economists argued that the high-wage policy had contributed to the Depression, most notably Benjamin Anderson, Murray Rothbard, and W. H. Hutt.[69]

Nevertheless, the neoclassical/Austrian interpretation of the 1930s was largely ignored or dismissed. Keynesians developed demand-side evidence purportedly supporting their position. An early convert to the Keynesian position was Alvin Hansen with his "secular stagnation" thesis.[70] In a series of studies, Robert A. Gordon argued that declining automobile and housing demand was the root cause of the downturn after 1929.[71] E. Cary Brown demonstrated that fiscal policy had not been aggressively tried, a finding supported by other scholars.[72] Peter Temin presented a comprehensive Keynesian interpretation of the period, including purported evidence of insufficient consumption.[73] At least one historian interpreting the period blamed the Depression in part on the failure of businesses to keep their promise to maintain wages at 1929 levels![74]

Milton Friedman won the Nobel Prize for his pathbreaking analysis, with Anna Schwartz, of the period from the monetarist perspective.[75] Naturally, the Marxian economists also weighed in with explanations for the Depression.[76]

In the seventies and eighties, Keynesian economics underwent substantial attack, and it became popular to talk of the "microfoundations of macroeconomics." Interest in the role of wages in the Great Depression was revived. The New Classical Economics stressed the critical importance of *expectations*.[77] The New Classicals argued, in a manner reminiscent of the earlier market–oriented economic theory of Pigou, that "the unemployment rate [is] insensitive to demand policy choices."[78]

In a series of papers around 1970, Robert Lucas and Leonard Rapping introduced the wage rate into models explaining key economic variables, including the unemployment rate.[79] They appropriately raised the issue of expectations, suggesting that the unexpected deflation of the early 1930s had caught workers off guard, contributing to the wage and unemployment disequilibrium, particularly by impacting on labor supply. Yet, they did not seem to reject totally the basic negative wage–unemployment relationship observed in the Phillips-curve literature of the sixties, nor does one find a ringing defense of the neoclassical and Austrian view that wages and unemployment are positively related. Nor did their modeling do a good job in explaining the unemployment experience after 1933.

The New Classical view that evolved in the 1970s has been summarized by Eric Kades:

> Today's New Classicals must argue that recessions occur when *low* wages are expected; workers then find leisure less costly in terms of wages foregone and bide their time until remuneration rates improve. But can the Great Depression best be explained as a multi-year withdrawal from labor markets by most Americans because they expected an eventual wage rise? The other explanations that New Classical theory can offer seem no more credible. One is that the utility function of most laborers called for a ". . . spontaneous outburst of demand for leisure . . . from 1929–1939."[80]

Leading proponents of New Classical principles actually have said diverse things about the Depression experience. Lucas said that "there were a lot of decisions made, that, after the fact, people wished that they had not made. There were a lot of jobs people quit that they wished they had hung onto . . ."[81] People simply had too high "reservation wages," which led to increased unemployment. Robert Barro accepts the monetarist explanation: "The unprecedented monetary collapse over this period accords quantitatively with the drastic decline in economic activity."[82] Thomas Sargent throws up his hands, saying "I do not have a theory, nor do I know somebody else's theory that constitutes a satisfactory explanation of the Great Depression."[83] Thus, despite a revival of interest in the microeconomic dimensions of unemployment, there has been no renewed commitment to the halfheartedly accepted neoclassical notion that unemployment was caused by excessive wages.

Several scholars examining the Depression era empirically in recent years, however, have given the wages hypothesis new life, with respect to both Britain and the United States. For example, Richard Jensen, in assessing the period, said that "Hoover and Roosevelt both made matters worse and delayed recovery. Their successful efforts to keep wages high accelerated the transition and increased structural unemployment."[84] Like most recent writers on the topic, Ben Bernanke seems to accept the view that high real wages contributed to the Depression. Using individual industry data, Bernanke concludes that "the inertia of nominal wages must be given some role in the explanation of real wage behavior."[85] Bernanke also believes that shortening the workweek served to have a positive impact on real wages. Although the British experience was somewhat different (see below), several scholars believe that rising real wages were a major part of the unemployment problem.[86] Yet there still are major accounts of the period written in the past few years that pay little heed to this or earlier research in explaining the Depression.[87]

Unemployment and Wages: The European Experience

The evidence is compelling that the Depression in America was of American origin, the product of the disastrous high-wage policy of the government along with other forms of public involvement influencing relative prices, notably the Federal Reserve's role in the decline in the stock of money. Yet, the Depression spread overseas, and unemployment rose elsewhere, although generally not as much as in the United States. Can unemployment abroad be explained in terms of the adjusted real wage rising above a natural or normal rate?

To examine that question, we turned our attention to Great Britain, the leading European economic power and the home of the Keynesian revolution, the new departure in economic thinking that took the view that "wages don't matter." In addition, we have performed some econometric testing for fifteen European nations. It suggests that a large portion of the fluctuations in unemployment during the interwar era are explained by a model incorporating wages, prices, and productivity.

The story unfolds somewhat differently in Britain than in the United States. After 1920, Britain was subjected to very high unemployment, with the rate exceeding 10 percent except for one brief interval. This is rather extraordinary since real output growth from 1921 to 1929 was 2.75 percent a year—far in excess of the average for the 1900–1913 period.[88] A large part of the reason for the high unemployment was that the reservation wage of workers rose considerably as exceedingly generous unemployment insurance benefits increased the average duration of unemployment and thus the unemployment rate.[89]

The substantial unemployment insurance benefits go a long way toward explaining the high rate of joblessness in the 1920s, suggesting that the natural rate of unemployment may have been around 10 percent. But that does not explain the rise in unemployment to above 20 percent after 1930. The dole was not made more generous and indeed was reduced. Nor can one explain the rising unemployment in terms of underconsumption. On examining the painstaking research of Nobel laureate Richard Stone on consumer expenditure, we observe that between 1927 and 1932, when the unemployment rate more than doubled, real consumption expenditures per capita actually rose.[90]

On the other hand, the wages hypothesis does an excellent job in explaining the rise in unemployment after 1929, and the decline within five years after 1933 to the natural rate (unlike in the United States, where unemployment remained high for eight years, a subject that is discussed in chapter 7). Using data gathered by Mitchell and Brown and Browne for Britain, we are able to compare the U.S. and British experience with respect to the components of the adjusted real wage.[91] The findings, presented in table 5.5, suggest a somewhat different pattern in Britain than in the U.S.

While Hoover and other progressives delayed the adjustment in money wages in the United States, at least a partial wage adjustment occurred, especially after 1931. In Britain, however, money wages were almost completely inflexible downward, explaining, perhaps, Keynes's emphasis on wage inflexibility. Prices were more pliable than wages, falling significantly, and pushing up real wages in Britain, which may explain why real consumption rose. Unlike the United States, Britain already had large and militant labor unions; these organizations had shown their potential power only a few years earlier in the general strike of 1926. Their presence no doubt largely explains the failure of money wages to fall.

Dissimilar to the American experience, labor productivity in Britain actually rose, and rather sharply, during the downturn. This further refutes

TABLE 5.5

WAGES, PRICES AND PRODUCTIVITY: U.S. AND BRITAIN, 1929 TO 1938[a]

Year	Money Wages	Prices	Real Wages	Productivity	Adjusted Real Wage[b]
United States:					
1929	100	100	100	100	100
1933	85	76	112	92	122
1938	106	82	129	113	114
Britain:					
1929	100	100	100	100	100
1933	95	85	112	111	101
1938	106	100	106	116	91

[a]1929=100.
[b]Real wages divided by productivity.
Sources: See text.

the argument that the adjusted real wage model is not meaningful because productivity declines caused by shifts in aggregate demand cause the adjusted real wage rate to rise. The growth in labor productivity in Britain during the early years of the Depression was in excess of the long-run historic trend.

In a policy sense, there was a decline in the money stock after 1929 that, while modest, worked to lower prices. It probably reflected a determination on the part of the monetary authorities to maintain the pound at a $4.86 exchange rate in order to avoid going off the gold standard. In the view of W. H. Hutt, the inflationary bias in Keynesian-style thinking in Britain even before the *General Theory* "caused an otherwise avoidable deflation to be essential."[92] In any case, the unanticipated deflation tended to increase real wages, which rose nearly 3 percent a year between 1929 and 1933, far in excess of the long-term historical trend.

It is arguable that Britain, unlike the United States, did not have a Depression in an output sense. From peak (1929) to trough (1933), real output fell but 6 percent, and over the 1929–39 decade, it rose by 21 percent in real terms, with an annual growth rate of 1.94 percent, relatively high in a historical sense.[93] The Depression in Britain was an unemployment depression generated by out-of-equilibrium wages. Amidst general prosperity, a portion of the British public suffered enormously. The unjustness of this contributed to the political environment that led to the Keynesian revolution. Yet, what was involved here was less market failure than institutional failure—the workings of strong labor unions protected by government and a monetary policy that served to provide unanticipated real-wage windfalls for that portion of the population fortunate enough to be employed.

Turning to some fifteen European countries for which data are available (Austria, Belgium, Czechoslovakia, Denmark, Finland, France, Germany, Hungary, Italy, the Netherlands, Norway, Poland, Sweden, Switzerland, and the United Kingdom), the statistical estimation of a real-wage–unemployment model gives generally robust results:[94]

1. In ten of fifteen instances, the basic model explains a majority of the considerable variation in unemployment rates from the mid-1920s to the mid- or later 1930s;
2. In thirteen of fifteen instances, real wages are positively related to the rate of unemployment at the 1 percent level of significance, and in the remaining cases (Denmark and Hungary), the relationship is significant at the 5 percent level.

We are inclined to agree with the first part of a statement by President Hoover, speaking before the American Bankers Association in Cleveland early in the fall of 1930: "Our leading business concerns have sustained wages." He went on to say: "These measures have maintained higher degrees of consumption than would have otherwise been the case. . . . They have thus prevented a large measure of unemployment."[95] With this, of course, we most emphatically disagree. As Lester Chandler so accurately put it, Hoover "seems to have paid little attention to wage rates as a determinant of costs of production."[96] In focusing on demand, he ignored supply.

The Great Depression brought unprecedented misery to millions of unemployed Americans. The inequalities and inequities of life seemed to grow, as other millions of Americans lived normal, even prosperous lives. The common interpretation is that this Depression, this misery, this inequality, reflected rigidities and imperfections in the markets for goods and resources. Yet the evidence we have presented is more consistent with a far different story. The market, particularly the critical market for labor, was prevented from operating in a normal fashion by the interventions of government. These intrusions turned a severe shock that started a recession into a major depression. Government failure, not market failure, was the problem, but the "solutions" to the massive unemployment that were increasingly proposed by economists of varying political persuasions formed the basis of policy departures that contributed significantly to problems in labor markets for several decades. Before turning to that, however, we must first show how the interference in the labor market had a domino effect, leading to a banking crisis that took us one step further—from a major economic downturn right into the Great Depression.

NOTES

1. All of these economic statistics are found in U.S. Department of Commerce, Bureau of the Census, *Historical Statistics of the United States, Colonial Times to 1970* (Washington, D.C.: Government Printing Office, 1975). For a summary of several important economic indicators during this period, see Richard K. Vedder, *The American Economy in Historical Perspective* (Belmont, Calif.: Wadsworth, 1976), p. 371.

2. The statistics in this paragraph are all from Lester V. Chandler, *America's Greatest Depression, 1929–1941* (New York: Harper and Row, 1970), pp. 33–42. The high unemployment for female blacks in Detroit appears to be more a function of the highly depressed nature of employment in Detroit than a consequence of race or gender. On this latter point, see chap. 14.

3. *Historical Statistics of the United States*, pp. 695–96.

4. The data were originally developed for our paper "What Caused the Great Depression? A Half Century Reassessment" (Athens, Ohio: Ohio University Department of Economics Working Paper Series, no. 85-19, 1985.)

5. If the estimates for November and December are correct and if the BLS/Lebergott estimate of 3.2 percent for 1929 is also correct, the average unemployment rate for the first ten months of 1929 was 2.44 percent.

6. Studies conjecturing as to why the stock-market crash occurred are too numerous to mention. A couple of interpretations deserve mentioning. Alexander J. Field believes that the relatively stringent monetary policy followed in 1928–29 would not have been followed if the Fed had been aware of the sharp rise in the transactions demand for money after 1925 arising from increased stock-market activity. See his "A New Interpretation of the Onset of the Great Depression," *Journal of Economic History* 44 (1984): 489–98. A radical perspective is that declining profit rates in the 1920s led to the crash. See Gerard Dumenil, Mark Glick, and Jose Rangel, "Theories of the Great Depression: Why Did Profitability Matter?" *Review of Radical Political Economy* 19 (1987): 16–42. Of course, the present account differs fundamentally with that interpretation.

7. See Robert M. Coen, "Labor Force and Unemployment in the 1920s and 1930s: A Re-examination Based on Postwar Experience," *Review of Economics and Statistics* 55 (1973), 46–55, and Michael R. Darby, "Three-and-a-Half Million U.S. Employees Have Been Mislaid: Or, An Explanation of Unemployment, 1934–1941," *Journal of Political Economy* 84 (1976): 1–16. The official BLS estimates are found in *Historical Statistics of the United States*, p. 135. For a discussion of methodology in the construction of the official estimates, see Stanley Lebergott, *Manpower and Economic Growth* (New York: McGraw-Hill, 1964), pp. 355–418.

8. Gene Smiley, "Recent Unemployment Rate Estimates for the 1920s and 1930s," *Journal of Economic History* 43 (1983): 487–93.

9. Michael R. Darby, "The U.S. Productivity Slowdown: A Case of Statistical Myopia," *American Economic Review* 74 (1984): 301–22.

10. Arthur C. Pigou, *Industrial Fluctuations* (London: Macmillan, 1927). Pigou is probably the first writer, at least in the English language, fully and explicitly to

elucidate the neoclassical unemployment theory outlined in this book. However, see also Henry Clay, *The Post-war Unemployment Problem* (London: Macmillan, 1929).

11. Willford I. King, *The Causes of Economic Fluctuations* (New York: Ronald Press, 1938) (on wages); Geoffrey H. Moore, ed., *Business Cycle Indicators* (Princeton, N.J.: Princeton University Press for the National Bureau of Economic Research, 1961) (on output and factory employment).

12. See *Historical Statistics of the United States*, p. 259, col. F-84 for data on net stocks of industrial equipment.

13. Ibid.

14. See our "Wages, Prices, and Employment: Von Mises and the Progressives," *Review of Austrian Economics* 1 (1987): 32–80, for greater detail.

15. Peter Temin, *Did Monetary Forces Cause the Great Depression?* (New York: W. W. Norton, 1976). Temin's limited discussion of the role of wages can be found on pp. 138–41.

16. Ibid., chap. 3 and the statistical appendix.

17. Frederic S. Mishkin, "The Household Balance Sheet and the Great Depression," *Journal of Economic History* 38 (1978): 918–37.

18. Hyman P. Minsky, "Banking and Industry Between the Two Wars: The United States," *Journal of European Economic History* 13 (1984): 235–72.

19. Thomas Mayer, "Consumption and the Great Depression," *Journal of Political Economy* 86 (1978): 139–45.

20. A. E. Gandolfi and J. R. Lothian, review of "Did Monetary Forces Cause the Great Depression?" *Journal of Money Credit and Banking* 9 (1977): 679–91.

21. The standard statement of Austrian economic theory is Ludwig von Mises, *Human Action* (New Haven, Conn.: Yale University Press, 1949).

22. See Murray N. Rothbard, *America's Great Depression* (Kansas City: Sheed & Ward, 1963), especially chaps. 1, 4, and 5.

23. Arthur M. Schlesinger, Jr., *The Crisis of the Old Order* (Boston: Houghton Mifflin, 1957), p. 241.

24. See Herbert Hoover, *The Memoirs of Herbert Hoover*, vol. 3, *The Great Depression, 1929–1941* (New York: Macmillan, 1952), p. 195. According to Hoover, an apple growers' association in the Northwest, seeing public sympathy for the unemployed, started marketing apples on street corners to increase sales.

25. William E. Leuchtenburg, "The New Deal and the Analogue of War," in *Change and Continuity in Twentieth-Century America*, ed. John Braeman, Robert H. Bremner, and Everett Walters (Columbus: Ohio State University Press, 1964).

26. *New York Times*, November 22, 1929, p. 1.

27. Ibid., p. 2.

28. John Kenneth Galbraith, *The Great Crash* (Boston: Houghton Mifflin, 1961), p. 143.

29. "This Time They Did Not Cut Wages," *Business Week*, January 1, 1930, pp. 23–24.

30. Carter Goodrich, "The Business Depression of Nineteen Hundred Thirty: Discussion," *American Economic Review* 21 (1931): 183–201; Joseph Schumpeter,

"The Present World Depression: A Tentative Diagnosis," *American Economic Review* 21 (1931): 179–82.

31.   Leo Wolman, *Wages in Relation to Economic Recovery* (Chicago: University of Chicago, 1931), pp. 2–3.

32.   As quoted in "Must Wages Fall?," *Literary Digest*, March 14, 1931, p. 9.

33.   Don Lescohier, "Working Conditions," in *History of Labor in the United States, 1896–1932*, ed. John R. Commons et al., vol. 3 of 4 (New York: Macmillan, 1918–1935), p. 92.

34.   "Davis Says Hoover Saved Wage Cuts," *New York Times*, May 22, 1930, p. 32.

35.   "Stabilization of Unemployment Makes Prosser Report Timely," *Business Week*, January 13, 1932, p. 27.

36.   "The Debate Over Pay Reduction," *New York Times*, June 7, 1931, sec. 9, p. 3.

37.   As quoted in "Wage-Slashing as a Great National Issue," *Literary Digest*, October 10, 1931, p. 5.

38.   Ibid.

39.   "Would Keep Scale of Present Wages," *New York Times*, August 7, 1930, p. 23.

40.   "Keeping Wages Up in the Business Dip," *Literary Digest*, August 16, 1930, p. 7.

41.   Robert Ozanne, *Wages in Practice and Theory: McCormick and International Harvester* (Madison: University of Wisconsin Press, 1968), p. 52.

42.   Anthony P. O'Brien, "A Behavioral Explanation for Nominal Wage Rigidity During the Great Depression," *Quarterly Journal of Economics* 104 (1989): 719–35.

43.   George D. Green, "The Ideological Origins of the Revolution in American Financial Policies," in *The Great Depression Revisited*, ed. Karl Brunner (Boston: Martinus Nijhoff, 1981), p. 244.

44.   Charles P. Kindleberger, *The World in Depression, 1929-1939* (Berkeley: University of California Press, 1973), p. 132.

45.   Joseph M. Jones, Jr., *Tariff Retaliation, Repercussions of the Smoot-Hawley Bill* (Philadelphia: University of Pennsylvania Press, 1934), passim.

46.   Hoover, *Memoirs*, 3:291.

47.   Jude Wanniski, *The Way the World Works*, rev. ed. (New York: Simon and Schuster, 1983), chap. 7.

48.   Christian Saint-Etienne, *The Great Depression, 1929–1938* (Stanford, Calif.: Hoover Institution Press, 1984), especially pp. 29–33.

49.   The wage, productivity and price level variables are indexed with 1982 = 100.

50.   It is possible to test statistically whether the observed deviation of actual from predicted rates is significant, even taking into account the forecast error existing in years prior to the out-sample prediction. Such testing confirms that the wage shock observed after 1929 is indeed statistically significant. See J. Johnston, *Econometric Methods*, 2d ed. (New York: McGraw-Hill, 1972), pp. 38–43.

51. Total profits fell from $10.5 billion to $7.0 billion. See *Historical Statistics of the United States*, p. 236, series F-178.

52. Ibid., p. 888, series U-212.

53. A large number of economists and public figures blamed international conditions and events for contributing to the Great Depression. See Charles Kindleberger, *The World in Depression, 1929–39* (Berkeley: University of California Press, 1973). Many, of course, argue that the American downturn was transmitted to the rest of the world. For another view, however, see Gertrud M. Fremling, "Did the United States Transmit the Great Depression to the Rest of the World?" *American Economic Review* 75 (1985): 1181–85.

54. For a discussion of reactions of economists to both Smoot-Hawley and the high-wage policy, see William J. Barber, *From New Era to New Deal* (Cambridge: Cambridge University Press, 1985), pp. 87–91.

55. Irving Fisher, *The Stock Market Crash—and After* (New York: Macmillan, 1930), pp. 268–69.

56. See Barber, *From New Era to New Deal*, p. 88.

57. "4,000 Hear Debate on Capitalist System," *New York Times*, February 3, 1930, p. 23.

58. Frank W. Taussig, *Principles of Economics*, 3d ed., 2 vols. (New York: Macmillan, 1923), 2: 364.

59. Irving Fisher, *Elementary Principles of Economics* (New York: Macmillan, 1923), pp. 443–44.

60. Thomas N. Carver, *Principles of National Economy* (Boston: Ginn and Co., 1921.)

61. Fred Rogers Fairchild, Edgar S. Furniss, and Norman S. Buck, *Elementary Economics* (New York: Macmillan, 1927), vol. 2, chap. 51.

62. Ibid., p. 498.

63. Ibid., pp. 501–2.

64. See J. Ronnie Davis, *The New Economics and the Old Economists* (Ames: Iowa State University Press, 1971), pp.157–58. The Davis volume is the definitive study of the thinking of economists during this period. Interestingly, few economists protested along neoclassical supply-side lines in 1932, when income-tax rates were raised drastically.

65. Ibid., p. 40.

66. On Pigou, Cannan, and Clay, see Mark Casson, *The Economics of Unemployment* (Cambridge, Mass.: MIT Press, 1983). See also Lionel Robbins, *The Great Depression* (London: Macmillan, 1933), and William H. Beveridge, *Unemployment: A Problem of Industry* (London: Longmans Green, 1930). The most extensive theoretical analysis of unemployment in a neoclassical tradition is Pigou's *The Theory of Unemployment* (London, Macmillan, 1933).

67. For Mises's view on unemployment, see his *Human Action*, 3d ed. (Chicago: Henry Regnery, 1960), or his *Theory of Money and Credit* (New Haven, Conn.: Yale University Press, 1953).

68. Jacob Viner, *Balanced Deflation, Inflation, or More Depression* (Minneapolis: University of Minnesota Press, 1933), especially pp. 12–13, and Willford I. King, *Causes of Economic Fluctuations*, especially chap. 8.

69. Benjamin Anderson, *Economics and the Public Welfare* (Princeton, N.J.: Van Nostrand, 1949); Murray Rothbard, *America's Great Depression* and W. H. Hutt, *The Keynesian Episode: A Reassessment* (Indianapolis: Liberty Press, 1979).

70. Alvin H. Hansen, "Economic Progress and Declining Population Growth," *American Economic Review* 29 (1939): 1–15.

71. Robert A. Gordon, "Business Cycles in the Interwar Period: The Quantitative Approach," *American Economic Review* 39 (1949): 47–63, or his *Economic Instability and Growth: The American Record* (New York: Harper and Row, 1974). A number of studies question Gordon's conclusions. See, for example, Lloyd J. Mercer and W. Douglas Morgan, "The American Automobile Industry, Investment Demand, Capacity and Capacity Utilization, 1921–1940," *Journal of Political Economy* 80 (1972): 1214–31; see also their article "Housing Surplus in the 1920s? Another Evaluation," *Explorations in Economic History* 10 (1973): 295–304.

72. E. Cary Brown, "Fiscal Policy in the 'Thirties: A Reappraisal," *American Economic Review* 46 (1956): 857–79; Larry Peppers, "Full-Employment Surplus Analysis and Structural Change: The 1930s," *Explorations in Economic History* 10 (1973): 197–210.

73. Ibid.

74. Irving Bernstein, *The Lean Years: A History of the American Worker, 1920–1933* (Boston: Houghton Mifflin, 1960), pp. 313–16, 506.

75. Milton Friedman and Anna J. Schwartz, *A Monetary History of the United States, 1867 to 1960* (Princeton, N.J.: Princeton University Press for the National Bureau of Economic Research, 1963). See also Schwartz's paper "Understanding 1929–33," in *The Great Depression Revisited*, ed. Karl Brunner (Boston: Martinus Nijhoff, 1981), pp. 5–48.

76. Paul A. Baran and Paul M. Sweezy, *Monopoly Capital: An Essay on the American Economic and Social Order* (New York: Monthly Review Press, 1966), pp. 238–44.

77. For an excellent survey of contemporary developments in economic theory, see Jerome L. Stein, *Monetarist, Keynesian and New Classical Economics* (New York: New York University Press, 1982).

78. Bennett T. McCallum, "Rational Expectations and Macroeconomic Stabilization Policy: An Overview," *Journal of Money, Credit and Banking* 12 (1980): 724.

79. Robert Lucas and Leonard Rapping, "Real Wages, Prices and Inflation," *Journal of Political Economy* 77 (1969): 721–54, and "Unemployment in the Great Depression: Is There a Full Explanation?" *Journal of Political Economy* 80 (1972): 186–91.

80. Eric Kades, "New Classical and New Keynesian Models of Business Cycles," *Economic Review, Federal Reserve Bank of Cleveland* 4 (1985): 30.

81. Quoted in Arjo Klamer, *The New Classical Macroeconomists: Conversations with the New Classical Economists and Their Opponents* (Totowa, N.J.: Rowman and Allanheld, 1983), p. 41.

82. Robert J. Barro, "Second Thoughts on Keynesian Economics," *American Economic Review* 69 (1979): 58.

83. Klamer, *The New Classical Macroeconomists*, p. 69.

84. Richard J. Jensen, "The Causes and Cures of Unemployment in the Great Depression," *Journal of Interdisciplinary History* 19 (1989): 582.

85.   Ben S. Bernanke, "Employment, Hours and Earnings in the Depression: An Analysis of Eight Manufacturing Industries," *American Economic Review* 76 (1986): 82–109.

86.   See Michael Beenstock and Peter Warburton, "Wages and Unemployment in Interwar Britain," *Explorations in Economic History* 23 (1986): 153–72, and T. J. Hatton, "A Quarterly Model of the Labour Market in Interwar Britain," *Oxford Bulletin of Economics and Statistics* 50 (1988): 1–23. For a more agnostic but not hostile perspective, see Barry Eichengreen, "Unemployment in Interwar Britain: Dole or Doldrums?" *Oxford Economic Papers* 39 (1987): 597–623. Another study emphasizing real wages that provides an excellent discussion of the thinking of British economists is Casson, *The Economics of Unemployment*. Finally, Jim Symons and Andrew Newell, "The Macroeconomics of the Interwar Years: International Comparisons," seem to confirm the wages hypothesis in an analysis of fourteen countries that was part of an excellent volume edited by Barry Eichengreen and Tim Hatton. See Eichengreen and Hatton's *Interwar Unemployment in International Perspective* (Norwell, Mass.: Kluwer Academic Publishers, 1988), pp. 61–96, especially p. 86.

87.   A particularly noteworthy book in this regard is Michael A. Bernstein, *The Great Depression* (New York: Cambridge University Press, 1987). Another pro-Keynesian perspective is provided by Tyler Cowen. See his "Why Keynesianism Triumphed Or, Could So Many Keynesians Have Been Wrong?" *Critical Review* 3 (1989): 518–30.

88.   See C. H. Feinstein, *National Income, Expenditure and Output of the United Kingdom, 1855–1965* (Cambridge: Cambridge University Press, 1972).

89.   Daniel K. Benjamin and Levis A. Kochin, "Searching for an Explanation of Unemployment in Interwar Britain," *Journal of Political Economy* 87 (1979): 441–78. Benjamin and Kochin provide strong statistical evidence supporting the assertion of numerous writers and politicians, among them Winston Churchill, that the existence of the dole greatly aggravated unemployment. See, for example, Edwin Cannan, "The Problem of Unemployment," *Economic Journal* 40 (1930): 45–55.

90.   Richard Stone et al., *The Measurement of Consumers' Expenditures and Behaviour in the United Kingdom, 1920–1938*, 2 vols. (Cambridge: Cambridge University Press, 1954 and 1966), 2: 110; see also Feinstein, *National Income*. For economic statistics, including unemployment rates, for this period, see Brian R. Mitchell, *Abstract of British Historical Statistics* (Cambridge: Cambridge University Press, 1988), p. 124.

91.   Ibid., and E. H. Phelps Brown and Margaret Browne, *A Century of Pay* (London: Macmillan, 1968), appendix 3, p. 446.

92.   W. H. Hutt, *The Keynesian Episode: A Reassessment* (Indianapolis: Liberty Press, 1979), p. 63.

93.   See Feinstein, *National Income*, p. T16.

94.   Data were assembled from a variety of sources, most importantly, Brian R. Mitchell, *European Historical Statistics 1750–1970* (New York: Columbia University Press, 1978), especially Section C, pp. 49–84. Data limitations were substantial. For most countries, the model examines variations in unemployment for the period 1925 to 1939, but for some countries data problems restricted analysis to a slightly

shorter period. In most cases, the annual measure of labor productivity was not provided, so the model merely relates real wages unadjusted for productivity to the rate of unemployment.

95. *Banker's Magazine*, November 1930, pp. 693–94.

96. *America's Greatest Depression, 1929–1941* (New York: Harper and Row, 1970), pp. 33–34.

6

The Banking Crisis
and the Labor Market

The initial determinant of the labor-market disequilibrium that produced the unprecedented unemployment of the Great Depression was the high-wage, underconsumptionist policy followed by the Hoover administration, which manifested itself in jawboning and tariff increases that kept wages remarkably high into 1931. Yet money wages did finally begin to fall considerably, and by 1931 Hoover and his policy were increasingly viewed with disdain. To the extent that high wages were maintained by "moral suasion," that tactic was increasingly ineffective as the Depression worsened. Despite the inability to maintain wages after 1931, the fall in money wages was inadequate to return the system to equilibrium, and unemployment continued to increase. Why?

Milton Friedman and Anna Schwartz have effectively argued that the Depression largely reflected the effects of the sharp decline in the stock of money after the fall of 1929 and, in particular, after late 1930.[1] The statistical evidence is strongly consistent with the view that the economic decline was closely correlated with a decrease in the stock of the medium of exchange.[2] For example, a very simple regression relating the magnitude of money (M2) to the quarterly unemployment rate from the fourth quarter of 1929 to the first quarter of 1933 is extremely robust, with a R^2 of .951; the relationship is also statistically significant at the 1 percent level.

We believe that the Friedman and Schwartz story is important and indeed helps in understanding the Great Depression. Yet we would stress that the distress arising from the decline in the stock of money arose because of the impact that the monetary disturbance had on the relative price of labor and, to a much lesser extent, capital. In addition, we believe that the monetary decline was in large part a by-product of the Hoover high-wage policy. The banking crisis of late 1930 began what was to be a rather steady shrinkage of the stock of money. The evidence is rather convincing that the banking crisis was largely caused by the consequences of the ill-conceived high-wage policy.

Financial Dimensions of the High-Wage Policy

Not only did the Hoover high-wage policy raise, rather than lower, unemployment, it also contributed mightily to the rapidly deteriorating financial condition of American business after the stock-market crash of 1929. By mid-1930, a massive profit squeeze was under way. Before-tax corporate profits fell 63 percent from 1929 to 1930, and given that dividends were maintained at essentially their 1929 levels (also a part of the Hoover program), undistributed corporate profits fell from $2,820 million in 1929 to a *negative* $2,613 million the following year.[3]

The number of firms posting actual losses mounted sharply. While in mid-1929 less than 6 percent of firms surveyed by the First National City Bank of New York were losing money, by the third quarter of 1930 the proportion of losers had increased to 29 percent and a large percentage of the remainder were not covering dividend payments.[4] Profits in the second quarter of 1930 were estimated to have been less than half of what they had been but nine months earlier.[5]

The same reasoning that led Hoover to urge firms to maintain wages also led firms to maintain dividend payments. According to Benjamin Anderson, "the poor old St. Louis and San Francisco railroad, impressed with its duty to keep purchasing power high, thereupon proceeded to declare its preferred dividend a full year in advance—with unsatisfactory consequences."[6] The maintenance of dividends in 1930 at nearly 95 percent of the 1929 level was consistent with underconsumptionist reasoning, but it very severely aggravated the financial strain on corporations, setting the stage for the onset of the financial crisis that began in late 1930.

The Impact on Banks

Most commercial bank assets at the outset of the Great Depression were in the form of loans and investments (primarily bonds). For example, the

June 30, 1929 call date revealed that commercial banks had 79.7 percent of assets in the form of loans and investments, with loans ($36.1 billion) being far more important than investments ($13.7 billion.) The banks had real-estate loans alone that equaled 72 percent of total bank capital.[7]

There was considerable variation among banks in the composition of their portfolios. Larger urban banks tended to make more security loans, while more longer-term real-estate loans were made by country banks. For example, in 1930, New York and Chicago national banks had less than 1 percent of their loans in the form of real estate, compared with more than 13 percent for the country banks with national charters.[8] With respect to bank investments, national banks kept fully 40 percent in the form of United States government bonds, compared with only 17 percent for the state banks.[9] Lower-quality securities (investments other than U.S. government, municipal, railroad, and public utility bonds) accounted for some 68 percent of holdings of state-chartered banks, but only 16 percent of investments of New York and Chicago banks with a national charter.[10] While national banks in 1930 had only 42 percent of their portfolios in unsecured or real-estate loans, some 64 percent of state bank portfolios were in this category.[11]

In short, the big city banks had more high-quality assets. While both the state and national banks had reported capital averaging 14 percent of assets in 1930, the state and smaller national banks were more vulnerable to loss owing to the nature of their loan and investment portfolios. As C. D. Bremer, a leading student of bank failures in this period, put it, "From . . . figures of the relationship between net capital funds and securities investments it may be concluded that the ability to absorb losses on account of the depreciation in the price of . . . securities has been particularly small among state banks in general, and among country banks in particular."[12] Another writer, Charles Popple, noted that "many country bankers expert in local finance were hopelessly incompetent in selecting bonds. With few exceptions, the quality of bonds they purchased was low."[13]

The decline in the financial condition of the nation's businesses following the adoption of the Hoover wage policy increased the risks to banks associated with loans and securities held, and thus lowered the true market value of those assets below book value, leading the reported capital of banks to be overstated. Both Peter Temin and Eugene White provide evidence consistent with this hypothesis. Temin observes a 60 percent increase in risk premiums from the end of 1929 to the end of 1930.[14] He notes that "the decline in the value of bank portfolios started well before the bank panic of 1930," and "the . . . downward pressure on the value of bank portfolios was a cause of the bank panic of 1930."[15] White generally agrees with "Temin's hypothesis that poorly performing assets were an important

TABLE 6.1

INTEREST RATE DIFFERENTIALS ON BANK LOANS: NEW YORK BANKS VS. 27 BANKS IN
SOUTHERN AND WESTERN CITIES

Quarter	Year	Interest Rate Differential[a]
III	1929	21
IV	1929	31
I	1930	69
II	1930	101
III	1930	116
IV	1930	127

[a]In basis points (100 basic points equals one percent); number reported is the median figure of three monthly figures
and is obtained by subtracting the reported interest rate on bank loans at New York banks from the similar figure for
southern and western banks.
Source: Authors' calculations from data in the *Federal Reserve Bulletin*, various issues.

contributing factor" in the bank crisis.[16] He also presents some data from
Vermont describing the estimated deviation of bonds held continuously
from June 30, 1928, from their book value.[17] By 1930, that deviation was
7 percent. Moreover, that statistic was for national banks, and state banks
were supposedly on the whole more invested in higher-risk bonds than
national banks, so the undervaluation may in fact have been greater for
many banks.

Given the apparent fact that country banks made loans that were less
well collateralized and to riskier customers than the New York banks, one
would expect a rise in risk premiums to be reflected in a growing differential in the interest rate charged on loans between New York and other areas
of the country. Using data in the *Federal Reserve Bulletin*, we observed the
interest-rate differential on bank loans in New York and in twenty-seven
southern and western cities (see table 6.1).[18] The differential widened by
ninety-six basis points from the fourth quarter of 1929 (when the Hoover
wage policy was enunciated) to the last quarter of 1930. Commercial failures were sharply higher in 1930 than in 1929, justifying the increased
differential. Realized loan losses for Federal Reserve member banks rose
from $87.5 million in the first half of 1929 to $213.1 million in the last half
of 1930. The latter figure so lowered profits that in the last half of 1930
profits only covered 44 percent of bank dividend requirements, compared
with 193 percent coverage in the first half of 1929.[19]

The deterioration in bank assets should have led to a significant decrease
in prices of bank stocks, to the extent that the market accurately perceived
the decline in the real value of bank capital. To ascertain whether this was
in fact the case, we gathered information on the price of bank shares for
twenty-eight banks, including nine in New York City, three in Chicago,
and banks in Los Angeles, San Francisco, the District of Columbia, Atlanta,

TABLE 6.2

TWO INDICES OF BANK STOCK PRICES RELATIVE TO INDICES OF INDUSTRIAL AND
CANADIAN BANK STOCK PRICES, 1930

Date	Stock Index:			
	12 Banks[a]	28 Banks[a]	25 Industrials[b]	4 Canadian Banks
12/27/29	100.0	100.0	100.0	100.0
3/28/30	110.6	101.4	102.2	99.9
6/27/30	85.5	90.0	96.6	95.4
9/26/30	73.2	76.8	94.4	89.9
12/26/30	64.7	72.6	73.4	91.3

[a]For details, see text.
[b]*New York Times* index of 25 industrial corporations.
Source: Authors' calculations from data in the *Bank and Quotation Record,* and from the *New York Times,* various issues.

New Orleans, Boston, Detroit, Minneapolis, Baltimore, Kansas City, St. Louis, Newark, Buffalo, Winston-Salem, Cleveland, Philadelphia, Pittsburgh, Providence, Dallas, and Milwaukee. Data are available in the *Bank and Quotation Record.*[20]

It should be pointed out at the outset that there are several deficiencies in the data, but these defects work in the direction of understating the true decline in security prices occurring in 1930. Most banks, even some large ones, were closely held, and shares traded infrequently. As a consequence, the quoted prices tended to reflect trades made days, weeks, or even months earlier. Thus the quoted price of the Wachovia Bank of Winston-Salem moved very little, and probably represented what the editors of the data source acknowledged were sometimes "nominal values." Fortunately, the shares of the big New York and Chicago banks were more frequently traded, so the trends in stocks of those banks are more likely to reflect true trends in prices. Even here, however, the sample was a nonrandom compilation of banks that had orderly markets for their stocks, which probably excludes smaller and in some cases less sound banks. We deliberately excluded, for example, the Bank of the United States from our sample, since it failed in December 1930, before the last date in our sampling period.

With these caveats in mind, the data of table 6.2 support the contention that investor uneasiness over bank assets and capital led to deterioration in share prices, in advance of a more generalized concern by depositors. The fact that investor uneasiness preceded depositor confidence loss is a reflection not of the relative astuteness of those two groups, but rather of the fact that shareholders have less secure claims on bank resources than do depositors, and are thus likely to become uneasy earlier.

Table 6.2 reports stock price indices for twenty-eight banks, and also for the twelve large New York and Chicago banks whose stock traded regularly. Between the end of March and the end of September 1930, bank stock prices fell about one-fourth or one-third, depending on the stock index used. This is three to four times the decline in stock prices of leading industrial corporations. Investor confidence was waning rapidly.

Between the end of March and the end of December 1930, the prices of shares of large New York and Chicago banks declined more than 41 percent, far more than the prices of industrial stocks generally. A more appropriate comparison, however, might be with the shares of Canadian banks. Canadian banks in our sample were all large (the Bank of Toronto, Imperial Bank of Canada, Bank of Montreal, and Royal Bank of Canada), like their New York and Chicago counterparts, and were engaged in similar business activities. The U.S. banks were operating in a country where the Hoover wage policy was in operation, however, while the Canadian economy did not face the jawboning and the wage-cutting strictures from Washington. At the end of 1930, Canadian bank shares were less than 9 percent below what they were at the beginning of the year, a modest decline that no doubt reflected declining business in the face of the depression in the neighboring U.S. (and its subsequent spread to Canada). This was only one-third to one-fourth the decline in the prices of U.S. stocks, a decrease that, we submit, reflected a progressive loss of confidence on the part of investors in the underlying values of bank assets.

There is some independent evidence consistent with our view that our sample probably, if anything, understates the decline in U.S. bank stock prices. A survey of the market values of the stocks of some one hundred banks and trust companies located in New York City was conducted by *American Banker* magazine for a period almost exactly coinciding with the second quarter of 1930. The aggregate market value of the stocks fell by about 27 percent, which is somewhat more than the decline recorded for our twelve-stock index of New York and Chicago banks.[21]

The examination of stock prices is instructive if modern-day experiences are at all relevant. There is abundant evidence in recent times that stock markets recognize deterioration in the financial condition of banks. A study by Margaret J. Smith for the Comptroller of the Currency shows that the market accurately anticipated seven large bank failures between 1974 and 1983.[22] Months before the public recognition of the run on the Continental Illinois bank in May 1984, that bank's common stock was selling for only about one-half of its book value at a time when most bank shares were selling close to their book value. The discount from book value was even greater in the case of the 1990 failure of the Bank of New England, which was largely anticipated.

How much impact could the deterioration in asset quality have had on the soundness of banks? Let us consider a hypothetical state bank with $10 million in assets at the start of 1930 that had a typical financial structure, meaning it had $1.4 million in capital, about $6.0 million in loans, $2.5

million in investments, and $1.5 million in cash and other assets, such as the bank building and equipment. If, during the course of 1930, interest rates on new loans rose by one percentage point, say from 6 to 7 percent, simply because of rising risk premiums, this would imply a decline in the market value of older, long-term loans of up to 14 percent, since a $1,000 loan paying $60 annual interest would have to decline to less than $860 (a 14 percent decline) for the yield to go from 6 to 7 percent.

For new loans, or old loans that were heavily collateralized or nearing maturity, the probable decline in asset value was no doubt less. Suppose the average decline was 10 percent, and that a 5 percent decline in the market value of investments also occurred (for the same reason)—not an unreasonable possibility in light of the evidence presented by White on Vermont.[23] The true (market) value of assets would then be reduced by $600,000 for loans and $125,000 for investments, reducing true capital by some $725,000, or more than 50 percent.

The above example represents what might be viewed as a typical state-chartered bank. But not all banks were typical. Suppose a bank had the asset portfolio reported above but only $1 million in capital at the beginning of 1930. The true value of capital by the end of 1930 would have been only $275,000—less than 3 percent of assets. Suppose a bank had above-average loans and investments of a highly risky nature. It is easy to imagine situations where total capital would be wiped out (e.g, where capital was 11 percent of assets, and loans deteriorated 15 percent and investments 10 percent below book value).

While the scenario just presented seems to accord with the evidence, there are at least two other explanations of bank failures in the early 1930s besides the Temin-White hypothesis relating to the deterioration of asset values. Friedman and Schwartz emphasize the importance of declining depositor confidence and give special attention to the failure of the large Bank of the United States in December 1930.[24] A key variable, they believe, is the deposit-currency ratio, which begins to fall sharply after October 1930.

Elmus Wicker attacks this line of reasoning in at least two different ways, arguing first that the banking crisis was not precipitated by the failure of the Bank of the United States in December, but rather by the Caldwell and Company bank chain's collapse in the South in November, a failure that reflected bad loans made in the twenties (a notion consistent with our previous hypothesizing about deterioration in asset values) and a decline in regional income.[25] Second, in his work with Boughton, Wicker shows by regression analysis that less than 30 percent of bank failures are explainable in terms of the decline in the ratio of deposits to currency, leading to the conclusion that depositor confidence was a secondary factor.[26] White, in his analysis of failures of national banks, uses a logit model that yields conclusions similar to Wicker's regarding the depositor confidence hypothesis, stating that the character of bank failures was not significantly different in a statistical sense from those that preceded 1930.[27]

All of these writers, in our judgment, are partly right, but they fail to perceive the possibility that the genesis of the whole crisis was the labor-market discoordination resulting from jawboning on the part of Hoover and the industrial elite. With respect to the Temin-White "asset deterioration hypothesis" we have already presented some supporting evidence, although it seems to us that Wicker has a point in stating that the deterioration in asset values reflected "bad" loans more than low-grade corporate bond investments as Temin alleges.[28]

With regard to the Friedman and Schwartz "loss of depositor confidence hypothesis," we believe that our scenario is perfectly compatible with it. In a world of small uninsured unit banks, the main depositor protection against loss is bank capital. A deterioration in the capital-asset ratio will lead to increasing depositor wariness, and a conversion of deposits to currency that makes depositor fear a self-fulfilling prophecy. "Sound" banks become "unsound" because of unanticipated depositor withdrawals. The decline in bank stock prices, almost certainly understated in our table, reflected shareholder wariness that probably paralleled the growing concerns of the other major group of actors on the right hand of the balance sheet, namely the depositors. The fall in the deposit–currency ratio after October 1930 is consistent with the view that growing depositor concerns about the decline in the true capital-asset ratio were raising the probability of failure, leading the risk-averse to withdraw their funds in increasing amounts. An econometric test of the relationship between depositor confidence and labor-market discoordination is presented shortly.

With regard to Wicker, we agree that the real decline in the banking system is not related to an isolated development in the nation's financial center, but reflected more generalized rising distress in such remote regions (to those living east of the Hudson River) as the South or the West. At the same time, however, our stock-market data suggest that investor wariness of the big financial-center banks may have been greater. One plausible explanation for this is that the big New York (and Chicago) banks lent heavily to large corporations that were more likely to be pressured to follow the Hoover high-wage policy than less visible smaller regional firms.

Concerning Wicker's "income decline hypothesis," we would concur, noting that the fall in incomes of businesses and unemployed individuals reflected in large part growing labor-market disequilibrium, and that this led to falling incomes and a resultant deterioration in asset quality. Along the same lines, we cannot ignore the wealth effects on aggregate demand, a point made so well by Frederic Mishkin in his excellent 1978 study on household balance sheets.[29] The decline in stock prices that Mishkin believes is important in explaining declining consumer durable-goods spending after 1930 probably in itself resulted in large part from the wage-induced profit squeeze. It is easy to formulate a counterfactual proposition where, in the absence of the Hoover wage policy, profits in 1930 would have been 30 or 40 percent higher than reported (or even more), and that, in turn, would have reduced the decline in stock prices, led to a smaller decrease in household wealth, and prevented any fall in autonomous consumption (which in any case we argue was not systematically related to business cycle changes during this era).

Perhaps, however, we have the scenario all wrong. Could it be that agrarian distress in the South and the West set off the 1930 banking crisis, and that the Hoover wage policy caused financial stress only in the nonagricultural portion of the economy, a sector that was not a party to the beginnings of the banking crisis? It is true that agricultural income was severely depressed in 1930, but we are skeptical of this alternative line of reasoning for three reasons.[30]

First, more than 45 percent of the deposits in banks failing in 1930 were in seven highly industrialized states: New York, Pennsylvania, Massachusetts, Connecticut, Illinois, Indiana, and Ohio.[31] Deposits in failed banks in those states exceeded those in suspended banks in the fourteen comparatively less industrialized states comprising the South Atlantic, East South Central, and West South Central census regions often cited as the area where the banking crisis began. Even in November and December 1930, almost precisely one-half of the deposits of suspended banks were in the comparatively highly industrialized Federal Reserve districts of Boston, New York, Philadelphia, Cleveland, and Chicago.[32]

Second, even banks in heavily agricultural regions deployed assets into nonagrarian pursuits. Small banks owned privately issued corporate bonds just like larger banks, although they often were of lower quality than those owned by the city banks. A deterioration in the value of these assets at the margin may have made some barely solvent banks insolvent. Also, even in the rural states a significant proportion of the labor force was engaged in nonfarming work for wages. For example, census data for 1929 reveal that 377,870 "wage earners" were involved in manufacturing alone in the East South-Central states of Kentucky, Tennessee, Alabama, and Mississippi.[33] Moreover, it appears that at least some farmers heeded the call for high wages as did their counterparts in industry. Indeed, the standard *Historical Statistics* series (D-739) on average annual earnings of full-time employees in "agriculture, forestry and fisheries" shows a decline of 3.2 percent from 1929 to 1930, which in real terms is a fall of well under 1 percent.

Third, the rising unemployment and falling production associated with the high-wage policy probably led, *ceteris paribus*, to some softening in the demand for agricultural products, aggravating the decline in agricultural prices that worsened conditions for farmers. For example, the fall in wheat prices from $1.04 to 67 cents a bushel from 1929 to 1930 almost certainly, in part, reflected a leftward shift in the demand curve arising from declining national income.[34] The farming sector was not isolated from the deleterious effects of policies that impacted perhaps more directly on industry.

An Econometric Test of the Wage-Banking Relationship

While there are various interpretations of the cause of the banking crisis, most writers would agree that declining depositor confidence was a major phenomenon, and that this development had some role to play in producing the crisis. The major disagreement is over the extent of the relationship, with scholars such as Boughton and Wicker saying that only a minority (29 percent) of the rise in failures is explainable by this phenomenon, while others (Friedman and Schwartz) assign it a rather more important role.[35]

Our analysis to this point has emphasized the fact that the decline in stockholder confidence in banks developed during the heyday of the high-wage policy in 1930. We assumed that a cause-and-effect relationship existed, but did no econometric testing. To remedy this deficiency, we decided to examine the relationship between the adjusted real wage and the deposit-currency ratio. When depositor confidence declines, there is a shift from bank deposits into currency, lowering that ratio. A decline in the deposit-currency ratio lowers the monetary base and thus has a potential multiple contractionary impact on the stock of money. If the shift is abrupt in a given banking area, banks may be forced to close because of inadequate liquidity, given the fractional reserve nature of banking. A bank run is reflected in an abrupt and sharp decline in the deposit-currency ratio. The decline in the ratio from over eleven to one in late 1930 to only slightly over four to one in March 1933 is the single most important proximate determinant of the fall in the money stock in that period.

We gathered monthly data on the ratio of deposits to currency and the adjusted real wage.[36] With these, we have estimated several different regressions where the dependent variable is the deposit-currency ratio. The time period is 1929 to March 1933, with the starting month in 1929 varying with the different models. The findings are:

1. In every model, there is a statistically significant (at the 1 percent level) negative relationship between the adjusted real wage and the deposit-currency ratio.
2. While there is some immediate impact, some of the effect of changing adjusted real wages is felt after a lag. A nine-month lagged relationship shows the most robust fit. It took the better part of a year for rising wages to be fully felt in declining depositor confidence as reflected in a falling deposit-currency ratio. At the same time, however, there was some near-immediate impact.
3. The explanatory power of the models is quite high, with the R^2 statistic exceeding .91.

The results, using a nine-month lag, are reported below. *DEPCUR* denotes the deposit-currency ratio, and is indexed with January 1929 equalling 100. The adjusted real wage variable, *WAGE*, is similarly indexed. The findings are extremely robust:

(1) $$DEPCUR = 294.776 - 1.913\ WAGE\ (-9),$$
                    $$(27.775)\quad (20.382)$$

          $$\overline{R}^2 = .916,\ F = Stat. = 224.894,\ DW = 1.944,$$

where the numbers in parentheses are t-statistics, and where an autoregressive adjustment term is omitted.

These findings provide econometric support for the view that the financial deterioration resulting from high real wages contributed to the decline in depositor confidence that was an important (some would say dominant) cause of bank failures after 1930.

The High-Wage Policy and Financial Markets

While the largest indirect effect of the high-wage policy was in contributing to the banking crisis, the abnormally low profits generated from that policy also impacted on interest rates and security prices. The supply of loanable funds declined dramatically between 1929 and 1931, with over 70 percent of the fall attributable to the decline in corporate retained earnings (see table 6.3).

TABLE 6.3

SAVINGS IN THE UNITED STATES, 1929 TO 1931

| | In Billions of Dollars | | |
Form of Savings	1929	1930	1931
Personal Savings	4.2	3.4	2.6
Capital Consumption Allowances	7.9	8.0	7.9
Corporate Retained Earnings	2.8	-2.6	-4.9
Net Government Savings[a]	0.7	0.7	-0.6
TOTAL	15.6	9.5	5.0

[a]Excludes state and local governments.
Source: U.S. Department of Commerce, Bureau of Economic Analysis.

The decrease in the supply of loanable funds contributed to a large increase in real interest rates.[37] Money interest rates changed little, with the yield on Corporate Aaa (Moody's) bonds falling only fifteen basis points (from 4.73 to 4.58 percent) from 1929 to 1931. This was despite the fact that massive deflation made bonds extremely attractive. The real interest rate (money rate minus the annual rate of change in prices) for highest-grade corporate bonds went from 4.73 percent in 1929 to over 13 percent in 1931 (using the CPI as our measure of price change.) Real interest rates nearly tripled. This, in turn, contributed to the decline in stock prices, a decrease in real wealth, and a fall in consumer spending. We would estimate that stock-market wealth alone declined by $88.7 billion between 1929 and 1931.[38] That alone should have reduced consumption by about $5.3 billion, or nearly one-third the reported decline in consumer spending.[39]

Recently, Stephen Cecchetti has argued that real interest rates were extremely high in 1930, as deflation could have been largely anticipated. He supports the monetarist perspective on the role of monetary forces, yet ignores the important labor market.[40] James Hamilton looks at commodity markets to gauge expectations. He concludes: "It is . . . difficult to blame the bank panics of late 1930 solely on bankruptcies caused by an unanticipated drop in the price level of only 5 percent. I conclude that decreases in particular relative prices, rather than overall consumer prices, are key to understanding this year."[41]

The major effect of the rise in real interest rates was on investment spending. Gross private domestic investment fell over 65 percent from 1929 to 1931 and net investment (after allowances for depreciation) turned negative. Thus the capital stock began to fall, which had a negative impact on productivity after 1930.

The Depression Scenario: A Summary

Summarizing the story of the past two chapters, as we see it the Depression unfolded as follows.

1) Beginning in late 1929, a series of price and productivity shocks produced a labor-market disequilibrium that led to falling levels of output and employment.
2) The Hoover administration's attempt to forestall money-wage reduction was successful, generating a rise in real wages (both adjusted and unadjusted), and hence a massive profit squeeze in American industry. This ultimately led to substantial layoffs of workers.
3) The decline in business profits had an adverse impact on the quality of bank portfolios, causing depositors to become wary and leading to a fall in the deposit-currency ratio in the economy.
4) Consistent with Friedman and Schwartz, the Federal Reserve System did not take steps to counteract the declining monetary base resulting from depositor fear.
5) The bank crisis produced a contraction in the money supply and a sharp fall in prices, a decline that offset the positive benefits of the downward money-wage adjustments that finally became substantial in 1931, the effects of which were materially reduced by the impact of the Smoot-Hawley tariff.
6) The combination of public-policy blunders (Hoover's high wages, the Congress's high-tariff policy, the deflationary actions or non-actions of the Federal Reserve) led to constant interferences with the mechanism that normally would have led real-wage rates to fall to equilibrium.
7) The disappearance of profits in industry led to a decline in investment and, in 1931 and after, a decline in the real capital stock. It also contributed to higher real interest rates which aggravated the investment and consumption decline.
8) Very consistent with the findings of Michael Darby, the declining real capital stock generated a further decline in productivity, and thus employment, that led us to the nadir of the Depression in 1933.[42]

NOTES

1. See Milton Friedman and Anna J. Schwartz, *A Monetary History of the United States, 1867–1960* (Princeton, N.J.: Princeton University Press for the National Bureau of Economic Research, 1963). Friedman and Schwartz have amplified their findings and responded to critics in several works. Two particularly interesting examples are Anna J. Schwartz, "Understanding 1929–1933," in *The Great Depression Revisited*, ed. Karl Brunner (Boston: Martinus Nijhoff, 1981), pp. 5–48, and Milton Friedman and Anna J. Schwartz, *Monetary Trends in the United States and the United Kingdom and Their Relation to Income, Prices, and Interest Rates, 1867–1975* (Chicago: University of Chicago Press for the National Bureau of Economic Re-

search, 1982). Their most recent commentary is found in Milton Friedman and Anna J. Schwartz, "Alternative Approaches to Analyzing Economic Data," *American Economic Review* 81 (1991): 39–49.

2.   There is, of course, a huge literature on both the accuracy of the Friedman and Schwartz conclusions and the reasons monetary policy was so contractionary. On the latter point, the "regulatory capture" hypothesis has received much attention: the Federal Reserve Board was "captured" by the banking industry. See, for example, Gerald Epstein and Thomas Ferguson, "Monetary Policy, Loan Liquidation, and Industrial Conflict: The Federal Reserve and the Open Market Operations of 1932," *Journal of Economic History* 44 (1984): 957–83; David C. Wheelock, "The Strategy Effectiveness and Consistency of Federal Reserve Monetary Policy, 1924–1933," *Explorations in Economic History* 26 (1989): 451–76; Gary M. Anderson, William F. Shughart, and Robert D. Tollison, "A Public Choice Theory of the Great Contraction," *Public Choice* 59 (1988): 2–23; and Philip R. P. Coelho and G. J. Santoni, "Regulatory Capture and the Monetary Contraction of 1932: A Comment on Epstein and Ferguson," *Journal of Economic History* 51 (1991): 189.

3.   U.S. Bureau of the Census, *National Income and Product Accounts of the United States, 1929–1976* (Washington, D.C.: Government Printing Office, 1981), p. 308.

4.   Geoffrey H. Moore, ed., *Business Cycle Indicators*, vol. 2, *Basic Data on Cyclical Indicators* (Princeton, N.J.: Princeton University Press for the National Bureau of Economic Research, 1961), p. 106.

5.   Harold Barger, *Outlay and Income in the United States, 1921–1938* (New York: National Bureau of Economic Research, 1942), appendix B, table 28. A smaller profit decline is reported in a less comprehensive survey conducted by the Federal Reserve Bank of New York. See Irving Fisher, *Booms and Depressions: Some First Principles* (New York: Adelphi, 1932), p. 98.

6.   Benjamin Anderson, *Economics and the Public Welfare* (Princeton, N.J.: Van Nostrand, 1949), p. 225.

7.   U.S. Bureau of the Census, *Historical Statistics of the United States, Colonial Times to 1970* (Washington, D.C.: Government Printing Office, 1975), p. 1021, series X-589 to X-594.

8.   C. D. Bremer, *American Bank Failures* (New York: Columbia University Press, 1935), p. 115.

9.   Ibid., p. 116.

10.   Ibid.

11.   Ibid., pp. 116, 117.

12.   Ibid., p. 120.

13.   Charles Popple, *Development of Two Bank Groups in the Central Northwest* (Cambridge, Mass.: Harvard University Press, 1944), p. 105.

14.   Peter Temin, *Did Monetary Forces Cause the Great Depression?* (New York: W. W. Norton, 1976), p. 107. The exact increase in risk premiums depends on whether one uses Temin's "fixed sample" or his "Baa sample." Ben S. Bernanke, "Nonmonetary Effects of the Financial Crisis in the Propagation of the Great Depression," *American Economic Review* 73 (1983): 262, shows a smaller (but still positive) widening of the risk differential by December 1930. Another study that deals with

the financial sector's role in the start of the Depression is Alexander J. Field, "Asset Exchanges and the Transactions Demand for Money," *American Economic Review* 74 (1984): 43–59.

15. Temin, *Monetary Forces*, p. 108.

16. Eugene Nelson White, "A Reinterpretation of the Banking Crisis of 1930," *Journal of Economic History* 44 (1984): 119–38.

17. Ibid., p. 129.

18. These data were reported monthly in the *Federal Reserve Bulletin*. We calculated the differential from the raw yield data reported in several different issues.

19. Authors' calculations from data in the *Federal Reserve Bulletin* for July 1930, February 1931, and July 1931.

20. *Bank and Quotation Record*, various issues in vols. 3 and 4.

21. Our index declines 23 percent. The *American Banker* survey is discussed in the *New York Times*, June 23, 1930, p. 30. It reported the fall in the overall value of bank shares, and the average per-share price may have fallen more if any new shares were issued in this period. Implicitly, the *American Banker* approach weights stocks according to their value, unlike our approach which weights each bank equally.

22. Margaret J. Smith, "Market Recognition of Changes in Financial Condition of Large Banks," *Comptroller of the Currency Staff Papers*, 1983-1, photocopied.

23. White, "A Reinterpretation of the Banking Crisis."

24. Friedman and Schwartz, *Monetary History*, chap. 7.

25. Elmus Wicker, "A Reconsideration of the Causes of the Banking Panic of 1930," *Journal of Economic History* 40 (1980): 571–83. See also his "Interest Rate and Expenditure Effects of the Banking Panic of 1930," *Explorations in Economic History* 19 (1982): 435–45.

26. James M. Boughton and Elmus Wicker, "The Behavior of the Currency Deposit Ratio During the Great Depression," *Journal of Money Credit and Banking* 11 (1979): 405–18.

27. "A Reinterpretation of the Banking Crisis," p. 137. See also Eugene N. White, *The Regulation and Reform of the American Banking System, 1900–1929* (Princeton, N.J.: Princeton University Press, 1983) for more insight into changes in American banking occurring before the banking crisis.

28. For one thing, the sheer volume of loans greatly exceeded that of bonds.

29. Frederic S. Mishkin, "The Household Balance Sheet and the Great Depression," *Journal of Economic History* 38 (1978): 918–37.

30. Farm income in the national income accounts declined by 30 percent from 1929 to 1930, from $6.2 to $4.3 billion. While this is a much sharper decline than the 12 percent fall in nonagricultural income, the fall in farm income accounted for less than 17 percent of the total income decline. See *Historical Statistics of the United States*, Series F-176 and F-163.

31. *Federal Reserve Bulletin*, February 1931, p. 113.

32. Ibid., December 1930, p. 7883; January 1932, p. 26.

33. U.S. Bureau of the Census, *Biennial Census of Manufactures, 1931* (Washington, D.C.: Government Printing Office, 1935), pp. 1188–1207.

34. *Historical Statistics of the United States*, Series K-508, p. 511. Output rose by less than 8 percent from 1929 to 1930. For prices to fall as much as they did without any shift in demand, the price elasticity of demand would have had to be very low, about $-.22$. If demand elasticity were, say $-.40$ or $-.50$ (still highly inelastic), a significant proportion of the decline in prices would have had to reflect a leftward shift in the demand curve for wheat. Of course, international shifts in demand no doubt also played an important role.

35. Boughton and Wicker, "The Behavior of the Currency Deposit Ratio," and Friedman and Schwartz, *Monetary History*, chap. 7.

36. The deposit-currency ratio data are from ibid., pp. 803–4. Wage and price data are from Willford I. King, *The Causes of Economic Fluctuations* (New York: Ronald Press, 1938), pp. 182–84. The standard NICB wage data are used. The productivity measure used to adjust real wages is output per factory worker, derived from Federal Reserve Board data reported in Moore, *Business Cycle Indicators*, 2: 118, 119.

37. A secondary reason for the decline in savings between 1929 and 1931 was the federal government budget deficit. Gene Smiley makes a good case that governmental fiscal policy was largely ineffective where used because of the "crowding out" problem, consistent with the argument here. See Gene Smiley, "Some Austrian Perspectives on Keynesian Fiscal Policy and the Recovery in the Thirties," *Review of Austrian Economics* 1 (1987): 145–80.

38. Raymond Goldsmith estimates stock-market wealth in 1929 at $186.7 billion. If that wealth declined proportionally with the Standard and Poor's Stock Market Index, wealth in 1931 would have been $98.0 billion, or $88.7 billion less. For Goldsmith's estimates, see *Historical Statistics of the United States*, p. 253. For greater detail, see Raymond W. Goldsmith and Robert Lipsey, *Studies in the National Balance Sheet of the United States*, 2 vols. (Princeton: Princeton University Press for the National Bureau of Economic Research, 1963), vol. 2, tables I and Ia.

39. That assumes that the marginal propensity to consume out of wealth over one year is .06. See Albert Ando and Franco Modigliani, "The Life Cycle Hypothesis of Savings: Aggregate Implications and Tests," *American Economic Review* 53 (1963): 55–84.

40. Stephen Cecchetti, "Prices During the Great Depression: Was the Deflation of 1930–32 Really Unanticipated?" *American Economic Review* 82 (1992): 141–56.

41. James D. Hamilton, "Was the Deflation During the Great Depression Anticipated? Evidence from the Commodity Futures Market," *American Economic Review* 82 (1992): 157–78.

42. Michael R. Darby, "The U.S. Productivity Slowdown: A Case of Statistical Myopia," *American Economic Review* 74 (1984): 301–22. Darby analyzed the period 1929–48 and concluded that "measured capital growth variations can explain all of the 1929–48 slowdown in quality-adjusted labor productivity growth. . . ." (p. 309).

7

The New Deal

"The only thing there is to fear, is fear itself!" So said Franklin D. Roosevelt on his inauguration as president of the United States on March 4, 1933. Roosevelt's charisma, his vigor, the activist policies he pursued—all contributed to a decline in fear and the beginning of an economic recovery. The change in the direction of economic activity had an enormously positive psychological impact that probably contributed to the economic recovery that followed. This was certainly a not inconsiderable achievement.

While Roosevelt may have helped initiate recovery, there is overwhelming evidence that newly instituted policies of his administration served to weaken that recovery and prolong the misery of the Great Depression. In this chapter we will demonstrate how governmental intervention in labor markets contributed in an important way to the continuing double-digit unemployment. Of the ten years of unemployment rates over 10 percent during the Depression, fully eight were during the Roosevelt administration (counting 1933 as a Roosevelt year). Moreover, institutional changes begun during the Roosevelt years had a long-lasting impact on the American economy, and on unemployment in particular. So not only was the record of the New Deal rather poor in terms of achieving economic recovery, the New Deal legacy is with us today in an increased natural rate of unemployment.

The Unemployment Experience, 1933–1941

Previously, we have emphasized unemployment up to March 1933. While there is some disagreement on the measurement of unemployment, all mea-

128

sures show very high rates of joblessness for the remainder of the 1930s. The lowest rate of annual unemployment recorded before 1941 using the official estimates was 14.3 percent in 1937. The median annual rate for the seven years of double-digit unemployment during recovery (1934–40) was 17.2 percent. By contrast, during the nation's worst downturn before the Great Depression, double-digit unemployment lasted only four years after recovery began, with the worst year having but 14.5 percent unemployment—almost the same as the best year during the 1933 recovery.

While the recovery experience of other nations varied considerably, as a generalization it is safe to say the American recovery was more sluggish and slower in coming than that of most European nations. By 1937, Britain's unemployment was down to 10.3 percent, fully four points lower than the American rate. Moreover, the natural rate of unemployment in Britain at this time was about 10 percent (the rate prevailing in 1929), so one could argue that Britain had fully recovered by 1937 (although it had a brief relapse to 12.3 percent unemployment in 1938).[1] Britain recovered far more in five years from its trough in 1932 than the United States did in seven years from its trough in 1933. Compared with some other nations, notably Germany, the U.S. recovery looks even more anemic. While generalization is dangerous, on the whole the U.S. recovery took longer and was more tepid than that of other major industrialized nations of the world.

Trends in Wages, Prices, and Productivity

The expanded unemployment model with multiple lags introduced in chapter 3 does an excellent job of explaining the New Deal–era experience. In no single year from 1933 to 1940 does the predicted unemployment rate vary as much as 10 percent from the actual rate. 1936 is fairly typical: the actual rate of 16.9 percent was rather less than 8 percent more than the predicted rate of 15.7 percent.

Looking in a broad sweep over the period 1933 to 1940, the adjusted real wage underwent a significant decline. That decline reflected most importantly a rise in labor productivity, and, to a much lesser extent, an increase in prices. Productivity rose 28.9 percent from 1932 to 1940 according to the measure used in our model; from 1933 (the trough in the business cycle) to 1940, labor productivity rose at an average compounded annual rate of 3.99 percent a year, high by historical standards. From 1932 to 1940, consumer prices rose by somewhat less than 3 percent. Measured from the trough in 1933, however, the price increase to 1940 averaged 1.14 percent a year.

With rapid productivity advance and moderately rising prices, one might have expected unemployment to fall rather dramatically. While there was some decline, it was relatively modest because money wages, for the first time in American history, rose significantly during this period of double-digit unemployment. While money wages rose "only" 15.9 percent from 1932 to 1940 using the broad-based wage measure used in our model, wage payments in some unemployment-sensitive industries rose far more, as will be demonstrated shortly. Using our measure, money wages rose 25.8 percent, from the trough in 1933 to 1940, or 3.34 percent a year. Even using this conservative measure of compensation change, real wages (unadjusted) were rising well over 2 percent a year during this period of massive unemployment. Put differently, real wages were rising faster during this New Deal era than was the long-term historic trend, despite extraordinarily high levels of unemployment.

A more detailed examination suggests that the adjusted real wage fell slightly (about 1 percent) in 1933, entirely reflecting a fall in money wages of nearly 8 percent that was not completely offset by deflation (about 5 percent) and productivity decline (2 percent.) The money-wage numbers, however, are somewhat misleading. While money wages in some sectors of the economy did decline significantly in 1933, wages began rising sharply in the mass-production industries in the last several months of the year, a matter to which we later return.

The broad-based data suggest that the adjusted real wage fell slightly further in 1934 (1.3 percent). An enormous productivity advance of over 10 percent, and some inflation (3.4 percent) was nearly offset by an unprecedented (for peacetime) increase in money wages of 12.3 percent.

The adjusted real wage fell sharply in both 1935 and 1936, and with it, unemployment declined significantly. Productivity and prices continued rising, albeit at slower rates in 1934. The key factor was that the sharp run-up in wages was abruptly halted, and indeed money wages fell by about 4 percent in 1936. Supreme Court decisions casting doubt on New Deal wage-raising legislation served, in our judgment, to bring some wage reduction and with it a decided decline in unemployment.

The picture abruptly changed again, however, in 1937 and 1938, this time for the worse. The adjusted real wage rose sharply. Productivity played little role, declining inconsequentially in 1937 (0.2 percent), and actually rising by over 3 percent in 1938. Prices, too, played a minor role, actually rising slightly over the two-year period (going up 3.6 percent in 1937, and falling 1.9 percent the following year.) The driving force in the rise in the adjusted real wage, and also unemployment, was a dramatic increase in money wages. Wages increased by 11.6 percent in 1937, the second double-digit annual increase in wages during the Depression. The increase for the next year was 5.2 percent. Even these numbers understate the wage gains in the important unemployment-intensive manufacturing sector. The 1937–38 wage hike reflects the impact of the upholding by the Supreme Court of the constitutionality of the National Labor Relations Act of 1935, the impact of the Social Security Act on wages, and possibly other legislation, as will be discussed later.

In 1939, 1940, and 1941, the adjusted real wage showed a steady decline, measured on an annual basis. In 1939, real wages were slightly lower than in 1938 (with both wages and prices moving modestly), while productivity rose 4 percent. Real wages rose slightly in 1940, but that was more than offset by another 3 percent productivity increase. As war approached in 1941, a significant productivity increase (5.6 percent) far more than offset a modest increase (1.4 percent) in real wages. A hefty money-wage increase (6.5 percent) was largely matched by 5 percent inflation.

If the wages theory of unemployment is basically valid, it is very clear that the prolonged nature of the Great Depression in the United States was the result of rapidly rising money wages. Moreover, the numbers above may well understate the extent to which wages increased. Using the alternative David-Solar index, hourly wages rose every year from 1934 to 1941, with the annual increases ranging from 1.3 to 19.1 percent. Helped by three years of double-digit wage increases, that index rose an extraordinary 69.5 percent from 1933 to 1941, an annual increase of 6.8 percent a year, whereas our index used in statistical estimation showed an increase of only 19.3 percent over the same period. In real terms, unskilled workers had increases in wages exceeding 5 percent a year—for seven years. Thus wages for blue-collar workers increased dramatically relative to those of white-collar workers. The Lebergott annual wage series rose "only" 43 percent, an increase of 4.6 percent a year. With the possible exception of the experience of the 1970s, this period probably had the largest sustained peacetime increase in money wages in the nation's history—during the nation's worst depression!

The orthodox classical and neoclassical theory that was then being overthrown suggested that real wages should have fallen, as unemployed workers competing for jobs bid down the price of labor. The failure of that to happen is, in our judgment, the major reason that the Depression was so prolonged. Yet the evidence strongly suggests that the failure of wages to adjust downward was not an affirmation of the Keynesian principle that wage adjustments cannot eliminate unemployment, even though some thought so at the time. Government failure, not market failure, was the problem. New Deal policies (and some Hoover-era policies predating the New Deal) systematically used the power of the state to intervene in labor markets in a manner to raise wages and labor costs, prolonging the misery of the Great Depression, and creating a situation where many people were living in rising prosperity at a time when millions of others were suffering severe deprivation.

Factory Employment Trends

While the Depression hit agriculture hard, nowhere was unemployment a greater problem than in America's factories. Manufacturing was the core of the modern urban economy, and was far more susceptible to cyclical fluctuations than the service sectors or trade.

Accordingly, trends in factory employment are important in explaining overall patterns of unemployment. Moreover, examining factory employment using the real-wage approach will provide another test of the validity of the wages hypothesis in explaining labor-market phenomena. Also, data are available allowing us to analyze employment trends on a quarterly rather than an annual basis, thereby permitting some microanalysis at the industry level.

Data on factory employment, industrial production, wholesale and consumer prices, and wages may be found in a variety of sources: the data we selected were collected and/or reported by the Federal Reserve Board, the National Industrial Conference Board, the Department of Commerce, and the Department of Labor.[2] Productivity can be estimated rather crudely by dividing industrial production by factory employment, which gives a measure of output per worker. For wages, we use the hourly earnings figures for twenty-five industries collected by the Conference Board.

The approach above suffers from one deficiency, namely that our measures of total employment and labor productivity may be viewed as being incorrectly stated to the extent that workers varied their workweek over time. In the 1920–22 downturn, this variability was not very great, and perhaps could be ignored. During the recovery from the Great Depression, however, the average workweek varied considerably. Fortunately, the National Industrial Conference Board compiled monthly workweek data for twenty-five major industries.[3]

We multiplied the average workweek data for each quarter by total factory employment to obtain a measure of employment in man-hours. We also defined our productivity variable to correct for shortening of the workweek by dividing industrial production by man hours to get a measure of productivity per unit of labor input. We indexed both modified variables on the first quarter of 1936 = 100.

We used regression analysis to examine quarterly variations in factory employment (F):

(1) $F = -493.611 - 1.172\ W_m + 2.259\ P_w + 2.494\ P_c$
           $(-6.684)\ (-4.201)\qquad (3.229)\qquad (2.713)$

           $+ 2.358\ O,\ \overline{R}^2 = .776,\ D - W = 1.282,$
           (4.557)

where W_m, P_w, P_c, and O denote money wages, wholesale prices, consumer prices, and productivity, respectively. The findings are highly consistent with the wage hypothesis, and the statistical relationships between the various independent variables and the dependent variable are all statistically significant (with the expected sign) at the 1 percent level. The results above do not use an autoregressive adjustment procedure and suggest a possible autocorrelation problem. Making such an adjustment eliminates concerns about autocorrelation, and all variables still have the anticipated signs, although the productivity and one of the price measures are not significant statistically. On the whole, however, the revised data add to our confidence in the validity of the adjusted real wage model as an explanation of employment trends in American industry during the prolonged recovery from the Great Depression.

A closer look at changes over the period reveals that factory hourly wages soared in late 1933, rising about 20 percent in the six months between the second and fourth quarters. To a considerable extent, this followed from the passage of the National Industrial Recovery Act in June. That act provided for wage floors for firms displaying the Blue Eagle, minimums that were well above prevailing wages for low-paying jobs. Moreover, hourly productivity actually fell slightly during this period. It is not surprising, then, that factory employment, which had risen robustly in the second and third quarters of 1933, actually declined in the fourth quarter, not recovering to the third quarter 1933 levels until the beginning of 1935. Money wages rose sharply again in 1934, albeit at a slower rate (almost 9 percent) than in 1933. Prices and productivity moved little, so the adjusted real wage increased.

From the last quarter of 1934 to the last quarter of 1936, factory employment expanded more than 23 percent. Since the average workweek also lengthened, man-hours of work increased even more, 45 percent. Real wages were virtually unchanged, with both money wages and prices rising slightly over the two-year period. Yet productivity showed a steady increase, moving up by 6 percent on an hourly basis over the period. The adjusted real wage fell. The job expansion coincided with a leveling-off in the sharp money-wage growth observed in 1933 and 1934. This was probably because one wage-increasing piece of legislation, the National Industrial Recovery Act, was found unconstitutional, and a second such piece of

TABLE 7.1

FACTORY EMPLOYMENT AND WAGES IN THE UNITED STATES, 1937–38[a]

Quarter	Factory Employment	Hourly Money Wages
1937 I	103.6	103.0
1937 II	106.1	110.7
1937 III	106.4	113.7
1937 IV	99.3	114.2
1938 I	89.0	113.4
1938 II	84.9	114.5
1938 III	86.8	113.7
1938 IV	92.1	113.9

[a]1936 IV =100.

Source: Survey of Current Business, Federal Reserve Bulletin, various issues.

legislation, the National Labor Relations Act of 1935, had not yet had any real effect, as its constitutionality was still uncertain.

The rise in factory employment continued into the first half of 1937, but a second money-wage shock was beginning that led to a "depression within a depression" beginning in late 1937. Table 7.1 shows the trends in factory employment and wages during this period. The initial surge in wages in the first quarter of 1937 was roughly offset by wholesale-price inflation, but the even larger run-up in money wages in the second quarter was largely real, as was the increase in the third quarter. In three quarters, money wages rose 13.7 percent, well over twice the rise in wholesale prices, and triple the rise in consumer prices. The wage run-up was not followed immediately by employment decline; indeed employment actually rose in early 1937. The fall in employment followed the increase in wages by about three quarters. After the third quarter of 1937, money wages stabilized, showing essentially no sustained movement until late 1939. While prices declined moderately (meaning real wages rose somewhat), productivity rose even more, so the adjusted real wage began to fall. This was followed by rising factory employment beginning in the last half of 1938.

The money-wage shock of 1937 was no random occurrence. It was the direct result of the influence of two institutional structures on the labor market, namely the federal government and labor unions. The National Labor Relations Act (Wagner Act) had been signed by President Roosevelt on July 27, 1935. But many eminent legal scholars considered the law unconstitutional; the Supreme Court had found the National Industrial Recovery Act unconstitutional and there was ample reason to believe that the Wagner Act would suffer the same fate. The National Lawyers Committee of the American Liberty League issued a 132-page statement arguing that the legislation "constitutes an illegal interference in the individual freedom of employees."[4]

Because of uncertainty over the law, there was no immediate impact of the Wagner Act on wages and the labor market. Labor-union membership climbed less than 10 percent in 1936, and at slightly more than four million, was less than it had been in 1920. Strike activity was actually less in 1936 than in 1935.[5] In April 1937, however, in *National Labor Relations Board* v. *Jones & Laughlin Steel Corporation* and four related cases, the Supreme Court ruled that the Wagner Act was constitutional.[6] The increase in wages, which had begun the previous quarter, surged amidst rising union militancy in the wake of the Supreme Court decision. Labor strife doubled over the levels of the previous years as organizing campaigns in the basic industries were mounted. Work days idle from work stoppages were at the highest level in the Depression era, not equaled again until 1946. Union membership rose over 40 percent, the largest annual growth recorded in the twentieth century.[7]

After the huge rise in money wages in the first three quarters of 1937, wages stabilized until 1941, at no time increasing by more than 3 percent above the level of a year earlier. Money wages on an hourly basis in the fourth quarter of 1940 were only slightly over 3 percent higher than three years earlier, suggesting annual wage growth of about 1 percent a year. Prices similarly showed little movement. Labor productivity rose significantly (over 5 percent a year) in both 1938 and 1939, before leveling off in 1940. The adjusted real wage declined significantly. Accordingly, factory employment at the beginning of 1941 was fully one-third higher than three years earlier. At last the nation was on its way out of the Great Depression.

A Tale of Two Industries: Steel and Autos

The pattern in American industry generally holds if one looks at individual industries. To further test the validity of our basic model, we regressed the adjusted real wage against factory employment for both the steel and auto industries using quarterly data from the second quarter of 1933 (steel) or first quarter of 1934 (autos) until late 1941. All told, we ran seven different regressions, using different dependent variables (auto employment and steel employment), as well as different measures of the independent variables. For example, the adjusted real wage was calculated using wholesale prices, consumer prices and, for the steel industry, a measure of steel prices. We also calculated employment and productivity using an annual measure rather than the hourly measure that was most often employed.[8] In all seven regressions, the expected negative relationship between steel or auto factory employment and the adjusted real wage was obtained. This greatly allevi-

TABLE 7.2

WAGES AND EMPLOYMENT IN THE STEEL INDUSTRY, U.S., 1934–1940

Quarter	Employment (Manhours)[a]	Money Wage[b]	Real Wage[c]	Adjusted Real Wage[d]
1934.1	73.3	89.2	94.2	93.6
1934.4	61.2	99.2	101.7	109.0
1936.1	100.0	100.0	100.0	100.0
1936.4	130.8	104.4	103.1	83.3
1938.2	62.8	126.8	123.8	139.0
1940.4	130.4	129.5	127.2	84.0

[a]FRB factory employment data multiplied by BLS average weekly hours data. All data are seasonally adjusted and indexed with 1936.1 = 100.
[b]Hourly wages, BLS.
[c]Hourly wages (BLS) divided by the BLS cost of living index.
[d]Real wage divided by hourly productivity, obtained by dividing the industrial production index for iron and steel by employment in manhours.
Source: Authors' calculations from BLS and FRB data.

ated any concern that somehow the results obtained earlier reflected some peculiar form of aggregation bias.

Table 7.2 shows the wage–employment relationship in greater detail for the steel sector, the larger of the two industries involved and the one for which data are available beginning in 1933. Note how peaks in the adjusted real wage tend to occur at about the same time as troughs in employment. Note also how changes in the adjusted real wage tend to lead to obvious changes in employment of a significant magnitude. For example, from the fourth quarter of 1936 through the second quarter of 1938, the adjusted real wage rose by about two-thirds, and as a consequence, employment fell by over one-half. Similarly, from the second quarter of 1938 to the last quarter of 1940, the adjusted real wage fell sharply (about 40 percent), and employment more than doubled, returning roughly to the level of 1936, and the adjusted real wage level of late 1936.

Productivity plays a role in the observed changes. The rise in productivity during 1936, and from late 1938 through 1940, was a significant factor in rising employment in those periods, just as falling productivity in 1934 and in 1937–38 contributed importantly to the decline in steel industry jobs during those years. At the same time, however, the abrupt increases in money wages were probably the largest single factor in the rises in adjusted real wages in 1934 and 1937–38, increases that had very profound effects on employment and unemployment in the industry.

There was much bitter complaining in this period about the rich economic "royalists." The New Deal had a strong income redistribution dimension. Yet not all the redistribution was along intended lines. Within the working population, the poor and the lower middle class, there was probably a growth in disparity in living standards in the thirties. The NIRA and the Wagner Act did lead to increases in wages, contributing to a doubling in hourly wages for many workers from early 1933 to late 1941. Yet these wage increases contributed to continued substantial unemployment in industry. Those who worked were better off than ever before, buying consumer durable goods in amounts rivaling those of the Roaring Twenties. In 1935, when the unemployment rate exceeded 20 percent, Americans bought more than twice as many refrigerators as in 1929, when the unemployment rate was 3.2 percent. A majority of the nearly two million buyers of refrigerators in 1935 were certainly not rich coupon clippers.[9] Yet for those millions without jobs, misery and poverty continued. The working laborer got richer, but the unemployed did not. The New Deal was far less friendly toward the poor and downtrodden than popular legend leads us to believe.

The Impact of the New Deal on Unemployment

Even in the late Hoover administration, new labor laws were adopted that had labor-market implications. The Davis–Bacon Act of 1931 required the federal government to pay "prevailing" (meaning union-scale) wages on construction contracts. The Norris–LaGuardia Act of 1932 was a pre–New Deal step to strengthen the hand of organized labor, restricting the use of injunctions and outlawing "yellow dog" contracts (contracts that prohibited workers from belonging to unions.)

As pointed out earlier, the major rise in wages in 1933, however, is attributable to the National Industrial Recovery Act (NIRA) enacted in June. We are not alone in making this argument. For example, two Nobel laureates, Paul Samuelson and Robert Solow, in introducing the American economics profession to the Phillips curve in its contemporary form, concluded: "Money wages rose or failed to fall in the face of massive unemployment. One may attribute this to the workings of the New Deal (the 20 percent wage increase of 1934 must represent the NRA codes) . . ."[10] Two decades later, after intensive research, Michael Weinstein essentially concluded the same thing.[11]

Under the NIRA, any business wishing to qualify for the right to display the Blue Eagle symbol had to adhere to industry codes agreed upon, generally, by industrial trade associations. In some respects, the government was permitting firms to engage in sanctioned cartels. For that privilege, however, firms had to adhere to wage practices favored by organized labor, including very high minimum wages. The floor of forty cents an hour established as a general minimum was nearly 90 percent of the *average* hourly wage prevailing in mid-1933, according to the NICB data.

The minimum wage under NIRA was less comprehensive than the one arising under the Fair Labor Standards Act five years later, but it was far higher in both an absolute and a relative sense. The minimum wage in 1938 was established at 25 cents per hour, and throughout the history of the minimum wage the minimum has seldom far exceeded one-half the average wage. The NIRA legislation, then, had a substantial impact, highly consistent with the Hoover high-wage policy adopted in 1929. Moreover, most codes provided for substantial increases for workers earning above-minimum wages (e.g., the 15 percent increase in the steel industry mentioned earlier).

There is absolutely no doubt that Roosevelt viewed the National Industrial Recovery Act as a way to raise hourly wages. He noted that the NIRA program was a program "to shorten the working week, to pay a decent wage for a shorter week, and to prevent unfair competition and disastrous overproduction."[12]

Prior to 1933, money wages had been falling. From the time of the passage of the NIRA to the end of 1933, factory wages rose by 22.2 percent.[13] In the absence of the legislation, wages more likely would have continued to fall as they had in 1931 and 1932. Thus the overall impact of the legislation probably far exceeds the 22 percent figure.

Aside from the wage floors, a second provision of the NIRA is of significance in explaining labor-market behavior. Section 7(a) was a seemingly innocuous statement guaranteeing workers the right to organize and engage in collective bargaining with employers. It was added to allay the fears of labor leaders that industry would act cooperatively against labor. It required that every industry code developed under the act include provisions guaranteeing the right of employees to organize and bargain collectively and that employees could not be required as a condition of employment either to join a company union or to refrain from joining a union of their choice. Thus NIRA was a clear forerunner of the National Labor Relations Act of 1935, and was in the so-called "pro-labor" spirit of such Hoover-era legislation as the Norris-LaGuardia Act and the Davis-Bacon Act.

While the questionable constitutionality of the legislation, as well as moves by companies to organize company unions, blunted the impact of Section 7a, some unions were successful in organizing workers, notably the Amalgamated Clothing Workers, the International Ladies' Garment Workers Union, and the United Mine Workers. John L. Lewis was particularly aggressive in obtaining higher wages for miners. The average hourly wage went from 49 cents an hour in 1933 to 72 cents an hour just two years later—before the Wagner Act had any impact.[14]

The Wagner Act can be viewed as a continuation of the underconsumptionist, high-wage policy initiated by Hoover and developed further by

Roosevelt. Not only did it establish collective bargaining as a matter of national policy, but it explicitly claimed that high wages helped fight depression. In the "Policy and Findings" portion of the law, it was stated that unequal bargaining power existing in nonunion situations "tends to aggravate recurrent business depressions, by depressing wage rates and the purchasing power of wage earners in industry."[15] Hence, by promoting unions and higher wages, recovery would be facilitated. The Wagner Act made explicit what had been implicitly accepted for years, namely the high-wage policy.

The Wagner Act provided the stimulus for several AFL unions to form the CIO in order to organize the mass-production industries. Significant organization attempts did not begin until the end of 1936. In the first half of 1937, the major automobile companies, excepting Ford, capitulated and recognized the United Auto Workers. Other important industries, most notably steel, were either unionized (U.S. Steel) or avoided unionization by paying union-scale wages.[16]

What evidence is there that the enactment of legislation such as the Wagner Act had any significant effect on wage levels? This issue has often been debated, and there is a substantial literature dealing with the question of the effect of unionism on wage levels.[17] Much of that literature focuses on the impact of unions on wages in the unionized sector of the labor market relative to wages in the nonunion sector. To give this previous research a greater historical dimension, consider the behavior since 1921 of a comprehensive measure of wage rates, compensation of full-time-equivalent employees, in those industries in the private sector that are traditionally regarded as being "unionized," that is, mining, construction, manufacturing, transportation, communications, and public utilities, vis-à-vis typically nonunionized industries (wholesale and retail trade, services, finance, and insurance and real estate.)

The wage differential between these two sectors is expressed as a percentage of the average wage for all workers, thus converting it into a relative wage differential. Figure 7.1 shows that the differential hovered between about 5 or 6 percent and slightly below zero prior to 1933, rising almost continuously in the late thirties and in 1940 and 1941, and reaching over 23 percent in the latter year. The trend continues after World War II to 24.45 percent in 1950 and 33.05 percent in 1960.[18] Formal statistical tests of these trends indicate a substantial change in the pattern of behavior of the union-nonunion wage differential commencing at approximately the time the nation's basic policy with respect to trade unions shifted from being one of reluctant toleration to one of legal encouragement.

While this evidence certainly is suggestive, it is possible to confirm the conclusions with a more formal statistical analysis. Again, multivariate

FIGURE 7.1

WAGES IN PREDOMINANTLY UNIONIZED AND NONUNIONIZED INDUSTRIES

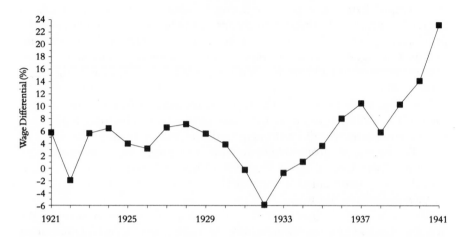

statistical techniques are employed to measure the relationship between money-wage rates on the one hand, and prices, productivity, and the extent of unionization in the labor force on the other.[19] The results confirm the existence of a statistically significant positive relationship between the portion of the labor force that is unionized and the level of money-wage rates. Knowing this relationship, and knowing the impact of changes in money-wage rates on unemployment (from our earlier statistical analysis), changes in the extent of unionism can be translated into estimated changes in employment.[20]

Before doing this, though, we wish to discuss certain other significant structural changes occurring at this time. Various governmental policies were contributing to increasing labor costs in ways that are not measured by the standard wage-rate statistics that have been used in our analysis. This was the era in which the great growth of supplements to wages and salaries ("fringe benefits") began. In 1929, supplements to wages and salaries were 1.2 percent of the total wage bill. Little change in this relationship occurred through 1935. In that year, for example, supplements were 1.4 percent of the annual wage bill.

In 1936, the fringe benefit portion of total compensation began to explode. Supplements as a percent of the annual wage bill rose as follows: 1936, 2.4 percent; 1937, 4.2 percent; and 1938, 5.1 percent.[21] At that point, supplements stabilized at about 5 percent of the total wage bill. The source of the rise in supplements is primarily employers' contributions for social insurance, required under the Social Security Act of 1935. In 1935, before

TABLE 7.3

ESTIMATES OF INDUCED UNEMPLOYMENT, UNITED STATES, 1934–1940

Year	Growth in Unionization (%)	Cumulative Unemployment Attributable to:	
		Old Age Retirement System (%)	Unemployment Compensation Costs (%)
1934	0.40	0.00	0.00
1935	0.91	0.00	0.00
1936	1.35	0.00	0.43
1937	4.65	0.60	1.09
1938	5.73	0.62	1.58
1939	6.28	0.66	1.55
1940	6.14	0.75	1.58

Source: Authors' calculations; see text.

that legislation was operative, they accounted for 25 percent of all supplements, while in 1938, they were some 71 percent of supplements.

Two aspects of social security contributed to the rise in supplemental compensation costs. The larger of the two new programs, at least initially, was the unemployment insurance program. In 1938, that accounted for 43 percent of supplements. Secondly, the old-age/survivors insurance program accounted for an additional 17 percent of supplements as of 1938. Thus, in 1938 the newly emerging national retirement system had raised wage costs by about 0.85 percent, while the unemployment system added another 2.2 percent.

With the aid of our initial statistical model of unemployment, the impact on unemployment of these various changes in wage costs can be estimated.[22] Year-by-year calculations are shown in table 7.3. They suggest that unionization was the more important cause of prolonged high unemployment, but that employer social security contributions raised the unemployment rate about another 2.2 percent. Put differently, nearly 1.2 million people were added to the unemployment rolls by 1938 because of the increases in labor cost associated with social insurance programs.

Figure 7.2 summarizes our findings graphically. The top line represents the actual unemployment rate, while the bottom line represents our estimate of what the unemployment rate would have been had unionization and social insurance programs not expanded. That line indicates that the economy would have returned to single-digit unemployment in 1937, not 1941, a year in which the unemployment rate barely made it into that range. It suggests that the Great Depression was very significantly prolonged in both its duration and its magnitude by the impact of New Deal programs.

The analysis above in some respects understates the effect of the New Deal, since it excludes the unemployment effects of other legislation. As Michael Weinstein has so well demonstrated, the NIRA greatly raised

FIGURE 7.2

ACTUAL AND COUNTERFACTUAL UNEMPLOYMENT RATES FOR THE UNITED STATES, 1934-40

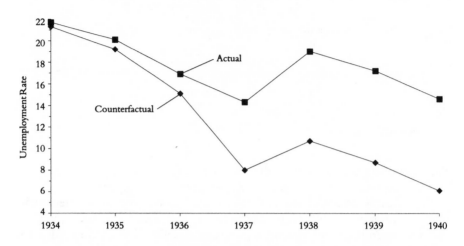

wages, and while it was ultimately found unconstitutional, that court decision did not reverse the upward wage shock that already had occurred.[23]
It is entirely possible that including the NIRA in our analysis above, we
would find that the Depression would have been completely over (less than
5 percent unemployment) by 1936. Likewise, the analysis ignores the impact of the Fair Labor Standards Act of 1938, which established a national
minimum wage.

Even with the conservative statement of the unemployment impact,
however, table 7.3 suggests that most of the abnormal unemployment of
the thirties would have been eliminated by 1937. The counterfactual unemployment rate closes most of the gap between the actual and natural unemployment rates by 1937, suggesting that the New Deal wage
cost–enhancing policies more than doubled the amount of abnormally large
unemployment in that year. Again, we view this as a conservative estimate.

Other Perspectives on New Deal Unemployment

While modern writers on the New Deal era have been increasingly sympathetic to the view that New Deal reforms delayed recovery, for the most
part, they have been unable to "cross the bridge," so to speak. They either
accept in some form the validity of the high-wage policy approach or
simply ignore the role of wages altogether. Particularly notable in that

regard is Peter Temin, perhaps the leading living proponent of the Keynesian perspective on the origins of the Depression. Temin admires Roosevelt, and believes that recovery began in the summer of 1933 because of a new macropolicy regime that Roosevelt initiated.[24] Yet he admits that U.S. employment growth was restricted by the high-wage policy of Roosevelt, although he ties his view to the Keynesian concept of efficiency wages (some wage growth would have raised productivity, but the New Deal went too far.)[25] Yet others appear to reject such a view. Bernanke and Parkinson, noting that there was a respectable amount of economic growth after 1933, have recently made an astonishing assertion: "Maybe Herbert Hoover and Henry Ford were right: Higher real wages may have paid for themselves in the broader sense that their positive effect on aggregate demand compensated for their tendency to raise costs."[26]

An alternative interpretation of the New Deal era has come from the Keynesian side. It claims that aggregate demand management in the form of fiscal policy was not really tried after 1933. E. Cary Brown found that, on balance, New Deal fiscal policy was stimulative in only one year, 1936.[27] Writing nearly two decades later, Larry Peppers essentially agreed with Brown.[28] This view is not consistent with that of Friedman and Schwartz, who attribute the revival of the economy to the recovery of the banking system.[29] They demonstrate that monetary growth seemed to coincide reasonably closely with patterns of unemployment.

THE 1937–1938 DOWNTURN

The sharp economic downturn in 1937 and 1938 has been explained in a variety of ways.[30] Early on, Benjamin Anderson espoused the wages hypothesis discussed above.[31] Yet this view has commanded less attention than other perspectives, particularly that of Keynesians.[32] Brown had noted that in 1936, there was some fiscal-policy stimulus because of veteran's bonus payments. Yet this stimulus disappeared by 1937, a point stressed by Alvin Hansen.[33] Payroll tax increases for social security (from 1 to 3 percent) in that year added to the contractionary nature of fiscal policy, leading to a full-employment budget surplus. New capital gains and corporate profits taxes were enacted, which both Joseph Schumpeter and Charles Hardy think contributed importantly to the decline.[34] Income-tax receipts in 1937 were up some 65 percent over the previous year, at a time when absolute federal spending was declining.[35] The federal deficit contracted sharply.

Monetary policy was clearly restrictive. On three occasions between August 1936 and May 1937, the Federal Reserve Board raised reserve requirements, flexing new regulatory muscle provided by the Banking Act of 1935. The doubling of reserve requirements led banks to scramble for reserves, and to rebuild previously existing excess reserves. This, to monetarists such as Milton Friedman, led to a decline in the stock of money and a resulting economic contraction. It is true that the money stock (M1) declined by over 6 percent from March 1937 to December of that year, and did not exceed the March 1937 levels until November 1938.[36]

What did people at the time say caused the downturn? As in 1929, wage-oriented explanations were mentioned occasionally, but they did not dominate the discussion. To be sure, a few prominent economists and businessmen recognized the problem. The president of the Brookings Institution, Harold Moulton, in early 1938 blamed the downturn on "the aggressive labor movement's" role in reducing hours and increasing pay without regard to increased efficiency.[37] A strong proponent of the wages hypothesis was Willford I. King of New York University and the National Bureau of Economic Research, who said that "wages have been forced up to levels which cannot be maintained and keep all the laboring force of the country at work."[38] The First National Bank of Boston in its newsletter commented that to "arbitrarily . . . impose shorter hours or higher wages without a corresponding increase in productivity throws the whole mechanism out of gear. . . ."[39]

Yet just as many seemed to argue the opposite: that high wages helped the nation, and that they were not rising enough in real terms. Chief among these was Roosevelt himself. He publicly developed what today would be called an efficiency-wage argument, suggesting that higher wages are associated with greater productivity.[40] He also advocated cutting prices, in effect raising real wages even further.[41] Roosevelt's chief political adviser (and Postmaster General) James Farley said that business "took advantage of the progress we have made to retain more than a wise share of the profits."[42] To Farley, the problem was that profits were too high, which is another way of saying adjusted real wages were too low. A few business leaders (although far fewer than in 1930) still argued that wages contributed to buying power. Edward Filene, the Boston merchant, for example, said that "employers make no greater error than to assume that wages come out of profits. The fact is profits come out of wages."[43]

Most business leaders, increasingly bitter and outspoken about the New Deal policies, blamed the decline on higher taxes and falling confidence arising from the administration's antibusiness, "soak the rich" philosophy. General Motors' Alfred Sloan declared that "confidence must be reestablished."[44] Lamont du Pont said that "Congress must dispel the 'fog of uncertainty' over taxes, prices, strikes, money, regulation of business."[45]

Some of the analysis had a modern ring to it. Take the objections over taxation: higher taxes meant lower rates of return, reducing the provision of capital and other resources. At least one critic, New York State Controller Morris S. Termaine, even anticipated the Laffer curve, arguing that a very high marginal tax rate (up to 79 percent from 1936 onward) "undoubtedly tends to reduce revenues."[46] Regarding monetary policy less was said, although prominent economist Irving Fisher attributed the downturn in large part to monetary contraction: "Reduction of our checkbook money . . . is the most basic cause of our trouble. . . ."[47]

Others, though, complained about fiscal policy in conventional Keynesian terms, emphasizing the reduced stimulus to aggregate demand associated with moving from a large budget deficit to a small one. In a letter to the London *Times*, John Maynard Keynes himself observed that the present "setback" in the United States resulted from a failure to have public-works projects on tap in sufficient quantity.[48] Roosevelt's son James publicly expressed similar views, which were in line with those of many cabinet members.[49] Federal Reserve Board Chairman Marriner Eccles blamed the recession in part on sharp reductions in federal "contributions to general buying power."[50]

There were still other explanations for the decline. For example, Sumner Slichter emphasized the importance of the collapse of commodity prices after the middle of 1936, which he believed unsettled business expectations.[51] In short, a variety of supply-side, monetarist, Keynesian, and neoclassical views were expressed to explain the 1937–38 downturn. Kenneth Roose concluded that "The causation of the recession of 1937–38 was complex rather than simple."[52] An examination of the viewpoints of leaders of the era reveals, however, that the huge wage run-up in 1937–38 was viewed by most persons as only a secondary cause of the renewed depression. The neoclassical approach to unemployment, never deeply embedded in the minds of most economists or businessmen, was not appealed to during this period of extraordinary wage increases. Already, the Keynesian aggregate-demand approach was becoming dominant in the thinking of intellectuals, disdained only by some business leaders who were increasingly viewed as mindless reactionaries.

The tragedy of the New Deal era was that well-intentioned programs undertaken in the name of relief (unemployment insurance) or reform (the Wagner Act and old-age insurance under social security), so retarded the second "R" of the New Deal program, namely recovery. While any thoughts about the counterfactual world that would have existed in the absence of the New Deal are necessarily somewhat speculative, there is little doubt that the New Deal's continuation of the Hoover high-wage policy meant that the Depression was prolonged by several years, and that several million people remained unemployed who otherwise would have worked. These social costs of the New Deal reforms were hidden, but were nonetheless very real.

There is little doubt that Franklin D. Roosevelt's policies added to the difficulties of the period. At the same time, however, in a very real sense Roosevelt merely continued and expanded upon the high-wage doctrine first articulated by Hoover. Far from being the bold new reformer saving the nation from the laissez-faire prescriptions of a reactionary president, Roosevelt was a chief executive who adroitly and charismatically expanded the legacy left by his progressive, if colorless, predecessor. He was aided and abetted in this by the emerging respectability of underconsumptionism (later called Keynesianism) in the intellectual community. The underconsumptionist, high-wage policy was triumphing in the world of ideas at the very time that it was failing in the real world of human behavior. The legacy of this intellectual triumph played an important role in the war and postwar era, even down to this day.

NOTES

1. For British unemployment, wage, and price data, see Derek H. Aldcroft, *The Inter-War Economy: Britain, 1919–1939* (New York: Columbia University Press, 1970), p. 352.
2. Data on industrial production, factory employment, and wholesale prices were obtained from Geoffrey H. Moore, ed., *Business Cycle Indicators*, 2 vols. (Princeton: Princeton University Press for the National Bureau of Economic Research, 1961), vol. 2. Consumer price data were largely derived from various issues of the *Federal Reserve Bulletin*. Consumer prices are the basic CPI measure of the Department of Labor; for four quarters, however, no CPI figures were available. For the missing quarters, values were estimated using changes in an alternate cost-of-living index constructed by the National Industrial Conference Board. That index and estimates of hourly earnings were derived from Willford I. King, *The Causes of Economic Fluctuations* (New York: Ronald Press, 1938), and various issues of the *Survey of Current Business*.
3. The data were regularly reported in the *Survey of Current Business*. We compiled the data from the special statistical supplemental volumes published in 1936, 1938, 1940, and 1942.
4. Philip Taft, *Organized Labor in American History* (New York: Harper and Row, 1964), p. 461.
5. U.S. Department of Commerce, Bureau of the Census, *Historical Statistics of the United States, Colonial Times to 1970* (Washington, D.C.: Government Printing Office, 1975), p. 179.

6. For a good discussion of the case and a synopsis of the decision, see Robert Cushman, ed., *Leading Constitutional Decisions* (New York: Appleton-Century-Crofts, 1958), pp. 348–62.

7. Ibid., pp. 177–79.

8. Data sources were the same as indicated earlier, except that Bureau of Labor Statistics data on money wages were used instead of Conference Board data. The BLS was also the data source for the steel price series used. Auto industry hourly wage and weekly hours worked data were not available for the automobile industry for 1933. All data were seasonally adjusted, either by the agency compiling the statistics or by the authors.

9. See *Historical Statistics of the United States*, p. 695, for statistics on refrigerator production.

10. See Paul A. Samuelson and Robert M. Solow, "Our Menu of Policy Choices," in *The Battle Against Unemployment*, ed. Arthur M. Okun (New York: W. W. Norton, 1965), p. 73. For the longer paper from which this article is drawn, see their "Analytical Aspects of Anti-Inflation Policy," *American Economic Review* 50, Supplement (1960): 177–94.

11. Michael M. Weinstein, "Some Macroeconomic Impacts of the National Industrial Recovery Act, 1933–1935," *The Great Depression Revisited*, ed. Karl Brunner (Boston: Martinus Nijhoff, 1981), pp. 262–81, or his *Recovery and Redistribution under the National Industrial Recovery Act, 1933–1936* (New York: Elsevier, 1980).

12. See Lester V. Chandler, *America's Greatest Depression, 1929–1941* (New York: Harper and Row, 1970), p. 223.

13. See King, *The Causes of Economic Fluctuations*.

14. *Historical Statistics of the United States*, p. 170.

15. See Glenn W. Miller, *American Labor and the Government* (New York: Prentice-Hall, 1948), p. 569. For a discussion of this and other legislative acts of the New Deal era see chaps. 15–20.

16. See Philip Taft, *Organized Labor in American History* (New York: Harper and Row, 1964), or his *The AF of L from the Death of Gompers to the Merger* (New York: Harper and Brothers, 1959).

17. The classic study is H. Gregg Lewis, *Unionism and Relative Wages in the United States* (Chicago: University of Chicago Press, 1963). There have been a number of subsequent attempts to measure the wage effects of unions. For one survey, see C. J. Parsley, "Labor Union Effects on Wage Gains: A Survey of Recent Literature," *Journal of Economic Literature* 18 (1980): 1–31.

18. The basic data employed in these calculations are taken from Lowell E. Gallaway, "Trade Unionism, Inflation, and Unemployment," in *Monetary Process and Policy: A Symposium*, ed. George Horwich (Homewood, Ill.: Richard D. Irwin, 1967), pp. 60–66. Prior to the New Deal, there were substantial numbers of non-union members in the work force of what we call unionized industries. For example, in 1920, when trade-union membership peaked at over five million, only about one-fourth of the workers in our unionized industries were union members. See Leo Wolman, *Ebb and Flow in Trade Unionism* (New York: National Bureau of Economic Research, 1936), appendix, table V, pp. 217–21. Actually, we feel that

we may have underestimated the union impact by employing a relative wage measure rather than focusing on the absolute real differential. For a theoretical discussion,
see Gallaway, "Trade Unionism, Inflation, and Employment." It is interesting to
note that wage flexibility tended to be greater in the early 1930s in the industries
that became unionized (and lost some wage flexibility) in the late 1930s.

19.   Specifically, the level of wage rates (measured on both an hourly and an
annual basis) was regressed against the rate of change in average labor productivity,
the rate of change in the wholesale price index, and the fraction of the labor force
that was unionized, for the years 1901 to 1941. The coefficient on the unionization
variable was used to calculate the impact of increased unionization on wages. For
further details, see our "Wages, Prices, and Employment: Von Mises and the Progressives," *Review of Austrian Economics* 1 (1987): 70.

20.   Ibid., pp. 55–57. The data used in computing the findings were somewhat
different from those generally used in this book, but visual inspection indicates that
the results would not likely be materially different from the data used here.

21.   Total supplements are from *Historical Statistics of the United States*, series D-
893. Average annual earnings are from series D-722. See also Albert Rees, *New
Measures of Wage-Earner Compensation in Manufacturing, 1914–1957*, Occasional Paper
no. 75 (Princeton, N.J.: Princeton University Press for the National Bureau of
Economic Research, 1960).

22.   Detailed supplement data are from *Historical Statistics of the United States*,
series D-907 and D-908.

23.   See Michael Weinstein, *Recovery and Redistribution Under the National Industrial Recovery Act, 1933–1935* (New York: Elsevier, 1980). See also his "Some Macroeconomic Impacts of the National Industrial Recovery Act, 1933–1935."

24.   Peter Temin and Barrie A. Wigmore, "The End of One Big Deflation,"
Explorations in Economic History 27 (1990): 483–502.

25.   Peter Temin, "Socialism and Wages in the Recovery from the Great Depression in the United States and Germany," *Journal of Economic History* 50 (1990):
297–307. See also his *Lessons from the Great Depression* (Cambridge, Mass.: MIT
Press, 1989), pp. 120–21.

26.   Ben Bernanke and Martin Parkinson, "Unemployment, Inflation and
Wages in the American Depression: Are There Lessons for Europe?" *American Economic Review* 79 (1989): 210–14.

27.   E. Cary Brown, "Fiscal Policy in the Thirties: A Reappraisal," ibid., 46
(1956): 857–79.

28.   Larry Peppers, "Full-Employment Surplus Analysis and Structural
Change: the 1930s," *Explorations in Economic History* 10 (1973): 197–210.

29.   Milton Friedman and Anna J. Schwartz, *A Monetary History of the United
States, 1867–1960* (Princeton, N. J.: Princeton University Press for the National
Bureau of Economic Research, 1963).

30.   For an excellent discussion of the various arguments about the 1937–38
downturn, see Gene Smiley, "Can Keynesianism Explain the 1930s?" *Critical Review*
5(1991): 81–114.

31. *Economics and the Public Welfare: A Financial and Economic History of the United States, 1914–1946* (Indianapolis: Liberty Press, 1979), chaps. 66–71. Additional support for the wages hypothesis was provided by Melvin D. Brockie, "Theories of the 1937–38 Crisis and Depression," *Economic Journal* 60(1950): 291–310.

32. A good general account of the period with a pro-Keynesian perspective is Broadus Mitchell, *Depression Decade: From New Era Through New Deal, 1929–1941* (New York: Rinehart, 1947), especially p. 22.

33. Alvin Hansen, *Full Recovery or Stagnation?* (New York: W. W. Norton, 1939), chap. 17.

34. Joseph A. Schumpeter, *Business Cycles*, 2 vols. (New York: McGraw-Hill, 1939), 2: 1038–40; Charles O. Hardy, "An Appraisal of the Factors ('Natural' and 'Artificial') Which Stopped Short the Recovery Development in the United States," *American Economic Review* 29, Supplement (1939): 170–182.

35. The "cash" deficit of the federal government fell dramatically, from $3,775 million to $650 million from fiscal year 1936 to fiscal year 1937. *Business Week*, March 26, 1938, p. 11.

36. Friedman and Schwartz, *Monetary History.*, p. 715.

37. *New York Times*, January 27, 1938, p. 1.

38. *Literary Digest*, December 25, 1937, p. 21.

39. *New York Times*, February 2, 1938, p. 29.

40. *New Republic*, March 2, 1938, p. 88.

41. Ibid., February 9, 1938, p. 4.

42. *New York Times*, August 9, 1938, p. 4.

43. Ibid., July 15, 1937, p. 37.

44. *Literary Digest*, January 8, 1938, p. 19.

45. Ibid.

46. Speech to the American Management Association; *New York Times*, December 15, 1937.

47. *Literary Digest*, December 25, 1937, p. 22. The idea that consumer installment credit played an important role, implied by commentators like Fisher, was generally rejected by Gottfried von Haberler. See his *Consumer Installment Credit and Economic Fluctuations* (New York: National Bureau of Economic Research, 1942), especially p. 12.

48. *New York Times*, January 3, 1938, p. 5.

49. Ibid., April 21, 1938, p. 3.

50. *Business Week*, January 8, 1938, p. 55.

51. Sumner H. Slichter, "The Downturn of 1937," *Review of Economics and Statistics* 20 (1938): 97–110.

52. Kenneth D. Roose, *The Economics of Recession and Revival: An Interpretation of 1937–38* (New Haven, Conn.: Yale University Press, 1954), p. 246.

8

The
Impossible Dream Come True

If the thirties were years of unequaled high unemployment, the forties were almost precisely the opposite. Unemployment fell to levels that compared favorably with the Gilded Age of a generation earlier. For the only time in American history, before or since, the nation had three consecutive years with an unemployment rate below 2 percent, and six consecutive years with a rate below 4 percent. This was all the more remarkable because the decade began with the Great Depression still very much present, with unemployment around 15 percent. It was not until mid-1941 that it returned to the single digits.[1] Table 8.1 details the remarkable fall in unemployment, and its failure to rise in the immediate aftermath of the war.

This was the era when Keynesians won the final intellectual battles in the war for supremacy in macroeconomic theory. Helping them in the struggle was the widespread perception that the wartime experience proved beyond doubt the efficacy of the Keynesian model and the potency of deficit spending as a countercyclical fiscal-policy device. By 1947, future Nobel laureate Lawrence Klein was able to write a book entitled *The Keynesian Revolution* without the title causing a stir, and the following year another future Nobel Laureate, Paul Samuelson, had the first edition of his enormously successful Keynesian-style principles textbook appear. Anti-Keynesians despaired, but were increasingly ignored. Friedrich von Hayek, for example, simply turned his considerable intellectual talents to writing in the field of philosophy. While at least one wrote a somewhat classical

150

TABLE 8.1

UNEMPLOYMENT IN THE UNITED STATES, 1940 TO 1947

Year	Quarter	Unemployment Rate[a]
1940	I	15.4
	II	14.8
	III	13.8
	IV	14.2
1941	I	12.2
	II	10.9
	III	9.0
	IV	7.4
1942	I	6.9
	II	5.0
	III	3.7
	IV	3.1
1943	I	2.3
	II	1.9
	III	1.8
	IV	1.5
1944	I	1.3
	II	1.3
	III	1.2
	IV	1.0
1945	I	1.1
	II	1.2
	III	2.1
	IV	3.6
1946	I	4.1
	II	4.0
	III	3.7
	IV	4.1
1947	I	3.8
	II	4.1
	III	4.1
	IV	3.7

[a]Seasonally adjusted; the 1947 data are not strictly comparable to earlier years.
Source: U.S. Department of Labor, Bureau of Labor Statistics

treatise on the Depression era (Benjamin Anderson), non-Keynesians were increasingly viewed as reactionaries out of step with new advances in economic knowledge. In a way, this is not surprising. Massive budget deficits equal to 20 percent or more of gross national product occurred at the same time that unemployment fell rapidly. It appeared that the Germans and Japanese had shocked America into an intelligent, job–creating fiscal policy. When Keynes died in 1946, his theories had already dominated economic thinking far more than those of the most influential economists of the previous two centuries, Adam Smith and Karl Marx, had in their lifetimes.

So persuasive did the evidence seem to be that virtually no one bothered to examine an alternative possibility, namely that the fall in unemployment during the war era reflected a decline in the real wage adjusted for productivity. And even those who did look at the wage data probably found little to suggest the appropriateness of the neoclassical framework. On the surface, it seemed that real wages rose at the very time that unemployment was falling, a phenomenon that was enough to turn any neoclassical into a Keynesian, as widening government deficits seemed to indicate the superiority of the income–expenditures approach to national income determination and unemployment. We would submit, however, that government-induced distortions in the data aided in the downfall of the neoclassical microeconomic approach to economics, and contributed to the high tide of Keynesianism.

Wartime-Era Unemployment and the Adjusted Real Wage

Before turning to the very serious data problem, we present for the record what official data suggest happened to unemployment and the components of the adjusted real wage. The data used are those employed in establishing the basic model, namely government data sources such as the consumer price index to measure price change.

TABLE 8.2

PREDICTED AND ACTUAL UNEMPLOYMENT, 1940 TO 1947

Year	Actual Unemployment Rate	Predicted Unemployment Rate
1940	14.6	14.5
1941	9.9	11.7
1942	4.7	6.5
1943	1.9	3.9
1944	1.2	3.6
1945	1.9	1.9
1946	3.9	3.2
1947	3.9	3.6

Source: Authors' calculations from model developed in chapter three.

As table 8.2 shows, the adjusted real wage model does a reasonably good job of explaining unemployment in the 1940 to 1947 period. The model, based on data for 1900 to 1989, captures the major decline in unemployment from the Depression era, although it tends to overpredict systematically unemployment for the war years (the 1944 prediction error is the third largest for the ninety years 1900 to 1989.) The model has unemployment bottoming out in 1945 at 1.9 percent, instead of in 1944 at 1.2 percent. The moderate rise in unemployment immediately after the war (in 1946 and 1947) is observed, albeit the rise appears slightly less than actually occurred.

The model indicates declines in unemployment in part because of the impact of lagged values of the components of the adjusted real wage. In the middle of the war, the adjusted real wage as measured is not declining, and it actually increases during the early part of the conflict. The reason for this is that money wages continue the rapid rise of the Depression era, increasing by double-digit amounts in three years (1942, 1943, and 1946.). Reported inflation, however, is less, and the real wage rises sharply, especially in the midwar period, increasing by about 6 percent a year in both 1943 and 1944, and in the 4 percent range in 1945 and 1946. Fortunately, productivity rises every year except 1947, so the adjusted real wage in 1947 is about the same as in 1940, with some decrease observed in 1941, an increase from 1941 to 1943, and a slight decline from 1943 to 1945, followed by a big one-year rise in 1946 that reverses itself the following year.

Statistical Problems in the Command Economy of the Wartime Era

The results above are highly suspect because the underlying data are almost certainly replete with significant distortions. Fortunately, in terms of the calculation of the aggregate adjusted real wage, these distortions tend to cancel each other out, meaning that the overall adjusted real wage measure calculated using the poor data may be reasonably accurate. For example, if inflation was understated during World War II (as we believe), productivity gains were overstated. Downward shifts in the adjusted real wage attributable to productivity increases in fact should have been attributed to inflation.

Independently, both Robert Higgs and ourselves have written critiques of the data of this era, Higgs concentrating on the GNP statistics for the wartime years, while we have concentrated on the postwar reconversion to peace.[2] Three unusual characteristics of this period make conventional statistics suspect. First, the existence of price and to a lesser extent wage controls makes the official price indices highly misleading. Second, the huge shift from civilian to military production distorts the calculation of gross national product and other economic aggregates, particularly since civilian activity is almost entirely evaluated at true market prices, whereas military activity is not. Third, the labor market underwent a dramatic transformation, including the employment of millions of military personnel at below-equilibrium wages via military conscription.

THE EVOLUTION OF WAGE AND PRICE CONTROLS

As early as May 1940, the organizational structure for future price controls was established by President Roosevelt.[3] The original Price Stabilization Division was headed by Leon Henderson, a veteran of wage and price manipulations from his days as chief economist for the National Recovery Administration. Henderson was one of the New Deal economists who believed that the 1937–38 downturn had come because prices (and profits) had risen too much—in other words that adjusted real wages were too low.[4]

The first actual price regulations began in 1941. They were generally met with approval from businessmen; one survey indicated that 82.5 percent of businessmen favored controls.[5] The Office of Price Administration, or OPA, was created in 1941, with its price administration division headed by John Kenneth Galbraith. Congress formally ratified Roosevelt's actions shortly before Pearl Harbor. Public opinion strongly favored controls.[6]

Truly comprehensive price controls began with the General Maximum Price Regulation of April 1942. Price increases under the first year of this regulation were fairly substantial: the consumer price index rose over 7 percent, and Hugh Rockoff believes this actually understates the true figure.[7] In May 1943, Galbraith resigned and was replaced by the energetic and relatively more effective Chester Bowles. The previous month, Roosevelt had issued a Hold-the-Line Order largely freezing prices and wages, a move that was generally accepted, although there were some exceptions.[8] From that point on, price controls seemed to be more rigorously enforced. Requests for price increases were generally denied if they would raise profits above the average for the 1936–39 period. Wage increases had to be approved, in general, by the National War Labor Board. Labor leaders, such as Philip Murray of the CIO, while generally adhering to a no-strike pledge, were from the beginning outspoken in their opposition to wage controls.[9]

Public acceptance of controls declined somewhat as the war came to a close, particularly with regard to wages. President Truman in August 1945 in effect removed direct wage controls but maintained price controls, allowing for wage increases to serve as a basis for price increase requests. A significant liberalization of controls occurred in February 1946, leading prices to rise at an annual rate of over 8 percent even before the price-control law expired in June 1946.[10] A relatively weak extension of the law was vetoed by President Truman, at Bowles's urging. Interestingly, even toward the end of the control period, many leading economists strongly favored continued price regulations, including such distinguished conservatives as Frank Knight and Henry Simons, Keynesians like Alvin Hansen and Paul Samuelson, the Marxist Paul Sweezy, and other eminent economists such as Simon Kuznets and Arthur Burns.[11]

THE DISTORTIONAL EFFECT OF PRICE CONTROLS

If price controls are to be meaningful, ceiling prices must be established below the equilibrium prices that would otherwise prevail. These below-

TABLE 8.3

U.S. PRICE AND REAL OUTPUT TRENDS: 1941–48; THREE INTERPRETATIONS

	Real GNP [a]			GNP Price Deflator[a]		
Year	1960 Data	1990 Data	Authors' Estimates	1960 Data	1990 Data	Authors' Estimates
1941	100.0	100.0	100.0	100.0	100.0	100.0
1942	111.5	118.8	117.1	113.2	106.5	108.0
1943	122.7	140.3	128.0	124.2	109.4	119.7
1944	132.4	151.8	127.6	126.4	110.9	131.7
1945	130.4	149.0	116.1	129.7	113.8	146.1
1946	120.3	120.6	108.5	141.0	140.6	155.6
1947	119.4	117.3	115.3	154.9	160.1	161.6
1948	125.7	121.9	125.6	163.7	171.0	165.6

[a]Numbers are indexed, with 1941=100.
Source: See text.

equilibrium prices, in turn, provide incentives for illegal trades (black markets), and typically have other effects (imposition of rationing to deal with shortages, a decline in the quality of services or products). Controls disguise the inflation outwardly, sweeping the underlying inflationary pressures under the rug.

Distortions in prices bring out distortions in real output (which is defined by dividing money GNP by a price index) and therefore productivity, and also in real wages. To deal with this problem, we constructed an estimate of the GNP price deflator that would have existed if various historical relationships had held during the 1940s. Using these forecasted prices, we can estimate trends in real GNP using the money GNP statistics on which there is general agreement (although see the argument below.)

For the years 1916 to 1941, we regressed the GNP price deflator against four independent variables (the money stock M2, interest rates on four-to-six month commercial paper, ton-miles of class A railroad volume, and the total number of employed workers).[12] Actual values for the independent variables were used with the estimated regression coefficients and constant term to calculate forecasted values of the GNP price deflator for the years 1942 through 1948. The forecasting was aided by the fact that the estimated regression had a relatively good statistical fit ($R^2 = .822$), with actual and estimated values being rather close for the years immediately preceding the war.

Taking the predicted GNP price deflator numbers for 1942–48, along with the official nominal GNP numbers, we calculated real GNP by year (table 8.3). We then compared our estimates with those of the Department of Commerce as reported in both 1960 and 1990. The official 1990 estimates show sharply lower inflation in World War II than the 1960 estimates. Elsewhere, we have demonstrated that the discrepancy between the 1960

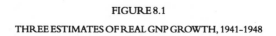

FIGURE 8.1

THREE ESTIMATES OF REAL GNP GROWTH, 1941-1948

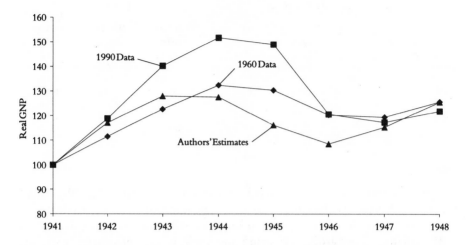

and 1990 official estimates is a pure statistical artifact.[13] In figure 8.1 we compare our estimate of real GNP growth using the official nominal GNP numbers and our price deflator with the government estimate as calculated in 1960 and 1990.

While we observe some dramatic increase in real output early in the war (to 1943), we see output starting to decline in 1944 and falling significantly in 1945. Total output growth from 1941 to 1945 is estimated at slightly over 16 percent, or 4 percent a year—a very good growth rate, but hardly the growth that the official estimates suggest. Similarly, the dramatic postwar drop in output recorded in official statistics is much reduced in our estimates.

Moreover, even our estimates of real GNP may be significantly distorted because of inappropriate calculation of nominal GNP. If Higgs is right (and he makes a good case for his perspective), then the Department of Commerce overvalued the government-produced wartime output significantly. Correcting for that distortion, real output does not show a major upsurge in the early 1940s, postwar output grows significantly, and the Great Depression does not really end until the close of World War II. If Higgs is right, however, the adjusted real wage does not fall in the early 1940s, as productivity per worker actually declines, more than offsetting the effects of inflation.

Making sense out of the World War II era, then, is difficult because of the enormous distortions associated with the substitution for market-valued economic activity of command–economy activity not formally measured at true market prices. This holds for the labor market as well. By 1943, a double-digit percentage of the labor force were "workers" in the military who were offering their labor services involuntarily at a wage below the equilibrium compensation level.

With these huge caveats, we do have some impressions about the World War II era. Real "economic activity" increased in the sense that more resources were being utilized. To the extent that the war economy led to price distortions, waste, inefficiency, the loss of consumer surplus, etc., however, real output grew far less than official statistics indicate. Moreover, inflation was far greater than the official numbers state, because it was disguised by controls. We derive comfort in the fact that our inflation estimates are remarkably close to those independently derived by Friedman and Schwartz.[14] Employment growth is exaggerated in an upward direction to the extent that millions were forced to work at below-equilibrium wages; consequently, the unemployment rate is understated.

Thus the World War II era is less of an economic success story than is often portrayed. Real wages probably fell in some meaningful sense, since consumers could not buy many desired goods at controlled prices. Both price controls and the move to a command economy have led us to overstate the productivity gains of the wartime era, although the precise magnitude of the overstatement is subject to debate. Nonetheless, even with all the distortions of the period, it appears that workers responded to changes in the adjusted real wage as predicted by the neoclassical theory.

The Postwar Recovery

The official government statistics at present state that real GNP fell 19 percent in 1946, 22.7 percent from 1944 to 1947, and over 25 percent on a per capita basis over that three-year period. The 1946 drop is the largest single yearly decline ever recorded. Earlier governmental statistical accounts, however, record a much weaker decline. For example, when the 1960 edition of *Historical Statistics of the United States* was released, the 1946 decline in real GNP was stated to be 7.8 percent.[15]

What is extraordinary, however, is that this severe drop in output occurred with unemployment rates under 4 percent, far below the normal peacetime rate in the twentieth century, either before or after the 1946 "depression."[16] Moreover, this relatively full employment was achieved despite an extraordinarily contractionary fiscal policy. The federal budget deficit on a national income accounts basis in 1944 was some $54.5 billion, equal to 25.8 percent of GNP. That would be the equivalent in 1991 (in relation to GNP) of a deficit of over $1,400 billion. By 1947, the federal budget was in surplus by $13.4 billion, or 5.7 percent of GNP.[17] The equivalent today (in relation to GNP) would be well over a $300 billion surplus. Among other things, the government in pursuing this extraordinarily contractionary fiscal policy fired (or "released from employment") roughly 20 percent of the total labor force. All of this had little impact on unemployment.

We know of no episode in American economic history that more clearly illustrates several neoclassical and Austrian economic insights than the 1944–47 business cycle experience. The ultimate irony is that the modern historical interpretation of that era suggests that it was a period that demonstrated the superiority of Keynesian economic doctrines. It was this period that saw the death of residual sentiments in the American economics profession that market coordination is the most appropriate and efficient means to assure reasonably "full" employment of productive resources. Politically, it was during this period that the federal government institutionalized Keynesian-style macroeconomic intervention with the Employment Act of 1946.

Despite the statistics cited above, conventional modern wisdom is that the transition from war to peace proceeded without a major downturn after World War II, and certainly that there was no "depression."[18] Our subsequent discussion will show that that interpretation is essentially correct. However, it is generally accepted that the smooth economic conversion resulted from "pent-up" demand for consumer goods offsetting the reduction in defense spending. In other words, the Keynesian prescription that "demand creates its own supply" worked after World War II.

After studying this historical episode, we conclude that:

1) Conventional wisdom is correct on one thing: there was no depression in 1946, or anything resembling one;
2) The failure of the nation to enter a depression after 1944 reflected not pent-up consumer demand so much as the substantial ameliorating effects of changing relative prices on the macroeconomy;
3) The smooth transition to peace was accomplished despite the existence of a fiscal policy that was the very antithesis of Keynesian economic prescriptions to deal with falling aggregate demand. The most dramatically contractionary fiscal policy in modern American history failed to alter materially the pace of economic activity;
4) Keynesian economics triumphed in politics and among academic economists at the very time that empirical evidence was clearly exposing its explanatory weaknesses. The very empiricist-quantitative economists

who rhetorically were selling the new economics of Keynes on the grounds that the evidence of the 1929–41 downturn showed the empirical bankruptcy of market-oriented economic doctrines were ignoring, perhaps deliberately, the 1944–47 empirical evidence that was devastating to the Keynesian paradigm.

5) A market-Austrian interpretation of this historical episode is very much more in keeping with the evidence.

STATISTICAL PROBLEMS

Between 1960 and 1990, government economists approximately doubled their estimate of the inflation occurring from 1944 to 1947, thereby causing the estimated real GNP decline to increase accordingly. After taking appropriate account of price controls, which were essentially removed in 1946, we estimate that while inflation continued after the war, in a meaningful sense it was far less than what has been reported, since repressed, disguised inflation came out in the open. We estimate that prices rose about 13 percent from 1945 to 1948, a rather substantial inflation rate, but far less than observed during the war or reported by government officials (26 to 50 percent, depending on the date of the statistics).

Using our GNP price deflator, the estimated 1946 output drop was only 6.5 percent, less than that for 1945. Moreover, we estimate that output rose rather than fell in 1947. Since we calculated that the 1947 output increase almost offset the 1946 decline, we suggest that there was virtually no decline in output from 1945 to 1947, compared with the current statistical data's suggestion of a decline of 21 percent (the 1960 data revealed a fall in output of slightly over 8 percent.)

Certainly our estimates are more consistent with the written commentary of the period, which emphasized the comparative smoothness of the transition from war to peace. They are also about what one would expect if one accepts the premise that wartime inflation was understated because of price controls, and consequently postwar inflation, while real, was overstated. Our estimates would seem consistent with the 1960 Department of Commerce data modified to take account of price interventions by the federal government. Whether our estimates are correct or not, it is clear that the aggregate government statistics on output, prices, etc., must be used with extreme caution, and that data "revisions" do not always bring about improved insight into historical phenomena.

WHY THE ERROR IN THE GOVERNMENT'S REVISED STATISTICS?

As indicated above, examination of the calculation procedures used reveals that the recent estimates are a complete statistical artifact. The aggregate

GNP price deflator is the weighted sum of several component price indices, such as the personal consumption expenditures index (which, in turn, has several components), and the indices for exports, imports, government purchases of goods and services, and private investment. Numbers are indexed around a base year, currently 1982. Over time, the price index for the government purchases of goods and services has risen significantly more than for other components. For example, in 1982 it is estimated that the aggregate price of government goods and services averaged 8.13 times the 1946 level, compared with "only" a 4.55-fold increase in the price of consumer goods. Since 1982 is set equal to 100, that means that the 1946 index number for the government goods and services price deflator is 12.3 (100 divided by 8.13); the figure for the personal consumption expenditure deflator is 22.0.[19]

As reconversion proceeded, the weights used to measure consumption's contribution to the aggregate price index dramatically increased, while the weights used to measure the government purchases contribution dramatically decreased. Since the consumption index had a bigger number (22 in 1946) than the government purchases index (only 12.3), the calculated aggregate GNP deflator rose in part merely as a result of the shift from government spending to consumer spending.

The 1990 data show that the total GNP price deflator rose from 15.7 to 19.4 from 1945 to 1946, an increase of 23.6 percent. Yet the subcomponents of the index are all reported to have increased less—consumption by less than 9 percent, investment by about 15 percent, government purchases by 4 percent, etc. Only by changing the weights and by arbitrarily giving higher numbers to the nongovernment purchases component of the index does one get this type of result, which is then used with nominal GNP data in calculating equally artificial real GNP. Had prices of governmental purchases risen exactly the same as other components in the index over time, the distortion would not have been observed. In earlier years, the distortion was smaller because the disparity between the government purchases price index and the other index components was much smaller than observed now. Since then, the series have diverged more over time because of consistently faster increases in the prices of government goods and services.

As indicated above, the true postwar picture may have been even more robust than the very modest decline already indicated for 1946, to the extent that government-produced output had a value less than that indicated by government expenditures on that output. Taking this factor into account, it is easy to derive estimates that show no GNP decline in 1946 and a major upsurge by 1947. Rather than a postwar depression, we entered a boom.

ECONOMIC INTERPRETATIONS OF THE POSTWAR RECONVERSION

It was widely believed during the latter part of World War II that substantial unemployment would develop after the war. A review of forecasts by Michael Sapir confirms the fact that many economists believed that a severe recession or depression was coming.[20] That view was held by most federal officials as well; as one of the nation's foremost experts on business cycles, Robert A. Gordon, put it, "In the summer of 1945 the belief was fairly widely held in Washington that unemployment would be a serious problem during the winter of 1945–46 and a strong deflationary tendency was predicted."[21]

In part, the prediction of depression reflected the influence of the secular stagnationists, led by leading Keynesian disciple Alvin Hansen, who argued that the investment boom that had stimulated American economic growth had stalled after the closing of the frontier and the slowdown in population growth.[22] In part, it reflected a more short-term Keynesian concern with falling aggregate demand in the face of decreased government expenditures. The thought of a rapid reduction in government military spending was a nightmare for some Keynesians. In 1943, Hansen wrote: "When the war is over, the Government cannot just disband the Army, close down munitions factories, stop building ships, and remove all economic controls."[23] Yet that is precisely what the government did, although it took a year to remove most controls.

Politicians took the dire predictions of economists seriously. Speaking to the Congress a few days after the Japanese surrender, President Truman said of reconversion, "Obviously during the process there will be a great deal of inevitable unemployment."[24] Truman was concerned that a fall in purchasing power would retard recovery. In calling for an increase in the minimum wage and extended coverage, Truman said that "the existence of substandard wage levels sharply curtails the national purchasing power and narrows the markets for the products of our firms and factories."[25]

A few days earlier, the prestigious Committee for Economic Development, representing twenty-nine hundred businessmen and headed by prominent industrialist Paul G. Hoffman, chairman of the Studebaker Corporation, called for federal aid to assist the newly created jobless to move to areas where jobs were created.[26]

At the same time, however, the use of two conventional Keynesian unemployment remedies, tax cuts and public-works projects, was largely rejected. Truman did call for the passage of a Full Employment Act, but proposed little in the way of new public-works spending or tax relief to stimulate aggregate demand.[27] Indeed, prominent Republicans were more

vehement in calling for income-tax cuts than the Democrats, with the rank-
ing Republican member of the House Ways and Means Committee calling
for a 20 percent cut.[28] The *New York Times*, summarizing congressional
feelings on public-works spending, concluded:

> Only a short time ago, the tendency at the nation's capital was to think in
> terms of public works as a major factor. It now seems to be agreed that they
> should be regarded only as a part of a broad program, or as a last resort in
> an emergency, and that private enterprise must be relied upon to provide the
> large-scale employment necessary."[29]

Despite the pessimistic concerns of economists and politicians, most of
the news around the time of the Japanese surrender was upbeat with regard
to the reconversion process. Within three days of VJ Day, the *New York
Times* wrote that "reports indicate that industry is reconverting its plants
from war to peace much more quickly and early, and that reconversion
unemployment is much smaller than anticipated."[30]

This did not stop the economic forecasters from predicting massive unemployment. Indeed, the faster-than-expected discharge of soldiers led
some forecasters to revise their estimates of unemployment upward. For
example, on September 1, *Business Week* predicted that gross national product in 1946 would be 20 percent below the 1944 levels and that unemployment would peak "closer to 9,000,000 than 8,000,000."[31] The nine million
figure represented about 14 percent of the projected civilian labor force.

Businessmen and Wall Street did not listen to the economists. The Standard and Poor industrial stock index rose more than 30 percent from the fall
of 1945 to the fall of 1946. As one commentary put it, "the simple fact is
that the transition from war to peace production isn't proving too rough."[32]
As early as September 1945, *Business Week* was revising its estimate of
unemployment for the end of 1945 down to 4.0 to 4.5 million from 6.0
million.[33] A CED survey of top businessmen predicted relatively high employment levels, with the number of jobs to rise 24 percent above the 1940
level and only 12 percent below the wartime peak.[34]

Still, even in December 1945 economists were predicting that "depression is just around the corner." Robert Nathan saw six million unemployed
by the spring of 1946, implying an unemployment rate of 10 percent.[35]
Veteran Department of Labor economist Isidore Lubin decided, in *Business
Week*'s opinion, to "play it safe," predicting a wide range: six to nine million
unemployed.[36] Even the minimum estimate turned out overly pessimistic
by a factor of nearly three.

THE REVISED KEYNESIAN INTERPRETATION OF RECONVERSION

Within a year of the war's end, it was clear that the pessimistic predictions were spectacularly wrong. Accordingly, economists rushed to put a new interpretation on events consistent with the new Keynesian theology that had become deeply instilled in many of them. The postwar prosperity (they did not have the benefit of the statistics in the *1990 Economic Report of the President*) was attributed to pent-up demand. In December 1946, the first report of the newly created Council of Economic Advisers, drafted primarily by Edwin Nourse, was representative of the new interpretation: "We have a postponed consumer demand, enterpriser ambitions, and purchasing power which hold the potential of some years of great activity. . . ."[37]

The view expressed by the council quickly became enshrined in much-cited works published in this period. According to Robert A. Gordon, "Even with the decline in government spending, aggregate demand was sufficient to maintain full employment. . . . Consumption increased rapidly in the face of a decline in GNP. Here lies the main part of the answer to the mildness of the reconversion recession."[38] Alvin Hansen said much the same thing: "The country came out of the war rich in monetary assets and monetary savings and desperately short of consumers' durables, houses, business plant and equipment. This laid the ground work for a vast postwar prosperity. . . ."[39]

The Hansen-Gordon interpretation quickly found itself a part of the standard surveys of American economic history published in the 1950s and later. In the popular second edition of the textbook edited by Harold Williamson on American economic history, Harold Somers noted: "A striking aspect of the postwar economy was the failure of predictions of postwar depression made by most economists. In general, the effect of deferred demand, financed by accumulated liquid holdings, was underestimated."[40] The author of the best-selling textbook for many years, Harold Faulkner, echoed this theme, somewhat perceptively, however, giving rather more emphasis to the investment and export-demand dimensions of aggregate demand: "The 'temporary props' for this prosperity were mainly three: business expenditures for reconversion and for new construction and equipment; heavy consumer spending, much of it for commodities unobtainable during the war, and heavy export of goods and services. . . ."[41]

While modern textbook authors, perhaps bewildered by the contemporary statistics for that era, now play down the postwar reconversion experience, there still seems to be acceptance of the notion that consumers spent America into prosperity. Jonathan Hughes, who sensibly still uses the less-biased 1960 data in analyzing the period, says that "consumers now could find something to own: new cars, refrigerators, soft goods. The country went off on a well-earned spending binge."[42] We could find no textbook that explicitly rejected the Hansen-Gordon interpretation.[43]

Thus within a few years of the end of World War II, the orthodox Keynesian demand explanation for the low unemployment during the postwar transition had become conventional wisdom in the literature and in the training of more than a whole generation of economic historians. The postwar experience was cited as further evidence of the efficacy of demand-management macroeconomic policies, when in reality overwhelming empirical evidence refuted that very conclusion.[44]

ASSESSING THE KEYNESIAN INTERPRETATION

There are two empirical problems with the "pent-up demand" explanation of the postwar reconversion: timing and magnitude. It is alleged that consumption and investment spending rose dramatically to offset declining government spending, so that aggregate demand was maintained, thereby permitting essentially full employment. Table 8.4 gives data on some key economic statistics, on a quarterly basis, for the 1945–47 period. By most indicators, the economic decline associated with the postwar reconversion reached its trough no later than the first quarter of 1946. In that quarter, the civilian unemployment rate peaked, while industrial production and nominal GNP moved to their business cycle lows.

Keynesian analysis argues that changes in aggregate demand determine the level of both nominal and real economic activity. Using armed forces employment as our measure, military activity peaked in the second quarter of 1945. From that time to the trough of the mild downturn in the first quarter of 1946, government purchases of goods and services fell an extraordinary 67.5 percent, or $65.7 billion. Over the same period, consumption spending rose but $14 billion, barely 20 percent of the fall in government spending. Whatever the merits of the pent-up demand argument, there was only a modest increase in consumption during the critical period of demobilization and reconversion, to be sure in part because of capacity constraints on consumer goods industries. Investment spending rose a more robust $21.6 billion, and net exports by $9.8 billion, but collectively the increases in demand fell about $20 billion short of the decline in government spending, leading money GNP to fall a rather sharp 10 percent.

By the end of the first quarter of 1946, the process of reconversion was largely completed. Nearly seven million people had left the armed forces, and government spending had fallen well over 90 percent of the way from

TABLE 8.4
EIGHT KEY AMERICAN ECONOMIC INDICATORS, QUARTERLY DATA, 1945 TO 1947

Quarter	Money GNP ($)[a]	% Unemployment Rate[b]	Corporate Profits ($)[c]	Industrial Production[d]	Layoff Rates[e]	Average Work Week Manufacturing[f]	Government Purchases ($)[g]	Housing Starts[h]
1945								
I	217.6	1.10	10.2	123	0.67	45.4	98.6	123
II	219.2	1.17	9.6	117	1.23	44.6	97.3	156
III	210.4	2.11	6.9	98	5.57	42.0	80.2	191
IV	206.8	3.66	6.5	86	1.77	41.4	55.2	393
1946								
I	197.7	4.14	8.8	84	1.77	40.7	31.6	718
II	205.3	4.02	11.5	87	1.37	40.1	26.2	685
III	215.6	3.66	15.5	93	0.77	40.2	25.5	630
IV	220.7	4.07	18.0	96	0.90	40.5	26.9	625
1947								
I	225.1	3.81	18.4	98	0.87	40.5	24.6	702
II	229.3	4.08	17.6	98	1.17	40.2	25.4	747
III	233.6	4.06	17.6	99	0.90	40.1	25.5	912
IV	244.0	3.72	19.3	101	0.87	40.8	26.1	1,007

[a]Not seasonally adjusted, in billions.
[b]Civilian unemployment rate, seasonally adjusted.
[c]After-tax corporate profits, in billions, seasonally adjusted.
[d]Industrial production, seasonally adjusted. 1947–49=100.
[e]Layoff rates per 100 workers in manufacturing, not seasonally adjusted.
[f]Average hours of worked per week, manufacturing, not seasonally adjusted.
[g]Government purchases of goods and services, not seasonally adjusted, in billions.
[h]Housing starts, in thousands, seasonally adjusted.

Sources: Geoffrey H. Moore, ed., *Business Cycle Indicators* (Princeton: Princeton University Press for the NBER, 1961); GNP: Department of Commerce, *National Income & Product Accounts of the United States* (Washington: GPO, 1981); Government Purchases: *1949 Statistical Supplement to the Survey of Current Business* (Washington, D.C.: GPO, 1950).

the wartime peak to what would be the postwar low in 1947. Federal finances had moved from a massive deficit position (equal to 20 percent or more of GNP) to a budget surplus. Monetary policy also moved toward a much more contractionary stance, although monetary growth was still high by long-term historical standards. Bank deposits and currency grew slightly over 7 percent from the second quarter of 1945 to the first quarter of 1946, less than half the nearly 15 percent growth observed over the preceding three quarters (the third quarter of 1944 to the second quarter of 1945.) The growth in bank reserves similarly declined by about 60 percent.[45]

As the nation moved from a radically expansionary to a contractionary fiscal policy in less than a year, and as the extraordinary monetary expansion slowed markedly, did the nation witness what the Keynesian paradigm suggested would happen, and what virtually all economists predicted? No. Unemployment in the first quarter of 1946 averaged slightly over 4 percent. To be sure, that was more than the rate of less than 2 percent in early 1945. Also, even our revised national income statistics would indicate there was some output decline. Yet unemployment peaked at a low rate by historical norms, below the average of the prosperous 1920s or the 1950s. Unemployment was low, long before any pent-up demand had an opportunity to play a role. Automobile production was still depressed in early 1946, and expenditures on other major consumer goods were still well below normal peacetime levels.

The latter point is empirically verified by the ordinary least squares estimation of simple consumption functions using three data sets for other (presumably "normal") periods, then estimating what consumption should have been for the 1945–47 period assuming that the consumption-income relationships of the other periods held. Specifically, we examined annual data for 1929–41 and for 1948–70, and quarterly data for the first quarter of 1948 through the fourth quarter of 1959.

The findings are interesting:

1) All three data sets show that actual consumption did not rise above predicted levels until 1947, well after reconversion was largely over and after the labor-market adjustment was completed.

2) In 1946 consumption spending was still several billion dollars below predicted ("normal") levels by all three data sets. In that connection, in the first quarter of 1946, the personal savings rate (personal savings as a percent of disposable personal income) was still nearly 11 percent, well above historical norms.[46]

3) The quarterly data suggest that actual consumption rose above "normal" or predicted levels only in the second quarter of 1947, nearly a year after

TABLE 8.5

SELECTED CHARACTERISTICS OF THE AMERICAN LABOR FORCE, JUNE 1945 AND 1946

Labor Force Characteristic	June 1945[b]	June 1946[b]
Noninstitutional Population[a]	105,290	106,210
Total Labor Force	67,590	62,000
Total Employment	66,700	59,430
Federal Employment	15,849	5,879
Armed Forces	12,130	3,070
Civilian	3,719	2,809
Non-Federal Employment	50,851	53,551
Civilian Employment	54,570	56,360
Male	34,710	39,650
Female	19,860	16,710
Female Civilian Employment (As % of Total)	36.39	29.65
Unemployment	890	2,570
Male	460	2,010
Female	430	560
Unemployment Rate (As % of Civilian Labor Force)	1.60	4.36
Unemployment Rate (As % of Total Labor Force)	1.32	4.15
Labor Force Participation Rate (%)	64.19	58.37
Employment-Population Ratio (%)	63.35	55.96

[a]Aged 14 or over.
[b]Numbers are in thousands.
Source: 1949 Statistical Supplement—Survey of Current Business, p. 53; Monthly Labor Review, August and September, 1946.

demobilization was essentially completed, a year after real GNP had started to rise, and 19 months into a postwar labor-market experience in which the unemployment rate had never exceeded 4.2 percent.

The Postwar Reconversion and the Adjusted Real Wage Model

Turning our attention back to labor markets and the adjusted real wage model, it is interesting to compare labor-force statistics at the height of mobilization, June 1945, with statistics exactly one year later, June 1946 (see table 8.5).

The total labor pool grew by nearly 1 million over the year, yet the labor force fell by nearly 5.6 million. The end of the war was accompanied by an enormous drop in the labor force participation rate. In particular, millions of women voluntarily decided to withdraw from the labor force and reverted to their traditional roles as mothers, wives, and housekeepers. About 56 percent of the potential unemployment created by the almost 10-million-person decline in federal employment was absorbed by voluntary exit from the labor force.

The word "voluntary" in the preceding paragraph is important. It is presumed in a free society that labor voluntarily enters into labor-market decisions. Yet during World War II, millions of men were drafted and became part of the labor force; some of them might not have voluntarily been part of that labor force in the absence of conscription. The wartime unemployment rates of under 2 percent were low, at least in part, because the normal rules of noncoercive labor-market participation did not apply. Thus the postwar rise in the reported unemployment rate, modest as it was, still overstated the true recessionary conditions that existed.

Yet, the sudden reversion of labor supply to more normal levels was not the only factor in the moderate postwar unemployment. Nonfederal employment grew 2.7 million in this first postwar year, in a period before the major consumer goods industries had resumed full production. Indeed, factory employment in June 1946 was still more than 10 percent below the June 1945 levels (because of declining defense-related production), implying that the growth in nonmanufacturing, nonfederal employment was actually more than 4 million jobs. More than 27 percent of the problem that the release of 10 million government employees created was eliminated by increased civilian employment, most of it in the private sector. If defense industries are considered, demobilization from June 1945 to June 1946 meant the loss of over 11 million jobs, about 4 million of which (about 36 percent) were absorbed in the civilian economy.

Why was nonmanufacturing civilian employment soaring by over 10 percent in one year, particularly when one considers that economists were widely predicting a resumption of the Great Depression, and that the main-line durable-goods industries (which were in manufacturing in any case) were still at below-normal production? How could millions of new civilian jobs be created when there was "underconsumption" by normal standards? The answer, of course, is that adjusted real wages fell.

Directly calculating what happened to the adjusted real wage is difficult for a variety of reasons. There is no accepted data series giving hourly wages for the entire labor force before 1947. Annual earnings figures are of questionable value because of a major reduction in overtime work at the conclusion of the war. Regarding prices, the deficiencies of price indices, particularly in a period when price controls are changing, are well known. Similarly, deficiencies in price indices impact on the calculation of labor productivity.

Nonetheless, we calculated the adjusted real wage for labor in eighteen different ways, using three different measures of hourly wages, three different price indices, and two different estimates of changing labor productivity. Specifically, we used hourly earnings in manufacturing, retail trade, and contract construction for our money-wage measure; the consumer price index, wholesale price index, and GNP price deflator in calculating real wages; and real private gross domestic product per man-hour, and real private gross domestic product per unit of labor input as our measure of labor productivity.[47]

The calculations reveal that for 1946, some fourteen of eighteen estimates show a decline in the adjusted real wage from 1945 levels, with the median decline being 2.35 percent. In no case was there an estimated increase in the adjusted real wage of greater than 2 percent. Similarly, making calculations for 1947 reveals even more striking results. Some seventeen of eighteen estimates of the adjusted real wage for 1947 are below 1945 levels (the single exception showed a 0.5 percent increase), with the median estimate recording a decline of 7.15 percent. Using the median, it would appear that the adjusted real wage tended to fall some in 1946, and continued to fall in 1947, perhaps explaining the continued robust growth in employment that year.

Some dimensions of reconversion served to reduce (although not eliminate) some deleterious unemployment effects of the New Deal legislative initiatives. For example, the peacetime transition meant a fall in the average workweek, as weary wartime workers sought an increase in leisure time. With a fall in the length of the average workweek came a decline, other things equal, in money wages. Suppose a worker making one dollar per hour worked a forty-five-hour week in early 1945. Because of the Fair Labor Standards Act of 1938, the worker received $1.50 per hour for hours worked past forty, or a total of $47.50 for a forty-five-hour week, slightly over $1.05 in average hourly pay. A reduction in hours to forty, with the nominal hourly wage left unchanged, lowered the paycheck to $40 ($1.00 per hour), a decline of over 5 percent in the average hourly wage. This example was a common occurrence.

Another development, unrealized at the time, was the relative decline in the importance of labor unions in the economy. Labor-union membership as a percent of civilian employment reached a peak in 1945 and declined after the war (and has continued to decline ever since). For example, in 1945, union membership equaled 26.59 percent of the civilian labor force; in 1946, the proportion had fallen fairly noticeably, to 25.03 percent, and then to 24.58 percent in 1947.[48] The decline occurred despite a rise in the proportion of workers who were male (more inclined to unionize). The decline in the relative importance of unions reduced somewhat the pressures on wage levels that collective bargaining imposes.

At least two factors contributed to the erosion of union strength. First, the shift in employment from the relatively union-intensive manufacturing sector to the less unionized service sector was a major element. Even within manufacturing, however, the demise of the War Labor Board after late

TABLE 8.6

COMPENSATION AS A PERCENT OF GNP AND PERSONAL INCOME, 1945 TO 1947

Quarter	Employee Compensation[a]	Personal Income[a]	Money GNP[a]	Compensation As % of: Personal Income	GNP
1945					
I	122.5	174.4	222.6	70.2	55.0
II	121.6	174.2	225.0	69.8	54.0
III	117.4	170.7	213.0	68.8	55.1
IV	109.1	168.6	200.3	64.7	54.5
1946					
I	105.1	168.5	199.1	62.4	52.8
II	109.8	173.5	206.3	63.3	53.2
III	114.0	181.4	221.1	62.8	51.6
IV	116.7	183.8	224.0	63.5	52.1
1947					
I	118.5	187.8	228.2	63.1	51.9
II	119.8	187.6	233.6	63.9	51.3
III	123.1	196.6	232.4	62.6	53.0
IV	127.7	201.7	248.6	63.3	51.4

[a]In billions of dollars.
Source: 1949 Statistical Supplement, Survey of Current Business (Washington, D.C.: Government Printing Office, 1950), pp. 6,7; authors' calculations. GNP statistics differ from those used elsewhere in the book because of more recent revisions; data for 1945 are not available in those revisions.

1945 removed a pro-union form of governmental intervention. The WLB consistently promoted collective bargaining in war plants, and the end of the war brought a close to this activity.

Because of the data problems mentioned earlier in the paper, however, we have only limited faith in the estimates of falling adjusted real wages given above. Fortunately there is an alternative way of discerning the change in adjusted real wages that avoids some of the problems associated with using such measures as price indices. As noted earlier, when the same price index used in calculating real wages is utilized in determining what happened to labor productivity, the adjusted real wage is simply equal to money-wage payments divided by total output or, more appropriately, personal income.

Table 8.6 gives data on employee compensation, personal income, and gross national product by quarters. Note that the ratio of employee compensation to income or output falls after the conclusion of the war. Using labor's share of personal income, the decline is from the 69–70 percent level late in the war to about 63 percent in the 1946 and 1947 quarters. Using labor's share of GNP, the decline is from 54–55 percent in the late war (first three quarters of 1945) to 51–53 percent in the 1946 and 1947 quarters. However calculated, labor's share declined, meaning the aggregate adjusted real wage tended to fall. These findings thus are consistent with the results suggested by wage, price, and productivity data. Millions of workers were

hired by business despite an uncertain economic future, in large part because the price was right.

The fall in the adjusted real wage meant an increase in the remuneration
of capital. After-tax corporate profits, never much over $11 billion on an
annualized basis during the war, rose to about $18 billion (on an annual
basis) by the last quarter of 1946.[49]

Nominal interest rates remained extremely low, increasing the spread
between the anticipated return on invested capital and the cost of borrowed
funds. For example, the average interest yield on an Aaa (Moody's) corporate bond in 1946 was 2.53 percent, the lowest of any year since that statistic
has been kept.[50] A major factor in the low interest rates, despite a relative
tightening in monetary policy, was the government budget surplus that
developed in 1946. The federal government, in effect, moved to being a
supplier rather than a demander in the loanable funds market. Perhaps the
most massive move toward a contractionary (in a Keynesian perspective)
fiscal policy in the nation's history helped to create conditions in capital
and money markets that assisted in the transition. The postwar era was a
classic case of "reverse crowding-out." Rising profits, and the anticipation
of future increases, stimulated investment spending (the only truly robust
major component of aggregate demand).

Rising profits led to rising equity values and higher net worths. Raymond
Goldsmith estimates that the national wealth rose far more in the two years
from 1945 to 1947 (46.4 percent) than in the sixteen years from 1929 to
1945 (31.1 percent.)[51] Whereas the anticapitalist innovations of the New
Deal probably caused what was in real terms a decline in per capita national
wealth in the 1929–45 era, the modest but real retreat from interventionism
along with a fall in the adjusted real wage and the associated rise in returns
to capital led to a significant growth in wealth in the demobilization period.

An excellent case can be made, indeed, that the increase in autonomous
consumption in the postwar era reflected increased spending induced by
rising wealth. About two-thirds of the shift in autonomous consumption
from 1945 to 1947 can be explained by the $267 billion growth in national
wealth during that period, if one accepts the Ando and Modigliani view
that the marginal propensity to consume out of wealth is about .06.[52]

In short, rather than pent-up demand preventing a depression, the evidence supports a distinctly non–Keynesian interpretation: a downward adjustment in labor supply and real wages, accompanied by a less stimulative
(nondeficit) fiscal policy, served to stimulate investment and consumption
spending. Relative price adjustments brought about what Keynesians considered an increase in aggregate demand, rather than the other way around.

While the empirical evidence is strong that the postwar conversion was
not a triumph of Keynesian demand-management theory but rather a con-

firmation of the powerful workings of the market, the Keynesian revolution was nonetheless in full swing. In spite of this, Keynesian-style fiscal and labor-market activism actually declined in the early postwar years.

NOTES

1.   The Bureau of Labor Statistics, U.S. Department of Labor, began to collect monthly unemployment-rate statistics beginning in March 1940. The estimate for that month, seasonally adjusted, was 15.35 percent. The lowest unemployment rate recorded in 1940 was 12.94 percent. Sustained unemployment reduction began in November 1940, and by the end of 1941, the unemployment rate was slightly over 7 percent. See Geoffrey H. Moore, ed., *Business Cycle Indicators*, 2 vols. (Princeton, N.J.: Princeton University Press for the National Bureau of Economic Research, 1960), 2: 122.

2.   Robert Higgs, "Wartime Prosperity? A Reassessment of the U.S. Economy in the 1940s," *Journal of Economic History* 52 (1992): 41–60; Richard K. Vedder and Lowell Gallaway, "The Great Depression of 1946," *Review of Austrian Economics* 5 (1991): 3–31. We borrow extensively from our paper throughout the remainder of this chapter.

3.   This historical narrative draws heavily on Hugh Rockoff, *Drastic Measures: A History of Wage and Price Controls in the United States* (Cambridge: Cambridge University Press, 1984).

4.   Ibid., p. 87.

5.   Ibid., p. 89.

6.   Ibid., p. 92.

7.   Ibid., p. 96.

8.   John L. Lewis, president of the United Mine Workers, was one of the less obedient individuals when it came to wage and price measures. He bitterly attacked the "Hold the Line" executive order of Roosevelt. See the *New York Times*, April 10, 1943, p. 1; April 11, 1943, p. 1.

9.   Ibid., May 4, 1942, p. 1; May 19, 1942, p. 21; September 6, 1942, p. 24.

10.   Ibid., p. 100.

11.   Ibid., pp. 101–2.

12.   All statistics are from U.S. Bureau of the Census, *Historical Statistics of the United States, Colonial Times to 1957* (Washington, D.C.: Government Printing Office, 1960).

13.   Vedder and Gallaway, "The Great Depression of 1946," pp. 11–12. The increase in the relative price of government purchases of goods and services since 1945, along with the dramatic increase in the relative importance of these purchases in the wartime years, caused the statistical problem.

14.   See Milton Friedman and Anna J. Schwartz, *Monetary Trends in the United States and the United Kingdom* (Chicago: University of Chicago Press for the National Bureau of Economic Research, 1982), pp. 102–4, 107.

15.   *Historical Statistics of the United States, Colonial Times to 1957* (Washington, D.C.: Government Printing Office, 1960), series F-3.

16. *Historical Statistics of the United States, Colonial Times to 1970* (Washington, D.C.: Government Printing Office, 1975), series F-86.

17. See the *Economic Report of the President 1990* (Washington, D.C.: Government Printing Office), pp. 379, 288.

18. This is not to deny, however, that there was a fair amount of economic discontent in the period. Because of continuing price controls into 1946, there were shortages of many consumer goods; labor strife ran high, with days missed because of work stoppages reaching a new peak.

19. A numerical example, suggested by an anonymous referee, might help the reader see the point.

	1946 as Base Year		1949 as Base Year	
	Consumption Deflator	Government Deflator	Consumption Deflator	Government Deflator
1946	100	100	40	25
1947	150	200	60	50
1948	200	300	80	75
1949	250	400	100	100

If the weights of the consumption- and the government-expenditures components of the GNP deflator in this hypothetical example were 60 percent and 40 percent, respectively, in 1947, and 80 percent and 20 percent in 1948, then the deflator would have risen by 29.4 percent (from 170 to 220) between 1947 and 1948 using 1946 as the base year. If one uses 1949 as the base year, however, we would have calculated an increase of 41.1 percent (from 56 to 79) for the same period.

20. Michael Sapir's "Review of Economic Forecasts for the Transition Period," National Bureau of Economic Research, *Studies in Income and Wealth* 11 (1949): 275–351. See also Lawrence Klein's reply, "Comment", ibid., pp. 352–57. One forecaster who correctly foresaw the low postwar unemployment was W. S. Woytinsky. See his "What Was Wrong in Forecasts of Postwar Depression?" *Journal of Political Economy* 55 (1947): 142–151, 143.

21. Robert A. Gordon, *Business Fluctuations*, 2d ed. (New York: Harper and Row, 1961), p. 464. Everett Hagen's forecast, for example, predicted an unemployment rate of 14.8 percent for the first quarter of 1946. See Sapir, "Review of Economic Forecasts," p. 332.

22. Alvin Hansen, "Economic Progress and Declining Population Growth," *American Economic Review* 29 (1939): 1–15.

23. Alvin Hansen, *After the War, Full Employment* (Washington, D.C.: United States National Resources Planning Board, 1943), p. 5. For a fuller discussion of the thinking of economists in this era, see Hugh S. Norton, *The Employment Act and the Council of Economic Advisers, 1946–1976* (Columbia, S.C.: University of South Carolina Press, 1977).

24. *New York Times*, September 7, 1945, p. 16.

25. Ibid.

26. Ibid., August 28, 1945, p. 38.

27. Ibid., September 7, 1945, p. 16. The original proposed full-employment legislation, however, would have mandated countercyclical fiscal-policy measures if necessary to obtain full employment. We are indebted to our colleague and Truman scholar Alonzo Hamby for this insight.

28. Ibid., August 28, 1945, p. 1. Rep. Harold Knutson repeated his call for a 20 percent individual income tax reduction plus an end to the corporate excess profits tax in late September, to no avail.

29. Ibid., September 2, 1945, section 4, p. 10.

30. Russell Porter, ibid., September 2, 1945, section 3, p. 1.

31. *Business Week*, September 1, 1945, p. 9.

32. Ibid., September 15, 1945, p. 9.

33. Ibid., September 29, 1945, p. 9.

34. *New York Times*, September 10, 1945, p. 32.

35. *Business Week*, December 27, 1945, p. 10.

36. Ibid.

37. Council of Economic Advisers, *First Annual Report to the President* (Washington, D.C.: Government Printing Office, 1947), p. 18.

38. Gordon, *Business Fluctuations*, pp. 465, 467.

39. Alvin Hansen, *The Postwar American Economy: Performance and Problems* (New York: W. W. Norton, 1967), p. 5.

40. Harold Somers, "The Performance of the American Economy Since 1919," in *The Growth of the American Economy*, ed. Harold F. Williamson (Englewood Cliffs, N.J.: Prentice-Hall, 1954), p. 713.

41. Harold U. Faulkner, *American Economic History*, 7th ed. (New York: Harper, 1954), p. 713.

42. Jonathan Hughes, *American Economic History*, 3d ed. (Glenview, Ill.: Scott Foresman, 1990), p. 522.

43. Robert C. Puth, however, shows some skepticism with the data. Using the modern data developed in the mid-1980s, Puth says that the 1945 GNP figures "may have substantially overstated the level of economic welfare." See his *American Economic History*, 2d ed. (Chicago: Dryden Press, 1988), p. 537. We would also concede that had consumer goods been more readily available in 1946, consumption spending would have been greater, so the demand-side story could have been more factually accurate. The fact, remains, however, that high-level consumption spending did not occur, even if the public was willing for it to do so.

44. As an anonymous referee perceptively pointed out, the adoption of the pent-up demand line of defense meant a theoretical retreat for Keynesians. Previously, the view had been that increases in aggregate demand could lead to almost infinite increases in total output (implying a positively sloped aggregate supply curve at all price levels). Implicitly, Keynesians were accepting the view that consumption spending during World War II had been "crowded out" by increased government spending, and that reduced government spending after 1945 led to a reversal of this process. Of course, proponents of the Keynesian perspective never pointed out this theoretical weakness.

45.   See Milton Friedman and Anna J. Schwartz, *A Monetary History of the United States, 1867–1960* (Princeton, N.J.: Princeton University Press for the National Bureau of Economic Research, 1963), pp.717–18, 741–42.

46.   See U.S. Department of Commerce, Bureau of Economic Analysis, *The National Income & Product Accounts of the United States, 1929–76* (Washington, D.C.: Government Printing Office, 1981), p. 76.

47.   The 1975 edition of *Historical Statistics of the United States* was used in the calculations. With that source, the price distortions with respect to the GNP price deflator were modest compared with later revisions.

48.   Total membership in U.S. unions rose only 77,000 in 1946, even as nonagricultural employment grew by nearly 2.7 million workers. Ibid., pp. 126, 178.

49.   The exact profit figure depends on whether the data are seasonally adjusted, or take into account inventory evaluation adjustments, taxes, etc. See the *1949 Statistical Supplement to the Survey of Current Business* (Washington,D.C.: Government Printing Office, 1948), p. 6.

50.   *Historical Statistics of the United States,* 1975 ed., p. 1003.

51.   Ibid., p. 255.

52.   Albert Ando and Franco Modigliani, "The 'Life Cycle' Hypothesis of Savings: Aggregate Implications and Tests," *American Economic Review* 53 (1963): 55–84.

9

The Gentle Time

Subsequent to the unexpectedly easy transition from war to peace that followed the cessation of hostilities in World War II, there were three relatively brief perturbations in a sustained period of fairly high levels of economic growth and low levels of unemployment. In 1949, unemployment rose from 3.8 to 5.9 percent but fell back the next year to 5.3 percent and continued to decline to a post–World War II low of 2.9 percent in 1953. After an increase to 5.5 percent in 1954, it hovered in the low 4 percent range for the next three years and then surged to 6.8 percent in 1958. Even with these periodic swings in unemployment, the average unemployment rate for the twelve years 1947–58 was 4.4 percent. Compared to the 1930s, it was a remarkable change.

In particular, the performance of the American economy in these years almost totally destroyed the "stagnationist" arguments of the late 1930s and early 1940s.[1] The post–World War II era had not become a mere reprise of the Great Depression. Why had this happened? A commonly expressed view at the time was that the failure to return to the economic conditions of the 1930s was the product of a remaking of the American economy. For example, Alvin Hansen, described by Arthur Okun as being "generally regarded as the dean of American Keynesian economists,"[2] argued this view as early as 1957. His thesis was a simple one. The difference in the American economy, beginning with the outbreak of war in Europe in 1939, was the presence of adequate aggregate demand.[3] Furthermore, the stimulus for the provision of adequate aggregate demand had come from the Keynesian revolution. The mythology of the success of the Keynesian

176

ideas was being extended to embrace the early post–World War II period. A classic version of this argument is provided by Hansen:

> Just as the decade before the Second World War deepened the conviction that the classicals were wrong, so the last fifteen years have strengthened the conviction that Keynes was right with respect to his positive program. Governments throughout Western Europe and the United States have, on an unprecedented scale, augmented aggregate demand beyond that generated by private enterprise. And all over the free world, but especially in the United States, we have witnessed what the economy can do when it is put under pressure. Government expenditures, government borrowing, government guarantees and lending operations, government policies in the area of social security, agriculture, public power, rural electrification, securities regulation, deposit insurance, and monetary, banking, and fiscal policies have provided much of the *fuel* needed for the full use of the productive capacity created by technology and capital accumulation.[4]

This appraisal, by the man who was the intellectual interpreter of the Keynesian framework for a whole generation of graduate students in economics, carried substantial weight in the world of ideas. For many, the immediate post–World War II era was viewed as something of a Keynesian tour de force, laying to rest once and for all any doubts about the efficacy of the Keynesian system.[5] Was it, though? Or do we have here another instance of the wish being father to the thought, another case of the data being twisted and tortured to yield the Keynesian "truth"?

The National Income Account Data

Some tentative answers to these questions can be found in the national income statistics for the era. Clearly, the basic thrust of the Hansen position is that the key to the relative prosperity of the time lies in the increasing use of the instrument of government to stimulate spending. If this is the case, the national income account data should show some clear signs of increased government activity, not compared to the unusual wartime levels, of course, which have already been shown to be markedly greater than those of 1946 and 1947, but certainly compared to what was happening at the end of the 1930s. In 1939, the standard measure of the government portion of the "autonomous" expenditures that are the key to the determination of national income in the Keynesian analysis, government purchases of goods and services, stood at $13.6 billion, or 14.9 percent of the 1939 gross national product (GNP) of $91.3 billion. In 1946, in the early portion of the transition period, government purchases of goods and services represented a somewhat smaller portion of GNP, 13.2 percent ($29.1 billion out of $212.4 billion) than in 1939. Moreover, in 1947, when the transition was well underway, government purchases of goods and services amounted to $26.4 billion, which translated into 11.2 percent of the GNP of $235.2 billion. In the years following, government purchases of goods and services as a share of gross national product did not reach the 1939 level until the buildup of military spending during the Korean War years. Thus, when viewed as a share of GNP, government purchases of goods and services actually declined, which does not seem to accord with Hansen's notion that government spending was augmenting private spending to an "unprecedented" degree. In fact, in 1947, government purchases of goods and services were significantly less than the combined total of gross private domestic investment and net exports, whereas in 1939 the opposite was true.

A slightly different picture of the relative importance of government as a source of spending activity emerges if the "official" estimates of real government spending, especially the most recent versions of those statistics, are used. In 1939, for example, the most recent data indicate that government purchases of goods and services claimed 20.1 percent of GNP, instead of the 14.9 percent shown by the nominal income account information. For 1946, the government share is actually higher than in 1939, being 21.6 percent, while in 1947 it is 16.9 percent. The larger shares of government in GNP reflect data distortions similar to those discussed in chapter 8. Our preference is to regard the nominal gross national product data as providing a more accurate picture of the relative importance of government. However, even if the real estimates are employed, between 1939 and 1947 the relative importance of government in the economy declines.

Attitudes Toward Economic Policy

So much for the national income account data. What about the attitudes of the public policymakers of the period? After all, at the beginning of the years immediately following World War II, a new "mechanism" for articulating and forming national economic policy was in place. Established by the Employment Act of 1946, the Council of Economic Advisers was functioning during the postwar transition years in time for President Harry Truman to submit the first *Economic Report of the President* to the Congress of the United States in January 1947.[6] Thus, formal economic policy recommendations were being made before the full transition from war to peace had been completed.

That first report is heavily influenced by the Employment Act's injunction to create "conditions under which there will be afforded useful employment opportunities, including self-employment, for those able, willing, and seeking to work, and to promote maximum employment, production, and purchasing power."[7] The expression "purchasing power" in the language of the enabling legislation became something of a leitmotiv in the early *Economic Reports*. The following assortment of statements in the January 1947 *Economic Report* is illustrative of the interest in the purchasing power aspect of national economic affairs:

> It is . . . of the utmost importance that at all times we be concerned as to the volume of purchasing power of the Nation and its relation to the volume of production of goods and services (p. 2).

> It is plain . . . that if employment is to remain high and if production is to increase in 1947, real purchasing power must rise sufficiently to take increased production off the market (p. 10).

> Chief among the unfavorable factors is the marked decline in real purchasing power of great numbers of consumers. . . . Maximum production and employment this year would yield a substantial increase in the available supply of consumer goods and services, especially in the area of durable goods. This requires higher real purchasing power to take the goods off the market (p. 19).

References such as these bear an uncanny resemblance to much of the rhetoric of the Hoover and New Deal years. In fact, there does not seem to be much difference between the views of Herbert Hoover, Franklin Roosevelt, and Harry Truman. The similarity between the views of Truman and Roosevelt is to be expected, not that with Hoover. Yet, it seems clear that in many ways Truman's views on economic affairs were quite like those of Hoover. For example, on the relationship between wage rates for labor and general levels of economic activity, Truman was as much of an underconsumptionist as Hoover on the matter of wage reductions. In his statement to Congress days after VJ Day in 1945, Truman spoke of the need to "prevent rapid decrease of wage incomes or purchasing power."[8] In the 1947 *Economic Report*, the following statement can be found: "The relation of wages, prices and productivity is the key to the maintenance of purchasing power. . . . If prices are too high in relation to wages, they restrict the market and reduce employment, as well as causing suffering to individual consumers" (p. 2).

Herbert Hoover might have made those remarks. Henry Ford did, in 1929. What those advocates of the underconsumptionist doctrines of the

1920s did not say, though, was what lies in between the two sentences just quoted, namely: "If prices are too low in relation to wages, they squeeze or eliminate profits, stifling the initiative of business, interfering with production, and reducing or retarding employment."

That has a decidedly neoclassical ring to it. Higher real wage rates will reduce, not stimulate, unemployment. Will the real Harry Truman (or Council of Economic Advisers) please stand up? A more detailed reading of the 1947 *Economic Report* suggests that the real Harry Truman was an underconsumptionist when it came to wage policy. He truly wanted higher real wages, but in the spirit of Franklin Roosevelt in 1938, wanted to obtain them by reducing prices. Lower prices would be the key. The language of the *Economic Report* is specific: "A major approach to bringing real purchasing power of consumers into balance with productive capacity this year must be through reduced prices. . . ." (p. 11). Harry Truman was the direct heir to the high real wage doctrine that was passed from Hoover to Roosevelt and, finally, to him.

THE INTELLECTUAL VIEW

The position on the linkage between wage rates and economic activity espoused in the first *Economic Report* was echoed in the views of members of the intellectual community. By now, almost everyone had abandoned the notion of Say's Law. Aggregate demand was the key. No longer was it assumed that "supply would create its own demand." Nor was it taken for granted that there was an inherent tendency for economies to operate at a full-employment level. The Keynesian revolution was an accepted fact. By 1947, intellectuals were already reflecting on the rapidity with which Keynes's notions had carried the day. Paul Samuelson summed up this triumph by remarking: "The *General Theory* caught most economists under the age of 35 with the unexpected virulence of a disease first attacking and then decimating an isolated tribe of south sea islanders. Economists beyond fifty turned out to be quite immune to the ailment. With time, most economists in-between began to run the fever, often without knowing or admitting the condition."[9]

Wage rates had a role to play in this new emphasis on aggregate demand. Now, one often heard the argument that there were two dimensions to wages, one as a cost of production but the other as a source of purchasing power. A case in point was Abba Lerner, an intellectual giant of the era, who offered almost the exact same perception of the role of wage rates that would appear later in the first *Economic Report*: "Looking at wages as costs of production we can see that if they are too high labor will be pricing itself out of the market and so defeating the objective of full employment. But if we consider wages as the source of demand for products on the market, it seems that we would be threatened with unemployment if they are too low."[10]

Lerner, though, put more emphasis on the cost side, suggesting that wage rates be left to adjust to movements in labor productivity with government policies in areas such as taxation, social service, and transfer payments being used to ensure that total income of workers was sufficient to provide a satisfactory level of aggregate demand.

Meanwhile, the academic establishment had been hard at work refining and extending the concepts of the *General Theory*. In the process, a more imposing and arcane technical apparatus had come into being, including extensions of the multiplier concept and the addition of an accelerator principle. Moreover, throughout this burst of intellectual activity, the role of wage rates in the macroeconomy faded further and further into the background, ultimately being regarded as merely an aspect of the overall distribution of income whose macroeconomic importance was felt through their impact on the nature and character of the Keynesian consumption function.

With the turning away from wage rates and market adjustments toward the principle of aggregate demand came a general pessimism about the post–transition era prospects for the American economy. Undismayed by the failure of the Keynesian apparatus to forecast the relatively painless transition from war to peace, the intellectual community in general saw bleak times ahead. On two successive pages of the March 1947 issue of the *American Economic Review* this view was expressed. On the last page of an article by C. Reinhold Noyes, president of the National Bureau of Economic Research, is the prediction that "after a short burst of apparent rejuvenation, we will arrive at a state of slow growth," while on the first page of a piece written by Evsey Domar, there is a reference to "the widely held belief that the present inflation is a temporary phenomenon, and that once it is over, the old problem of deflation and unemployment may possibly appear before us again."[11]

In all fairness, there were economists who saw a different prospect. As early as 1946, W. S. Woytinsky painted a decidedly rosy scenario for the years ahead. In a critique of a pessimistic view of events to come in the United States that had been offered by Michael Kalecki,[12] Woytinsky argued that Kalecki's forecast of oversaving in the American economy and a consequent lack of aggregate demand by the year 1950 was inappropriate.[13] If anything, he maintained, there would be a slight abundance of aggregate demand, creating an inflationary rather than a deflationary situation. Nevertheless, the Woytinskys of the world, the optimists, were in a decided minority compared with the Domars and Kaleckis, the pessimists.

The Real World: What Happened?

Back in the real world of events, Truman's worst fears were being realized as the United States moved through the postwar transition period. After the relaxing of wage and price controls in 1946, prices and wages began to rise quite rapidly. Indices of the month-to-month movements in wages and prices between June 1946 and January 1949 are shown in table 9.1, with June 1946 set equal to 100. The wage series is hourly earnings of manufacturing workers and the price series is the consumer price index. Between the last month in which the wartime controls were in effect, June 1946, and December 1946, consumer prices rose by 15.0 percent and manufacturing hourly wages by only 5.9 percent. According to the purchasing power interpretation of the importance of wage rates, this should have had a devastating effect on the overall level of employment. However, as we already know, it did not.

Subsequent to December 1946, the rate of increase in wage rates generally exceeded that of consumer prices. Price levels continued to rise through August 1948. At that point, compared to June 1946, the real wage rate had fallen by 4.5 percent. The great inflationary episode was over. In a sense, the late summer of 1948 can be viewed as the time at which a new equilibrium set of relative commodity and factor prices had been established in the United States, prices that reflected all the structural changes that had been introduced into the American economy during the Great Depression and World War II years. Now the question would be whether this new set of relative prices could be sustained in a fashion that would consistently yield something approximating full employment. The crux of the Keynesian critique of the classicals had been that full employment could not be maintained in the long run under a classical regime. In addition, the prevailing intellectual orthodoxy of the time, grounded in the Keynesian aggregate-demand notions, was consistently forecasting that this new "equilibrium" would not generate sufficient aggregate demand to sustain full employment on a permanent basis. Thus, this would only be a temporary interlude, a brief respite from the chronic unemployment that was endemic in the American economy, unless there was substantial supplementing of aggregate demand through government spending. Kalecki's estimates implied that a government deficit amounting to more than 7 percent of GNP would be necessary by 1950 if aggregate demand were to be adequate to provide full employment.[14]

The First Test: The 1949 Recession

The test of whether this new set of equilibrium prices was capable of producing sustained full employment came quickly. Whereas commodity

TABLE 9.1

MANUFACTURING WAGE RATES AND CONSUMER PRICES: JUNE 1946–JANUARY 1949[a]

Month	1946		1947		1948		1949	
	Wage	Prices	Wage	Prices	Wage	Prices	Wage	Prices
January	—	—	107.1	115.0	118.5	126.6	127.9	128.2
February	—	—	107.9	114.9	119.1	125.7	—	—
March	—	—	108.9	117.3	119.3	125.2	—	—
April	—	—	109.4	117.2	119.6	127.0	—	—
May	—	—	111.3	117.0	120.5	127.9	—	—
June	100.0	100.0	113.1	117.9	122.0	128.8	—	—
July	100.8	105.9	113.5	118.8	123.5	130.3	—	—
August	102.6	108.1	114.0	120.3	125.0	130.9	—	—
September	103.9	109.5	115.2	122.9	126.2	130.9	—	—
October	104.2	111.5	116.1	122.9	126.6	130.2	—	—
November	105.1	114.2	117.0	123.7	127.2	129.2	—	—
December	105.9	115.0	117.9	125.3	127.5	128.6	—	—

[a]Numbers are indexed, with June 1946=100.
Source: Bureau of Labor Statistics.

price levels had peaked in August 1948, money wage rates continued to rise through January 1949. In those few months, manufacturing wage rates rose by 2.7 percent and prices fell by 2.0 percent. Almost all of the decline in real wage rates subsequent to June 1946 had been erased. If the purchasing power doctrine with respect to the role of wage rates were valid, there should have been a surge in economic activity. However, there was not. Apparently, the cost side of real wage rate increases was dominant. Commencing in the first quarter of 1949, unemployment rates began to rise.

Within the framework of the wages hypothesis, it is easy to see what happened in 1948–49. Money wage rates tend to adjust to price changes in a lagged fashion.[15] In this particular case, labor markets were anticipating a certain amount of additional price inflation that was not realized. The unanticipated deflation of the late 1948 period produced the downside effects of the temporary money illusion implicit in the lagged adjustment of money, and, by definition, real wage rates. The manner in which this process works is quite simple. When prices are falling, as they were in late 1948, there is a tendency for both money and real wage rates to reach levels that are higher than what is warranted by current levels of commodity prices and productivity, increasing the adjusted real wage rate. In turn, according to the wage hypothesis, employment will fall and unemployment will rise.

How well does the wage hypothesis perform in explaining the economic downturn that took place in early 1949? To explore this, we have estimated a very simple form of our model using quarterly data.[16] The model may then be used to predict unemployment rates for the period of the downturn. These may then be compared with the actual data to obtain some sense of how well the model performs in accounting for movements in the unemployment rate. Figure 9.1 compares the predicted and actual unemployment rates for the period beginning with the first quarter of 1949 and running through the third quarter of 1951. The correspondence between the two rates is striking. What is particularly impressive is the extent to which the adjustment mechanisms that link levels of money wages, prices, and labor productivity appear to have asserted themselves by the beginning of 1950 in a fashion that triggers a return to full employment. Between the fourth quarter of 1949 and the third quarter of 1950, the adjusted real wage rate fell by 4.5 percent.

While the evidence from the simple regression model lends substantial support to the wage hypothesis, there are alternative arguments that might be made. Of particular importance in 1950 is a possible source of substantial stimulus to aggregate demand in the form of a surge in government purchases of goods and services associated with the hostilities in Korea. However, this event can be completely discounted as a factor in triggering the

FIGURE 9.1

ACTUAL AND PREDICTED UNEMPLOYMENT RATES, UNITED STATES,
FIRST QUARTER, 1949, THROUGH THIRD QUARTER, 1953

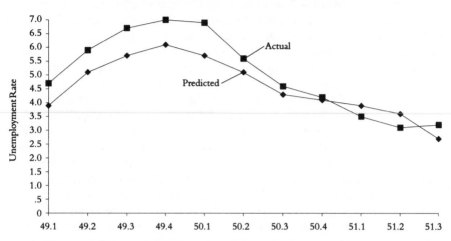

economic recovery in 1950. The unemployment rate in the fourth quarter
of 1949 averaged 7.0 percent. In the second quarter of 1950, it had already
declined to 5.6 percent. Since the North Korean incursion into South Korea
began on June 25th, any buildup of government purchases of goods and
services as the result of this military action had nothing to do with the
initial stages of the recovery. Even more telling is the fact that for the entire
year 1950, government purchases of goods and services, in nominal terms,
were slightly less than they were in 1949. The impact of Korea on the
aggregate-demand side was not felt until calendar year 1951.

There is still another possibility. Could it be that there was some form
of decisive action by the federal government that provided a stimulus to
aggregate demand sufficient to produce the observed recovery? There does
not seem to be any persuasive evidence to support such a hypothesis. A
reading of public documents does not indicate that there was any overwhelming sense of urgency associated with the economic downturn that
began in early 1949. In the midyear *Economic Report of the President*, submitted in July 1949, at least halfway through the run-up in the unemployment
rate, President Truman states, "The kind of government action that would
be called for in a serious economic emergency would not be appropriate
now."[17]

Truman's lack of a sense of emergency at this time is confirmed by the
rather pallid set of legislative recommendations he passed on to Congress
in this report. In the realm of explicit fiscal policy, he wanted to repeal the

tax on the transportation of goods, liberalize the carry-over provisions for dealing with losses by corporations, and raise estate and gift taxes. More revealing is his one clear concession to Keynesian orthodoxy, a recommendation that "no major increase in taxes should be undertaken at this time."[18] Rather than considering stimulating aggregate demand by running deficits in the federal budget, Truman was concerned primarily with developing surpluses in the budget that could be used to retire the national debt. These are not the policy recommendations of someone who has accepted the Keynesian framework for dealing with variations in economic activity.

The absence of a sense of urgency in the White House was confirmed by other observers. In an extensive study of the use of fiscal policy in the post–World War II recessions done for the Brookings Institution, Wilfred Lewis, Jr., remarked that Truman's advisers, including those from the Council of Economic Advisers and Treasury Secretary John W. Snyder, welcomed a "recession" as an antidote to the inflationary conditions that had been dominant in the postwar era.[19] More specifically, Lewis concluded that "deliberate counterrecession expenditure actions played an insignificant role in the recovery" from this recession.[20] His final assessment of this episode was simple and direct: "The administration's diagnosis that this was not the long-feared postwar depression—but only a temporary adjustment that would be brief, mild, and self-correcting without drastic federal action—proved to be essentially accurate."[21] "Self-correcting without drastic federal action" hardly fits the notion that the pattern of this economic cycle provided a confirmation of the validity of the Keynesian paradigm.[22]

The 1953–1954 Recession

While the Korean War played an insignificant role in producing the economic recovery of 1950, it made an important contribution to the onset of the next post–World War II business cycle, the 1953–54 downturn. The surge in government purchases of goods and services generated substantial inflationary pressures in the years 1951 and 1952, leading to a reprise of the pattern of events that marked 1948 and 1949. In the years 1951–52, the implicit price deflator for the business sector increased at an average annual rate of 4.3 percent. However, in 1953 and 1954 the average increase was only 1.0 percent a year. The average rates of change in the consumer price index were even more dramatically different, 5.1 percent in 1951–52 and 0.7 percent in 1953–54. Thus, once more, a significant gap opened up between anticipated and actual rates of price inflation. In this case, the result is unanticipated disinflation, which led to a rise in the adjusted real wage rate. It increased by 3.1 percent between 1952 and 1954.

FIGURE 9.2

ACTUAL AND PREDICTED UNEMPLOYMENT RATES, UNITED STATES,
FIRST QUARTER, 1953, THROUGH SECOND QUARTER, 1955

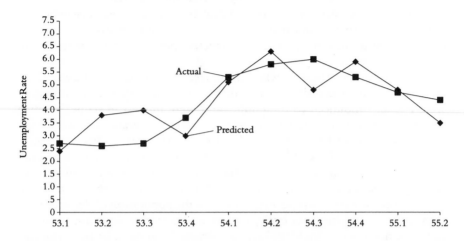

As to specifics, by late 1953, as the inflationary pressure generated by the Korean War wound down, money wage rates increased much more rapidly than prices. For the entire year 1953, average money wage rates for the economy as a whole rose by 7.1 percent, while prices moved upward at 0.9 percent a year measured by the implicit price deflator for the business sector, and 0.6 percent a year over the period December 1952 to December 1953, according to the consumer price index. Finally, the real wage rate "overhang," the gap between the actual and the equilibrium real wage, became sufficiently large to produce a rise in unemployment. In the fourth quarter of that year, the average unemployment rate rose by a full percentage point. It was another 1.6 percentage points higher in the first quarter of 1954 and by third quarter 1954 peaked at 6.0 percent, a rise of 3.3 percentage points since third quarter 1953. Our simple version of the wage-rate model accounts for this upswing in unemployment quite well. See figure 9.2 for a comparison of the actual unemployment rates, quarter by quarter, with those predicted by the model. Again, labor markets reacted to these conditions and the adjusted real wage rate began to change. In the last half of 1954 it began to back off from its mid-1954 peak. From the first half of 1954 through the first half of 1955, it fell by about 3 percent, and the unemployment rate began to decline in the latter part of 1954.

By that time, Dwight Eisenhower was president and, being the first Republican president since Herbert Hoover, was somewhat sensitive on the issue of unemployment. He did not wish to preside over a serious recession.

Nevertheless, his key advisers, especially George Humphrey, secretary of the treasury, sounded much like John Snyder. According to Robert Donovan, Humphrey felt that "a few adjustments were not to be feared. Employment could decline for six or seven months without becoming critical."[23] To be sure, within the administration there was discussion of public-works projects and from outside there were cries that disaster was upon us.[24] Still, no concerted set of corrective policy actions emerged, and as already noted, the recovery came.

In his Brookings study, Lewis summarized this episode as follows: "Discretionary counterrecession expenditure actions were slow to be initiated, were not all announced to the public, and were modest in scope."[25] Even "modest in scope" is perhaps something of an exaggeration. Lewis's own calculations revealed that the sum total of "discretionary" fiscal expenditures through the third quarter of 1954 was $300 million, less than one-tenth of one percent of GNP for that year.[26] It is extremely difficult to argue that the economic recovery that began in 1954 represented a triumph of Keynesian demand management through the application of discretionary fiscal policy. This business cycle, like its immediate predecessor, appeared to fit the description "mild and self-correcting." Far from being a vindication of the Keynesian model, it is better interpreted as being supportive of the wages hypothesis that we have advanced.

The 1958 Recession

The third business downturn of the decade was the 1958 rise in unemployment. In this case, the scenario was only slightly different. First, there was a steady escalation in the rate of price inflation after 1954. The implicit price deflator rose by 1.6 percent in 1955; by 3.3 percent in 1956; and by 3.5 percent in 1957, followed by a slowing to a 1.3 percent increase in 1958. As this happened, the rate of increase in money wage rates surged to 6.4 percent a year in both 1956 and 1957. By itself, this might not have created any problems. However, 1956 and 1957 were years of relatively low productivity gains. Beginning with 1949 and moving through 1955, the annual average increase in the productivity of labor was 4.0 percent. In 1956 it was 1.4 percent and in 1957 2.7 percent. This combination of wage, price, and productivity increases led to an upward movement in the adjusted real wage rate, increasing it by 3.9 percent over its 1955 level and triggering the 1958 recession.

Turning to the specifics of this cycle, unemployment began to edge up in late 1957, rising from 4.2 to 4.9 percent between the third and fourth quarters. Even sharper increases followed. In the first quarter of 1958,

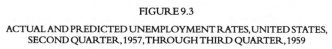

FIGURE 9.3

ACTUAL AND PREDICTED UNEMPLOYMENT RATES, UNITED STATES,
SECOND QUARTER, 1957, THROUGH THIRD QUARTER, 1959

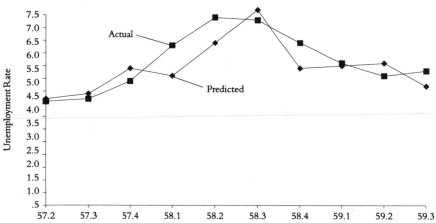

another 1.4 percentage points were added to the unemployment rate, taking it to 6.3 percent, and in the second quarter it rose to 7.4 percent. This was the peak. The third quarter was marked by a fall to 7.3 percent and by the second quarter of 1959 the unemployment rate stood at 5.1 percent. The quarterly version of our wages model tracks this cycle quite well, as is shown in figure 9.3.

What was the reaction of the economic policymakers to this downturn? As usual, recognition of it was somewhat belated and the actual debate over what, if any, policy measures to take did not become serious until the early months of 1958. The outside pressures were even greater than in the past. Arthur Burns—who perhaps should have been more understanding, having sat in on the White House debates during the previous recession—proclaimed in the *New York Times* that the recession would continue until the government intervened on a large scale.[27] Lewis summarizes the situation well: "The AFL-CIO charged the administration with seeking to tranquilize the public; the Democratic National Committee attacked Eisenhower's 'Hoover-like' approach; and former President Truman asserted that five years of Republican misrule had brought the country to the brink of depression."[28]

Within a few months, though, it was clear that the recovery was underway. Again, we can ask the question: did deliberate countercyclical fiscal policy make any contribution to this recovery? The answer is similar to that obtained with respect to the previous two business cycles, namely, that the contribution was quite small. Lewis estimated that the total volume of discretionary budget expenditures through the quarter in which the recovery began was about $400 million, once more about one-tenth of one percent of GNP.[29] Thus, this business cycle looked much like its two immediate predecessors.

What About Monetary Policy?

There is a possible criticism of our description of the role of conscious economic policy in accounting for the rather quick recoveries from business cycle downturns in the immediate post–World War II era. What about monetary policy? We have said nothing about its possible role in producing the results we have observed, largely because we think it was relatively ineffective in reducing the severity of business cycles in this period. In the early postwar years monetary decisions were subordinated to the Treasury's desire to keep interest rates low so as to reduce the cost of financing the federal government's debt. This was no longer the case after 1951, when an accord was negotiated between the Treasury and the Federal Reserve that freed the latter to engage in countercyclical monetary policy.

The accord generated optimistic expectations about the future of monetary policy, expectations that were to be unrealized. One assessment stated that "the post-Accord decade began with mounting enthusiasm for the general instruments of monetary control—the so-called 'rediscovery of money.' It ended with confidence in a predominantly monetary approach considerably shaken. The desirability of heavy reliance on fiscal methods was increasingly accepted, and sentiment for judicious resort to selective controls appeared to be mounting."[30]

Milton Friedman and Anna Schwartz shared this view. In their *Monetary History of the United States*, they provide a detailed description of how the actions of the Federal Reserve system in the 1950s following the accord probably exacerbated business cycle swings due to the lag between the initiation of monetary actions and their final effect. They conclude: "If this interpretation has any validity, it leads to the somewhat paradoxical conclusion that confidence in the efficacy of monetary policy in the 1950s was inversely related to monetary stability. As that confidence has grown, it has produced a growing instability in the stock of money."[31]

They then added a wish that would be prophetically unfulfilled: "Hopefully, the process is not explosive but self-limiting."[32]

What generalizations emerge from this experience? Apparently partly by accident, and partly due to executive indecision, the American economy was left to its own devices in responding to the economic instabilities of the immediate postwar era. Following the reestablishment of a new set of equilibrium commodity and factor prices during 1948, there was a series of relatively brief business cycle downturns, each followed by a recovery that would seem to have little relationship to the discretionary actions advocated by Keynes and his followers. Rather, the economy showed a systematic self-correcting tendency, contrary to the Keynesian wisdom. Moreover, this tendency was manifested through money-wage adjustments in the labor market.

In this respect, the immediate postwar era is rather similar to the first three decades of the century. Between 1900 and 1929 there were a number of economic ups and downs that resulted in an average unemployment rate of 4.73 percent. In the later period, 1946–59, the unemployment rate averaged 4.49 percent. Contrary to the mythology of Keynesians such as Alvin Hansen, this era does not provide a striking and powerful vindication of the Keynesian orthodoxy. Quite the opposite, it supports the notion that there are self-correcting tendencies in the American economy which, if permitted to operate, will drive it toward full-employment outcomes.[33]

NOTES

1.   Stagnationist notions were widespread in the late 1930s. In his presidential address to the American Economic Association on December 28, 1938, Alvin H. Hansen remarked that

> a full fledged recovery . . . requires a large outlay on new investment, and this awaits the development of great new industries and new techniques. But such new developments are not currently available in adequate volume. It is my growing conviction that the combined effect of the decline in population growth, together with the failure of any really important investment innovations of a magnitude sufficient to absorb large capital outlays, weighs very heavily as an explanation for the failure of the recent recovery to reach full employment.

"Economic Progress and Declining Population Growth," *American Economic Review* 29 (1939): 11. Hansen was not alone in his views. A number of other economists were espousing similar notions. One of the most precise statements of the stagnationist hypothesis came from Oskar Lange: "The events since 1929 in the United States and in other countries with an advanced industrial capitalism show that private capitalism suffers from a lack of sufficient inducements to invest which prevent it from securing full employment of the existing private resources." "Is the American Economy Contracting?" Ibid., p. 513.

2.   Arthur Okun, *The Battle Against Unemployment* (New York: W. W. Norton, 1965), p. 53. This remark is made in an editorial introduction to an excerpt from one of Hansen's writings.

3. For detailed insights into Hansen's views, see his *The American Economy* (New York: McGraw-Hill, 1957), chaps. 2 and 3.

4. Ibid., chap. 2, p. 41.

5. This idea has had substantial staying power among intellectuals. Just recently, we had the opportunity to review a book that unhesitatingly and fully accepted as established truth the Hansen view of the post–World War II era. See Herman Van der Wee, *Prosperity and Upheaval: The World Economy 1945–1980* (Berkeley: University of California Press, 1987). Our review appears as "The Keynesian Performance," *Critical Review* 3 (1989): 488–504.

6. The report was submitted on January 8, 1947. In private conversation with the authors, Truman biographer Alonzo Hamby stated that the first report was written, for the most part, by Edwin G. Nourse of the Council of Economic Advisers. Other members of the council were Leon Keyserling and John D. Clark.

7. As quoted in *Economic Report of the President* (Washington, D.C.: Government Printing Office, 1947), p. 9.

8. Harry S. Truman, *Memoirs*, vol. 1, *Years of Decision* (Garden City, N.Y.: Doubleday, 1955), p. 484.

9. Paul A. Samuelson, "The General Theory," in *The New Economics*, ed. Seymour Harris (New York: A. A. Knopf, 1947), p. 146.

10. Abba P. Lerner, "An Integrated Full Employment Policy," in *Planning and Paying for Full Employment*, ed. Abba P. Lerner and Frank D. Graham (Princeton, N. J.: Princeton University Press, 1946), p. 183.

11. C. Reinhold Noyes, "The Prospect for Economic Growth," *American Economic Review* 37 (1947): 33, and Evsey D. Domar, "Expansion and Unemployment," ibid., p. 34.

12. Michael Kalecki, "The Maintenance of Full Employment after the Transition Period," *International Labour Review* 75 (1945): 449–64.

13. W. S. Woytinsky, "The Maintenance of Full Employment After the Transition Period: Notes on Mr. Kalecki's Models," *American Economic Review* 36 (1946): 641–45.

14. Kalecki, "The Maintenance of Full Employment," pp. 449–64. Kalecki estimated GNP for the United States in 1950 to be $178 billion (in 1943 prices) and felt that as much as a $13 billion budget deficit would be required to have full employment.

15. We present a wage-adjustment function that contains lagged price and productivity terms in an appendix to our *The "Natural" Rate of Unemployment*, Staff Study, Joint Economic Committee of Congress (Washington, D.C.: Government Printing Office, 1982).

16. The regression model is a bivariate one with the unemployment rate as the dependent variable and the adjusted real wage rate as the independent variable. The data embrace the period beginning with the first quarter of 1949 and extend through the first quarter of 1961. The relationship between the adjusted real wage rate and the unemployment rate is positive and the t-statistic associated with the regression coefficient is 7.09. The coefficient itself is 0.39. Thus, a five-percentage-point shift

in the real wage is estimated, *ceteris paribus*, to produce about a two-percentage-point movement in the same direction in the unemployment rate.

17. *The Midyear Economic Report of the President* (Washington, D.C.: Government Printing Office, July 1949), p. 5.

18. Ibid., pp. 13, 14.

19. Wilfred Lewis, Jr., *Federal Fiscal Policy in the Postwar Recessions* (Washington, D.C.: The Brookings Institution, 1962), pp. 106–20.

20. Ibid., p. 124.

21. Ibid., p. 125.

22. To be fair, other explanations of a decidedly Keynesian nature have been offered to account for this business cycle. Rendigs Fels, "The U.S. Downturn of 1948," *American Economic Review* 60 (1965): 1059–76, provides a wide-ranging discussion of the literature on this subject as well as his own interpretation. Interestingly, in Fels's discussion and in the twenty-one-equation model he provides to interpret this cycle, the word "wage" never appears. At the very least, we would argue that our interpretation is superior on at least three counts: (1) It incorporates a variable that accounts for about two-thirds of the total cost of producing output, (2) Our model is applicable for all the data that we have available to analyze, and (3) The simplicity of our version conforms to the principle of Occam's razor.

23. Robert J. Donovan, "The Formation of Fiscal Policy: 1953–1954," in *The Battle Against Unemployment*, ed. Arthur Okun (New York: W. W. Norton, 1965), p. 128.

24. For example, Colin Clark, writing in the *Manchester Guardian*, forecast unemployment rates in the United States in excess of 10 percent unless the government engaged in large spending programs. Clark's forecast was reported in the *New York Times*, November 18, 1953, p. 5. Several weeks later, Senator Paul Douglas of Illinois echoed Clark's prognosis. Ibid., January 3, 1954, p. 5.

25. Lewis, *Federal Fiscal Policy*, p. 185.

26. Ibid., p. 184, table 24.

27. *New York Times*, February 16, 1958, p. 56.

28. Lewis, *Federal Fiscal Policy*, p. 206.

29. Ibid., p. 232, table 28.

30. Charles R. Whittelsey, Arthur M. Freedman, and Edward S. Herman, *Money and Banking: Analysis and Policy* (New York: Macmillan, 1963), p. 514.

31. Milton Friedman and Anna Schwartz, *A Monetary History of the United States, 1867–1960* (Princeton, N.J.: Princeton University Press for the National Bureau of Economic Research, 1963), p. 638.

32. Ibid.

33. Substantial portions of the foregoing discussion are from our "The Keynesian Performance."

10

The Camelot Years

By historical standards, things were going swimmingly. On a decade-by-decade basis, the 1950s shows one of the best records in terms of unemployment in this century. However, recall our earlier comments about the psychology of unemployment. If you are accustomed to and expect 10 percent unemployment, 5 percent seems a delight. But once you become accustomed to 5 percent, it is no longer so desirable. You begin to yearn for 4 percent, or 3 percent, or ultimately none. Besides, the Great Depression was fading in memory. No longer would its average unemployment of over 18 percent serve as a yardstick by which we would gauge the positive dimensions of the immediate post–World War II unemployment experience. From here on, the role of the Great Depression would be to serve as the ultimate justification for government action designed to reduce unemployment below the levels to which we had now become accustomed. And, since we now expected such unemployment, almost by definition it had to become unsatisfactory in the minds of those with an economic policy agenda to advocate.

By the middle to late 1950s, there were signs of an emerging tide of discontent with even the economic performance of that decade. In 1957 the dean of Keynesian economists, Alvin Hansen, while acknowledging that things had not gone too badly since the 1930s, was arguing that we could do better, if we could shed ourselves of our fears of inflation.[1] By the standards of the years to come, especially the 1970s, the inflation of the late 1950s seemed trivial. However, for a brief period, as that decade neared its close, the question of the propriety of inflation was at center stage among economists, with some arguing that a "little" inflation was not so bad and others arguing for the importance of price stability.[2]

It was also a different generation of economists. Those "youngsters" who had been under the age of thirty-five in the 1930s, and who Samuelson felt had been extremely prone to catching the Keynesian fever, were now at the height of their powers. They had known little else in their professional lifetime but the Keynesian prescription, which, by now, they had transformed into a neo-Keynesianism that recognized few limits to the possibilities of controling and manipulating a modern economy.[3] The neo-classical constraints supposedly no longer existed, and with their passing, the potential for using inflation to stimulate the economy began to acquire a certain irresistible quality for many economists.

If the outcome of a debate is judged by what happened in a policy sense, the "inflationists" scored a decisive victory. Two things account for this. First, there was the brief business cycle of 1958–61. In terms of its immediate actual impact on society, it was a truly minor event in the history of business cycles. From a longer-term perspective, though, it is arguably one of the major occurrences of this century.

The facts of this cycle are very straightforward. After the 6.8 percent average unemployment rate of 1958, there is a decline to 5.5 percent in 1959 and the usual pattern of economic recovery seemed to be underway. However, the recovery stalled in 1960, with unemployment remaining the same. Also, 1960 is a year in which labor productivity grew at only a 1.4 percent rate while money wage rates were advancing at a 4.0 percent rate. With a more normal increase in productivity, the adjusted real wage rate would have fallen, setting the stage for a resumption of the economic recovery in 1961. As it is, the adjusted real wage rate rose by 1.0 percent, generating a rise in unemployment and the recession of 1961.

The specifics of the 1958–61 period are worth describing in more detail. The recovery from the 1957–58 surge in unemployment had been somewhat spotty. By the second quarter of 1959 the unemployment rate had fallen to 5.1 percent, but in the next two quarters it rose, first to 5.3 percent and then to 5.6 percent. However, in the first quarter of 1960 it returned to the 5.1 percent level. From there, it increased steadily through the next five quarters, peaking at 7.0 percent in the second quarter of 1961. Again, the recovery from this cycle downturn was mild, with the unemployment rate returning to 5.5 percent by the second quarter of 1962. The simple form of the wage-rate model employed in the previous chapter accounts for the behavior of the unemployment rate in this period quite well, as is shown in figure 10.1. Once more, the recovery seemed to be driven by labor-market adjustments, rather than by discretionary monetary or fiscal policy. On the fiscal-policy side, for example, Lewis estimates that discre-

FIGURE 10.1

ACTUAL AND PREDICTED UNEMPLOYMENT RATES, UNITED STATES,
FIRST QUARTER, 1960, THROUGH FIRST QUARTER, 1962

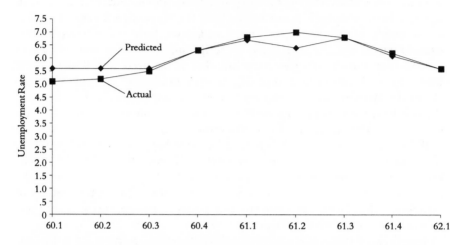

tionary budget expenditures totaled $800 million, between one- and two-tenths of one percent of Gross National Product (GNP).[4]

The brief interval encompassing 1958 through 1961 provided ammunition that the advocates of greater governmental involvement in macroeconomic affairs used effectively. Two major lines of criticism of the performance of the American economy emerged in the early 1960s: (1) a "structural change" argument, and (2) a "deficiency of aggregate demand" hypothesis. Both of these carried overtones of the stagnationist views that dominated the late 1930s and early post–World War II period.

The first of these observed that the unemployment rate at the most prosperous point of the last three business cycles had risen from 2.6 percent in the second quarter of 1953 to 3.9 percent in the first quarter of 1957, and then to 5.1 percent in the third quarter of 1959 and first quarter of 1960. From this, it was inferred that "structural" unemployment in the United States was on the increase, largely as the result of technological change imposing greater and greater demands for skilled labor.[5] This was nothing more than a restatement of the argument that technical progress is a threat to the jobs of workers, a notion that seems to have been with us since the beginning of written economics.

By contrast, the "deficiency of aggregate demand" thesis was purely Keynesian in spirit. One of its more eloquent proponents was Arthur Okun who, in a 1962 paper, presented estimates of the gap between potential and actual GNP in the United States beginning with 1953.[6] His calculations argued that, commencing with 1958, actual GNP began to deviate markedly, on the downside, from potential GNP. This is not surprising. His definition of potential GNP assumed a 4 percent unemployment rate, which he argued represented full employment at that time.[7] Since the unemployment rate had been above 4 percent ever since 1953, although only marginally in 1955, 1956, and 1957, potential GNP had to be systematically greater than actual as the decade progressed.

There was little evidence to support the technological progress version of the structural change notion and, consequently, almost by default, the "deficiency of aggregate demand" explanation for the behavior of unemployment in the late 1950s became the most cited one.[8] Not that it was necessarily correct. However, the argument of the day was couched in either-or terms. It was either structural change in the economy or a deficiency of aggregate demand that explained the observed rise in unemployment. The possibility that it was merely an aberration produced by a particular confluence of movements in wages, prices, and productivity was not entertained as a competing hypothesis. The neo-Keynesians had captured almost uncontested possession of the high ground in the policy debates that would characterize the 1960s.

Adding to the strength of their position was another development of the period, one mentioned earlier in this book—the Phillips curve concept. When Paul Samuelson and Robert Solow popularized the idea in their paper at the 1959 annual meetings of the American Economic Association, the last piece of the neo-Keynesian puzzle was put in place.[9] The Phillips curve seemed to suggest that expansionary aggregate-demand policies that were inflationary could eliminate unemployment. To be sure, some saw the Phillips curve as defining constraints. Okun, for example, stated that Samuelson and Solow "present us with a menu of policy choices that will not permit us to have our cake and eat it too."[10] This, however, was akin to looking at a glass half-filled with water and observing that the glass is half-empty. Others looked at the Phillips curve glass and saw it as being half-full. To them, it represented not a set of constraints but a set of possibilities. Now, it could be said with greater definition what was attainable and at what cost in terms of price inflation. Moreover, given the proclivity of economists to think in marginal terms, the temptation to purchase more real output, and less unemployment, at the expense of a "little more" inflation ultimately would become overwhelming. Arguments such as Hansen's had suddenly acquired a greater vitality and a certain element of precision. And, as noted earlier, any remaining notions of constraints, such as an equilibrium or "natural" rate of unemployment, were now relegated even more completely to the junk pile of discredited economic ideas.

The Phillips curve represented the final renunciation of the classical view of the role of money wage rates in the economy. Now, the relationship was perceived to be one in which the greater the rate of increase in money wage rates (and, by implication, prices), the lower the level of unemployment. Money wage rate adjustments were dismissed as far as being a mechanism through which unemployment levels are determined. Instead, they were seen as a residual effect of the tightening and loosening of labor markets in response to changing levels of aggregate demand.

The final triumph of the Keynesian revolution was at hand. All that was needed to make it possible was a sympathetic political administration, one that would act on the convictions of the mainstream economists. This vital element came with the 1960 presidential election. John F. Kennedy was receptive to Keynesian notions. Besides, much of the campaign rhetoric that had carried him, by a narrow margin, to the seat of power had focused on the economic performance of the waning years of the Eisenhower administration. John Kennedy was the answer to the prayers of the neo-Keynesians.

Kennedy's basic economic philosophy was well articulated in his first *Economic Report of the President*.[11] Invoking the experience of the Great Depression as the rationale for federal government policies oriented toward improving aggregate economic conditions, the report admitted that things were better than they were in the 1930s, but followed this with the necessary qualification that there were still problems. Specifically, the report noted that "though the postwar record is free of major depression, it is marred by four recessions."[12] Obviously, new departures would be required to rectify this shortcoming in the American economy. Finally, there was the claim that already events were moving in a desirable fashion. It was confidently stated that "the economy has regained its momentum," and that it was "responding to the Federal Government's efforts . . . 'to promote maximum employment, production, and purchasing power. . . .'"[13]

The claims of success in moving the economy forward are interesting. As to unemployment, the rate still stood at the cyclical peak of 6.9 percent in July and August of 1961, fell to 6.8 percent in September and October, and then showed the first marked decline, to 6.1 percent, in November and December. For the year, the average was 6.7 percent, just one-tenth of a percentage point less than the 1958 average. Perhaps, though, those late 1961 declines in the unemployment rate were the harbingers of better days. A certain folklore has developed about the early 1960s. This was Camelot, a warm breath of spring after the dreary late 1950s. Everything was moving forward apace. We were now substituting economic "knowledge" for myth.[14] Progress was in the air.

The reality of the Kennedy years, however, was something else. A careful examination of the 1961–63 period shows that it was almost an exact duplicate of what had occurred in the previous three years, 1958–60. In 1958, the unemployment rate rose to 6.8 percent. In 1961, it was 6.7 percent.

FIGURE 10.2

UNEMPLOYMENT RATES, UNITED STATES, 1957.4–1960.3
AND 1960.3–1963.2 BUSINESS CYCLE

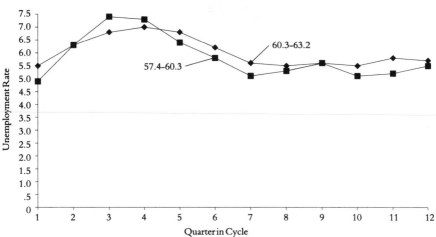

1959 and 1960 saw unemployment rates of 5.5 percent in both years. The 1962 rate was also 5.5 percent and that of 1963 was an even higher 5.7 percent. From the standpoint of the unemployment experience, it is impossible to distinguish between the two eras. This is illustrated dramatically by simply plotting the quarter-by-quarter unemployment rates for two different three-year periods, one beginning in the fourth quarter of 1957 and the other starting with the third quarter of 1960. The results of doing this are shown in figure 10.2. The two unemployment cycles match each other almost exactly.

Even the particulars of the pattern of movement in the key variables that influence the unemployment rate are almost identical, with one notable exception. Table 10.1 summarizes the year-by-year behavior of all the pertinent measures for these two periods of time. The lone significant difference between the two periods occurred in the behavior of the rate of change in the average productivity of labor in the third year, 1960 and 1963 respectively. In 1960, it rose by only 1.4 percent which, as we noted previously, led to a rise in the adjusted real wage rate and the recession of 1961. In 1963, though, it increased by 3.7 percent and, rather than increasing, the adjusted real wage rate declined by 1.1 percent, setting the stage for a continuation of the economic recovery on beyond 1963. In fact, the unemployment rate reversed itself and fell to 5.2 percent in 1964.[15]

It is also interesting to compare the cumulative unemployment performance of the American economy in the first half decade of the 1960s with

TABLE 10.1

THE MAGNITUDE OF DETERMINANTS OF UNEMPLOYMENT, 1958–60 AND 1961–63

Year in Period	% Unemployment Rate		% Change Money Wages		% Change Prices		% Change Productivity		Adjusted Real Wage	
	58–60	61–63	58–60	61–63	58–60	61–63	58–60	61–63	58–60	61–63
1	6.8	6.7	4.3	3.8	1.2	0.6	3.1	3.4	100.6	100.6
2	5.5	5.5	4.5	4.5	2.0	1.3	3.2	3.7	99.8	100.1
3	5.5	5.7	4.0	3.8	1.6	1.1	1.4	3.7	100.8	99.0

Source: Authors' calculations from U.S. Department of Labor data.

that for the latter half of the 1950s. In the first five years of the 1960s, the unemployment rate averaged 5.7 percent. In the last five years of the 1950s, the average was 5.0 percent. The "golden age" began somewhat inauspiciously.

While the behavior of the American economy in the Kennedy years was not notably different from that in the preceding period, the goals of the new administration were ambitious. That first *Economic Report* confidently remarks: "In the existing economic circumstances, an unemployment rate of about 4 percent is a reasonable and prudent full employment target for stabilization policy. If we move firmly to reduce the impact of structural unemployment, we will be able to move the unemployment target steadily from 4 percent to successively lower rates." It continues: "The recent history of the U.S. economy contains no evidence that labor and commodity markets are in general excessively 'tight' at 4 percent unemployment."[16] The latter comment was to allay any fears of overheating the economy through stabilization policy. Faith abounded. Two pages later in the *Economic Report* the goal of 4 percent unemployment was described as a "modest" one.

Confirming the belief of the time, Okun's estimates of the gap between potential and actual output were reported and there was talk of a "full utilization" economy in 1963, i.e., a 4 percent rate of unemployment. Of course, as we already know, the reality was far from the hope. Unemployment was much closer to the 6 percent level. In short, the optimistic expectations of the first Kennedy *Economic Report* were not realized. However, to a very real extent, the rhetoric of the time transcended the previous concern about dealing with the phenomena of business cycles once they occurred. More and more, the emphasis seemed to be shifting toward producing a "cycle-proof" economy, one that moved steadily along its full-employment growth path.

Subsequent to 1963, dramatic changes occurred. To begin, a major cut in income taxes was enacted. Proposed under President Kennedy and enacted in the early months of Lyndon Johnson's administration, the cut was based on the theory that it would provide a classic Keynesian-style stimulus to aggregate demand by encouraging consumption spending. While the marginal-rate reductions proposed were significant, with the top rate falling from 91 to 70 percent, while the lowest rate declined from 20 to 14 percent, the actual revenue impact of the tax cut was relatively small, amounting to a 5.4 percent decrease in federal taxes as a percent of GNP between 1963 and 1965. Based on statistical estimates of consumption functions, the maximum stimulus to consumption occurred in 1965 and amounted to an additional $1.3 billion of consumption spending.[17] By itself, this could hardly be the basis for a powerful economic recovery. That the tax cut had

TABLE 10.2

RATE OF CHANGE IN THE MONETARY BASE IN THE U.S., 1961–70

Year	% Rate of Change in Monetary Base
1961	1.7
1962	3.0
1963	4.2
1964	5.0
1965	5.3
1966	4.6
1967	5.4
1968	7.1
1969	5.5
1970	5.4

Source: Board of Governors of the Federal Reserve System.

a powerful fiscal stimulus from the aggregate-demand side seems especially doubtful when the overall nature of the federal budget is considered. In 1963 the federal government ran a $4.8 billion deficit in its budget. In 1964 the deficit was only $1.1 billion higher and in 1965 it fell to $1.4 billion.[18] However, it could have had substantial supply-side effects. Arguments for the tax cut were made at this time that have a distinct supply-side flavor. For example, President Kennedy himself, in a public speech, made the following statement:

> Our true choice is not between tax reduction, on the one hand, and the avoidance of large federal deficits on the other. It is increasingly clear that, no matter what party is in power, as long as our national security needs keep rising, an economy hampered by restrictive tax rates will never produce enough revenue to balance the budget—just as it will never produce enough jobs or enough profits. In short, it is a paradoxical truth that tax rates are too high today and tax revenues too low—and the soundest way to raise government revenues in the long run is to cut rates now.[19]

There is support for the argument that there were supply-side effects associated with this tax cut. The evidence for the post–World War II era indicates that the aggregate level of taxation is negatively related to the productivity of labor.[20] Very simply, the reduction in the degree of taxation that occurred in the mid-1960s fostered increases in the average productivity of labor. At the peak of the impact of the tax reduction, in 1965, it had the effect of increasing GNP by 0.4 percent, solely through the impact on labor productivity.[21] Again, by itself, this would not have produced a strong surge in economic activity. However, the cumulative effects of small changes operating in the same direction can be powerful.

Even more substantial events were occurring in the realm of monetary policy. Beginning in 1962, the rate of growth in the monetary base, sometimes called "high-powered" money, began to accelerate. Table 10.2 details the rate of change in this measure from 1961 through 1970. In 1961, the growth in the monetary base was 1.7 percent over the previous year. In 1962, it was 3.0 percent. 1963, 1964, and 1965 show respective rates of growth of 4.2, 5.0, and 5.3 percent.

The significance of the increase in the rate of growth in the monetary base lies in its impact on prices in the economy. Other things equal, a 1 percent increase in the monetary base is associated with a 1 percent increase in the implicit price deflator for GNP.[22] If nothing else had changed, the escalation in the monetary base would have produced a price explosion. However, other things did not remain the same. Largely as a result of increases in labor productivity that averaged 3.7 percent a year for 1962–65, the real output of goods and services was growing rapidly. And, again, other things equal, every percentage point of growth in real GNP tends to reduce the rate of growth in the GNP deflator by 0.6 percentage points.[23] Since the average rate of growth in real GNP for 1962–65 was 5.8 percent, the rate of growth in the deflator was held to an average of 1.5 percent a year. However, by 1965, it had climbed to 2.3 percent.

The 1962–65 interval is characterized by a subtle form of "money illusion" in labor markets. Ordinarily, we think of money illusion as occurring when money wage rates do not move along with variations in the price level. However, it also may be present when money wage rate changes do not accurately reflect movements in the average productivity of labor. In general, the money wage rate adjustment mechanism captures productivity changes in only a partial fashion in the short run. As we have already pointed out, labor productivity increased at an average of 3.7 percent a year and the implicit price deflator by 1.5 percent a year. Money wage rates, though, rose by only 4.4 percent a year, 0.8 percentage points less than the sum of the increments in prices and productivity. Table 10.3 provides details of these movements for the years in question.

The failure of money wage rates to advance as rapidly as prices and productivity in combination produced a significant fall in the adjusted real wage rate. It stood at 100.8 (1977 = 100) in 1961 but had declined to 97.4 by 1965. Accompanying this drop was a downward movement in the unemployment rate to 4.5 percent. Not surprisingly, a further fall in unemployment, to 3.8 percent, occurred in 1966. The secret of beating down the unemployment rate to below 4 percent by the mid-1960s lay in workers' real wage rates not advancing as rapidly as the average productivity of labor. In the process, the corporate profit share of national income increased from 11.7 to 13.5 percent between 1961 and 1966.[24] As business profits rose, employment expanded and unemployment fell.

In a world of lagged labor-market adjustments, money illusion is a temporary phenomenon. After 1965, the rate of change in money wage rates

TABLE 10.3

UNEMPLOYMENT AND CHANGES IN MONEY WAGE RATES, PRODUCTIVITY, AND THE
GNP PRICE DEFLATOR, U.S., 1962–1970

| | | Rate of Change in | | |
Year	% Unemployment Rate	% Money Wage Rates	% Productivity	% GNP Deflator
1962	5.5	4.7	3.6	1.9
1963	5.7	3.8	4.0	0.9
1964	5.2	5.2	4.3	1.0
1965	4.5	3.8	3.0	2.3
1966	3.8	6.9	2.8	3.3
1967	3.8	5.4	2.7	2.5
1968	3.6	7.9	2.7	4.6
1969	3.5	7.0	0.1	5.1
1970	4.9	7.3	0.7	4.7

Source: Bureau of Labor Statistics.

began to escalate. Over the next four years, it would average 6.8 percent. Combined with a slowing in the average rate of growth in labor productivity to 2.2 percent a year, this should have led to a significant rise in the adjusted real wage rate. This did not occur until 1969, however. The inflationary pressure implicit in the higher rates of growth in the monetary base now began to surface and the average rate of increase in the GNP deflator was 3.7 percent, with a peak of 4.8 percent in 1969. Again, detailed movements in the pertinent statistics are provided for the individual years in table 10.3.

The quarter-by-quarter pattern of events for the period beginning with the first quarter of 1963 and running through the first quarter of 1969 is explained quite well by the simple bivariate version of the adjusted real wage model. Figure 10.3 compares the unemployment rates estimated from the model with the actual rates for this twenty-five-quarter period. The correspondence between the predicted and actual rates of unemployment is quite close.

Beginning with 1969, though, there was a sharp change in the pattern of events. Productivity gains were minimal, 0.1 percent, and money wages rose by 7.0 percent. Despite the 5.1 percent increase in prices, the adjusted real wage rate rose by 1.8 percent. The story was repeated in 1970. Productivity increased by 0.7 percent, prices rose by only 4.7 percent, and money wages climbed at a 7.3 percent pace. The adjusted real wage rate moved upward another 1.9 percent. One year later, the unemployment rate stood at 5.9 percent. The heady days of Camelot were over.

While it had lasted, it had been a fascinating experience. Inflation had become the key. Beguiled by the concept of the Phillips curve, economic policymakers had been willing to pursue courses of action that produced

FIGURE 10.3

ACTUAL AND PREDICTED UNEMPLOYMENT RATES, UNITED STATES,
FIRST QUARTER, 1963, THROUGH FIRST QUARTER, 1969

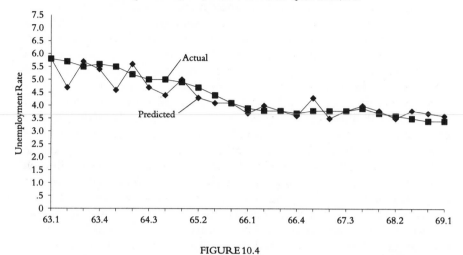

FIGURE 10.4

RATES OF INFLATION AND UNEMPLOYMENT, UNITED STATES, 1961-1969
AND SAMUELSON-SOLOW VERSION OF PHILLIPS CURVE RELATIONSHIP

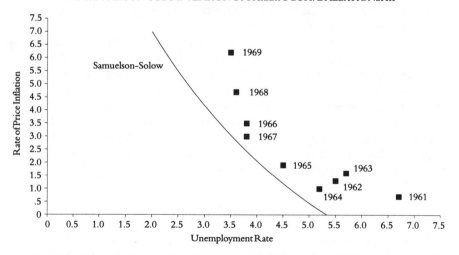

greater and greater rates of price inflation in an attempt to "buy" a little less unemployment. For a while it had seemed to work. Figure 10.4 portrays the behavior of the rates of price inflation and unemployment for the years 1961–69. If ever there were a Phillips curve, this would seem to be one—not quite that portrayed in the Samuelson-Solow article, but close. For purposes of comparison, their version is also shown in figure 10.4. Of course, the critical dimension of the Phillips curve is whether a relationship like that shown in figure 10.4 is stable. If it is, perhaps the Hansen-type argument that a little inflation can be a good thing has validity. After all, the output gains implied in lower rates of unemployment are "real" while the price movements are purely nominal in character. If a steady rate of price inflation in the 4.5 to 5.0 percent range will yield a permanent 3.5 percent unemployment rate while price stability gives a significantly higher rate, why not? Maybe there is such a thing as a free lunch, after all.

As we know by now, the flaw in this argument is that the existence of the apparent Phillips curve depicted in figure 10.4 depends on the presence of some degree of money illusion in labor markets. If that money illusion is permanent in character, the Phillips curve relationship has the potential of being stable. However, empirical evidence tells us that money illusion in labor markets is only temporary in character. Markets adjust over the longer run and the money-wage adjustment to rising price levels becomes almost complete with a very short lag. This means that any steady rate of price inflation will quite quickly produce the neoclassical equilibrium unemployment rate in labor markets. In order to maintain an unemployment rate that is less than the equilibrium one, it is necessary steadily to escalate the rate of price inflation.[25] Labor markets must be "surprised" by unanticipated price inflation if the adjusted real wage rate is to be kept below its equilibrium level.

The difficulties associated with accomplishing this feat are no better illustrated than by the experience of the 1960s. What began, with great expectations, as a magnificent experiment in applying the neo-Keynesian mode of analysis to the formulation of economic stabilization policy ended as a disturbing testimonial to the inadequacies of that theoretical paradigm. More than that, it left behind a legacy that defined the macroeconomic policy-making role of the central government in much more limited terms, a fact that becomes all the more obvious when the unemployment experience of the decade of the 1970s is considered.

NOTES

1.   Alvin H. Hansen, "The Case for High Pressure Economics," in *The Battle Against Unemployment*, ed. Arthur Okun (New York: W. W. Norton, 1965), pp. 53–64.

2.   For the other side of the argument, see Arthur F. Burns, "Monetary Policy and the Threat of Inflation," an address to the Fourteenth American Assembly, October 18, 1958, reprinted in *United States Monetary Policy*, ed. Neil H. Jacoby, 1st ed. (New York: The American Assembly, Columbia University, 1958), pp.

207–18, and Henry C. Wallich, "Postwar United States Monetary Policy Appraised," ibid, pp. 91–117.

3.   Perhaps the quintessential statement of neo-Keynesianism is the Paul Samuelson and Robert Solow paper on the Phillips curve. It completes the total reversal of the classical form of the relationship between wages and unemployment. See their "The Analytics of Anti-Inflationary Policy," *American Economic Review* 50 (1960): 177–194. Add to this Samuelson's views on government budget deficits, expressed in his 1962 Wicksell lectures in Sweden, and you have the full neo-Keynesian view. See "Functional Fiscal Policy for the 1960s," in Paul A. Samuelson, *Stability and Growth in the American Economy* (Stockholm: The Wicksell Lecture Society, 1963), pp. 23–60.

4.   Wilfred Lewis, Jr., *Federal Fiscal Policy in the Postwar Recessions* (Washington, D.C.: The Brookings Institution, 1962), p. 270, table 30.

5.   Probably the leading exponent of the "structural change" hypothesis was Charles Killingsworth. See his testimony in *The Nation's Manpower Revolution*, Subcommittee on Employment and Manpower of the Committee on Labor and Public Welfare, United States Senate, *Hearings*, part 5, 88th Congress, 1st session (Washington, D.C.: Government Printing Office, 1965), pp. 1461–83.

6.   Arthur Okun, "Potential GNP: Its Measurement and Significance," *Proceedings, Business and Economics Section, American Statistical Association*, 1962, pp. 98–104.

7.   In an address before the American Bankers Association Symposium on Unemployment in February 1964, Albert Rees argued for the 4 percent unemployment goal. This address is reprinted as "Dimensions of the Unemployment Problem," in *The Battle Against Unemployment*, ed. Arthur Okun (New York: W. W. Norton, 1965), pp. 23–31.

8.   For evidence that contradicts the "structural change" hypothesis, see the analysis of Edward Kalachek, reported in *Higher Unemployment Rates, 1957–1960: Structural Transformation or Inadequate Demand*, study for the Subcommittee on Economic Statistics of the Joint Economic Committee of the Congress (Washington, D.C.: Government Printing Office, 1961), and Lowell E. Gallaway, "Labor Mobility, Resource Allocation, and Structural Unemployment," *American Economic Review* 53 (1963): 694–716.

9.   The basic Phillips curve citations are A. W. Phillips, "The Relation Between Unemployment and the Rate of Change in Money Wage Rates in the United Kingdom, 1862–1957," *Economica* 25 (1958): 283–99; Richard G. Lipsey, "The Relation Between Unemployment and the Rate of Change in Money Wage Rates in the United Kingdom, 1862–1957: A Further Analysis," ibid., 27 (1960): 1–31; and Samuelson and Solow, "The Analytics of Anti-Inflationary Policy."

10.   Okun, *The Battle Against Unemployment*, p. xi.

11.   *Economic Report of the President*, transmitted to the Congress January 1962 (Washington, D.C.: Government Printing Office, 1962).

12.   Ibid., p. 4.

13.   Ibid., p. 3.

14.   For a sense of the political (and academic) attitudes of the time, see John F. Kennedy, "Mythology and Economic Knowledge," in Okun, *The Battle Against*

Unemployment, pp. 1–5. This selection is from Kennedy's commencement address at Yale University on June 11, 1962.

15.   The quarterly values of the adjusted real wage rate follow this same pattern. In the first eight quarters of the two three-year periods for which unemployment rates are shown in figure 10.2, the adjusted real wage rates move in virtual unison (simple correlation of 0.95). It is only in the last four quarters of these periods that any divergence appears. The higher rate of productivity growth in the second period begins to move the adjusted real wage rate downward and sets the stage for the prolonged recovery that marks the remainder of the decade.

16.   *Economic Report of the President*, 1962, p. 46.

17.   These estimates are calculated from the consumption functions previously employed to evaluate the pent-up consumer demand explanation of the unexpected ease of the transition from war to peace following World War II. See chapter 8.

18.   Data from the Department of the Treasury, Office of Management and Budget, as reported in various issues of the *Economic Report of the President*.

19.   Speech to the Economic Club of New York, December 14, 1962.

20.   See our *Poverty, Income Distribution, the Family and Public Policy*, study for the Subcommittee on Trade, Productivity, and Economic Growth, Joint Economic Committee of Congress (Washington, D.C.: Government Printing Office, 1986), p. 99.

21.   This is based on the authors' calculations using the regression model reported ibid.

22.   This calculation is based on David Klingaman and Rajindar Koshal, "A Model of United States Inflation," *Atlantic Economic Journal* 10 (1982): 100.

23.   Ibid.

24.   These estimates are based on the national income accounts data reported by the Department of Commerce, Bureau of Economic Analysis, in various issues of the *Economic Report of the President*.

25.   This argument is articulated in a prescient fashion by Milton Friedman, "The Role of Monetary Policy," *American Economic Review* 58 (1968): 1–17.

11

"Pride Goeth Before a Fall"

There is often a peculiar irony in human affairs. Just as it seems that we have acquired mastery over our fate, we find that we have miscalculated. The 1960s was the decade in which the business cycle was to be dispatched ceremonially to the realm of historical curiosity. With our present knowledge, we know that this was not to be. However, that is an account of events that has the benefit of hindsight. After the fact, it may be clear why the great promises of the 1960s were not to be realized. At the time, though, things seemed otherwise to most economists.

Consider the following thought experiment. It is 1969. Assume that you know in advance what the rate of price inflation will be, year by year, throughout the decade of the 1970s. This is all the advance information at your disposal. You are then asked to predict what unemployment rates will occur in the coming years. What will your answer be?

A very reasonable approach to responding to that question would seem to involve an assessment of the current theoretical notions concerning the relationship between inflation and unemployment and a review of the historical experience in this respect, especially the most recent events. The dominant theory of the time, neo-Keynesianism, is consistent with the notion of a stable Phillips curve relationship. Further, the behavior of unemployment and inflation rates in the period 1961–69 is highly consistent with that theoretical framework. This being the case, why not invoke the empirical evidence of 1961–69 and use it to predict unemployment rates for the 1970s?

TABLE 11.1

ACTUAL AND PREDICTED UNEMPLOYMENT RATES FOR THE U.S. 1970 TO 1979

		Predicted Unemployment:			Forecasting Error:		
Year	Actual Unemployment (%)	Keynesian Model(%)	Neoclassical Model: (%) #1	#2	Keynesian Model (%)	Neoclassical: (%) #1	#2
1970	4.9	3.4	5.4	4.8	-1.5	+0.5	-0.1
1971	5.9	3.3	5.3	5.4	-2.6	-0.6	-0.5
1972	5.6	3.8	5.2	6.6	-1.8	-0.4	+1.0
1973	4.9	3.0	5.1	4.7	-1.9	+0.2	-0.2
1974	5.6	2.2	6.3	5.7	-3.4	+0.7	+0.1
1975	8.5	2.2	5.1	6.4	-6.3	-3.4	-2.1
1976	7.7	3.3	5.3	9.6	-4.4	-2.4	+1.9
1977	7.1	3.0	5.0	7.2	-4.1	-2.1	+0.1
1978	6.1	2.6	5.3	7.8	-3.5	-0.8	+1.7
1979	5.8	2.3	6.0	4.8	-3.5	+0.2	-1.0

Source: Authors' Calculations.

What would have been the results of doing this? Table 11.1 contains a set of estimates of what unemployment would have been for the 1970s if the Phillips curve relationship characteristic of the interval 1961–69 had remained in operation. The maximum unemployment rate under these conditions is 3.8 percent in 1972 and the minimum is 2.2 percent in both 1974 and 1975. When these rates are compared with the actual behavior of the unemployment rate, it becomes clear that there is a pronounced underprediction of unemployment rates, with the worst being in 1975. In that year, the predicted rate is 2.2 percent and the actual rate is 8.5 percent, a difference of 6.3 percentage points. For the entire decade, the Phillips curve–style predictive mechanism yields an expected unemployment rate that averages 2.9 percent. The observed rate averaged 6.2 percent.

Of course, it might be argued that this was an unusual period; that the emergence of the cartel of the Organization of Petroleum Exporting Countries (OPEC) was sufficient to produce a supply shock that shifted the Phillips curve to the right from the position it held during the 1960s. However, the escalation of oil prices is largely confined to the middle of the decade. Between 1970 and 1973, the price of a million BTUs' worth of crude oil rose by 3.9 percent (actually falling relative to prices generally) and between 1975 and 1978 it fell by 3.5 percent. The rise in oil prices between 1973 and 1975 was 64.4 percent, certainly a possible source of an increase in the rate of price inflation in that era.[1] But why would the movement to a new price level at this point in time impart an upward bias to the rate of inflation for the next several years? That requires substantial lags in price adjustments to the oil shock. Besides, the Phillips curve model was systematically underpredicting the unemployment rate well before there was any pronounced surge in oil prices. The oil-price shock does not seem to be a promising explanation for the failure of the Phillips curve model to accurately predict unemployment rates in the 1970s.

Let us now conduct a second thought experiment. Assume that in addition to knowing in advance the behavior of price levels, you also know the behavior of money wage rates and the average productivity of labor over the ensuing decade. Also, you are constrained to using the parameters of the neoclassical labor-market-oriented model for explaining unemployment that has been advanced throughout this book, an approach that in 1969 is regarded as totally discredited by nearly everyone. What will the unemployment predictions for the 1970s be? We calculated the neoclassical predictions first using a simple model with single-year lags, confining our analysis to data for the period 1947–69. We then used the more complex multilagged model introduced in chapter 3, based on data for the period 1900–1989.

As Table 11.1 indicates, for either version of the model, the neoclassical approach is substantially superior to the Phillips curve method in predicting the unemployment rate. Turning to the first version, for the initial five years of the decade, the neoclassical prediction is generally quite close to the true rate, missing by at most 1.0 percentage points. On average, the absolute value of the error in the neoclassical prediction is 0.5 percentage points per year. In the interval 1975–79, the absolute value of the prediction error is larger, averaging about 1.8 percentage points per year. In particular, there is an underprediction of the unemployment rate in the years 1975 through 1977. But, by the end of the decade, 1979, the predicted rate, 6.0 percent, is very close to the actual rate of 5.8 percent. By comparison, in that same period, the Keynesian model errs, on average, by 4.4 percentage points and predicts an unemployment rate for 1979 of 2.3 percent.

Using the second, more complex version of the model, the neoclassical approach performs even better. In the first half of the decade, the mean absolute forecasting error is a very small 0.4 percentage points, rising to 1.4 points in the last half of the decade. In the worst year relative to the Keynesian model, the complex neoclassical model's forecasting error is 44 percent less than than of the Keynesian model.

Returning to the first version of the neoclassical model and looking at the entire decade, it predicts an average unemployment rate of 5.4 percent, less than one percentage point below the true average. Figure 11.1 illustrates the differences in the results of these two thought experiments even more strikingly.

The neoclassical model does an even better job of accounting for the behavior of unemployment in the 1970s when the data observations from that period are included for purposes of making statistical estimates. Using the second version of the neoclassical model, the predicted values for unem-

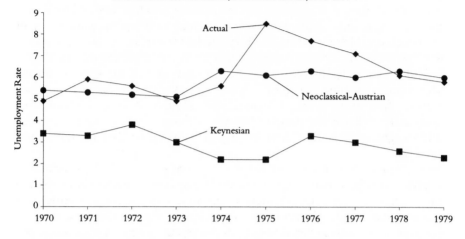

FIGURE 11.1

COMPARISON OF ACTUAL UNEMPLOYMENT RATE WITH UNEMPLOYMENT
RATE FORECAST BY NEOCLASSICAL-AUSTRIAN AND
KEYNESIAN PARADIGMS, UNITED STATES, 1970-1979

ployment for the years 1970–79 that result from a multiple regression equation that employs data from the entire twentieth century, including
1970–79, are quite close to the actual and, over the entire decade, average
6.3 percent, compared to the actual average of 6.2 percent.

The 1970s in Detail

As described in the previous chapter, unemployment began to increase in
1970, rising to 4.9 percent in that year and to 5.9 percent in 1971 as a result
of the adjusted real wage rate increasing by about 3 percent between 1967
and 1970. The upward movement in adjusted real wages was reversed in
1971. Prices rose by 4.4 percent and the average productivity of labor
increased by 3.2 percent. Meanwhile, money wage rates rose by only 6.5
percent.

If we turn from the annual to the quarterly data, the impact of movements in wages, prices, and productivity on levels of unemployment are
described quite well by the simple bivariate quarterly model relating movements in the adjusted real wage rate to the unemployment rate. Figure 11.2

FIGURE 11.2

ACTUAL AND PREDICTED UNEMPLOYMENT RATES, UNITED STATES,
FIRST QUARTER, 1970, THROUGH THIRD QUARTER, 1973

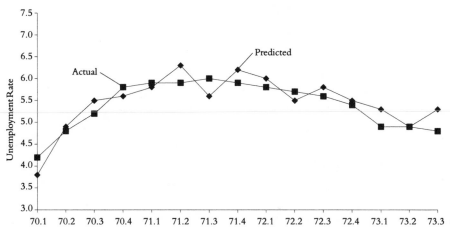

compares the quarterly unemployment rates predicted by that model with the actual rates. Again, the correspondence is dramatic. The cycle peaks in the third quarter of 1971 and by mid-1973 recovery has been achieved. For the full calendar year 1973, the unemployment rate averages 4.9 percent, its 1970 level.

After 1973, unemployment never regained that level, the closest being in 1979, when it averaged 5.8 percent. This is an intriguing development, given that the average rate of price inflation, as measured by the implicit GNP price deflator, was 7.4 percent per year for the seven years 1973–79. Moreover, unemployment averaged 6.8 percent for the years 1974–1979. This is the era that led to the coining of the term "stagflation," which is more of a descriptive term than an explanation for this emerging phenomenon.

"Stagflation" described a state of affairs in which, despite persistent price inflation, the unemployment rate remained at levels substantially greater than those occurring in the mid-1960s. Of course, such a concept absolutely contradicts the predictions of neo-Keynesian macroeconomic thinking. Interestingly, though, the events of this period are thoroughly compatible with a neoclassical labor-market conception of economic affairs. This is demonstrated quite convincingly by once more comparing the actual unemployment rate, quarter by quarter, with the predicted values for the unemployment rate derived from our simple quarterly adjusted real wage rate model of unemployment. This is done in figure 11.3 for the period

FIGURE 11.3

ACTUAL AND PREDICTED UNEMPLOYMENT RATES, UNITED STATES,
FOURTH QUARTER, 1973, THROUGH SECOND QUARTER, 1979

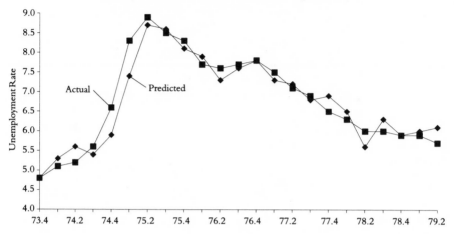

beginning in the fourth quarter of 1973 and running through the second quarter of 1979.

What happened here? Why did the phenomenon of stagflation emerge at this time? There was a quickening of the pace of money wage rate increases as inflationary expectations became pervasive in the economy. Ordinarily, increases in unemployment produce a marked slowing of the rate of increase in money wage rates, but not in the 1970s. Between 1969 and 1973, money wage rates advanced at an average of 7.1 percent a year, with a minimum of 6.5 percent in 1971 and a maximum of 8.0 percent in 1973.

The steady escalation of the rate of price inflation during the 1960s was now being reflected in the labor market in the form of pronounced inflationary expectations. All through the 1970s, the rate of increase in money wage rates showed a general upward trend until, as we enter the 1980s, it exceeded 10 percent.

Even more important, though, is the fact that the rate of change in money wage rates began to diverge rather systematically from the sum of the rates of change in productivity and prices. Table 11.2 shows the pertinent data for the 1960–69, 1969–73, and 1973–79 business cycles, measuring from peak to peak. In the first of these cycles, the average rate of change in money wage rates was 5.3 percent a year, exactly equal to the sum of the average yearly rates of change in prices and productivity. However, in the 1969–73 cycle, the rate of change in money wage rates exceeded the sum of the rates of change in prices and productivity by 0.2 percentage

TABLE 11.2

CHANGING WAGES, PRICES AND PRODUCTIVITY, U.S., 1960–79

Time Period	Mean Annual Rate of Change in:	
	Money Wage Rates (%)	Prices Plus Productivity (%)
1960–1969	5.3	5.3
1969–1973	7.1	6.9
1973–1979	9.0	8.6

Source: Authors' calculations from U.S. Department of Labor data.

points a year. Between 1973 and 1979, that disparity widened to 0.4 percentage points a year. This suggests an upward drift in the equilibrium real wage rate and possibly a corresponding increase in the equilibrium, or natural, rate of unemployment.[2]

What might have been the root cause of this change? A possible explanation for the rise in the equilibrium wage rate was a shift in workers' labor-supply responses. A number of factors were at work that could alter these responses in a fashion that would affect the intensity of workers' job search efforts, once they became unemployed, as well as their reservation wage. A major factor in this regard was the existence of substantial unemployment compensation programs. The evidence is clear that the availability of unemployment compensation programs is positively related to the level of unemployment.[3] Also, there is a sizable body of research that substantiates the premise that there is a predictable work-incentive response at the level of the population as a whole to the availability of transfer payment income. This was demonstrated rather early on by Carl Brehm and Thomas Saving with respect to the response to general assistance payments and has been confirmed by additional analysis through the years.[4] Further, in a more specific sense, the work of Benjamin and Kolchin, dealing with Britain between the wars, is particularly supportive of this argument.[5] The critical thing is that the accessibility of unemployment compensation benefits in the United States has been rising. Over the course of the 1961–69 business cycle, about two-thirds of the civilian labor force was in employment covered by unemployment compensation programs. Contrast this with the more than 80 percent in covered employment in the years 1974–79.[6]

In addition to unemployment compensation benefits, there are other social transfer payment systems to consider. The food stamp program did not exist in the 1960s. By the 1979–80 fiscal year, payments under this program amounted to over $9 billion, annually.[7] Vendor medical payments more than quadrupled during the 1970s. All told, social welfare expenditures by all governments in the United States rose from about 13 percent of personal income in 1960 to about 22 percent at the end of the 1970s.[8] Such a growth in the relative importance of "safety-net" expenditures alters people's attitudes with respect to what is an acceptable job, increasing the volume of structural unemployment associated with any given wage rate in the economy. This increases the equilibrium unemployment rate in the economy.

How much did the equilibrium unemployment rate rise over its 1960s level? That depends on how much the equilibrium real wage rate rose. Some insight into the magnitude of the upward drift in that measure can be obtained by comparing the relationship between real wage rates and levels of productivity at comparable points in the business cycle. To assist in making this comparison, we have expressed both real wages and productivity in index number form with 1949 being set equal to 100. At the time of the cyclical downturn of 1961, the real-wage index was 1.3 percent greater than the productivity index. Nineteen years later, when unemployment began to rise in 1980, the real-wage index exceeded the productivity index by 4.3 percent. On the basis of the parameters of our statistical model of unemployment, this difference of 3.0 percentage points translates into almost a 2.5 percentage point rise in unemployment. Thus, if the equilibrium unemployment rate was 4 percent in the 1960s, it would be 6.5 percent at the end of the seventies. Since a 4 percent value for the equilibrium unemployment rate in the 1960s is quite probably an underestimate, the equilibrium unemployment rate at the conclusion of the decade of the 1970s may well have been 7 percent or more.

How Well Did Demand Management Work?

If there ever was a period in which deliberate government policy aimed at managing the American economy was employed, it is the decades of the 1960s and 1970s. In the seventies the compulsion to manage, to attempt to replicate the economic successes of the sixties, was apparently irresistible. Richard Nixon is a case in point. In his very first *Economic Report*, the language is that of a nonmanager. He stated:

1. We l ιve learned that Government itself is often the cause of wide swings in the ecoι.ɔmy.
2. We nave learned that . . . the economy cannot be managed mechanistically and will not suspend its laws to accommodate political wishes.
3. We have learned that 1-year planning leads to almost as much confusion as no planning at all . . . ."9

Yet, by the end of 1971 there were in place the first wage and price controls in American history that were not a direct outgrowth of a wartime situation, and by the time of Nixon's fourth *Economic Report* the administration boasted, "The economic performance of 1972 owed much to sound and forceful Government policy."[10]

While Nixon had for years professed skepticism about governmental intervention, he had begun his public service working in the Office of Price Administration in 1941, helping to enforce tire rationing. Some of the men whom he trusted in economic policy measures, notably Secretary of the Treasury John Connally, were activists who were temperamentally impatient with laissez-faire market approaches. Nixon claims that the August 1971 decision to enact wage and price controls had "relatively strong, though skeptical, support among those present" at a Camp David summit of top advisers held immediately before the announcement.[11] Interestingly, the advisers (including Paul McCracken, Paul Volcker, Herbert Stein, Arthur Burns, George Shultz, and others in addition to Connally) disagreed over the closing of the "gold window," a move leading to freer markets in foreign exchange.[12]

In any case, the Nixon (and later the Ford and Carter) teams became accustomed to serving as economic "managers" and, more often than not, their management of the economy translated into imparting an inflationary bias to it. The leading self-styled "inflation fighter" of the era, Arthur F. Burns, chairman of the Board of Governors of the Federal Reserve system from 1970 to 1978, presided over a substantial increase in the rate of growth in the money supply. In five of the nine calendar years that he headed up the Federal Reserve, there was a double-digit rate of growth in the most generally accepted measure of the money supply.[13] This was unprecedented outside of periods of total defense mobilization.

It was the same on the fiscal side. After being critical of the government spending excesses of the period 1965–68, when federal spending exceeded receipts by 7.1 percent, Nixon offered federal budgets for the years 1970–74 in which spending exceeded receipts by 7.2 percent.[14] His successors followed the same path, pumping up the economy in nominal terms. The 1970s was the first decade in the history of the Republic in which the federal government did not balance its budget in a single year. Prior to 1970, federal budget deficits of more than 2 percent of gross national product were very rare. In the 1970s, such deficits existed in six of the ten years.[15] In short, there was no deficiency of aggregate demand in the seventies.

By now, we know that these policies did not work in the same way they had in the 1960s. In fact, the stagflation of the 1970s was sufficient to make the combined performance of the two decades a not particularly impressive one. The unemployment rate in 1961 was 6.7 percent, up to then the highest rate for the post–World War II period. In 1980, it was 7.1 percent and rising. At that, it was lower than it had been in 1975 and 1976. As to

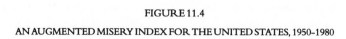

FIGURE 11.4

AN AUGMENTED MISERY INDEX FOR THE UNITED STATES, 1950-1980

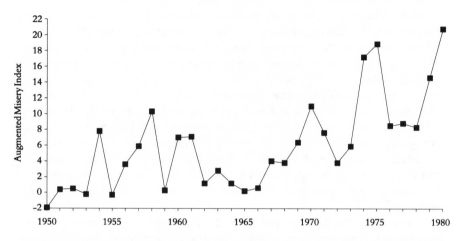

inflation, in 1961 the rate of price inflation was 1.0 percent. In 1980, it was 11.1 percent and had been as high as 13.0 percent. Real economic growth across the two decades was adequate, but not spectacular by historical standards—running at 3.55 per cent per year, just slightly less than the long-term historical average of about 3.6 percent a year. Even the interval of greatest economic growth in this period, 1961–69, showed only a rate of growth of 4.7 percent, compared, for example, to the 6.0 percent that marked a similar period, 1921–29. Or take 1921–41, embracing the Great Depression of the 1930s. The real growth rate in that interval was slightly greater (3.60 percent) than it was in the two decades under discussion.[16]

The failure of macroeconomic policies in the 1970's is vividly illustrated using the device of the "misery index." The misery index was invented by Arthur Okun, and represented the sum of the unemployment and inflation rates. More recently, some economists have taken to subtracting the rate of economic growth from Okun's index in order to get an indicator that reflects performance on the three predominant economic goals: low unemployment, stable prices, and high output growth.

Figure 11.4 shows that the misery index tended to be in the low single digits for most years in the 1950s and 1960s (1958 is the most conspicuous exception), before rising to the double digits at the beginning, in the middle and at the end of the 1970s decade. The 1979–80 downturn culminated in an augmented misery index exceeding 20 in 1980, the highest level in decades. By this measure, at least, the 1970s were the most unsuccessful decade of the postwar era.

TABLE 11.3

ACTUAL VERSUS SIMULATED PERFORMANCE OF THE U.S. ECONOMY, 1961–80

Performance Statistic	Actual Performance (%)	Simulated Performance (%)
Real Growth Rate	3.55	3.57
Average Unemployment Rate	5.22	5.38
Average Rate of Inflation	4.73	0.78

Source: See Text

The rather mixed record of success in managing the American economy between 1961 and 1980 raises the issue of whether, given the existence of an equilibrium rate of unemployment, short-term manipulation and control of economic variables has much to offer from the standpoint of improving economic performance. Perhaps, it may be postulated, the economy would do just as well, or even better, if national economic policy focused more on providing conditions that are conducive to long-term economic growth rather than emphasizing the control of short-term economic conditions. To explore that possibility, the actual performance of the American economy in the period 1961–80 can be compared with the results of a simulation of the economy that assumes no attempt at managing it in the short run, except for a fixed rate of growth in the monetary base.[17]

A comparison of the results of the simulation, which assumes a 2 percent annual rate of growth in the monetary base, with the actual performance of the economy is shown in table 11.3. The only substantial difference is in the rate of price inflation. Two decades of attempts at short-term management of the American economy produced about 4 percent a year more price inflation with no appreciable effect on unemployment or the real growth rate, the latter two being determined by the underlying structural realities of the economy, that is, the forces that determine the natural rate of unemployment within the neoclassical framework. With a zero rate of growth in the monetary base, the comparison would be even more striking. Productivity gains would have been reflected in the form of falling prices and we would have experienced an era of price deflation (over 1 percent a year) rather than price inflation with, of course, little difference in the real level of economic performance.

Lest the foregoing remarks suggest that the rate of price inflation is totally irrelevant to the time path of the real magnitudes of an economy, it should be emphasized that our simulations assume no feedback between the price level and the processes of capital accumulation and technological change. What is evaluated is the usefulness of short-term attempts at managing the economy, given the level of labor productivity in the system. In the longer run, persistent price rises are likely to have negative impacts on levels of saving and, ultimately, investment; thereby shifting a society to a lower economic growth path. For example, it is probably no accident that over the period 1973–82, productivity in the nonfarm-business sector of the American economy increased by less than 5 percent. Indeed, for the last five years of that period, it actually declined very slightly.[18]

The State of Economic Thinking at the End of the Decade

By the end of the decade of the 1970s the optimism about the state of macroeconomic thinking and its implications for public policy that characterized the end of the previous decade was gone. It was obvious that problems had arisen with respect to the general applicability of the Keynesian framework. With the questioning of the theory came a questioning of its application to the American economy. The concern was deep and widespread. There was a sense of malaise in the air that had not been felt since the days of the late 1930s. For example, in March 1980, that venerable body, the American Assembly, with the sponsorship of the Annenberg School of Communication's Center for Study of the American Experience, convened a meeting to discuss the topic "Economic Issues and the President: 1980 and Beyond." The preface to the proceedings of this assembly contained the following assessment:

> When the United States entered the decade of the seventies, political leaders were divided in their views about the most effective measures to pursue in the management of the American economy . . . , but they all had one thing in common: the conviction . . . . that the American economy was manageable.
> As we enter the decade of the eighties, more and more Americans are beginning to question whether our economy is manageable. Some observers have suggested that our economy is "over the hill" and that we must either undertake fundamental changes to our whole system or else face the prospect of becoming a second-rate nation, watching others take over the primacy of world economic leadership.[19]

We have already provided ample evidence to explain why observers of the American economy might feel that it had become unmanageable. However, one more perspective on that issue might be helpful using the Phillips curve device. We know that at the end of the previous decade there was strong evidence of a systematic relationship between inflation and unemployment. However, as the "thought experiment" we described earlier indicates, the link between inflation and unemployment was quite different

FIGURE 11.5

RATES OF INFLATION AND UNEMPLOYMENT, U.S., 1970-1979

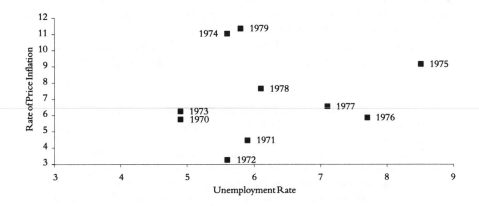

in the seventies, compared to the sixties. Figure 11.5 shows the nature of the unemployment–price inflation nexus for the seventies.

This diagram is revealing. Other than the interval 1975–77, there appears to be an underlying stability in the unemployment rate. It is not responsive to changes in the rate of price inflation. What about the years 1975–77, though? Our previous analysis has demonstrated that in this interval the economy had been shocked out of equilibrium by a rise in the adjusted real wage rate, but then returned to its basic underlying level of unemployment. Thus, there is a strong indication here that the equilibrium, or "natural" rate of unemployment is acting as a significant constraint on the actions of anyone attempting to manage the American economy.

Why then and not in the sixties? What was there in the seventies that made the constraint of the "natural" rate of unemployment operative? The key would seem to be changes in people's expectations with respect to the amount of price inflation that was typical for the economy. The beating down of the unemployment rate in the 1960s and the march up the Phillips curve had been based on the inflation of the period being unanticipated. Wage-rate adjustments lagged behind movements in prices and productivity and the adjusted real wage fell. In the seventies, though, the inflationary expectations of participants in labor markets had accelerated, and replicating the events of the 1960s would require a more substantial escalation of the rate of price inflation than what actually occurred. By decade's end, people were anticipating the double-digit price inflation of 1979 and 1980. Consequently, it was not possible to reduce the unemployment rate below its equilibrium level without an even further escalation of the rate of price inflation.

Further increases in the pace of inflation were not politically acceptable. As his term in office wound down, Jimmy Carter inveighed against the dangers of rising prices but saw little hope for containing inflation. With reference to the 1978 Humphrey-Hawkins Full Employment and Balanced Growth Act, which established "interim" goals of 4 percent unemployment and 3 percent price inflation by 1983, Carter conceded, in his 1980 *Economic Report*, that

> I have therefore been forced to conclude that reaching the goals of a 4 percent unemployment rate and 3 percent inflation rate by 1983 is no longer practicable. . . .
>
> Reducing inflation from the 10 percent expected in 1980 to 3 percent in 1983 would be an . . . . unrealistic expectation. Recent experience indicates that the momentum of inflation built up over the past 15 years is extremely strong. A practical goal for reducing inflation should take this fact into account.
>
> Because of these economic realities, I have used the authority provided to me in the Humphrey-Hawkins Act to extend the timetable for achieving a 4 percent unemployment rate and 3 percent inflation. The target year for achieving 4 percent unemployment is now 1985, a 2-year deferment. The target year for lowering inflation to 3 percent has been postponed until three years after that [1988].[20]

The way in which Carter altered the timetable for reaching the Humphrey-Hawkins goals is suggestive of his attitude, and that of his advisers, with respect to the possibility of reducing unemployment and inflation rates. Apparently, the feeling was that it would be easier to reach the unemployment goal than the inflation target. Yet, that runs contrary to the visual image created by figure 11.5. If anything, the figure suggests that the rate of price inflation was more volatile than the rate of unemployment. A simple statistical analysis confirms this. The coefficient of variation for the rate of price inflation is twice that of the unemployment rate during the 1970s.[21]

By the end of the seventies, the notion that there is something intractable about the rate of price inflation received support from the ranks of academic economists. Otto Eckstein elevated this view of the world to respectability with his concept of "core inflation." Eckstein developed the idea of core inflation in an analysis done for the Joint Economic Committee of Congress. His own description of it ran as follows: "It is the [inflation] rate that would occur if the economy were on its long-term equilibrium growth path, free of shocks and excess demand."[22] This is nothing more than the idea that there is a "natural" rate of price inflation in the economy. The development of the idea of core inflation may well be one of the most remarkable acts of juxtaposition ever performed in economic thinking. Working from a set of data observations that quite clearly suggest the existence of a "natural" rate of unemployment, the analysis is turned on its ear to make the basic constraint the "natural" rate of price inflation in the economy. In fact, in Eckstein's scheme of things, the unemployment rate still remained an important target variable to be influenced by economic policymakers. He revived the Phillips curve concept of a stable trade-off between unemployment and inflation by substituting the core inflation rate for the actual inflation rate.[23]

Admittedly, this procedure provided a much more restrictive set of choices than those that prompted Arthur Okun's complaints almost two decades earlier. According to Eckstein, achieving a 5 percent rate of unemployment would require a core inflation rate of about 10 percent. More interesting, the Humphrey-Hawkins goal of simultaneously attaining a 4 percent rate of unemployment and a 3 percent rate of price inflation was pure wishful thinking. In fact, Eckstein was perhaps the ultimate in pessimism about the future prospects for the United States from the standpoint of controlling inflation. He despaired of aggregate-demand management being able to deal with the problem of price inflation in any satisfactory way, remarking that

> In summary, the fiscal and monetary policies which the government employs to manage aggregate demand must create a constructive environment in which inflation can be improved, but they cannot, *by themselves*, solve the problem. Aggressive demand management, aiming at unemployment rates averaging 6 percent or less every year, makes it impossible to have any other policy succeed. The inflation will simply become worse and worse—until the public despairs and forces politicians to adopt price controls. But even if demand management sets its gauges to achieve unemployment in the 6.5 to 7 percent area, the inflation problem is not solved. Indeed, given the probable shocks from energy, with a real OPEC increase of 4 percent a year, there would be no improvement in the core inflation rate. These exercises demonstrate that demand management must be careful and somewhat more conservative than it has been, but that *it is beyond its capacities to accomplish an adequate improvement of inflation.*[24]

That is a grim scenario and Otto Eckstein was a man to be taken seriously. His academic credentials were impeccable and he was president of Data Resources Incorporated, one of the preeminent economic forecasting firms in the country. Very many people accepted his views as authoritative. Is it any wonder that there might have been pessimism abroad in the highest circles? Actually, compared to Eckstein's assessment of future prospects for the American economy, Jimmy Carter's views appeared to be quite optimistic. What remains to be seen is whether Eckstein's pessimism was warranted.

NOTES

1.   The oil-price data are taken from United States Department of Commerce, *Statistical Abstract of the United States 1990* (Washington, D.C.: Government Printing Office, 1990), table 955, p. 568.

2.   Estimates reported in our Joint Economic Committee of Congress Staff Study, *The "Natural" Rate of Unemployment* (Washington, D.C.: Government Printing Office, 1982), p. 28, indicate that the equilibrium rate of unemployment was about 4.4 percent in the 1960s, 5.7 percent in the early 1970s, and stood at 6.6 percent by the end of the decade of the 1970s.

3.   Some of the representative studies of this subject are the early work by Gene Chapin, "Unemployment Insurance, Job Search, and the Demand for Leisure," *Western Economic Journal* 9 (1971): 102–7, and later, Martin Feldstein, "Unemployment Compensation: Adverse Incentives and Distributional Anomalies," *National Tax Journal* 27 (1974): 231–44.

4.   C. T. Brehm and T. R. Saving, "The Demand for General Assistance Payments," *American Economic Review* 54 (1964): 1002–18. For further evidence along this line and additional literature references, see our *Poverty, Income Distribution, the Family and Public Policy*, Joint Economic Committee of Congress (Washington, D.C.: Government Printing Office, 1986).

5.   Daniel K. Benjamin and Levis A. Kolchin, "Searching for an Explanation of Unemployment in Interwar Britain," *Journal of Political Economy* 87 (1979): 441–78.

6.   For this and other statistics on labor markets in this era, the annual *Manpower Reports of the President* put out by the United States Employment and Training Administration are useful.

7.   *Statistical Abstract of the United States 1990*, p. 351.

8.   Total social welfare expenditure data are from the United States Social Security Administration and the personal income data are from the United States Department of Commerce. Ibid., p. 350.

9.   *Economic Report of the President* (Washington, D.C.: Government Printing Office, 1970), p. 3.

10.   *Economic Report of the President* (Washington, D.C.: Government Printing Office, 1973), p. 3.

11.   Richard M. Nixon, *The Memoirs of Richard Nixon* (New York: Grosset and Dunlap, 1978), p. 519.

12.   Ibid.

13.   The percentage figures for the rate of growth in the M2 money magnitude between 1971 and 1977 are: 1971, 13.5; 1972, 13.0; 1973, 6.9; 1974, 5.5; 1975, 12.6; 1976, 13.7; and 1977, 10.6. *Source*: Federal Reserve Board data, as reported in various issues of the *Economic Report of the President*.

14.   United States Office of Management and Budget, as reported in *Statistical Abstract of the United States 1990*, table 497, p. 309.

15.   *1991 Economic Report of the President* (Washington, D.C.: Government Printing Office, 1991), p. 375.

16.   The growth rates are calculated from the real gross national product statistics for the United States reported by the United States Department of Commerce, Bureau of Economic Analysis.

17.   The magnitude employed is the adjusted monetary base, which consists of (1) reserve accounts of financial institutions at Federal Reserve Banks, (2) currency in circulation (currency held by the public and in the vaults of all depository institutions), and (3) an adjustment for reserve requirement rate changes. A detailed description of the simulation can be found in our *The "Natural" Rate of Unemployment*, p. 29.

18.   See the standard average output of labor statistics reported by the United States Department of Labor. These are summarized in the Statistical Appendix to the *Economic Report of the President* for the appropriate years.

19.   The published proceedings bear a slightly different title than the conference itself, namely, *The Economy and the President: 1980 and Beyond* (Englewood Cliffs, N. J.: Prentice-Hall, 1980). See p. v.

20.   *Economic Report of the President, 1980* (Washington, D.C.: Government Printing Office, 1980), pp. 9–10.

21.   The coefficient of variation is the ratio of the standard deviation of a data set to its mean. For the rate of price inflation over the period 1970–79, it is 0.38. For the unemployment rate, it is 0.19.

22.   Otto Eckstein, "Choices for the Eighties," in *The Economy and the President*, p. 76.

23.   Ibid., fig. 5, p. 89.

24.   Ibid., pp. 90–91. (Emphasis added.)

12

The Winds of Change

As the decade of the eighties began, there was controversy and debate about the nature of the macroeconomic world. Among academic economists, new ideas had been surfacing throughout the seventies, especially the rational-expectations notions of Robert Lucas, Thomas Sargent, Robert Barro, and others.[1] Their basic premise, that participants in market processes accurately anticipate future market developments, especially price movements, put expectations at the forefront of economic analysis. Within the context of the macroeconomic conditions of the 1970s, it provided a much more appealing explanation for events than the negatively sloped Phillips curve of the sixties. It can be argued that the almost vertical Phillips curve of the seventies reflected anticipation by markets of the effect of the traditional tools of demand management—monetary and fiscal policy—on price levels and the like. If anticipated inflation is approximately equal to actual inflation, the impact of policies of demand management are effectively discounted by markets and it becomes impossible to drive the unemployment rate below its natural or equilibrium level, even temporarily. In short, it is not possible in a rational-expectations world to create the money illusion in labor markets that characterized the 1960s.

At the other extreme from the rational-expectations view were the Keynesians who, in the Eckstein mode, maintained their faith in the notion that the unemployment rate can be manipulated at will, even though the cost, in terms of price inflation, may be substantial. For the confirmed Keynesian or neo–Keynesian, there was still no equilibrium constraint on the unemployment side.

Reality, we feel, lies somewhere in between these two positions. We reject the rational-expectations view on the grounds that it cannot account for the existence of business cycles. In a rational-expectations world, all we should see is random variations around a long-term trend line in whatever measure of overall macroeconomic activity is being observed, whether it be the unemployment rate, per capita gross national product, industrial output, or something else. Our long-term historical experience tells us that the phenomenon of the business cycle does exist. The variations in economic activity that have been observed are not merely random variations around a long-term trend.

As for the Keynesian or neo-Keynesian position, we reject it on the grounds that it makes, either explicitly or implicitly, an unrealistic assumption about the nature and character of reactions to errors in forecasts of future events. Cycles are possible in this framework because there may be systematic errors in those forecasts. The key is the reaction of individuals to such errors. At the extreme, the forecasting error is either permanent or is only partially corrected. A full adjustment to such an error is never made. This produces the familiar Keynesian notion of a wide range of possible equilibrium situations, including those that may be regarded as providing an unsatisfactorily low volume of employment. For example, in labor markets, a failure to respond fully to the forecast error generates a permanent money illusion whenever there are incorrectly anticipated (or forecast) changes in the general level of prices and/or the productivity of labor.[2]

This is the source of the stable Phillips curve approach to interpreting the behavior of the macroeconomy. In such a scenario, unanticipated movements in prices and productivity will be translated into predictable movements in employment and total output. Such shocks to the macroeconomy may produce high levels of unemployment with no hope that the general forecast error will be fully corrected by market participants. The result is what is sometimes called a less-than-full-employment equilibrium in the economy. Of course, on the other side of the coin, the forecast error may be in a direction that generates a permanent decline in the unemployment rate, even to levels that are capable of satisfying the unemployment goals for the economy that are laid out in the Humphrey-Hawkins legislation of 1978.[3] Unfortunately, the implicit assumption that forecast errors are not corrected, especially in the market for labor, is not supported by the available data, especially the behavior of the rate of price inflation and the unemployment rate during the decade of the seventies.

Between these two views of the world is the reality alluded to previously. In it, there still are systematic errors in forecasts of market developments, but rather than the forecast error being permanent or only partially eliminated, it is corrected with the passage of time. This leads to a lagged response in markets to unanticipated changes in the conditions affecting those markets. Such a response tends to return a market to a unique equilibrium position, which, in the case of the labor market, can be thought of as a full-employment equilibrium. Of particular interest is the pattern of response of money wage rates to unanticipated changes in prices and labor productivity. A lagged response will produce displacements of the real wage from its equilibrium level, but as the forecast errors are corrected, there will be a tendency for the labor market to return to equilibrium. Such a theoretical framework is described quite well by Jerome Stein's notion of a world in which the rational-expectations outcomes are approached in an asymptotic fashion with the passage of time.[4]

While the jargon has changed, the rational-expectations and asymptotically-rational-expectations outcomes represent only modest variations on the basic neoclassical-Austrian view described earlier. Rational expectations is merely the neoclassical-Austrian model with instantaneous adjustment and random errors in the outcome. Asymptotically rational expectations is nothing more than the neoclassical-Austrian model emphasized here with lags in the adjustment mechanism.

In addition, at the beginning of the 1980s, there was serious questioning from outside the academic world of the demand-management view that had so dominated economic affairs in the United States since 1960. Supply-side economics emerged from the popular and political arenas, although there are certainly strong hints of it within the formal academic community.[5] For example, there was a substantial debate in the late 1970s in the pages of the *Wall Street Journal* about the validity of some supply-side ideas advanced by Representative Jack Kemp and Senator William Roth.

Kemp and Roth were arguing for very substantial reductions in income-tax rates in the United States. The rationale of their position was well expressed in a letter from Roth to the editor of the *Wall Street Journal* in July 1978:

> By imposing barriers between effort and reward, our present tax system is threatening to destroy the American dream of upward mobility. The excessive tax rates have stagnated our economy and too many Americans are facing the prospect of downward mobility. Substantial tax rate reductions are needed to encourage people to work harder, to be more innovative, to take risks, and to be able to lead a better life. These tax cuts are needed to breathe life into our free enterprise system and to increase the prospects for upward mobility and a higher standard of living for all Americans.[6]

Roth's letter is in response to a column by Walter Heller that took issue with Kemp and Roth's advocacy of a $114 billion reduction in income taxes in the United States. Heller's column began on a polemical note, expressing absolute scorn and disdain for the Kemp–Roth proposal:

> Sound the trumpets and hear the heralds: There is, after all, such a thing as a free lunch. . . .
> It is Congressman Kemp and Senator Roth with their $114 billion tax cut bill . . . who offer us this bonanza.
> And it won't cost us a thin dime. According to the Kemp–Roth June 1978 "Tax Cut News," their cuts "will increase the incentive to work, save and invest, resulting in higher growth, lower prices, more jobs, and high government revenues." . . . Lunch is not only free, we get a bonus for eating it. P. T. Barnum move over.[7]

What is ironic here is that Kemp had invoked the experience with the Kennedy–Johnson tax cuts of the 1960s, which had been engineered in large part by Heller, to argue for the validity of the Kemp–Roth proposal. Heller, though, could not escape his Keynesian heritage. Ignoring the surge in productivity that marked the mid-1960s, he flatly asserted that the success of the Kennedy–Johnson tax cuts was attributable purely to their providing a stimulus to aggregate demand. With this out of the way, he then claimed that the Kemp–Roth proposal would provide too much stimulus on the demand side and trigger a wave of inflation. He summed up his position very simply:

> To summarize, then, nothing in the history of tax cuts, econometric studies of taxpayer responses, or field surveys of incentives suggests that the effects of a big tax cut on the supply of output even begin to match its effects on the demand for output. A $ 114 billion tax cut in three years would simply overwhelm our existing productive capacity with a tidal wave of increased demand and sweep away all hopes of . . . containing inflation.[8]

Heller's standard Keynesian demand-management view of the world received support from a wide spectrum of economists. Gardner Ackley, his successor as chairman of the Council of Economic Advisers, echoed his views.[9] Even Herbert Stein, chairman of the Council during part of the Nixon-Ford years, chimed in: "I agree with almost everything that Walter Heller said on this subject [the Kemp–Roth proposal] in the *Wall Street Journal* of July 12. . . ."[10] Heller was in the same tradition as Eckstein. Later in the year, in another column in the *Journal*, he made it clear that he subscribed to the core-inflation notion when he referred to the "cost-push forces that form the hard core of the inflationary spiral."[11] Within this mindset, the economic problems facing the United States at this juncture seemed to be quite intractable. This pessimistic view of present and future prospects came through very clearly in some remarks made by Paul Samuelson during the interval between Ronald Reagan's election to the presidency and his taking office. Samuelson commented: "A basic fact about present-day Americans is our scaled-down expectations. This seems a rational rather than pathological reaction to what have been the actualities of the 1970s."[12] Samuelson's pessimism was reflected in his forecasts of what conditions were likely to be in the 1980s. What he saw was average levels of unemployment in excess of 8 percent, average rates of price inflation of more than 9 percent with frequent excursions into the double-digit range, and perhaps an average real growth rate in gross national product of 2 percent a year.[13] At least, though, he rejected such worst-case scenarios as the virtual zero growth suggested by Lester Thurow.[14]

By contrast, the supply-side view of the world was growth-oriented, rather than preoccupied with counteryclical demand-management problems. However, it did run contrary to the major thrust of mainstream thinking about macroeconomic matters since the days of the Great Depression. In the debate in the pages of the *Wall Street Journal*, Paul Craig Roberts perhaps put his finger on the basic dilemma facing the long-time Keynesians when he commented, "As the adage goes, it is hard to teach old dogs new tricks, and Keynesians, who have spent four decades thinking in terms of spending and demand, find it hard to understand arguments about incentive and supply."[15]

The Experience of the Eighties

Against this background of wide disagreement, some of it quite acrimonious, the 1980s began on something of a negative note. In the first year of the decade, the inflation rate averaged 1 percent a month, and beginning with the second quarter of the year, the unemployment rate began to rise. What occurred here was a minor business cycle that ran its course in about a year. During this cycle, the unemployment rate increased quite rapidly between March and July of 1980, rising from 6.3 to 7.8 percent. After July, there was a slow drift downward until the rate reached 7.2 percent the following March.

In a number of ways, this "mini" cycle is consistent with both the core-inflation and rational-expectations hypotheses for explaining the operation of the American economy in the aggregate. It is almost classic stagflation. The inflation rate stayed high, feeding inflationary expectations that were reflected in a rational-expectations manner in increases in money wage rates. For example, in the second and third quarters of 1981 the rates of increase in the GNP price deflator and worker compensation per hour

FIGURE 12.1

ACTUAL AND PREDICTED UNEMPLOYMENT RATES, UNITED STATES,
THIRD QUARTER, 1979, THROUGH FIRST QUARTER, 1981

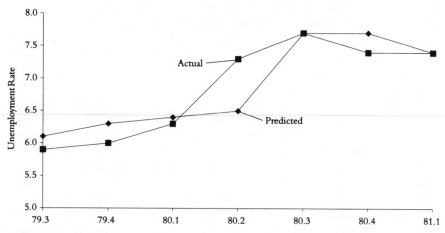

moved in virtual lockstep.[16] However, in addition to being consistent with the stagflation notions, the behavior of the American economy across this business cycle can also be explained in terms of the neoclassical-Austrian adjusted real wage approach. While money wage rates and prices moved fairly closely together in this interval, the adjusted real wage was shocked out of equilibrium by generally declining levels of productivity of labor. The years 1979 and 1980 both showed declines in productivity. How well the adjusted real wage hypothesis works in accounting for this cycle is suggested by figure 12.1 which compares the actual unemployment rate with that predicted by a simple version of the adjusted real wage rate model. The correspondence between the two is quite clear.

THE GREAT DISINFLATION

Through the spring and summer of 1981, the American economy drifted through a period in which inflation was still running at double-digit levels and the unemployment rate fluctuated between 7.2 and 7.6 percent. Toward the end of the year, though, there was a dramatic turn of events. During the fourth quarter of 1981 the rate of price inflation suddenly slowed, falling to levels that, according to Eckstein's estimates of core inflation, were not attainable in the American economy. This trend continued through the first quarter of 1982. In these six months, the average rate of price inflation fell from the 1 percent a month that had been common since the beginning of

1979 to 0.25 percent a month. There was a brief resurgence of inflation in late spring (May and June), but, even so, from mid-1981 through mid-1982, the rate of price inflation (measured by movements in the consumer price index) declined to 6.2 percent, some 40 percent less than the 10.3 percent rate that marked mid-1980 through mid-1981.[17] After the brief surge in inflation in the spring, the lower level of price inflation reasserted itself. In the last six months of 1982, the monthly average for the rate of price inflation was again 0.25 percent, and for the period mid-1982 through mid-1983, the CPI rose by only 3.2 percent.

The sudden decline in the rate of price inflation was quite inexplicable from the standpoint of some of the theoretical paradigms for explaining macroeconomic phenomena. It obviously did not fit Eckstein's core-inflation thesis. Nor, given the passage of the Economic Recovery and Tax Act of 1981, did it square particularly well with Heller's assertion that a major tax cut would "simply overwhelm our existing productive capacity with a tidal wave of increased demand." The 25 percent reduction in the federal income tax certainly qualified as a major tax cut, but it did not have the effect that Heller anticipated. Finally, the rational-expectations approach would seem to imply that the tax cut would be fully anticipated. That might have had a variety of effects. Combined with the aggregate-demand interpretation of the tax cut, it should have produced the burst of inflation forecast by Heller, Ackley, and Stein. A possible combination of theories that would fit the actual sequence of events is that of a fully anticipated tax cut that produces the supply-side effects described earlier. However, we know of no one who argued this position, and such an explanation does not fit other events that accompanied the decline in the rate of price inflation.

Why did this unanticipated disinflation occur? Was there a significant decline in the growth of the money supply? That seems unlikely. From 1978 through 1979, the M2 variant of the money supply grew at a rate of 7.8 percent; between 1979 and 1980, the growth was 8.9 percent; and between 1980 and 1981, it was 10 percent. If anything, the growth rate in the money supply was accelerating in the years immediately preceding the late-1981 disinflation.

However, there was one marked change on the monetary side. The velocity of money began to decline, following a protracted period of sustained increase. Something happened around 1980 that produced a significant alteration in the behavior of the population. The decline in velocity was consistent with a lowering of inflationary expectations. There was nothing in the pattern of growth in the money supply to suggest why this happened. There was, however, a significant alteration in the publicly announced philosophy of the Federal Reserve system with respect to monetary policy. In 1979, under the chairmanship of Paul Volcker, the

Federal Reserve announced that it would no longer conduct its monetary-policy operations with an eye to influencing, or "targeting," interest rates.[18] Instead, its monetary goals would be expressed in terms of influencing the rate of growth in the money supply.

This switch in objectives may have had a major effect on the level of inflationary expectations in the economy. It can be argued that attempting to influence interest rates generally means attempting to push them down, and that this introduces a systematic inflationary bias into the economy. Abandoning the goal of manipulating interest rates per se may well have been interpreted as a step that would remove this bias, thus lowering inflationary expectations, and ultimately reversing the long-term pattern of growth in the velocity of money.

THE RECESSION OF 1982

Whatever the source of the decline in the rate of price inflation, this disinflation was to a substantial extent unanticipated. Consequently, it was not accompanied by a similar reduction in the rate of increase in money wage rates. Consistent with the lagged adjustment version, and contrary to the rational-expectations models, wage rates adjusted only partially to unanticipated movements in prices and productivity. Therefore, although the rate of increase in money wage rates declined between 1981 and 1982 from 9.3 to 7.5 percent, this did not match the over-four-percentage-point drop in the rate of price inflation.[19]

In addition, the rate of growth in the average productivity of labor was slightly negative at this time. Obviously, this combination of events produced an upward surge in the adjusted real wage rate, triggering a dramatic rise in unemployment that began in the fourth quarter of 1981 (actually, in September). By the fourth quarter of 1982, the unemployment rate averaged 10.6 percent, compared to a rate of 7.4 percent in August 1981.[20]

The rhetorical response to this burst of unemployment was very pronounced in some quarters. The *Washington Post*'s coverage of the October 1982 hearing of the Joint Economic Committee of Congress at which the announcement was made that unemployment had increased to 10.1 percent in September (later revised to 10.2 percent) conjured images of a new Great Depression. An election was about a month away, and it was not lost on politicians and the news media that the last time unemployment had been officially recorded at 10 percent or more was prior to the United States' entry into World War II. That October hearing came complete with a huge photograph of Herbert Hoover, bearing the legend, "Prosperity Is Just Around the Corner," ensconced on an easel to remind all in attendance of the early 1930s. To ensure that no one missed the point, beside the Hoover photograph was one of Ronald Reagan, with its own caption, "Recovery Has Been Sighted." [21]

One after the other, five unemployed people testified before the committee regarding their plight. One of them, a steelworker from West Virginia who had lost his $3,000-a-month job, provided the most poignant testimony, describing how he had attempted suicide by putting a gun to his head and pulling the trigger. A shipbuilder from the Baltimore area told of being laid off from his $30,000-a-year job. [22]

Even by the standards of election-year political posturing, the response of public figures was sharp. Congressman Parren Mitchell, a Democrat from Baltimore, was "angry" and described the president as "this dreadful man." [23] The speaker of the House of Representatives, Thomas P. (Tip) O'Neill, Jr., called for immediate House action on "needed recovery measures," claiming that "the situation demands that Congress move directly to restore public confidence and regain control of the nation's economic destiny." [24] A sense of crisis pervaded the Washington atmosphere.

All that fall, suggestions for alleviating the situation abounded. There were calls for emergency public-works programs, repeal of the 10 percent cut in income taxes that was scheduled to go into effect in 1983, and faster growth in the money supply, among other things. The ghost of underconsumptionism was visibly present, as seen in the following evaluation of the administration's economic policies offered by Congressman Henry Reuss, chairman of the Joint Economic Committee:

> President Reagan's prosperity plan was called 'trickle-down' economics. . . .
> Well, it didn't work. . . .
> There was a shift in income *away* from *ordinary* people and toward the wealthy. The result was a boom market in luxuries. . . . Ordinary people started to run out of purchasing power. There just wasn't enough ordinary income for ordinary people to take ordinary goods off the shelves. That . . . brought us our hard times. [25]

Reuss's view was supported by labor economist and former Secretary of Labor Ray Marshall, who criticized the current economic policy for being "very inefficient, relying on the theory that tax breaks for the wealthy and big corporations will 'trickle down' to ordinary working people and the poor." [26] Walter Heller and John Kenneth Galbraith decried the magnitude of the federal budget deficit and the failures of supply-side economics. [27] Galbraith remarked, "We have shifted income from those whose spending and demand are assured to those whose spending and demand are discretionary." [28] Robert Eisner made an open plea for a deliberate inflation of the

FIGURE 12.2

ACTUAL AND PREDICTED UNEMPLOYMENT RATES, UNITED STATES,
SECOND QUARTER, 1981, THROUGH SECOND QUARTER, 1985

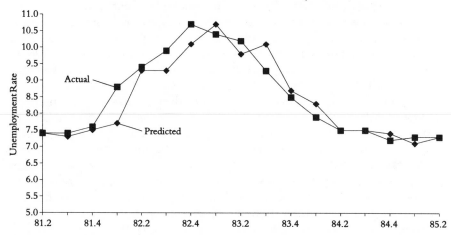

system in order to reduce real interest rates and Willard Wirtz, Secretary of Labor in the mid-1960s, stated that the only satisfactory unemployment rate was zero.[29] When it was pointed out by some that the rise in unemployment was a necessary consequence of reducing the rate of price inflation, Congressman Augustus Hawkins, co-author of the Humphrey-Hawkins amendments to the Employment Act of 1946, declared that it was "illegal" to practice "trade-off" economics.[30] The Congressman was right. The Humphrey-Hawkins legislation did make the Phillips curve illegal.

Fortunately for the nation, this outpouring of advice was largely ignored. Out in the real world, events that would reduce the level of unemployment were in progress. As the neoclassical-Austrian labor-market adjustment process asserted itself, the rate of change in money wage rates had already begun to slow, falling from an annual rate of 9.0 percent in the third quarter of 1981 to 4.5 percent in the fourth quarter 1982. Combined with some modest increases in labor productivity, the effect was first to halt the rise in the adjusted real wage rate, and then to produce a decline in this key statistic, beginning in the first quarter of 1983. Accordingly, the unemployment rate began to drop, falling to 7.2 percent by the fourth quarter of 1984.

Figure 12.2 depicts the relationship between the actual unemployment rate and that predicted by the simple bivariate model that employs the adjusted real wage rate to explain variations in the unemployment rate. As can be seen, for the period beginning with the fourth quarter of 1981 and ending with the second quarter of 1985, there is a remarkable correspondence between the actual and predicted values for the unemployment rate. Once again, the neoclassical-Austrian labor-market adjustment process provides an explanation for variations in the unemployment rate.

The recession of 1982 presents a classic case of the impact of unanticipated changes in the rate of price inflation. In this case, it was an unanticipated decline in the rate of change in prices, in contrast to the events of the 1960s, when there was an unanticipated rise in the inflation rate. However, the effects on the labor market in the two cases were qualitatively the same, although in opposite directions. In the 1960s, the unanticipated rise in prices produced a decline in the adjusted real wage rate and a decrease in unemployment, followed by a return of the adjusted real wage rate to its equilibrium level and a rise in unemployment at the beginning of the seventies. In the case of the downturn of 1982, the unanticipated decline in inflation led to a rise in the adjusted real wage rate and an increase in unemployment. Again, though, there was a market adjustment process at work. By the time unemployment surged past the 10 percent mark in the fall of 1982, recovery was already in sight. That such a recovery was in progress can be attributed primarily to the self-adjusting properties of the American economy, which were permitted to operate at this time with a minimum of governmental tinkering.

As we have already pointed out, unemployment peaked in that fall of 1982 and, just as the cacophony of complaints about the nature of economic policy reached a crescendo, the turnaround began. In January 1983, employment rose slightly and the unemployment rate fell back to 10.4 percent. This was to launch a prolonged period of rising levels of employment. Within three years of the cycle trough in December 1982, roughly nine million new jobs would be created and the unemployment rate would decline to about 7 percent.

The swiftness of the decline in unemployment surprised a number of forecasters. During the height of the 1982 recession, the Joint Economic Committee held a hearing at which five economic analysts offered their prognostications of future events. MIT economist Francis Bator described a number of possible scenarios, none of which fit what actually happened. He dismissed what would have been an accurate forecast with the following statement: "As of now, the hope that we could have both rapid recovery and a continued deceleration in core inflation without a serious policy of direct wage restraint [wage controls] strikes me as a low probability bet."[31]

The next witness, Raymond Dalio, was even more direct, stating that "the . . . forecast that the economy will turn up at the same time interest rates and inflation fall is impossible."[32] Michael Evans, responding to a request to state when the economy would reach the January 1981 unemployment rate of 7.4 percent, said: "We would not see a decline to the 7.4% rate of January 1981 until mid-decade at earliest, with the possibility that this might not occur until about 1990."[33] The final two witnesses, Donald Ratajczak and Allen Sinai, saw late 1985 at the earliest as the time at which the American economy might get back to the January 1981 level of unemployment.[34] For the record, the January 1981 unemployment rate was equaled in either May or June of 1984, depending on whether the original or the revised figure for the prerecession month is used.

THE SKY IS FALLING!

The economic recovery continued past 1985 on into 1987, the year for which Paul Samuelson had forecast an 8.3 percent unemployment rate and a 9.4 percent rate of price inflation, even in the absence of the 1981 cut in the federal income tax. By now, there had been a second round of reductions in the income tax, embodied in the Tax Reform Act of 1986. The unemployment rate had continued to fall, passing through the 7 percent mark in January 1986 and breaking through the 6 percent barrier in September of 1987.

The steady decline in unemployment was associated with a steady fall in the adjusted real wage. With the single exception of 1986, real wages changed less than 1 per cent a year from 1983 through 1988. In all those years except 1987, however, productivity rose more than 2 percent a year (in 1987 it rose about 1 percent). The adjusted real wage fell. Declining rates of inflation were accompanied by continued damping of inflationary expectations, with wage settlements falling to the 4 percent annual increase range.

In October 1987, however, an apparent disaster loomed, at least in the minds of many economists and journalists. There was a second Great Crash. Between August 25 and October 18, the Dow-Jones Industrial Average of stock prices fell by nearly 500 points. Then, on October 19, it went into a "free fall," declining by 508 points in that single day. At the moment of the crash, it was widely interpreted as signifying the end of the post-1982 recovery. The *Washington Post* and the *New York Times* sounded the trumpets of doom. Hobart Rowen, writing for the *Post* announced:

> Now the joyride is over, but so far, the staggering record stock market collapse has been met with government denial reminiscent of 1929. . . .
> "The economy is fundamentally sound," said Treasury Secretary James A. Baker III. And President Reagan, who gives every evidence of being totally out of touch with reality, told reporters, "I don't know what meaning it [the

October 19 decline in the Dow-Jones index] might have, all the business indicators are up—there's nothing wrong with the economy. . . ."[35]

Echoing this attitude, James Reston offered his views in the *Times*:

> At the time of the crash, the Secretaries of State and the Treasury were out of the country, and the President, as usual, was out to lunch.
> . . . it is not the mathematics of the crash that are worrying the leaders of both parties here and the allies abroad but a feeling that Washington is leaderless and following a policy of spend and spend, borrow and borrow, that is threatening not only the security of the nation but of the civilization it is supposed to lead.[36]

The doomsday forecasts were, of course, completely off the mark. The decline in aggregate demand implicit in a reduction in the market value of equities of over one trillion dollars either did not occur or was irrelevant to economic progress. As we know, there was no second Great Depression. The unemployment rate continued to decline, reaching a low of 5.1 percent in March 1989. The stock market recovered from its decline, and eventually surpassed the highs it had reached before the crash.

What happened? Basically, the behavior of the American economy at this time can be explained by the neoclassical-Austrian hypothesis. Nothing was happening that was capable of shocking the adjusted real wage rate into fundamental disequilibrium. There was "nothing wrong with the economy." In fact, the quarter-by-quarter movements in unemployment during the latter portion of the decade of the eighties can be explained quite well by the adjusted real wage rate model. This is shown in figure 12.3. The upward movement in economic activity that began after November 1982 continued onward into the nineties.

DOES KEYNES LIVE?

There is an aspect of James Reston's remarks about the Great Crash of 1987 that might suggest that we have systematically overlooked a major feature of the eighties, the growth in the federal deficit. Could it be, after all, that the post-1982 economic recovery is merely a classic case of Keynesian aggregate-demand management, with the impetus for prosperity coming from the excess of government expenditures over government revenues? Possibly. But if one wishes to play the Keynesian game, it must be played in full. The United States is not a closed economy. Quite the contrary. It was affected in a major way by the patterns of international trade that marked the eighties. Those patterns enter into the familiar Keynesian

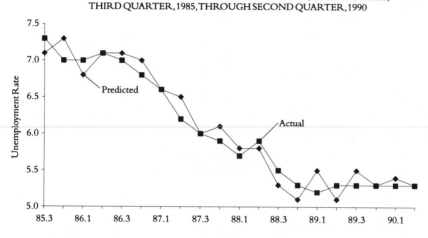

FIGURE 12.3

ACTUAL AND PREDICTED UNEMPLOYMENT RATES, UNITED STATES,
THIRD QUARTER, 1985, THROUGH SECOND QUARTER, 1990

spending equations in the form of net exports of goods and services (exports minus imports). During the bulk of the eighties, this was a negative figure, known simply as the "trade" deficit. What the United States experienced during the eighties was twin deficits—a fiscal one, emerging out of the nation's tax-and-spend policies, and a trade deficit, reflecting the excess of imports over exports.

The significance of the twin deficits is obvious. In a strict Keynesian sense, the effect of the trade deficit was to cancel the demand stimulus generated by the fiscal deficit. Over the years 1981–89, the total increments to the fiscal deficit, compared to its level in 1980, were $827.4 billion. In the same interval, the increments to the trade deficit, again compared to its 1980 level, were $718.4 billion. Since in the Keynesian model, these operate in opposite directions the combined additional demand stimulus from these two sources was $109 billion, or $12.1 billion a year. In a world in which the annual level of gross national product averaged a little more than four trillion dollars, this represents about three-tenths of one percent of GNP, hardly a major source of aggregate-demand stimulus. Besides, coincident with the presence of federal budget deficits were state and local government surpluses that amounted to an average of $48 billion a year during the eighties.[37] With these included, the combined stimulus from the fiscal and trade deficits is negative.

Beyond those simple aggregate numbers, there is an intriguing pattern in the movements of the fiscal and trade deficit. This year's fiscal deficit anticipates next year's trade deficit. This is shown in figure 12.4 where the

FIGURE 12.4

COMPARISON OF CHANGES IN FISCAL AND TRADE DEFICITS,
UNITED STATES, 1980-1989

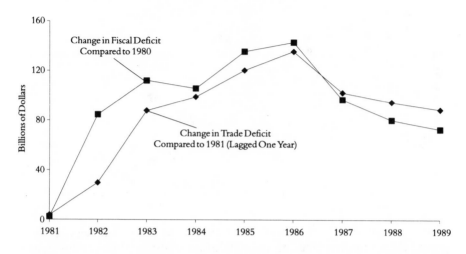

increase in the fiscal deficit in any given year is related to the trade deficit
of the following year. The similarity in the movements of the two data
series is clear. What this suggests is that any positive stimulus to aggregate
demand from the fiscal deficit this year is roughly canceled out next year
by a negative stimulus arising out of the trade deficit. Of course, this
relationship could be just a coincidental one. However, there is a line of
reasoning that would link the movements in the fiscal and trade deficits.
Fiscal deficits raise the real interest rate, which encourages capital inflows
into the United States, which influence exchange rates in a fashion that
encourages a greater volume of imports.[38] More than that, the nature of
the nation's balance of payments is such that the excess of imports over
exports should roughly equal the capital inflows. With an appropriate set
of elasticities in the markets for loanable funds, the linkage we have described in figure 12.4 is a possible one. However, the importance of the
observation that any aggregate-demand stimulus resulting from the fiscal
deficit was very largely canceled out by movements in the trade deficit does
not turn on the linkage between the two being systematic.

It is important to realize that aggregate-demand considerations are not
the only dimension of the trade deficit. Since the trade deficit is merely the
other side of the coin of capital imports, there is a supply-side effect that
may operate to increase levels of output and employment. If nothing else,
the excess of imports over exports that accompanies the capital imports has

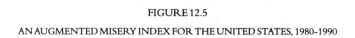

FIGURE 12.5

AN AUGMENTED MISERY INDEX FOR THE UNITED STATES, 1980-1990

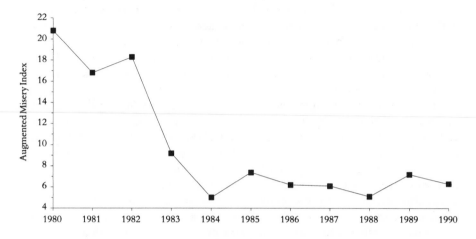

the effect of providing the United States with the services of a substantial volume of productive resources located abroad. This is a far more important facet of the trade deficit than any Keynesian aggregate-demand effects.

One final word on the deficit question. Robert Eisner has offered an interesting line of reasoning that maintains that, in a real sense, the whole issue of the federal deficit has been misstated.[39] He maintains that there really is no fiscal deficit problem. Accepting this has implications for the argument that government deficits "crowd out" private activity in the economy. Also, such a view is not consistent with the proposition that the fiscal activity of the federal government in the decade of the eighties produced Keynesian-style aggregate-demand stimulus sufficient to explain the prolonged economic recovery that followed the 1982 recession.

STABILITY IN THE EIGHTIES

How can the decade of the eighties be characterized? To borrow a phrase from the 1920s, it seems to represent a "return to normalcy." Viewed from the standpoint of the "augmented misery index" discussed in the previous chapter, there was a dramatic improvement in economic conditions in the United States. Figure 12.5 shows the behavior of the misery index during the 1980s. At the beginning of the decade it stood at 20.80, but within four years it had declined to 5.02. Further, 1984 is the beginning of a seven-year period, running through 1990, that shows the greatest stability of any interval of that length during the twentieth century. In those seven years, the misery index fluctuates, roughly, around a level that is very close to the median value of the index for this century, 5.92. At times, it seems as if the American economy had somehow achieved the classical stationary state. For example, between September 1988 and June 1990, inclusive, the civilian unemployment rate varied between only 5.1 and 5.4 percent. Only in one month was it at 5.1 percent and only in four months did it reach 5.4 percent. In the other seventeen months it was either 5.2 or 5.3 percent.

The behavior of unemployment in the United States during the eighties provides additional support for the premise that unemployment can be explained in terms of the basic neoclassical-Austrian model with modest lags in the basic adjustment processes. Especially convincing in this respect are the occurrences of the early 1980s. The neoclassical-Austrian paradigm indicates quite clearly why unemployment rose so dramatically in late 1982, while also accounting for the recovery from that recession. That experience confirms quite convincingly the existence of a tendency for the American economy to respond to a disequilibrium in labor markets with a series of adjustments that takes it back toward the equilibrium rate of unemployment, thereby producing stability of the type seen in the later portion of the eighties. Of course, such a sequence of events is conditioned on there being a minimum of governmental attempts to manage the economy.

Still, the myth that positive public policy is the key to macroeconomic stability persists. For example, on the occasion of the Keynes centenary, in the very midst of the surge in employment in the United States, Nobel laureate John R. Hicks made the remarkable statement, "The ship needs continual steering."[40] This remark embodies quintessentially the refusal by many economists to recognize the existence of a definable equilibrium, or natural, rate of unemployment to which the economy continually tends.

NOTES

1. See Thomas Sargent and Neil Wallace, "Rational Expectations, the Optimal Monetary Instrument and the Optimal Money Supply Rule," *Journal of Political Economy* 83 (1975): 241–54, and Robert E. Lucas and Leonard A. Rapping, "Real Wages, Employment, and Inflation," ibid., 77 (1969): 721–54.

2. The idea of a forecast error that is not corrected is sometimes expressed in the form of arguing that money wage rates are rigid in character, once they are agreed upon by market participants. Rigid money wage rates imply a lack of response to price and productivity shocks in the labor market.

3. In several ways, the Humphrey-Hawkins legislation is somewhat fatuous. It sets goals for the economy that simply are outside the realm of achievement. Its interim goals of 4 percent unemployment and 3 percent price inflation were so patently unfeasible that, as was discussed earlier, President Jimmy Carter felt compelled to postpone the achievement of such goals until well into the 1980s.

4. Jerome L. Stein, "Monetarist, Keynesian, and New Classical Economics," *American Economic Review* 71 (1982): 139–44, and *Monetarist, Keynesian, and New Classical Economics* (New York: New York University Press, 1982).

5. Of particular interest in the academic literature are analyses such as Michael J. Boskin, "Taxation, Saving, and the Rate of Interest," *Journal of Political Economy* 86 (1978): S3–S27; Martin Feldstein, "Does the United States Save Too Little?" *American Economic Review* 67 (1977): 116–21; and Feldstein, "Social Security and Saving: The Extended Life Cycle Theory," *American Economic Review* 66 (1976): 77–86, which challenge much of the prevailing wisdom about the relationship between saving and patterns of taxation.

6. Letter to the editor, *Wall Street Journal*, July 17, 1978, p. 11.

7. Walter Heller, "The Kemp-Roth-Laffer Free Lunch," ibid., July 12, 1978, p. 20.

8. Ibid.

9. In the August 1978 *Dun's Business Monthly*, Ackley is quoted as follows: "If Keynesians are correct that tax cuts increase demand by much more than they raise supply, a mammoth $120 billion tax cut (even if spread over three years) could produce an inflationary outburst that would dwarf anything we have seen up to now."

10. Herbert Stein, "The Real Reasons for a Tax Cut," *Wall Street Journal*, July 18, 1978, p. 20.

11. Walter Heller, "The Carter Program: Can It Work?" ibid., November 7, 1978, p. 20.

12. Paul A. Samuelson, "Outlook for the '80s," *Newsweek*, December 15, 1980, p. 88.

13. Ibid.

14. Lester Thurow, *The Zero-Sum Society* (New York: Basic Books, 1980).

15. Paul Craig Roberts, "The Economic Case for Kemp-Roth," *Wall Street Journal*, August 1, 1978, p. 16.

16. Compensation per hour in the business sector of the economy rose by 7.5 percent in the second quarter and 9.0 percent in the third quarter 1981. The GNP price deflator was 6.6 percent for the second quarter and 9.3 percent for the third. See *Economic Report of the President 1983* (Washington, D.C.: Government Printing Office, 1983), table B-41, p. 209.

17. The GNP implicit price deflator showed a similar pattern. From 1980 to 1981, it rose by 9.7 percent. From 1981 to 1982, the increase was 6.4 percent. See *Economic Report of The President 1991* (Washington, D.C.: Government Printing Office, 1991), table B-5, p. 293.

18. On October 6, 1979, the Federal Open Market Committee of the Federal Reserve unanimously approved the shift away from targeting interest rates. See

Lindley H. Clark, "Speaking of Business," *Wall Street Journal*, November 13, 1979, p. 23. In his article, Clark quoted Otto Eckstein's view of the shift in policy emphasis:

> The full implications of the change will not become visible for several years. . . . However, there should be little regret attached to the demise of the old approach. Interest rate management had meant in recent years that policy tended to move very late at every phase of the business cycle and that it would accommodate inflationary shocks and excess demand. It is no wonder that the surprises have been mainly on the inflation-side. . . .

We find Eckstein's position a persuasive one. For a detailed exposition of Federal Reserve Chairman Paul Volcker's views on this issue, see his statement before a November 24, 1982, hearing held by the Joint Economic Committee of Congress: *The Unemployment Crisis and Policies for Economic Recovery*, Ninety-Seventh Congress, Second Session, November 24, 1980 (Washington, D.C.: Government Printing Office, 1983).

19. See *Economic Report of the President 1991*, table B-47, p. 339. Measured by the GNP implicit price deflator, the decline in the rate of inflation in the business sector between 1981 and 1982 was only 3.7 percentage points—from 9.6 to 5.9.

20. *Economic Report of the President 1985* (Washington, D.C.: Government Printing Office, 1985), table B-29, p. 267.

21. The circumstances of this hearing are described in the *Washington Post* of Saturday, October 9, 1982. In addition, one of the authors of this book was present at the hearing in the capacity of a staff economist for the Joint Economic Committee.

22. Ibid, p. A-10.

23. Ibid.

24. Ibid.

25. Remarks of Representative Henry Reuss, Democratic response to President's radio address, Saturday, October 9, 1982; mimeograph, circulated within the Joint Economic Committee of Congress, October 1982.

26. Statement, before Joint Economic Committee of Congress, *Hearings, The Unemployment Crisis and Policies for Economic Recovery*, Ninety-Seventh Congress, Second Session, October 15, 1982 (Washington, D.C.: Government Printing Office, 1983), p. 32. Later that fall, Arthur Schlesinger, Jr., argued in a somewhat similar vein as follows:

> Some in high places today would have us abandon social responsibility in the name of unbridled individualism. They claim that the best way to treat our problems is to cut social programs for the poor and taxes for the rich. They would remove the protecting arm of the government from our industrial life, consign working people to the harsh mercies of the unregulated market, and redistribute income from the poor and middle classes to the already affluent. . . . Their policies are rekindling the fires of class war.

See "Statement," before Joint Economic Committee of Congress, *Hearings, Political Economy and Constitutional Reform*, Ninety-Seventh Congress, Second Session, Part

1, November 17, 1982 (Washington, D.C.: Government Printing Office, 1983), p. 227.

27.   Galbraith and Heller testified at a congressional hearing on October 15, 1982. *Hearings, The Unemployment Crisis and Policies for Economic Recovery.*

28.   Ibid., p. 21.

29.   Ibid.

30.   Ibid.

31.   Joint Economic Committee of Congress, *Hearings, The Unemployment Crisis and Policies for Economic Recovery*, Ninety-Seventh Congress, Second Session, October 20, 1982 (Washington, D.C.: Government Printing Office, 1983), p. 105.

32.   Ibid., p. 114.

33.   Ibid.

34.   Ibid.

35.   *Washington Post*, October 21, 1987, section A, p. 23.

36.   *New York Times*, October 21, 1987, section 1, p. 35.

37.   *Economic Report of the President 1991*, table B-79, p. 379.

38.   This line of reasoning is quite consistent with the formal economic theory that relates an external equilibrium in the balance of payments to internal equilibrium in the traditional IS-LM sense.

39.   Robert Eisner, "Which Budget Deficit? Some Issues of Measurement and their Implications," *American Economic Review* 74 (1984): 138–43; Eisner and Paul J. Pieper, "A New View of the Federal Debt and Budget Deficits," ibid. 11–29; and Eisner, *How Real is the Federal Deficit?* (New York: Free Press, 1986).

40.   John R. Hicks, "A Skeptical Follower," *The Economist*, June 18, 1983, p. 18.

13

The
Natural Rate of
Unemployment

Like most accounts of economic change, this book has emphasized short-run movements in economic variables, in this case unemployment. Yet in our concern for explaining variations in the amount of joblessness from one year to the next, we risk the possibility of ignoring longer-term shifts in the magnitude of unemployment. There has, in fact, been a fairly considerable variation in "typical" or "normal" rates of unemployment over the twentieth century. In this chapter, we return to a longer time horizon to attempt to suggest reasons for these changes. Our conclusions are, frankly, rather more speculative than those developed earlier, but we think highly plausible and defensible.

To begin, let us examine what has happened to "average" unemployment rates over time. In figure 13.1, we present a moving average of unemployment rates, where the average consists of ten years (the year in question plus the previous nine years.) This is a measure of the typical unemployment rate encompassing a period that usually includes at least two full business cycles. The conspicuous exception is the Great Depression era, where extremely high unemployment rates persisted for an entire decade. Our account begins with 1907 because the average unemployment rate for earlier years was heavily influenced by nineteenth-century unemployment experiences not discussed in this volume.

FIGURE 13.1

A 10 YEAR MOVING AVERAGE OF THE UNEMPLOYMENT RATE, 1907-1990

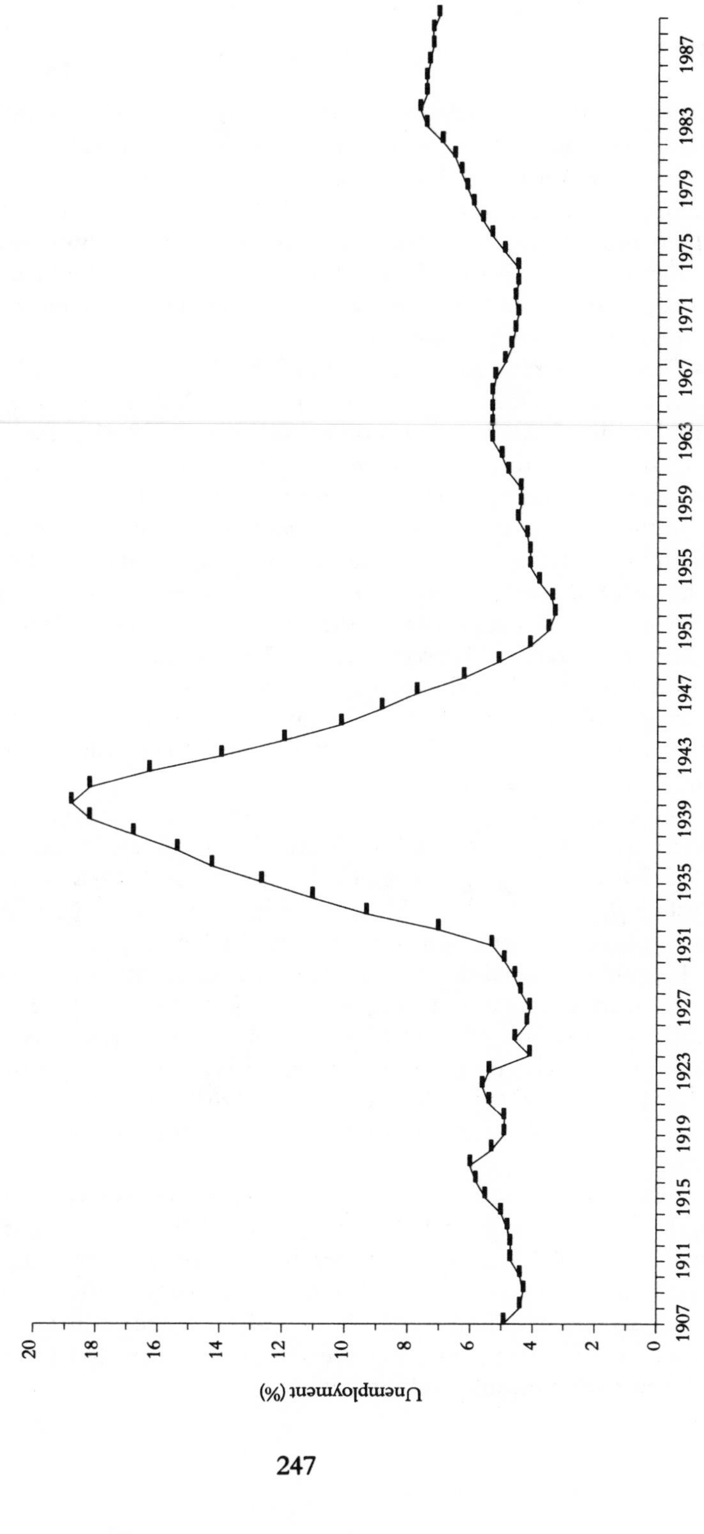

247

For the 1907 to 1929 period, the average long-run unemployment rate varies between 4.39 and 6.07 percent, with most of the years having a rate of less than 5 percent. There is no obvious tendency for the rate to rise or fall over time, although the lowest observed rates came comparatively late (1926 and 1927). It is not much of an exaggeration, however, to say that in the generation before the Great Depression, unemployment rates tended to oscillate around 5 percent, with no pronounced tendency for the long-term average rate to rise or fall.

The average rates for the period 1930 to 1954 are influenced by the abnormalities of the Great Depression and World War II. The range of ten-year average rates is astonishing, going from a low of 3.41 percent in 1952 to a high of 18.82 percent just twelve years earlier. It is no wonder that pressures to tame the business cycle were most intense in that era.

In the postwar era from 1955 to 1990, the swings in average unemployment rates narrow again, but not to the extent seen in the 1907–29 period. The range of average rates is 4.19 to 7.67 percent. Compared to the 1907–29 era, in a smaller proportion of the years, the average, or long-term, rate is less than 5 percent, 39 percent versus 57 percent. More strikingly, however, in fully one-third of the years the average rate exceeds 6 percent, which was true of only one year in the earlier era. This suggests that the long-term unemployment rate in modern times tends to be somewhat higher and less stable than in the earlier era.

Most disturbingly, the long-term unemployment rate has a distinct upward trend during the 1955–90 era. With the exception of the period 1963–73, it tends to rise over time until the mid-1980s, at which point a decline begins. By the 1980s, one might consider 7 percent a "typical" unemployment rate, compared with under 5 percent thirty years earlier.

It could be argued that ten years is not a sufficiently lengthy time horizon to measure a long-run average unemployment rate; ten-year averages are still fairly heavily influenced by specific business cycle episodes. Accordingly, we calculated a twenty-five-year moving average, presented in figure 13.2. Data limitations force us to begin with 1914. As it is, the early observations are moderately heavily influenced by the nineteenth-century experience.

Using this measure of long-term average unemployment, the rate started in the 7 percent range and fell until the late 1920s, bottoming at 4.59 percent in 1929. Then it began to rise, reaching a plateau in the 10 percent range by around 1940, where it remained to the early 1950s, when it began a sharp decline, reaching a century low of 4.18 percent in 1966. Since 1966, however, the average rate has risen in twenty-three of twenty-four years, passing the 6 percent level by 1990.[1]

FIGURE 13.2

A 25 YEAR MOVING AVERAGE OF THE UNEMPLOYMENT RATE, 1914-1990

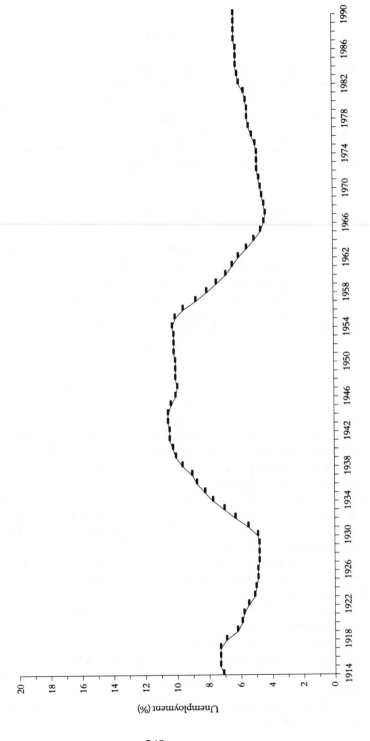

The two data sets agree on four points. First, we had a successful average unemployment experience in the 1920s, with the long-run average rate in most years being less than 5 percent. Second, we had a disastrous experience in the 1930s. Third, the 1950s was a successful era, with either a low (ten-year average) or rapidly falling (twenty-five-year average) long-run average unemployment rate. Fourth, the late 1970s and early 1980s were a period of a rising average rate of unemployment.

An Overview of the Natural Rate of Unemployment

The variations in the moving averages reported above reflect fluctuations in both cyclical unemployment, on the one hand, and frictional and structural unemployment on the other. We have extensively discussed cyclical unemployment in the previous twelve chapters. We wish to focus our attention here on changes in the noncyclical components of unemployment, that is, frictional and structural. In short, we wish to look at the natural rate of unemployment.

TRENDS IN CYCLICAL UNEMPLOYMENT BRIEFLY REVISITED

Before turning to structural and frictional conditions, however, some restatement of the nature of cyclical unemployment is in order. Reviewing for the noneconomist reader, the natural rate of unemployment is the unemployment rate that persists where there is no money illusion.[2] When unemployment is at the natural rate, the rate of price inflation is exactly where people expect it to be. When actual inflation is greater than expected, people are caught off guard. In the context of our model, real wages are pushed below the levels expected by workers, lowering the adjusted real wage and unemployment, and increasing output. Workers are tricked into accepting lower wages than those desired, given their tastes and behavioral patterns. Similarly, prices (interest rates) are pushed below expected levels in the loanable funds market.

According to this view, discussed in earlier chapters, unemployment rises when inflation rates are less than people anticipated; real wages are pushed up above the expected levels; and employment and output are reduced. Thus the business cycle can be viewed in large part as evolving out of the accuracy of the perceptions of economic agents regarding the rate of inflation.

We believe this basic theory is highly insightful, yet not a total explanation of cyclical behavior with respect to unemployment. For example, pro-

TABLE 13.1

LEVELS AND VARIATIONS OF AMERICAN UNEMPLOYMENT RATES, PRICES, WAGES,
MONEY, PRODUCTIVITY, DEFICITS AND GROWTH, 1900–1989

Variable[a]	Average			Standard Deviation:		
	1900–29	1930–59	1960–89	1900–29	1930–59	1960–89
Unemployment Rate	4.70	9.30	6.09	2.29	7.36	1.60
% Change, Money Wage	5.07	4.78	6.49	6.19	5.66	2.29
% Change, Consumer Prices	2.61	1.91	5.00	6.42	5.14	3.32
% Change, Productivity	2.11	2.54	1.87	4.09	3.24	1.55
% Change, M2	7.14	5.49	8.27	5.23	5.14	2.80
Federal Deficit As % of GNP	0.66	3.87	1.93	3.67	8.00	1.78
% Change, Real GNP	3.62	3.10	3.19	6.54	7.79	2.28

[a]Variables are expressed on an annual basis (e.g., the percent change per year in real GNP.)
Source: Authors' calculations from U.S. Department of Commerce, U.S. Department of Labor, and Federal Reserve System data.

ductivity growth over time is subject to fluctuations, and while one could extend the natural rate concept to incorporate "productivity illusion," that is not generally done. Some of the ebbs and flows in employment and thus output are reflected in productivity change. We have argued that Keynesian productivity change induced by aggregate-demand shifts is uncommon, but that on occasion there may be Smithian (induced by changing rates of capital formation) or Schumpeterian (induced by fluctuations in the pace of innovation) variations in productivity change. The "real business cycle" literature of modern times has rediscovered the latter form of change.[3]

We suggested at the outset that while the overall magnitudes of unemployment in recent decades do not compare favorably with the first three decades of the century, the variation in the rate of unemployment has actually been moderately reduced. Table 13.1 suggests why. The rates of change in the various components of the adjusted real wage, as measured by standard deviations, have declined. Prices, while rising faster than earlier in the century, are fluctuating less, even in an absolute sense. This, no doubt, has contributed in part to a decline in the fluctuations in wage increases. Also, productivity growth, while declining somewhat in absolute magnitudes in modern times, has at least tended to be less volatile than earlier.

These findings are consistent with the view that wage stability has promoted unemployment stability. Since, for example, inflation rates vary less than they used to, price increases are less likely to catch workers seriously off guard, a circumstance that leads to nonexpected (and nonequilibrium) wages, and thus to rising or falling cyclical unemployment. This greater certainty, in turn, probably has reduced labor militancy and, in turn, contributes to less volatility in money wages over time.

The table supports the basic validity of a fundamental monetarist principle, namely that the amount of inflation is tied to increases in the money supply. Note that while the magnitude of price increases is influenced by the amount of money created, there is some evidence that monetary policy has, on balance, become more stable, thus reducing employment instability through its impact on price-wage volatility.

Table 13.1 suggests, using long-term data, that the negative Phillips curve relationship is not a valid guide for policy. The 1960–89 period had significantly more inflation (via higher monetary growth) than the era 1900–1929, but also higher unemployment. While a short-run negative relationship between price inflation and unemployment often exists (as our own model demonstrates), it does not persist in the long run because of the fact that money illusion cannot be maintained permanently.

Regarding fiscal policy, note that the period with the most expansionary fiscal policy, 1930–59, had the highest average rate of unemployment, while the period with the least expansionary fiscal policy had the lowest average rate of unemployment.[4] Over the long run, it would appear that stimulating aggregate demand may sometimes enhance inflation, but not "real" variables such as economic growth and employment. Indeed, there is a perfect rank-order negative correlation in table 13.1 between fiscal policy stimulus and the average annual rate of economic growth.

TRENDS IN THE NATURAL RATE OF UNEMPLOYMENT

Since money illusion cannot be maintained indefinitely, the natural rate of unemployment over reasonably long time periods should approximate the average or median rate of unemployment. Based on figures 13.1 and 13.2, it would seem that the natural rate of unemployment in the early decades of the century probably exceeded 4 percent, but was less than 5 percent. Moreover, the natural rate in the 1950s and 1960s probably was also in that range. Over the entire period 1900–1969, the median annual unemployment rate was 5.1 percent; if the 1930s are excluded, the median falls to 4.6 percent. It probably would be safe to state that the natural rate of unemployment oscillated narrowly around a 5 percent rate over most of the period 1900–1969.

Since 1970, the median unemployment rate, based on data for twenty-two years (1970–91) is 6.65 percent. If one begins this latter period in 1974, the eighteen-year median is 7.1 percent. It seems likely that the natural rate has been in the 6–7 percent range in this period.[5] As suggested earlier, this rise occurred mainly in the 1970s, and it is possible that the natural rate actually began falling in the mid-1980s. Nonetheless, on balance, the natural rate has been noticeably higher in the last decades of the century than earlier.

Some writers of popular surveys of intermediate-level macroeconomic theory have suggested that the natural rate has slowly drifted upward over the twentieth century. For example, Robert Gordon thinks that the natural rate rose from 3.4 percent in 1900 to 6.0 percent by 1975, rising by no more than 0.4 points in any decade.[6] Looking at the post-1960 period and using a Data Resources Inc. model, Dornbush and Fischer seem to accept the same conclusion.[7] Indeed, their estimated rate never exceeds 5 percent.

Such estimates simply are inconsistent with the historical experience. If the DRI estimate were accepted, we would have passed through some twenty years with unemployment rather consistently above its natural rate. It requires a rather jaundiced view of human intelligence to accept the notion that people have been consistently fooled for decades, with inflation persistently being less than expected. This is particularly true when one considers that the actual average rate of inflation increased considerably over this period. The same criticism holds, albeit to a lesser extent, for Gordon's results.

Frictional Unemployment in Recent Decades

Why did the natural rate rise in modern times? The natural rate reflects frictional and structural unemployment. What has happened to frictional unemployment over time? Recall that frictional unemployment results when qualified workers are out of work temporarily because they do not have perfect labor-market information (e.g., it takes time and effort to learn about job opportunities.) With the significant decline in communication costs, given the advent of modern computers and electronics, it would seem that the long-run trend would be for frictional unemployment to decline, not increase.

One possible explanation for a rise in frictional unemployment would be increased geographic mobility. If a person moves to a new state looking for a job, he or she could well be frictionally unemployed for a time while exploring job opportunities in a new area in which the aspiring worker knows little about labor markets. Yet the evidence is fairly strong that geographic mobility has declined during the period in which the natural rate of unemployment has risen. Evidence from the annual *Current Population Survey* (CPS) suggests that in the mid- to late 1960s (near the end of the era of the 4–5 percent natural rate of unemployment), about 3.4 percent of the population made an interstate move annually. By the mid- to late 1980s, however, that proportion had fallen to under 3 percent per year.[8]

Looking at the 1950s and early 1960s, N. J. Simler concluded that short-term unemployment was about 2 percent of the labor force.[9] One could assume that short-term unemployment (under fifteen weeks) is essentially frictional in nature, whereas longer-term unemployment tends to be structural and cyclical. Simler regressed the percent of unemployment that was long-term (over fifteen weeks) against the total unemployment rate, with the intercept term providing what we regard as a crude but probably reasonably accurate estimate of frictional unemployment. Replicating the Simler procedure for the 1970–90 period yields:

(1) $U_t = 1.54 + 0.2012\ U_{1t}$, $\overline{R}^2 = .83$, $D-W = 1.923$,
                (2.26)   (7.58)

where U_t is the total unemployment rate, U_{1t} is the percent of the labor force unemployed for more than fifteen weeks, and the numbers in parentheses are t-values. An autoregressive term is omitted.

The replication of the Simler procedure suggests that frictional unemployment actually has fallen in recent decades, to slightly over 1.5 percent. This is consistent with the view that falling information costs have lowered frictional unemployment. Thus the rise in structural unemployment is probably even greater than the rise in the overall natural rate of unemployment.

The Increase in Structural Unemployment

It would seem likely, then, that the rise in the natural rate of unemployment has resulted from greater structural unemployment. Two types of explanation for that increase are worth noting: demographic changes reflecting the shift in the age composition of workers and the participation of citizens in labor-market activities; and the impact of public policies that have led to an increase in the equilibrium adjusted real wage.

AGE COMPOSITION OF THE LABOR FORCE

Some standard surveys of macroeconomics attribute the rise in the natural rate of unemployment largely to a shift in the composition of the labor force to proportionally more individuals for whom the incidence of unemployment is high, notably teenagers and young adults.[10] Our own research looking at data for 1960 and 1979 suggests that a secondary determinant of the rise in the natural rate of unemployment can be attributed to age-composition shifts.[11] Our estimates suggest that, at most, 40 percent of the rise in the natural rate was age-related.

Unemployment rates among teenagers tend to be dramatically higher than those of other segments of the population. We calculated what the aggregate unemployment rate would be for various recent years assuming that the 1960 proportion of teenagers in the labor force was maintained, but also that the interage unemployment differentials were as observed in the various years. From 1960 to 1973, the rise in the relative importance of teenagers is estimated to have raised the unemployment rate by about 0.3 points. Even if some other nonteenage compositional shifts were at work, it is hard to believe that the overall unemployment impact of the age factor exceeded 0.5 points. However, the natural rate probably rose by less than 1.0 percentage points over that period (rising no more than 0.07 points a year and probably less), so the age factor conceivably was an important determinant in the rise in unemployment.

The natural rate almost certainly rose rapidly from 1973 to 1980. The ten-year moving average unemployment rate rose by 1.86 points in this period, or nearly 0.27 points per year. The twenty-five-year moving average moved up by 0.70 points, a still impressive 0.10 points per year. Over this period, however, the proportion of teenagers in the labor force actually began to decline (albeit very little), so the age composition factor probably played no role in the observed increase.

In the 1980s, the declining proportion of teenagers in the labor force should have led to a decrease in unemployment exceeding 0.30 points; when other age groups are taken into account, it is conceivable that the age factor accounts for a 0.50 point drop in the natural rate of unemployment. We believe (and the ten-year moving average data confirm) that some fall in the natural rate may have set in by the mid-1980s which may be attributable, at least in part, to demographic factors.

Looking at the whole historical experience from 1960 to 1990, the natural rate of unemployment was clearly higher in the latter year than in the former, indeed one to two full percentage points higher. Yet the proportion of teenagers in the labor force in 1990 was actually slightly less than in 1960. Over the long term, it is hard to attribute increases in the natural rate to demographic factors, even though those factors may have explained some comparatively modest increases or decreases within the longer time frame.

GROWTH IN LABOR SUPPLY

Perhaps a better case can be made that the 1970s saw a rise in unemployment because of an unusually large amount of labor-force growth. The labor force in the 1970s grew by over 24 million, or 30 percent. In absolute terms, this was nearly twice the growth in labor-force participants observed in the 1960s, and three times the increase of the 1950s, and is, in fact, the largest growth for any decade in the twentieth century. In large part, this reflected a rise in female labor-force participation (which rose an extraordinary 35 percent.) Some might argue that the economy simply was not accustomed to such growth in labor supply, and that millions of new relatively unskilled workers could not find work given the slow growth in demand for those jobs. One might evoke a sex-compositional argument similar to that used for age composition to explain part of the rise in unemployment in the 1970s. Throughout that decade, the female unemployment rate was consistently (1.4 to 1.9 percentage points) above that for males. Yet, had the gender shift in the labor force not occurred between 1970 and 1980, the aggregate unemployment rate for 1980 would have been less than .20 points lower than what actually occurred.

Believers in the wage hypothesis emphatically reject this labor-absorption argument. An unusual increase in labor supply should have led to a downward drift in real wages adjusted for productivity to prevent unemployment from rising. After World War II, demobilization led to an even more dramatic increase in the civilian labor force than that of the 1970s, and the economy adjusted to it, with only minor unemployment effects, through a downward shift in real wages.

Over the critical years 1973–79, however, the adjusted real wage remained essentially unchanged in the face of the labor supply boom. Money wages rose by record peacetime amounts, exceeding 9 percent a year in a majority of years. This was despite the fact that a larger proportion of the labor force than previously was relatively inexperienced (new job entrants.) The median adjusted real wage for the 1970s (using annual data) was over 1 percent higher than for the 1960s. The dramatic increase in labor-force involvement did not have the expected impact on real-wage rates.

CHANGING COMPOSITION OF JOBS

It is possible that the apparent acceleration in the rise of the natural rate of unemployment in the 1970s is a consequence of changes in the occupational mix of the labor force that increased the mismatch of skills between unemployed and available jobs. For example, the number of operators of computers and peripheral equipment nearly tripled in nine short years between 1972 and 1981.[12] Could it be that the pace of technological change was accelerating, causing more structural unemployment problems?

To explore this possibility, we examined the changing proportion of the labor force in nine occupational categories in the 1950–60 decade, and again for the period 1970–81. Ignoring the direction of movement, we calculated the mean change in the percent of the labor force in the various categories. There was virtually no difference: interoccupational migration was about the same in the 1970s as in the 1950s. While a definitive evaluation of this issue would require analysis at a more detailed level of occupational groupings, we see no evidence that the pace of occupational change quickened significantly during the era of significant increases in the natural rate of unemployment.

Governmental Policies and Structural Unemployment

In several preceding chapters, we have suggested that various governmental policies have tended to increase unemployment. Considering that demographic and occupational compositional changes played a limited role, can the rise in the natural rate after the 1960s be attributed in part to governmental policies? We believe the answer to that question is "yes."

FIVE WAGE-ENHANCING POLICIES OF GOVERNMENT

Over the past six decades, the federal government has passed myriad forms of legislation that directly or indirectly had, and still have, the effect of increasing wages for some workers, contributing to a rise in the adjusted real wage, and leading to a higher measured unemployment equilibrium than would otherwise be the case. Let us cite five examples: the Davis-Bacon Act, the Fair Labor Standards Act, the National Labor Relations Act, the various civil rights acts, and the legislative enactments that have increased federal employment.

Passed in 1931, the Davis-Bacon Act provided for "prevailing wages" to be paid on federally funded construction projects. Prevailing wages were interpreted to be the union-scale wages existing in a locality. Over time, the impact of Davis-Bacon has expanded as federal funding for non–federally owned capital projects has grown, and as state governments have passed "little Davis-Bacon laws" to supplement federal legislation. This legislation originally had racial overtones and may have served to increase minority unemployment in the construction industry.

The Fair Labor Standards Act of 1938 established a federal minimum-wage law. Since then, the impact of the legislation has grown substantially as the result of coverage being expanded to include previously excluded groups as well as by increases in the minimum. There is a massive literature that suggests that the federal minimum-wage law adds to unemployment, particularly for teenagers and minorities.[13]

TABLE 13.2

GROWTH IN GOVERNMENTAL EMPLOYMENT IN THE UNITED STATES, 1929–1990

Year	Number [a] of Governmental Employees	Number[a] Employed	Government as a Percent of Total
1929	3,065	46,467	6.60
1940	4,202	48,060	8.74
1950	6,026	60,087	10.03
1960	8,353	67,639	12.35
1970	12,554	80,796	15.54
1980	15,837	100,907	15.70
1990	18,096[b]	119,550	15.14

[a]In thousands.
[b]Partly estimated from actual 1988 data.
Source: 1990 Statistical Abstract of the United States; 1991 Economic Report of the President.

The National Labor Relations Act (Wagner Act) of 1935 and other pieces of legislation had a major influence in an approximate tripling in the proportion of the nonagricultural labor force belonging to labor unions in the late 1930s and early 1940s. Later legislation (most notably the Taft-Hartley Act of 1947) reduced somewhat the power of unions (e.g., by outlawing the closed shop and secondary boycotts, and allowing states to dispense with the union shop via right-to-work laws). Nevertheless, legal protection for labor organizations today is far greater than in the first third of this century. H. Gregg Lewis and other scholars have found that, on balance, the economic impact of unions has been to increase wage rates.[14]

Although the first civil rights legislation was passed in the late 1950s, the major laws came with the Civil Rights Act of 1964 and subsequent legislation. The civil rights legislation made wage-based discrimination legally indefensible, and probably served to induce employers to increase wages for minorities and females relative to males. The affirmative action programs following from civil rights legislation tended to promote a numerical goal or quota approach to racial dimensions of labor markets, probably artificially stimulating the demand for minority employees in order to meet goals, and thereby increasing minority wages. While the precise dimensions of this wage effect are hard to quantify, there is widespread casual evidence that minority salaries in professional areas are thousands of dollars annually above white salaries for comparable individuals. The impact of this on unemployment is uncertain, but it likely has been wage-enhancing.

Lastly, the growth of government has led to a huge rise in both the absolute and relative importance of government employment (table 13.2.) The proportion of the labor force working for local, state, or federal governments has more than doubled since 1929. Data for recent years suggest that government employees earn somewhat higher salaries and more generous fringe benefits than workers in the private sector.[15] The low quit rates

TABLE 13.3

THE GROWTH IN WORKERS' COMPENSATION, 1940 TO 1988

Year	Workers Covered[a]	Benefits Paid[b] ($)	Benefits as % of Payroll
1940	25	256	0.72
1950	37	615	0.54
1960	45	1,295	0.59
1970	59	3,031	0.66
1980	79	13,618	1.07
1988	94	30,789	1.49

[a]In millions.
[b]In millions of dollars.
Source: 1991 Statistical Abstract of the United States.

and long list of applicants for such jobs as postal workers and teachers suggest that government employees are paid above-equilibrium wages.[16] Over time, public employees have been able to extract economic rents from the taxpayer. The end of the armed-forces draft has also led to compensation going from below-equilibrium levels to equilibrium or above levels of pay.

GOVERNMENTAL POLICIES RAISING THE RESERVATION WAGE

We suggested earlier that the duration of unemployment is determined by the interaction of job offers to prospective workers and the reservation wage of those workers. The higher the reservation wage, the longer an employee will remain unemployed. In fact, many workers counted in unemployment statistics are voluntarily unemployed in the sense that they have implicitly or explicitly turned down job opportunities that do not pay what they feel they deserve.

Three types of governmental policies raising the reservation wage in recent decades are worth mentioning: unemployment compensation, workers' compensation, and public-assistance payments. Following up on the pioneering research of Gene Chapin, Martin Feldstein estimated in the 1970s that unemployment insurance payments serve to raise the aggregate unemployment rate by the better part of one full percentage point.[17]

Less publicized is the extraordinary growth in workers' compensation payments particularly in recent years. In 1989, over 13.8 million Americans from sixteen to sixty-four were classified as having an employment disability, some 8.6 percent of that population.[18] As table 13.3 demonstrates, disability payments have exploded in recent years. In an earlier era, many persons who were unable to engage in heavy labor would have taken jobs requiring less physical effort. The establishment and expansion of the worker's compensation program has sharply raised the reservation wage of a segment of the population. Moreover, by directly increasing labor costs (average total workers' compensation premiums by employers now exceed 2 percent of payroll), the workers' compensation program has raised the adjusted real wage.

The area where government may well have had the greatest impact on labor markets is public assistance. The modern welfare state in America began in the 1930s, with a second huge expansion in the 1960s and 1970s. Expenditures for what the Social Security Administration terms "public aid" rose from 0.73 percent of GNP in 1953 to 2.73 percent by 1976, with nearly all of the increase coming after 1967. After holding relatively constant for a few years, the proportion fell slightly in the 1980s, reaching 2.47 percent in 1988.[19]

There is abundant evidence that public-assistance payments raise the reservation wage, reducing employment participation.[20] We regressed the unemployment rate against public aid as a percent of GNP and several other control variables for the period 1953–88. We obtained a consistently positive and highly significant, in a statistical sense, association between public assistance and unemployment.[21] In general, it appears that a one percentage point increase in the proportion of GNP devoted to public assistance is associated with about a one percentage point increase in the unemployment rate (e.g., from 5 to 6 percent.) This implies that the negative employment effects of public assistance are rather large.

Critics of this finding often raise the issue of causation: they claim that unemployment creates public assistance, rather than the reverse. To deal with this, we used regression analysis for the period 1954 to 1989 to relate public-assistance changes to later changes in unemployment, with statistically significant results obtained. Also, the use of cross-sectional data where public assistance is measured by average monthly AFDC benefits shows a statistically significant relationship with unemployment—a correlation that is hard to reconcile with causation running predominantly from unemployment to benefit levels.

It is true, almost by definition, that there is some reverse causality present: some people who become unemployed do seek public assistance. However, that does not detract from the existence of labor-market effects of welfare. The disincentive effects extend more generally to the willingness of welfare recipients to work. As Robert Moffitt recently concluded in a major survey article, "The literature on the incentive effects of the U.S. welfare system has shown unequivocal evidence of effects on labor supply. . . ."[22]

Minorities tend to have lower incomes, and thus use public-assistance benefits disproportionately. Figure 13.3 shows that in 1954, the employment-population ratio was higher for nonwhite Americans than for whites.

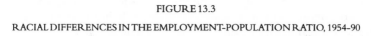

FIGURE 13.3

RACIAL DIFFERENCES IN THE EMPLOYMENT-POPULATION RATIO, 1954-90

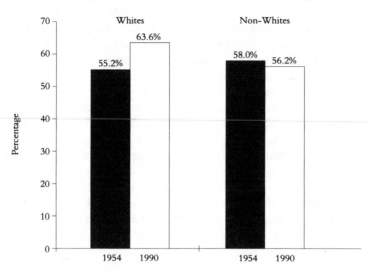

By 1990, the situation was dramatically reversed. We suspect that the reason relates largely to the differential impact of public-assistance payments on the two groups.

OTHER PUBLIC POLICIES

There are a variety of other government actions that have had an effect on labor-market conditions. For example, income and related taxes impact importantly on labor supply. On three occasions in the twentieth century, the Mellon tax cuts in the 1920s, the Kennedy tax cuts of 1964–65, and the Reagan tax cuts of 1981 and after, labor effort and income of the most impacted groups (upper-income Americans) expanded enormously after tax reductions.[23] In some instances, already employed individuals "employed" themselves more intensively, working harder to add to income after tax reductions increased the rate of return on labor services. Of course, when taxes rise, as they frequently do following significant reductions, the opposite effects are observed, including an increase in the reservation wage of many people.

Also, the Social Security Act of 1935 has had the long-term impact of increasing labor costs very significantly. To the extent that employers shift the burden of the employer share of social security taxes to the worker through lower money wages, it might be argued that social security has little or no unemployment impact. Yet it is probably true that the burden of increased social security taxes or coverage has not always been instantly shifted to employees. Also, there is a considerable literature that suggests that social security has impacted adversely on savings, private-sector capital formation, and consequently on labor productivity.[24] In addition, by providing an alternative source of income to potential workers, it has had an impact in producing higher reservation wage rates.[25]

Finally, an increasingly important cause of structural unemployment is job loss associated with governmental environmental or safety regulations. At this writing, thousands of jobs in the timber industry in the Northwest are in jeopardy because of proposed environmental regulations forbidding timber cutting to reduce damage to endangered animal species. Within miles of where this book is being written, some 1,260 coal-mining jobs are in jeopardy because the 1990 Clean Air Act's standards are forcing a utility to burn low-sulfur coal not available in southeastern Ohio. Not atypically, the coal mine operates in a sparsely populated area with thin labor markets, so closing it inevitably will create at least some additional structural unemployment.

Spatial Dimensions of American Unemployment

We originally suggested that while regional differences in unemployment do exist, over time they tend to narrow. At the same time, however, there are areas where the normal rate of unemployment tends to be relatively low, while other areas tend to have rather persistently high levels of unemployment. This is shown in table 13.4, which describes the median annual rate of unemployment for three years between 1930 and 1950 and ten years between 1961 and 1988 for the nine census regions of the country.

Regional disparities are noticeable in both periods. In the earlier interval, the highest unemployment region (the Mid-Atlantic states) had nearly double the unemployment rate of the lowest unemployment region, the West North-Central. For the more recent decades, the disparities narrowed somewhat, but the highest-unemployment region, the Pacific states, excluding Alaska and Hawaii, which were omitted from the sample because of data limitations, had unemployment well over 50 percent higher than the lowest-unemployment region, again, the West North-Central states. The median rates fell from the earlier period, which contains two Depression-era observations, for six of the census regions, but rose in the three southern regions.

TABLE 13.4

MEDIAN UNEMPLOYMENT RATES FOR CENSUS REGIONS, 1930–1988[a]

Region	Period:	
	1930–50 (%)[b]	1961–1988 (%)[c]
New England	8.15	5.84
Mid Atlantic	8.97	6.46
East North Central	7.10	6.07
West North Central	4.62	4.44
South Atlantic	4.78	5.55
East South Central	4.65	6.68
West South Central	5.58	5.84
Mountain	7.38	6.17
Pacific	7.77	6.97

[a]For each period, the average rate for the dates observed were calculated by state; the median of those averages was used here.
[b]Years observed were 1930, 1940, and 1950.
[c]Years observed were 1961 and every third year thereafter.
Source: Authors' calculations from U.S. Department of Labor data.

The West North-Central region had the lowest median unemployment rate in both periods; in the 1961–88 period, the rate in these states was fully 20 percent below that of the next lowest region, the South Atlantic area, which also was among the lowest regions in the earlier period. By contrast, the Mid-Atlantic and Pacific regions tended to have relatively high unemployment in both periods. Looking at individual states, the contrasts are even more striking. For example, for the 1961–88 period, the median unemployment rate was less than 4 percent in Nebraska and South Dakota, but exceeded 9 percent in West Virginia. If neo-Keynesian unemployment hysteresis exists anywhere, it is in West Virginia, whose median unemployment rate for the recent period was nearly 20 percent higher than in any other state.

Within regions, there are some interesting variations. Why was the typical unemployment rate in New Hampshire in the three recent decades more than 25 percent lower than in any other New England state? Why did Michigan have 20 percent more unemployment than Illinois? Why did Louisiana have nearly 50 percent higher unemployment than the three neighboring states in the West South-Central region? Why was New Mexico's rate significantly above that of any of its neighbors?

Looking at the regional data, it appears that the lowest unemployment areas are locations with relatively high agricultural employment, modest levels of unionization, and a comparatively modest incidence of public assistance.[26] This is confirmed by regression analysis that uses the state-level data. In this model, the unemployment rate for a recent year (1988) is explained by several variables: population density (a measure of agricultural activity and rural population), the proportion of manufacturing employ-

ment that is unionized, and federal expenditures on several income maintenance programs as a percent of personal income. All variables work in the
expected direction.[27]

Examples of specific states that reflect these factors are abundant. For
example, two states with rather high levels of welfare involvement (e.g.,
West Virginia or Vermont) tend to have higher unemployment relative to
states with low levels of such involvement (e.g., New Hampshire.) While
this correlation certainly does not prove causation, it is consistent with the
theorizing and discussion about the debilitating effects of public assistance
on labor-force participation. The rationale for the other explanatory variables included in this analysis is quite clear. Rural areas, which tend to be
less impacted by minimum-wage laws, affirmative action, unemployment
compensation insurance, etc., than urban areas, in general show less unemployment. As to the unionization variable, high levels of unionization are
associated with higher equilibrium real wages and a greater volume of
unemployment. While this brief examination of regional patterns of unemployment is far from exhaustive or definitive, the evidence at least suggests
that the patterns are consistent with the view that the natural rate of unemployment has increased in line with additional market rigidities that have
been imposed by governments and labor unions. To be sure, more work on
regional unemployment differentials needs to be done, and the conclusions
above are more suggestive than definitive. However, they are useful.

To close, these observations are also consistent with those we obtained
in a recent study with Robert Lawson using a model explaining interstate
variations in the labor-force participation rate.[28] In that study, we observed
also that unemployment rates seem to vary with the political complexion
of a geographic area. Areas that are relatively more conservative (as measured by the percent voting for Ronald Reagan in the 1984 presidential
election) tended to have a larger proportion of the population in the labor
force, consistent with the view that areas where there is a congenial political
environment for public intervention tend to have relatively less employment.

What final conclusion do we reach? It is a simple one. Observed variations in the natural rate of unemployment through time and over space are
quite consistent with the basic thesis that has emerged from our treatment
of the phenomenon of the business cycle. Government actions, as expressed
in a wide range of public-policy actions, generally have contributed to the
presence of higher levels of unemployment, rather than lower.

NOTES

1.   The long-term average rate will continue to rise in the early 1990s unless the
unemployment rate suddenly falls below four percent, a highly unlikely possibly.

2.   The father of the natural rate of unemployment concept is Milton Friedman. See his "The Role of Monetary Policy," *American Economic Review* 58 (1968): 1–17.

3.   See John B. Long and Charles J. Plosser, "Real Business Cycles," *Journal of Political Economy* 91 (1983): 39–69, or Edward Prescott, "Theory Ahead of Business Cycle Measurement," *Carnegie-Rochester Conference Series on Public Policy* 25 (1986): 11–44.

4.   If we were comparing short time periods, one could legitimately raise the possibility of lagged responses or question the direction of causation. We are comparing average behavior over long (thirty-year) time horizons, however. The effects of short-term economic phenomena related to business cycles are reduced. The data suggest that long periods of fiscal stimulus have been associated with high unemployment rates over those long periods.

5.   For a fuller explanation of our views, see our *The "Natural" Rate of unemployment*, Joint Economic Committee, Congress of the United States (Washington, D.C.: Government Printing Office, 1982). For some other estimates of trends in the natural rate, see Robert Gordon, *Macroeconomics*, 3d ed. (Boston: Little, Brown and Company, 1984), appendix B, table B-1, pp. xiv–xxi; Stuart E. Weiner, "The Natural Rate of Unemployment: Concepts and Issues," *Economic Review, Federal Reserve Bank of Kansas City*, January 1986, pp. 11–23; and Keith M. Carlson, "How Much Lower Can the Unemployment Rate Go?" *Review, Federal Reserve Bank of St. Louis*, July/August 1988, pp. 44–57. A good brief and simple survey of the findings in the above works is found in James Gwartney and Richard Stroup, *Macroeconomics*, 5th ed. (San Diego: Harcourt Brace Jovanovich, 1990), p. 192.

6.   Gordon, *Macroeconomics*, table B-1, pp. xiv–xv. Gordon inexplicably does have a sharp (0.8 point) rise in the rate occurring in the single year 1930.

7.   Rudiger Dornbush and Stanley Fischer, *Macroeconomics*, 5th ed. (New York: McGraw-Hill, 1990), p. 560.

8.   The average for four years in the late 1960s was 3.4 percent of the population changing states (per year). For three years in the late 1980s, the average was 2.8 percent. See the *Statistical Abstract of the United States*, various years, for information on this phenomenon.

9.   Norman J. Simler, "Long Term Unemployment, the Structural Hypothesis, and Public Policy," *American Economic Review* 54 (1964): 985–1001.

10.   See, for example, Gordon, *Macroeconomics*, or Gwartney and Stroup, *Macroeconomics*.

11.   See our *The "Natural" Rate of Unemployment*.

12.   *Statistical Abstract of the United States 1982–83* (Washington, D.C.: Government Printing Office, 1982), p. 389.

13.   See Charles Brown, Curtis Gilroy, and Andrew Kohen, "The Effect of the Minimum Wage on Employment and Unemployment," *Journal of Economic Literature* 20 (1982): 487–528, Douglas K. Adie, "Teenage Unemployment and Real Federal Minimum Wages," *Journal of Political Economy* 81 (1973): 435–41, and John M. Peterson and Charles T. Stewart, *Employment Effects of Minimum Wage Rates* (Washington, D.C.: American Enterprise Institute, 1969.)

14.   The definitive early study was H. Gregg Lewis, *Unionism and Relative Wages in the United States* (Chicago: University of Chicago Press, 1963). Later studies and

literature reviews include C. J. Parsley, "Labor Unions and Wages: A Survey," *Journal of Economic Literature* 18 (1980): 1–31; Richard B. Freeman and James L. Medoff, *What Do Unions Do?* (New York: Basic Books, 1984), and H. Gregg Lewis, *Union Relative Wage Effects* (Chicago: University of Chicago Press, 1986).

15. In 1987, the indicated average earnings for government workers were $22,486, compared with average annual pay of $20,847 for workers in the whole economy. Since, on average, fringe benefits of governmental employees tend to be more generous than those of the private sector, the differential in total compensation may be on the order of 15 percent or more. See *Statistical Abstract of the United States 1990* (Washington, D.C.: Government Printing Office, 1990), pp. 300, 408. The state and local earnings averages were calculated by multiplying average October earnings by twelve.

16. There is considerable evidence that federal workers are paid more than private-sector counterparts. For the latest research, see Brent R. Moulton, "A Reexamination of the Federal-Private Wage Differential in the United States," *Journal of Labor Economics* 8 (1990): 270–93. On postal workers, see Douglas K. Adie, *An Evaluation of Postal Service Wage Rates* (Washington, D.C.: American Enterprise Institute, 1977); on teachers, see Randall W. Eberts and Joe A. Stone, "Teacher Unions and the Cost of Public Education," *Economic Inquiry* 24 (1986): 631–43, and Richard Vedder, "The Economic Status of U.S. Teachers, 1870–1987," Ohio University Department of Economics Research Paper Series no. 89-06.

17. Gene L. Chapin, "Unemployment Insurance, Job Search, and the Demand for Leisure," *Western Economic Journal* 9 (1971): 102–7, and Martin Feldstein, "Unemployment Compensation: Adverse Incentives and Distributional Anomalies," *National Tax Journal* 27 (1974): 231–44.

18. *Statistical Abstract of the United States 1991*, p. 369.

19. Calculated from various issues or volumes of the *Social Security Bulletin*, the *Statistical Abstract of the United States*, and the *1991 Economic Report of the President*.

20. See Sheldon Danziger, Robert Haveman, and Robert Plotnick, "How Income Transfers Affect Work, Savings and the Income Distribution," *Journal of Economic Literature* 19 (1981): 975–1028; Mark Killingsworth, *Labor Supply* (Cambridge: Cambridge University Press, 1983); John Pencavel, "Labor Supply of Men: A Survey," in *Handbook in Labor Economics*, ed. Orley Ashenfelter and Richard Layard, 2 vols. (Amsterdam: North-Holland, 1986), 1: 3–102; Jerry Hausman, "Taxes and Labor Supply," in *Handbook of Public Economics*, ed. Alan Auerbach and Martin Feldstein (New York: Elsevier Science, 1987); Isabel Sawhill, "Poverty in the U.S.: Why Is It So Persistent?" *Journal of Economic Literature* 26 (1988): 1073–1119, and Lowell Gallaway, Richard Vedder, and Robert Lawson, "Why People Work: An Examination of Interstate Variations in Labor Force Participation," *Journal of Labor Research* 12 (1991): 47–59.

21. We tested many versions of the model, including versions where variables were expressed as ten-year moving averages, to deal with the criticism that unemployment determines public assistance rather than the other way around.

22. Robert Moffitt, "Incentive Effects of the U.S. Welfare System: A Review," *Journal of Economic Literature* 30 (1992): 56.

23.   See Christopher Frenze, *The Mellon and Kennedy Tax Cuts: A Review and Analysis*, Joint Economic Committee of Congress Staff Study (Washington, D.C.: Government Printing Office, 1982); Warren Brookes, *The Economy in Mind* (New York: Universe Books, 1982); Lowell Gallaway and Richard Vedder, *Poverty, Income Distribution, the Family and Public Policy*, Joint Economic Committee of Congress Staff Study (Washington, D.C.: Government Printing Office, 1986); and Lawrence Lindsey, *The Growth Experiment: How the New Tax Policy Is Transforming the American Economy* (New York: Basic Books, 1990.)

24.   Although much discussed and criticized, the standard study remains Martin Feldstein, "Social Security, Induced Retirement, and Aggregate Capital Accumulation," *Journal of Political Economy* 82 (1974): 905–26.

25.   For an example of how changes in the social security program impacted on people's labor-market behavior, see Lowell Gallaway, "Labor Supply Responses at Work: The Case of Early Retirement," in *War on Poverty—Victory or Defeat?* Hearing before Subcommittee on Monetary and Fiscal Policy, Joint Economic Committee, Ninety-Ninth Congress, First Session, June 20, 1985, pp. 140–50 (Washington, D.C.: Government Printing Office, 1986).

26.   A recent attempt to explain interstate variations in the natural rate of unemployment attributes a good portion of the differentials to varying degrees of unionization. See Paul R. Blackley, "The Measurement and Determination of State Equilibrium Unemployment Rates," *Southern Economic Journal* 56 (1989): 440–56.

27.   Excepting the unionization variable, they are all significant at the 1 percent level. Federal income maintenance expenditures per state are for the 1989–90 fiscal year and include federal payments for unemployment compensation, supplemental security income, food stamps, housing assistance, and black lung payments. Data come from standard U.S. Department of Commerce data sources.

28.   Lowell Gallaway, Richard Vedder, and Robert Lawson, "Why People Work: An Examination of Interstate Variations in Labor Force Participation," *Journal of Labor Research* 12 (1991): 47–59.

14

Who Bears the Burden of Unemployment?

The considerable variations in the aggregate magnitudes of unemployment over time and space and according to time horizon (long versus short run) disguise important demographic, racial, and gender differences in unemployment. In many recent years, teenage unemployment rates have been triple the overall unemployment rate, and at times there have been more modest, but noticeable, differences in unemployment by gender. Far and away the most interesting and potentially divisive differential, however, is that with respect to race.

Many writers have studied these differences intensively. In a general survey of a century of unemployment, we cannot hope to explore them in as much detail as some would think desirable. For example, we have not used the micro data sets available only for recent decades, since that departs from the historical nature of this volume, and those data are not strictly comparable to some earlier figures available from the census. At the same time, however, to ignore these differentials completely would lead us to neglect an important part of the twentieth-century unemployment story. Accordingly, we have decided to point out some facts on these demographic, gender, and race differences in a historical context, and suggest some reasons why they may exist.

White-Nonwhite Unemployment Differentials over One Hundred Years

In the more than forty-year period in which the Bureau of Labor Statistics has published unemployment data by race, the incidence of joblessness among nonwhites consistently has been substantially higher than that among whites.[1] Moreover, that differential has been increasing. In the first three years in which race-specific unemployment data were available, 1948–50, the nonwhite rate averaged 3.27 percentage points above the white rate; the nonwhite-white unemployment-rate ratio was 1.70 to 1. By contrast, in 1988–90, the nonwhite unemployment rate averaged 5.54 percentage points above the white rate, and the nonwhite-white unemployment ratio was 2.20 to 1.[2]

There is strong evidence, however, that dramatic racial differences in unemployment did not exist sixty to one hundred years ago. In the era from 1890 to 1930, the nonwhite unemployment rate seemed to be not materially different than the white rate. In a period in which Jim Crow laws were adopted, when the Ku Klux Klan and lynchings were well established, and when few black Americans could even vote, the relative employment opportunities of racial minorities, by one common measure, were greater than they are today.

Since 1940, the *Current Population Survey* (CPS) has provided monthly data on unemployment based on a sampling of households. The nature of the reporting improved further after 1947, with racial information available since 1948. The Lebergott/BLS annual data for the period before 1948, however, are not race-specific.

THE 1890 AND 1900 CENSUSES

Yet, there are some underutilized census data on unemployment dating as far back as 1890 that provide enormous detail, including racial information. Both the 1890 and 1900 censuses, however, calculate unemployment rates in a radically different fashion than that accepted today. Whereas the modern CPS and Lebergott/BLS data are stock or point-of-time estimates, the early census data are flow data, dividing all unemployment over a previous twelve-month period by the estimated labor force (actually, occupied persons, which presumably includes unemployed Americans.) Since a typical person remains unemployed but a few months out of a year, the reported unemployment rates based on the flow data tend to be dramatically larger than what modern point-of-time estimates would show.

With this in mind, the 1890 census data, after allowing for some corrections published in the 1900 census, show an unemployment rate for nonwhites of 15.8 percent, only 0.8 percentage points above the reported rate for whites of 15.0 percent.[3] For 1900, the reported differential is much greater, with the nonwhite rate of 28.8 percent exceeding the white rate of 21.2 percent by over seven percentage points.[4] Using the nonwhite-white unemployment-rate ratio as our guide, however, the 1900 ratio of 1.36 to 1 is markedly lower than reported in any year since CPS race-specific data are available.

Moreover, even these modest race differentials are overstated if the data are converted to approximate the present-day stock estimates. The assumption that the relative unemployment-rate differentials (measured by the nonwhite-white unemployment-rate ratio) between races would be the same regardless of the type of data holds only if the average duration of unemployment is the same for different racial groups. In fact, however, nonwhite workers had a materially smaller average duration of unemployment than whites, in both the 1890 and 1900 censuses.

Both censuses classify workers into three categories: those unemployed for one to three months during the previous twelve months; those unemployed four to six months, and those unemployed seven to twelve months. Making certain assumptions about the distribution of unemployed within each of these classifications, it is possible to calculate the average duration of unemployment for whites and for nonwhites. For 1890, for example, the estimated mean duration of nonwhite unemployment was 3.09 months, while for whites it was 3.50 months.[5]

The shorter unemployment duration for blacks and other nonwhites means that the unemployment-rate data based on twelve-month flows overstate relative nonwhite unemployment. To illustrate, recall the rather extreme example described in chapter 1. There, we assumed two groups of ten workers, one consisting of whites and the second of nonwhites. Suppose only one of the whites has been unemployed during the year, but he was unemployed for all twelve months. Further, assume that four blacks were unemployed for three months each. Using the 1890/1900 methods of calculation, the white unemployment rate for the group would be 10 percent (one divided by ten), whereas for blacks it would be 40 percent (four divided by ten.)

Using modern stock methods of calculation, however, the unemployment rates for the two groups would be identical (10 percent). The reason for this is very simple. The Bureau of Labor Statistics records unemployment on or around the twelfth day of each month; the annual unemployment rate is the simple average of the twelve monthly rates. For the group of whites, for each month the rate would be recorded as 10 percent (one of ten workers unemployed.) For the nonwhite group, suppose that unemployment among the four workers did not overlap. Then each monthly report would record a ten percent unemployment rate. If the unemployment overlapped, the monthly rates would vary from zero to, conceivably, 40 percent, but the average of the twelve monthly rates would be 10 percent.

This suggests a procedure for converting the flow unemployment rates to modern-day stock equivalents. First, calculate the mean duration of unemployment in months for each racial group. Second, divide twelve (for months) by the calculated mean duration to obtain the average number of workers in each group composing one worker-year of unemployed labor. Third, divide the reported unemployment rate based on flows by the statistic derived in the second step to obtain a point-in-time estimate.

We applied this procedure to the 1890 and 1900 censuses. In 1890, the estimated nonwhite unemployment rate of 4.07 percent is actually lower than the observed rate for whites, 4.41 percent.[6] The mean for all workers, of slightly under 4.4 percent, is highly consistent with Lebergott's 1890 annual unemployment rate estimate of 4.0 percent.

For 1900, the estimated nonwhite unemployment rate is 7.57 percent, modestly higher than the estimated white unemployment rate of 6.47 percent. The nonwhite-white unemployment ratio of 1.17 to 1, however, is dramatically lower than anything observed in the postwar era. The implied aggregate unemployment rate for the year is about one-third higher than Lebergott obtained.

THE 1930 CENSUS

The quality of census unemployment reporting declines after 1900 (nothing was reported in 1920) until the important fifteenth decennial census in 1930. Most people think of 1930 in terms of the Great Depression, and the official BLS estimate is that unemployment averaged 8.7 percent for the year. Yet the census enumeration was completed in April, at a time when the economy was recovering somewhat from the stock-market crash of the previous fall. We earlier estimated the April 1930 aggregate U.S. unemployment rate to be 6.6 percent, suggesting that at the time of the census the country was in the equivalent of a moderately severe recession.

The 1930 census uses modern point-of-time procedures. Several different classes of unemployment are identified. We defined unemployment to be the sum of the "Class A" unemployment, characterized as "persons out of a job, able to work, and looking for a job" and "Class B" unemployment, which included persons with jobs who were laid off without pay (excluding the sick or voluntarily idle) at the time of the census. The calculated unemployment rate for nonwhites was 6.07 percent, again below the 6.59 rate

TABLE 14.1

RACIAL DIFFERENCES IN UNEMPLOYMENT RATES IN THE U.S., 1890–1930

Year	% Unemployment Rate:		Difference (%)	Nonwhite–White Unemployment Rate Ratio
	White	Nonwhite		
1890	4.41	4.07	-0.34	0.92 to 1
1900	6.47	7.57	+1.10	1.17 to 1
1930	6.59	6.07	-0.52	0.92 to 1
Average, all years	5.82	5.90	+0.08	1.01 to 1

Source: Authors' calculations from U.S. Census of 1890, 1900 and 1930; see text for details.

TABLE 14.2

RACIAL DIFFERENCES IN UNEMPLOYMENT RATES IN THE U.S. 1940–1989

Year	% Unemployment Rate:		Difference	Nonwhite–White Unemployment Rate Ratio
	White	Nonwhite		
1940	9.50	10.89	1.39	1.15 to 1
1950	4.9	9.0	4.1	1.84 to 1
1955	3.9	8.7	4.8	2.23 to 1
1960	5.0	10.2	5.2	2.04 to 1
1965	4.1	8.1	4.0	1.98 to 1
1970	4.5	8.2	3.7	1.82 to 1
1975	7.8	13.8	6.0	1.77 to 1
1980	6.3	13.1	6.8	2.08 to 1
1985	6.2	13.7	7.5	2.21 to 1
1990	4.7	10.1	5.4	2.15 to 1

Source: 16th Census of Population; 1990 Economic Report of the President; authors' calculations.

calculated for white Americans. The aggregate unemployment rate, so computed, is within one-tenth of a percentage point of our earlier estimate which used quite a different calculation procedure.[7]

Summarizing, analysis of three rather comprehensive surveys of individual unemployment experiences in the 1890–1930 period leads us to believe that racial differences in unemployment rates were essentially nonexistent. As table 14.1 indicates, the mean rate of unemployment for the three dates differs by only 0.08 percentage points between whites and nonwhites. In every case, the nonwhite–white unemployment ratio is between .92 and 1.17, suggesting that the similarities between the races in terms of unemployment were more striking than the differences.

THE UNEMPLOYMENT-RATE DIFFERENTIAL SINCE 1940

The era of discernible race differentials in unemployment probably began in the 1930s, although it was not entirely obvious until a decade later (table 14.2). While the CPS began in 1940, race-specific data are not available, so again we rely on the census, choosing to count government emergency workers as employed.[8] Data for later years are based on the Bureau of Labor Statistics (CPS). Note that the race differentials widen over time in an absolute sense, but also in a relative sense as well.

Looking at the absolute unemployment differential between whites and nonwhites, it expands sharply (by almost five percentage points) between 1930 (from table 14.1) and 1950, shows a minor narrowing from 1950 to 1970 (0.4 points), and widens appreciably (over 3 points) in the 1970s, before narrowing slightly in an absolute (but not relative) sense in the 1980s. The 1990 rate was the fourteenth consecutive year in which the nonwhite-white ratio exceeded 2.0.

Searching for an Explanation for Widening Differentials

We now explore three possible explanations for the widening of racial differentials over time.

I. RACIAL DISCRIMINATION

It seems unlikely that in a truly color-blind society, unemployment rates for one racial group would average double or more that for the other group. Therefore, it seems intuitively very appealing to attribute the modern unemployment differences to racial discrimination. The discrimination might be direct, such as when an employer faced with two applicants chooses the less qualified white individual because of prejudice against nonwhites. Or it might be indirect, resulting from the fact that nonwhites lack training, education, or work experiences that whites have had, in part because of previous discrimination.

While the discrimination explanation is intuitively appealing, there is a huge problem with it: there were no major racial differences in unemployment between 1890 and 1930. Yet by most accounts, prejudicial conduct against racial minorities was much more intense in this earlier era than today. In the 1890–1930 period, blacks were lynched, subjected to Ku Klux Klan harassment, faced inferior segregated schools, had virtually no political role, and were largely unrepresented in many high-paying professional occupations. These problems were reduced in magnitude with the passage of time. For example, in 1900, the proportion of nonwhites working in professional and managerial occupations was less than 25 percent of that for whites. By 1980, the proportion of nonwhites working in the professions or managerial occupations exceeded 62 percent that for whites.[9] If racial

TABLE 14.3

RACIAL DIFFERENCES IN UNEMPLOYMENT RATES BY REGION, U.S., 1930

| Region | Unemployment Rates for: | | Nonwhite-White Unemployment Rate Ratio |
	Whites	Nonwhites	
New England	8.42	10.73	1.27 to 1
Mid Atlantic	8.01	10.74	1.34 to 1
East North Central	8.01	14.97	1.87 to 1
West North Central	4.28	9.07	2.12 to 1
South Atlantic	4.21	4.41	1.05 to 1
East South Central	3.40	2.67	0.79 to 1
West South Central	4.36	4.46	1.02 to 1
Mountain	5.97	9.16	1.53 to 1
Pacific	7.32	9.37	1.28 to 1
U.S.	6.59	6.07	0.92 to 1

Source: Authors' calculations, 1930 Census, Unemployment-General Report, pp. 232-234.

discrimination can cause unemployment, then the unemployment data suggest that discrimination should have grown over time; yet most observers would conclude that in fact it was reduced somewhat in magnitude.

We believe that the trend toward greater racial unemployment differentials is not consistent with the evidence that points to some reduction in racial discrimination over time. At the same time, however, we will argue below that even though the amount of discrimination almost certainly declined, the unemployment consequences of any given amount of discrimination possibly have increased because of changes in the legal and regulatory environment in which labor markets operate.

Alternatively, it is at least plausible that while overt public displays of discrimination have lessened (in part because of legislative enactments against discriminatory behavior), covert discrimination has grown—possibly as a backlash against the statutory changes designed to promote greater racial equality. The political successes of George Wallace in the 1960s and David Duke in the 1990s suggest that white resentment of affirmative action and other programs may be intense, possibly consistent with rising discriminatory behavior against blacks in hiring decisions.

2. CHANGING JOB AND LOCATIONAL CHOICES OF NONWHITES

In the early part of the twentieth century, most blacks lived and worked in the South. For example, in 1930, nearly 72 percent of nonwhites worked in the three census divisions constituting the South, compared with 23 percent of the white population. As table 14.3 demonstrates from the 1930 census data, unemployment rates there tended to be much lower than in other regions. By contrast, a majority of whites worked in the three census

TABLE 14.4

UNEMPLOYMENT DIFFERENTIALS BY RACE, 1930 AND 1980

Group or Statistic	% Unadjusted Unemployment Rate	% Geographically Adjusted Unemployment Rate
1930		
Whites	6.59	6.59
Non-whites	6.07	9.79
Nonwhite/white Unemployment Rate Ratio	0.92 to 1	1.49 to 1
1980		
Whites	5.43	5.43
Non-whites	9.49	10.13
Nonwhite/white Unemployment Rate Ratio	1.75	1.87 to 1

Source: Authors' calculations, 1930 and 1980 censuses.

regions constituting the Northeast and industrial Midwest, compared with only about 18 percent of the nonwhite population. Also, interestingly, the nonwhite-white unemployment-rate ratio, which was essentially one (or even less) in the South, approached modern day levels (two to one) in the Midwest.

What would the white-nonwhite unemployment differential have been in 1930 had the nonwhite labor force been geographically distributed in the same proportion as whites, assuming that the counterfactual distribution would not have changed observed regional unemployment rates? We calculated hypothetical numbers of unemployed nonwhites by regions using the white geographic distribution of workers, arriving at an adjusted unemployment rate of 9.79 percent, and a nonwhite-white unemployment-rate ratio of 1.49, some 57 basis points higher than the unadjusted ratio (0.92).Performing a similar counterfactual estimate with the 1980 census data, the nonwhite-white unemployment differential rises from 1.75 to 1.87. Adjusting for population distribution had far less impact in 1980 than in 1930 for three reasons: the 1980 nonwhite population distribution more closely approached that of whites; interregional differences in unemployment rates declined; and interregional disparities in the nonwhite-white unemployment ratio also fell. Table 14.4 summarizes the 1930 and 1980 evidence. Some 54 percent of the observed growth in the nonwhite-white unemployment differential is eliminated by adjusting for the disparities in the geographical distribution of the population.[10]

Geographical migration is, of course, related to occupational mobility. Looking at the occupational mix in 1900, table 14.5 indicates that blacks and other nonwhites were indeed heavily overrepresented in agriculture and domestic and personal service, and underrepresented in manufacturing, trade, and transportation. Yet the intraoccupational unemployment differentials are not dramatically large, except in the relatively minor category of

TABLE 14.5

WHITE AND NONWHITE UNEMPLOYMENT RATES BY OCCUPATION, U.S. 1900

Job Category	Percent of Labor Force in Category:		Percent Unemployment Rate:[a]		Nonwhite–White Unemployment Rate Ratio
	White	Nonwhite	White	Nonwhite	
Agriculture	32.69	53.03	5.39	7.18	1.33 to 1
Professional Service	4.85	1.16	8.30	12.80	1.54 to 1
Domestic and Personal Service	17.09	33.27	8.96	8.07	0.90 to 1
Trade and Transportation	18.17	5.41	3.34	4.66	1.40 to 1
Manufacturing/Mechanics	27.20	7.13	8.12	9.78	1.20 to 1

[a]Converted to point-in-time estimate by authors; see text.

Source: Authors' calculations from data in U.S. Bureau of the Census, Special Reports, Occupations at the Twelfth Census (Washington, D.C. Government Printing Office, 1904).

professional service. Indeed, in domestic and personal service the nonwhite unemployment rate is lower than the white.

As before, we calculated what the aggregate nonwhite unemployment rate would have been if the nonwhite labor force had had the same occupational distribution as the white. The result was that the nonwhite unemployment rate would have been raised by 0.26 points, and the nonwhite-white unemployment differential would have increased from about 1.17 to 1 to 1.21 to 1.

We repeated the same procedure, looking at the last census showing approximate racial parity in unemployment, 1930, as well as the first and the latest available postwar censuses.[11] The results are shown in table 14.6. The adjustment procedure raised the estimated unemployment rate for blacks relative to whites in 1930 somewhat more than in 1900. Taking the average of the 1900 and 1930 numbers again indicates that blacks and other nonwhites were heavily overrepresented in agriculture and domestic and personal service, and underrepresented in manufacturing, trade, and transportation. The intraoccupational unemployment differentials are again not dramatically large, except in the rather insignificant category of professional service; and in domestic and personal service the nonwhite unemployment rate remains lower than the white.

The impact of occupational structure works in the opposite direction in the postwar era, however. Blacks and other nonwhites moved in large numbers into such relatively high–unemployment fields as manufacturing. For example, in 1980 nearly 27 percent of nonwhites were "operatives and laborers" mostly in manufacturing, compared with less than 18 percent for whites. In 1980 nonwhites were relatively overemployed in this area where they were grossly underemployed in 1900. Yet the unemployment rate in this category was nearly double the average for the entire economy. The move of nonwhites out of agriculture was so complete that by 1980 a slightly smaller proportion of nonwhites than whites considered themselves

TABLE 14.6

OCCUPATIONALLY ADJUSTED UNEMPLOYMENT RATES BY RACE, 1900–1980

| | Unadjusted: | | | Adjusted: | | |
| | % Unemployment Rate: | | Nonwhite–White | % Unemployment Rate: | | Nonwhite–White |
Year	White	Nonwhite	Unemployment Rate Ratio	White	Nonwhite	Unemployment Rate Ratio
1900	6.47	7.57	1.17 to 1	6.17	7.85	1.21 to 1
1930	6.59	6.07	0.92 to 1	6.59	7.38	1.12 to 1
1950[a]	4.43	7.77	1.75 to 1	4.43	6.97	1.57 to 1
1980[a]	5.54	9.92	1.79 to 1	5.54	8.59	1.55 to 1

[a]Unemployment rates and the ratio differ from those reported in Table 14.2 for 1950 and 1980, since Table 14.2 relies on CPS data, while this table relies on Census data.
Source: Authors' calculations from the 1900, 1930, 1950 and 1980 censuses of population.

farmers.[12] Moreover, whites continued to be dramatically more strongly represented in low-unemployment managerial and professional occupations. As a consequence, taking the average of the 1950 and 1980 census data, the nonwhite-white unemployment rate ratio falls from 1.77 to 1.56 after occupational adjustment. All told, some 45 percent (.33 of .72) of the unadjusted increase in the nonwhite-white unemployment-rate differential is the consequence of the racial differences in the occupational mix of the labor force.

We have suggested that roughly half of the growth in the unemployment differential is explainable in terms of geographical mobility, and roughly half explainable by occupational movement. Those two factors are not strictly additive, since much occupational mobility accompanied geographical movement. On the other hand, the combined effect of the two forces is greater than indicated by either single factor, since intraregional occupational mobility had no impact on measured geographical migration but nonetheless impacted on the observed unemployment differential. It is probably safe to say that most—but not all—of the observed rising unemployment differential is explainable in terms of the migratory behavior of Americans, particularly minorities.

It would be possible, using more detailed data sources, to analyze many demographic and social characteristics simultaneously. Preliminary analysis suggests, for example, that the high pre-1940 relative labor-force participation of black women contributed modestly to a lowering of the aggregate unemployment rates of nonwhites early in the century, since female unemployment rates were lower than male rates. The gender-adjusted nonwhite-white unemployment-rate differential for 1930, for example, rises from 0.92 to 1 to 0.96 to 1. While not the whole story, the changing occupational mobility patterns of the population contributed importantly to the rise in nonwhite unemployment.[13]

3. DIFFERENTIAL RACIAL IMPACT OF GOVERNMENTAL POLICIES

Directly or indirectly, changes in the legislative and regulatory environment in which labor markets operate have impacted on unemployment. It is possible that one unintended consequence of much of the changing statutory and regulatory milieu has been a widening of the nonwhite-white unemployment differential.

As this book demonstrates throughout, much labor legislation has had the impact of raising wages for workers. The Fair Labor Standards Act of 1938, the Davis-Bacon Act of 1931, and state legislation that led to "little Davis-Bacon laws" are obvious examples. It is noteworthy that there is strong circumstantial evidence that antiblack sentiment played some role in the passage of the Davis-Bacon legislation.[14] The legislation strengthening collective bargaining, most notably the National Labor Relations Act, clearly led to higher wage levels in many industries as unionization gained strength. More recently, civil rights legislation in the 1960s imposed potential legal liability on employers who failed to pay qualified nonwhites as much as whites.

Actually, there are some good theoretical reasons for believing that these wage-enhancing policies might serve to increase unemployment differentials. Let us assume, to use Becker's phrase, that people have a "taste for discrimination."[15] Suppose that initially there are absolutely no legal restrictions on wage rates and that labor markets are reasonably competitive. Suppose further than an employer advertises for a job at a low wage, and draws one nonwhite applicant, who is hired. Suppose, however, that, instead, a minimum wage has been imposed that forces the employer to pay more; this leads to two workers applying for work, one nonwhite and one white. Having a preference for whites because of prejudice, the employer hires the white, since it is anticipated that that individual will provide more nonpecuniary income to the employer (or less nonpecuniary costs) than the nonwhite would.

Alternatively, suppose that two individuals, one white and one nonwhite, initially apply for the job. The employer is prejudiced against nonwhites, but, even more importantly, he is also a profit maximizer. Suppose he learns that the white will not work for less than $5 an hour, while the nonwhite, who appears to be roughly equally qualified, will work for $4. The employer may well decide that exercising his racial prejudice is too costly, so he will hire the nonwhite.[16] The imposition of civil rights legislation, however, makes it highly risky to appear to be paying nonwhites less than whites for similar work. The cost of hiring the nonwhite, including contingent legal liabilities, rises relative to hiring the white. Consequently, after such legislation the employer might play it safe and hire the white worker at $5 an hour. Thus the imposition of wage floors and laws against wage discrimination can serve to increase the unemployment consequences to minorities of any given amount of discrimination.

In this regard, it is interesting to note that the major increase in the nonwhite-white unemployment-rate ratio, even allowing for adjustment for racial differentials in occupational and migration patterns, came in the period between 1930 and 1950. This was an interval of rapidly increasing governmental involvement in the economy. Federal government outlays rose from slightly over 3 percent of GNP to about 16 percent of GNP in that period. The bulk of the legislation restraining private wage-setting behavior occurred during these two decades, including the previously mentioned Fair Labor Standards Act, the Davis–Bacon Act, the National Labor Relations Act, etc. Even the Social Security Act forced employers to pay a fringe benefit not previously provided.

As indicated in the last chapter, unemployment compensation has increased the average duration of unemployment; this has particularly raised black unemployment. For both 1890 and 1900, the mean duration of unemployment for nonwhites was estimated to be 12-13 percent less than for whites (13.4 weeks for nonwhites in 1890, 15.2 weeks for whites; 13.9 weeks for nonwhites in 1900, 16.0 weeks for whites). By contrast in recent years, the duration for nonwhites has been 15 percent or more greater than for whites (e.g., in 1980, the nonwhite duration was 13.4 weeks, the white duration 11.5 weeks.) Similarly, as the previous chapter indicated, the disincentive effects of public assistance have impacted more on nonwhites than on whites.

It is therefore a plausible hypothesis that governmental policies have raised the reservation wage of nonwhite Americans relative to the reservation wage of white Americans, increasing the relative duration of nonwhite unemployment and thus the nonwhite-white unemployment-rate differential.

In 1900, blacks and other nonwhites, being generally poorer than whites, could ill afford to be unemployed for long, and thus were less choosy than whites about accepting offers of employment. In recent years, lower-income Americans, who include a disproportionate number of nonwhites, can earn income not working, receiving a variety of forms of income assistance from the government. The opportunity cost of being unemployed has fallen for low-income Americans. This has raised the nonwhite unemployment duration (and thus unemployment rate) relative to that for whites.

Further Evidence: Changing Employment-Population Ratios

Some people argue that the unemployment rate is not the best measure of employment opportunity. An alternative measure is the employment-population ratio, the proportion of the population of work age that is actually working. Using employment instead of unemployment, one avoids some of the problems of defining unemployment, and takes into account the discouraged-worker phenomenon that sometimes distorts unemployment rates.

Using the census data for 1900 and 1930, along with Bureau of Labor Statistics data available since 1954, we can get a good picture of the changing employment-population ratio by race over time (table 14.7).

TABLE 14.7

THE EMPLOYMENT-POPULATION RATIO BY RACE, U.S. 1900 TO 1990

Year	% Employment-Population Ratio:[a]		Nonwhite to White Employment-Population Ratio
	Nonwhites	Whites	
1900	57.4	45.5	1.26 to 1
1930	60.2	44.7	1.35 to 1
1954	58.0	55.2	1.05 to 1
1975	50.1[b]	56.7	0.88 to 1
1990	56.2[b]	63.6	0.88 to 1

[a]For 1900 and 1930, the population was defined as persons aged 10 or over; for 1954 and later, the population includes those 16 and over, following census and BLS practices at the time.
[b]For blacks only; it would appear the ratio for nonwhites, including other races, would be slightly above the figures indicated, but only slightly since blacks numerically dominate the nonwhite category.
Source: Authors' calculations from the 12th and 15th censuses of population; *1990 Economic Report of the President*, p. 337.

There was a much higher incidence of participation in work by nonwhites than by whites in the early decades of the century. That changed decisively over the period 1930 to 1975, as the nonwhite employment-population ratio fell substantially at the very time that the white employment-population ratio was rising significantly. By 1975, blacks were less likely to work than whites. Since 1975, the ratio has risen for both whites and blacks.

Actually, if anything table 14.7 understates the decline in black involvement in employment activities after 1930. The 1930 employment-population ratio is calculated, following Census Bureau practice, by defining the work-age population as being ten years of age or over. whereas the later data refer to the over-sixteen population. Since employment among those aged ten to fifteen was relatively low in 1930, excluding that group would raise the employment-population ratio in that year noticeably.

In terms of the explanations mentioned above, it is noteworthy that the decline in relative nonwhite employment was happening at the very time that the civil rights movement was calling attention to discriminatory practices. It would be very hard to claim that the decline reflected growing discrimination, particularly since relative nonwhite participation in many relatively high-paying occupations was actually growing. The occupational-shift arguments that explain a good deal of changing unemployment differentials are less relevant here. It is noteworthy that the big deterioration in nonwhite employment came during the period between the New Deal and the implementation of the Great Society programs of the late 1960s. This is consistent with the view that some of these programs may have had negative effects on the employment opportunities or work incentives of blacks relative to whites.

To be sure, there are other factors at work. Looking at more disaggregated data (table 14.8) reveals that the rise in white employment involve-

TABLE 14.8

THE U.S. EMPLOYMENT-POPULATION RATIO BY SEX AND RACE, 1930–1989

Year	Whites:		Nonwhites:	
	Males (%)	Females (%)	Males (%)	Females (%)
1930	69.6	19.2	83.0	37.7
1954	81.5	31.4	76.5	41.9
1975	73.0	42.0	60.6[a]	41.6[a]
1989	73.7	54.6	62.8[a]	43.3[a]

[a]Blacks.

Source: Authors' calculations from 1930 Census, *1990 Economic Report of the President*, p. 337.

ment after 1930 reflects a dramatic growth in female labor-force participation, whereas nonwhite female participation, already high, does not show a substantial upward move. The household durable goods revolution and changes in social attitudes (in part shaped by World War II) may partly explain why wives from fairly affluent middle-class families, predominantly white, began working.

At the same time, however, the changing female role does not explain the very sharp difference in male employment behavior. From 1930 to 1954, the white employment-population ratio rose (even standardizing the age definition used), while the black ratio fell noticeably. From 1954 to 1975, the ratios fell for both groups, but nearly twice as much for nonwhite males.

On balance, then, the evidence supports the initial proposition that nonwhite involvement in the labor force declined significantly relative to that of whites, particularly in the critical period 1930 to 1975.[17] Since that era was one of relative government activism, the empirical evidence seems consistent with the view that public intervention in labor markets changed the relative racial involvement in the labor force. We admit that this conclusion is partly circumstantial, and that structural labor-market shifts such as migration and occupational movement are quite important. Nonetheless, the evidence points to some differential racial impact of government programs on job opportunities.

Gender Differences in Unemployment

While the major gender-related labor-market development of the twentieth century has been the convergence of male and female labor force involvement, there have been some noticeable gender unemployment differentials worth mentioning. Before 1940, the evidence suggests that the incidence of unemployment was similar between men and women. In the 1900 and 1940 censuses, the reported unemployment rate for women was very

TABLE 14.9

MALE AND FEMALE UNEMPLOYMENT RATES BY DECADES, 1950–1990

Decade	Differential:[a]		Female-Male Ratio:[b]	
	Range	Median	Range	Median
1950s	0.00–1.60	0.70	1.00–1.57	1.16
1960s	0.50–2.10	1.60	1.09–1.68	1.36
1970s	1.40–1.90	1.65	1.18–1.43	1.35
1980s	-0.70–0.50	0.20	0.93–1.07	1.04

[a]The female unemployment rate minus the male unemployment rate (for all age groups).

[b]The female unemployment rate divided by the male rate (if the female were 6 percent, the male 5 percent, the ratio would be 6 divided by 5, or 1.20).

Source: Authors' calculations from the *1991 Economic Report of the President* (Washington, D.C.: Government Printing Office, 1991), p. 330.

slightly higher than for men, but in 1930 it was markedly lower (see table 1.3.)

As table 14.9 indicates, from 1950 to the 1980s, the female unemployment rate generally exceeded that for males. The modest differentials of the 1950s expanded substantially in the 1960s and were maintained at fairly high levels throughout the 1970s, with the female rate typically exceeding the male rate by about 1.6 percentage points. In the 1980s, however, the differential largely disappeared, and in some years since the 1980s the female rate actually has averaged less than the male rate over the course of the year.

The causes of these trends are not entirely obvious. One explanation that would seem to fit the facts fairly well relates to the growth of governmental involvement in labor markets. The data for 1940 and earlier reflect a world without minimum wages, with minimal social security coverage (none before 1935), and little or no unemployment insurance. These programs grew during the 1940s and 1950s, perhaps impacting somewhat more on women than men, particularly since women were relatively low-paid workers. This might explain the moderate differential observed during the 1950s.[18]

According to this explanation, the growth in the differential in the 1960s and 1970s reflects in part the expansion of the traditional New Deal–era programs, particularly with respect to coverage. More importantly, however, it reflects the growth of Great Society programs that may have raised reservation wages of women relative to those of men. In particular, the growth of poverty programs such as Medicaid and food stamps was associated with the rise in single-female-parent families; the unemployment rate for women who maintain families has consistently been substantially higher than for women in general.[19]

According to this view, the decline in the differential in the 1980s coincides with the relative decline in federal labor-market involvement. Real federal public aid fell in relation to the gross national product. The minimum wage fell in real terms throughout most of the 1980s, and fell in relation to wages generally. Both of these factors would lead to a decline in reservation wages, and probably more so for women than men, given their generally lower income levels.

While this explanation seems to fit the facts reasonably well with respect to the increase in the female-male unemployment differential from 1940 to 1980, the 1980s decline contrasts vividly with the nonwhite-white differential, which did not show a similar movement. It is possible that the virtual disappearance of the gender differential in large part reflects structural changes, for example the growing professionalization of the female labor force. It also is plausible that affirmative action policies have had a different impact on females than on nonwhites.[20] We must state, however, that we are uncertain which, if any, of these explanations has the most validity.

Teenage Unemployment Differentials

In recent decades, teenagers have had the highest incidence of unemployment of any age group. The historical patterns of the development of the teenage unemployment differential seem to be similar to those observed for nonwhites. In the 1930 census, teenage unemployment was moderately (21 percent) above that for the population as a whole, with the absolute differential being slightly over 1.2 percentage points. By 1940, however, the teenage unemployment rate was well over double total unemployment, a pattern observed ever since.

In both an absolute and relative sense the differential widened significantly again in the 1960s, the median ratio of teenage to total unemployment going from 2.49 in the 1950s to 3.07 in the 1960s. The absolute differential widened again in the 1970s and, very modestly, in the 1980s, but given the rise in the natural rate of unemployment, the relative differential (measured by the teenage-total unemployment ratio) actually fell.[21]

A voluminous literature argues that minimum-wage laws have adversely impacted on teenage unemployment.[22] The adoption of the minimum wage in the 1930s (and the earlier precursor to that under the National Industrial Recovery Act) thus may explain the dramatic increase in the differential in the 1930s. The expansion of minimum-wage coverage and a continued increase in its level may also explain the further growth in the 1960s. The moderation in the relative differential in the past generation may reflect a decline in the minimum wage relative to wage levels generally. While that conclusion fits the general evidence relating to minimum wages, a detailed historical analysis of the teenage unemployment differential must await further study.

Race, gender, and age differentials in unemployment are considerably higher in the last third of the twentieth century than they were in the first third. While much of the explanation turns on changes in occupational composition, it seems almost certain that public policies have adversely impacted on minorities and youth relative to the population at large when it comes to unemployment. In that respect, these findings once more confirm the general proposition that public policy in the United States during the twentieth century has led to increases in unemployment.

NOTES

1. This section draws extensively on research reported in our paper, "Racial Differences in Unemployment in the U.S., 1890–1990," forthcoming in *Journal of Economic History* 52 (September 1992).

2. The post-1950 unemployment data on race, gender, and age used in this chapter are all taken from the *1991 Economic Report of the President* (Washington, D.C.: Government Printing Office, 1991), p. 330.

3. U.S. Department of Commerce and Labor, Bureau of the Census, *Occupations at the Twelfth Census* (Washington, D.C.: Government Printing Office, 1904), p. ccxxvi.

4. Ibid.

5. The 1890 census data come from U.S. Department of the Interior, Census Office, *Report on Population of the United States at the Eleventh Census: 1890*, Part II (Washington, D.C.: Government Printing Office, 1897), as well as other volumes from the same census.

6. In doing the calculation, some assumption had to be made about the number of unemployed of a given duration within each category of unemployed (e.g., unemployed for one to three months, four to six months, or seven to twelve months). Alternative assumptions were made. While changing the assumptions materially changed the reported absolute values, it did not alter by more than a negligible amount the nonwhite-white unemployment-rate ratio, the critical variable under investigation.

7. Several volumes were utilized from the 1930 census in making calculations used in this chapter, the most important of which was *Fifteenth Census of the United States: 1930, Unemployment, Volume II, General Report* (Washington, D.C.: Government Printing Office, 1932).

8. See *Sixteenth Census of the United States: 1940, Population, Volume III, The Labor Force* (Washington, D.C.: Government Printing Office, 1943).

9. As derived from census data.

10. This may approach an upper-bound estimate of the migration impact. Adjusting the white labor force to the nonwhite geographical distribution (the opposite

of the approach in the text), the estimated rise in the migration-adjusted nonwhite-white unemployment rate differential is greater, rising from 1.22 in 1930 to 1.76 in 1980. Using this approach, only 35 percent of the unadjusted rise in the differential is explainable by geographical mobility. Adjusting labor-force distributions of both racial groups to that of the total population, however, yields a result close to that reported in the text.

11.   In doing so, we switch to using the census rather than the CPS estimates for the postwar period. The reader may wonder why we did not average the 1900 and 1930 census results with respect to geographical distribution; the published race-specific unemployment data were not available for the earlier date.

12.   John Cogan believes the decline in demand for agricultural labor played a major role in the decline in black teenage labor-force involvement in the postwar era. See his "The Decline in Black Teenage Employment: 1950–70," *American Economic Review* 72 (1982): 621–38.

13.   The estimation of the impact of the changing compositional structure of the labor force on racial unemployment differentials involved calculating the proportions of individuals employed in each of several major occupational categories, along with unemployment rates for each category, for several census years. Occupational composition data came from the occupations volumes of several censuses, e.g. *Fifteenth Census of the United States: 1930, Population, Volume IV, Occupations By States* (Washington, D.C.: Government Printing Office, 1933), or *1980 Census of Population, Volume 1, Chapter D, Detail Population Characteristics, Part 1 United States Summary* (Washington, D.C.: Government Printing Office, 1984).

14.   A fuller discussion can be found in our as yet unpublished 1991 paper "Racial Dimensions of the Davis-Bacon Act."

15.   Gary Becker, *The Economics of Discrimination*, 2d ed. (Chicago: University of Chicago Press, 1971).

16.   Along these lines, Price Fishback demonstrates that coal companies competed vigorously for black labor in the early 1900s, despite the apparent existence of racial discrimination. See Price V. Fishback, "Can Competition among Employers Reduce Governmental Discrimination? Coal Companies and Segregated Schools in West Virginia in the Early 1900s," *Journal of Law and Economics* 32 (1989): 311–28. For a more comprehensive demonstration that blacks benefited from competition among white employers, see Robert Higgs, *Competition and Coercion: Blacks in the American Economy, 1865–1914* (Cambridge: Cambridge University Press, 1977). For a more elaborate analysis of the theory of employment discrimination, see Richard A. Epstein, *Forbidden Grounds: The Case Against Employment Discrimination Laws* (Cambridge, Mass.: Harvard University Press, 1992), especially chaps. 2–4.

17.   A particularly useful symposium on the economic status of African-Americans is included in the fall 1990 issue of the *Journal of Economic Perspectives*. In particular see Gerald D. Jaynes, "The Labor Market Status of Black Americans, 1939–1985," *Journal of Economic Perspectives* 4 (1990): 9–24, and Jonathan S. Leonard, "The Impact of Affirmative Action Regulation and Equal Employment Law on Black Employment," ibid., pp. 47–64.

18.   There is evidence that the female-male unemployment differential in neighboring Canada is explained in large part by minimum wages. A clearly secondary factor is the "loose attachment" of women to the labor force. See Anthony Myatt and David Murrell, "The Female/Male Unemployment Rate Differential," *Canadian Journal of Economics* 23 (1990): 312–22.

19.   In the 1970s, for example, the median annual unemployment rate for women maintaining families was 7.8 percent, compared with 5.7 percent for all women over twenty years of age (a category that includes many single female parents).

20.   For example, if an employer feels pressure to increase employment for groups protected under civil rights legislation, he may find it easier or cheaper to hire females to meet those requirements than nonwhites, in part because females are more numerous. Also, affirmative action pressures may have increased nonwhite wages relative to those of whites, more than the same pressures raised female wages relative to those of males.

21.   There is some cyclical dimension to the ratio of teenage to adult unemployment. Young black men, for example, do much better in terms of finding jobs when economic conditions are good. See Richard Freeman, *Employment and Earnings of Disadvantaged Young Men in a Labor Shortage Economy* (National Bureau of Economic Research Working Paper No. 3444, 1990).

22.   See, for example, Douglas K. Adie, "Teenage Unemployment and Real Federal Minimum Wages," *Journal of Political Economy* 81 (1973): 435–41. See also David Neumark and William Wascher, *Evidence on Employment Effects of Minimum Wages and Subminimum Wage Provisions from Panel Data on State Minimum Wage Laws* (Cambridge, Mass.: National Bureau of Economic Research Working Paper no. 3859, 1992).

15

Unemployment and the State

When reaching the conclusion of a book, one searches for broad themes, for a grand statement of the central thesis of the work. In this instance, the fundamental thrust of our effort may not have been totally obvious, having been somewhat submerged in the masses of statistical and theoretical discussion that have been a necessary feature of our argument. Basically, what we have been examining is the role that the state has to play in determining the level of unemployment in a free society. To provide a focus for dealing with that question, let us review the range of alternative views on this issue. We begin with a quotation from Professor Hayek. In his classic, *The Road to Serfdom*, published in 1944, he perceives the essence of the debate about the nature of what was becoming known as macroeconomic policy quite perceptively, to wit:

> There is, finally, the supremely important problem of combating general fluctuations of economic activity and the recurrent waves of large-scale unemployment which accompany them. This is, of course, one of the gravest and most pressing problems of our time. But, though its solution will require much planning in the good sense, *it does not—or at least need not—require that special kind of planning which according to its advocates is to replace the market.*[1]

The State and the Business Cycle

What Hayek had in mind when he penned these remarks was the growing movement toward advocacy of some form of centralized planning that

288

would inject the national government into the multiplicity of decisions that characterize a modern economic system. The tendency to move in this direction had begun early in the century. After the economic downturn that produced an increase in the unemployment rate to 8.0 percent in 1908, agitation for the creation of a central bank was very substantial. Ultimately, that led to the creation of the Federal Reserve system, which began operation in 1914 with the avowed purpose of stabilizing the economy by controlling variations in the money supply.

If the performance of the Federal Reserve is judged by the standard of the variability of the money supply, its first ten years rate as an unmitigated disaster. Growth in the money supply ranged from a negative 12 percent to a positive 30 percent. There was a sharp upswing in the monetary growth rate during and immediately following World War I. A common measure of the money supply, M1, grew by 16.2 percent in 1917, 11.0 percent in 1918, and 14.9 percent in 1919, a three-year average of 14.0 percent.[2] This average is greater than the rate of growth in the money supply in any single year of the twentieth century prior to the establishment of the Federal Reserve system.[3] Worse yet, the year 1921 saw an 8.9 percent decline in the money stock. This gives a range of variation in the rate of growth in the money supply of 25.1 percentage points within a five-year period. For the interval from 1900 to the creation of the Federal Reserve, this range was only 14.7 percentage points. The end result of these wild swings in money supply growth was an interval of severe price inflation, followed by sharp price deflation. These were decisive factors both in causing the 1920–22 business cycle and in making it as severe as it was. What is particularly significant is the interpretation that was ultimately put upon the 1920–22 business cycle by people who would be quite influential in years to come. There was a general tendency to ascribe the severity of the cycle, in which unemployment is estimated to have averaged 11.7 percent for the year 1921, to the harsh rigors of the marketplace. Future President Herbert Hoover was especially impressed by the magnitude of this business cycle, viewing the adjustment process that characterized it as the "liquidation" of labor, which he opposed on the grounds that "labor was not a commodity: it represented human bones."[4]

Reactions such as Hoover's represent a classic case of what was to become commonplace throughout the twentieth century. If an instrument of government intervention in the economy produced unanticipated, and unwelcome, results, some other factor or institution, more often than not the market mechanism, was assigned the responsibility for the undesired events and the stage was set for even more extensive government intervention at the next sign of an economic problem. The crisis of 1920–22 was found unacceptable by many people who had become infected with the planning mentality that marked the wartime conditions of 1917–18.[5] Despite the adjustment process of 1920–22 providing a striking testimonial to the efficacy of market mechanisms in correcting a fundamental condition of disequilibrium, its aftermath was marked by a turning away from this type of market adjustment. In its place came the underconsumptionism of industrialists such as Ford and Filene, politicians such as Hoover, and social commentators such as Foster and Catchings. Moreover, there was support from the intellectual community in the form of ideas such as those espoused by John Hobson. All of these views contributed to sowing the seeds of the disaster of the 1930s.

The process of refusing to blame government intervention for the economic failures that seem to follow in its wake was repeated in the 1930s. When the downturn began, the underconsumptionist hypothesis dominated public-policy actions. Money wage rates were held at levels that exceeded substantially what they would have been if normal market adjustments had been made. Underconsumptionism did not work. Yet, in the wake of its failure, responsibility for the debacle of the 1930s was ritualistically laid at the feet of the market mechanism. The inability of markets to override the impact of the meddling that characterized the initial years of the Great Depression was widely interpreted as providing definitive evidence of market failure. Therefore, it was argued that new tools of government intervention were needed. The ultimate intellectual rationale for such a view is, of course, Keynes's *General Theory*, a sophisticated reworking of the underconsumptionist notion. The problem was now defined in oversaving terms, rather than as underconsumption. However, these are merely two sides of the same coin.

The great irony in all this is that underconsumptionist thinking triumphed despite its manifest failure in the arena of public policy. For nearly half a century, it was able almost to totally vanquish the market adjustment approach to dealing with macroeconomic problems, no matter what the evidence said. Major public-policy initiatives, such as the National Labor Relations Act of 1935, were justified by underconsumptionist notions, and when the Employment Act of 1946 was drafted, underconsumptionist rhetoric dominated its language. Completing the underconsumption-Keynesian victory was the widely accepted interpretation that somehow the failure of the American economy to return to the conditions that marked the 1930s after World War II represented a vindication of Keynesian-style public-policy initiatives. As we demonstrated earlier, the truth is just the opposite. The relatively easy post–World War II adjustment to peacetime conditions and the character of the business cycles that marked the interval between the war and 1960 provide striking evidence of the capacity of market adjustments to provide stability in the American economy.[6]

In a sense, there was a schizophrenic character to the conventional wisdom that emerged during this period. On the one hand, the Keynesians wanted to take credit for the relatively smooth way in which things were going, but they also wanted to enhance the argument for additional government intervention and management of the economy. The solution was simple. Instead of focusing on the business cycle, shift attention to longer-term problems, namely, how to stimulate a greater amount of economic growth. In this way the United States launched on its third great period of intervention in the American economy during the twentieth century. The thrust of its approach, at least as espoused by the architects of the policy, such as Paul Samuelson, Robert Solow, and Walter Heller, would be conscious management of aggregate demand and a willingness to accept some degree of price inflation in the economy.

Once more, the interventionist mode led to an unanticipated outcome, the stagflation of the seventies. Not unexpectedly, the responsibility for this policy failure was assigned elsewhere, this time to underlying structural rigidities in the economy. Ad hoc theories were developed to explain why it had become so difficult to manage the economy. Eckstein's core inflation and the rational-expectations arguments specific to the seventies are good examples. We speculate that, given the appropriate set of circumstances, these views of the American economy would have become the foundation for a further extension of the role of government at the macroeconomic level. More often than not, the core inflation argument was used to suggest the possible need for wage-price restraint. It was argued that because of structural imperfections in the economy, traditional monetary and/or fiscal policy is incapable of providing a satisfactory combination of inflation, unemployment, and economic growth. Thus, if we are to be able to manage the levels of unemployment and economic growth, it will be imperative that wage-price controls be invoked. Add to this the rational-expectations view that monetary and fiscal policy are ineffective because they are fully anticipated by markets and the rationale for wage-price controls and perhaps even stronger forms of intervention, such as some variety of indicative planning or industrial policy, becomes apparent.

This time, though, before the argument for extending government manipulation of the economy even further could acquire sufficient momentum to ensure its adoption as policy, a sequence of events occurred that undercut its validity. The combination of the unanticipated disinflation that began in 1981 and the failure to engage in aggregate-demand management strategies during the recession of 1982 allowed market mechanisms to assert themselves once more. As the inflation rate fell from its double-digit 1979 and 1980 levels to 3.1 percent in 1983 and to as low as 1.9 percent in 1986, the alleged structural rigidities in the economy seemed to become less urgent than they had seemed at the beginning of the decade. Additional evidence of the relative lack of structural imperfections was provided by the unprecedented seven consecutive years of declining civilian unemployment rates that marked the years 1983 through 1989.

Clearly, the historic development of public policy of the macroeconomic variety in this century has produced alternating periods in which the federal government played an active role in the American economy and periods in which it did not. It is interesting to observe the relative consequences of this cycle of activism and nonactivism for the magnitude of business cycles since 1900. The first two unemployment peaks, those of 1908 and 1915, occur in a relatively nonactivist era. The unemployment rates in these two years are 8.0 and 8.5 percent, respectively. The next cycle, 1920–22, is an activism-induced one that has a peak unemployment rate of 11.7 percent in 1921. There follows a nonactivist cycle that drives the unemployment rate up to 5.0 percent in 1924. Then come the two major downturns associated with the activist era of the Great Depression, the slide from 1929 through 1933, during which unemployment rose from 3.2 to 24.9 percent, and the 1938 recession, which saw unemployment rise from 14.3 percent in 1937 to 19.0 percent in 1938. Next are the relatively non-activist cycle downturns of 1946, 1949, 1954, 1958, and 1961, with their respective peak annual average unemployment rates of 3.9, 5.9, 5.5, 6.8, and 6.7 percent, respectively. Finally, we have the cycle downturns that may be attributed to government actions during the last activist era, those of 1970–71, 1974–75, 1980–81, and 1982. The peak annual average unemployment rates during these cycles are 5.9, 8.5, 7.6, and 9.7 percent.

There is a rather obvious pattern in these cycles. The four that show the highest peak unemployment rates, 1929–33, 1937–38, 1920–21, and 1981–82, all may be traced in some substantial way to the effects of governmental activism. In the case of the fifth largest unemployment peak, there is a tie between a year from an activist era cycle, 1975, and one from a nonactivist cycle, 1915. Clearly, the periods in which governmental influence on macroeconomic events was the strongest are those marked by the poorest economic performance. As far as the business cycle is concerned, a strong case can be made that government intervention in the economy has made things worse, not better.

In the Long Run Many of Us Are Alive

One of the clichés that has emerged from the Keynesian episode is Keynes's remark to the effect that in the long run we are all dead. That comment, as much as any single remark, captures the mind set of the twentieth century, especially in the realm of making economic policy. The emphasis is on the short run, today, not tomorrow. Don't worry about the long run. You'll be dead then. Unfortunately, though, long runs do come, and when they arrive they are greeted by large numbers of people who are still alive and who are forced to deal with the full consequences of the short-run–oriented policy decisions of the past. And so, defunct academic scribblers and political dilettantes from distant ages continue to wield their influence on contemporary life, more often than not for the worse.

A striking example of this can be found in the case of unemployment. The level and pattern of unemployment in current American society carry the distinct imprint of past public-policy decisions, some taken more than half a century ago. Go back in time to the early years of the century, to the years before government intervention in macroeconomic affairs became more commonplace, to the years before the Great Depression. Typically, unemployment was in the 4 to 4.5 percent range with extreme values of 1.4 and 11.7 percent. The Great Depression decade (1930–39) is, to be sure, an aberration from the long-term trend in unemployment and, thus, it is appropriate to disregard it when assessing what has happened since 1929. Picking up the long-term unemployment story after the Great Depression had largely run its course, the typical unemployment experience of the forties and fifties is not measurably different from that of the pre–Great Depression decades. However, after that, the typical (or median) unemployment rate begins to drift upward over the next three decades, a half percentage point in the sixties, another percentage point in the seventies, and an additional 1.3 percentage points in the eighties. Systematically, the natural rate of unemployment has been moving upwards for at least a quarter of a century.

As described in earlier chapters, the origins of the rise in the natural rate of unemployment can be traced to a wide variety of public policies that have impacted on the labor-market behavior of individuals in the United States. The Norris-LaGuardia Act, the Davis-Bacon legislation, the National Labor Relations Act of 1935, the Social Security Act, unemployment compensation legislation, minimum-wage laws, and the whole apparatus of the modern welfare state have combined to make people more selective in their search for jobs, driving upward the unemployment rate recorded through our data collection process. Today, the typical unemployment rate is perhaps 50 percent greater than it was for the bulk of this century. In fact, the median unemployment rate for the eighties is about 65 percent higher than that for the fifties. This increase in the natural rate of unemployment represents a pure loss to the economy, which is ironic, given that so many of the public policies that produced it were justified at the time of their enactment by underconsumptionist arguments. They were supposed to be a positive stimulus to macroeconomic activity but have been just the opposite.

The impact of government policies on the structure of unemployment has been equally distorting. For example, prior to the development of the modern welfare state, there were no meaningful racial differentials in unemployment. However, throughout the post–World War II era, unemployment among nonwhites has systematically exceeded that among whites, currently by a ratio of more than two to one.

Particularly striking has been the deterioration in the relative unemployment position of young black males. In 1954, the first year in which annual unemployment data are available by race and age group, the unemployment rate for white males aged sixteen through nineteen was 13.4 percent. The similar rate for nonwhites was 14.4 percent. Eighteen years later, in 1972, the unemployment rate for white males aged sixteen through nineteen stood at 14.2 percent, 0.8 of one percentage point higher than it was in 1954. This was the first year in which data were available for blacks as a separate group, rather than just for nonwhites. The rate for black males aged sixteen through nineteen was 31.7 percent, more than twice the 1954 rate for nonwhites . Similarly, the female-male unemployment differential grew in the immediate postwar era, albeit to a much lesser extent.

Not only has the state aggravated the problem of unemployment for Americans, it has done so differentially. The biggest losers from state intervention have been the very people that advocates of activism have claimed need the most help, namely nonwhites, women, and unskilled and inexperienced youths. The strong, skilled, and comparatively affluent have managed to adjust to state intervention, although not without cost. The burden of the welfare state has fallen inordinately on those it was supposed to benefit the most.

The Contemporary Scene

So much for the past. It might legitimately be asked how our analysis and findings relate both to contemporary economic thinking and to the current and future economic scene. As to the first of these, we note Martin Bronfenbrenner's comment in the foreword that some readers might regard our efforts as "distillations from quaint and curious volumes of forgotten lore." That some might respond in this fashion would not surprise us, given that we place so much emphasis on the role of equilibrium wage rates in the business cycle. However, we think that such a view is misplaced. Rather, we prefer to view what we have done as quite mainstream with respect to the current discussions of macroeconomic matters. After all, a major present-day debate among macroeconomists is centered on the sources of shocks to the macroeconomy. Are they monetary in nature? Or do they reflect real phenomena, such as productivity changes, for example? In this respect, our arguments are couched in distinctly conventional terms. The one thing that all the cycles we describe have in common is their being set in motion by some kind of shock, some unanticipated event that generates a labor-market disequilibrium. Sometimes the shocks are monetary, sometimes real. Often, they have been reinforced by subsequent shocks generated by ill-conceived public policy. We find historical instances that are consistent with all of these possibilities, putting us on both sides of the current debate.[7]

Starting from this position, what we offer is an explanation for how business cycles are propagated, how perturbations of either a monetary or a real character are translated into variations in general levels of economic activity. Thus, we have gone the next step beyond the present debate to deal with the more critical issue of how shocks become cycles, with the emphasis being on the role played by labor markets in this process. To be sure, at first glance that may seem to be an argument out of the past, but we feel that it enables us to take a step into the future by providing a more general theory of how the macroeconomy functions, rather than relying on a series of special paradigms that apply only to specific sets of circumstances.

What about the pertinence of what we have done to the American economy of the 1990s? When the penultimate version of this work was being finished in the late spring of 1991, we wrote of how attention had shifted away from the unemployment problem during the 1980s, but speculated that the swings in the pendulum that brought the nonactivist era of the 1980s into being would again bring an activist period during which there would be a move to "do something" about unemployment. Those thoughts were prophetic. Events often move swiftly in the arena of public policy and this is one of those times. The public rhetoric associated with the, by historical standards, relatively mild recession that began in mid-1990 has been escalating rapidly, not unlike the events surrounding the weak business cycle that occurred at the very end of the 1950s and beginning of the 1960s. That earlier minor occurrence had a profound effect on our political culture, providing the impetus for the onset of the activist period that would ultimately produce the stagflation of the 1970s. The current response to what has been a modest increase in the unemployment rate is reminiscent of that time, raising the possibility that there will come into being a renewed sense of urgency about the macroeconomy that will create a consensus supporting governmental intervention to manage and stabilize the economic system.

The established record of the results of attempting such managing during this century, with its emphasis on the underconsumptionist/Keynesian forms of aggregate-demand manipulation, we already know. The methods of shaping the course of economic events that have been employed in the past will not work. Therefore, if once more we choose to walk down the path of attempting to provide central direction to the macroeconomy, the inevitable disappointments that will be encountered could well trigger a demand for new departures in economic interventionism, such as some form of industrial policy or, even worse, wage, price, and/or incomes control. There is no end to the possible forms of mischief that can be practiced in the name of stabilizing the economy. It is well to remember two things about the history of public policy of the macroeconomic variety. First, previous public-policy failures in the realm of economic stabilization generally have been used as the basis for arguing that even greater power to control and manage is required. Second, whenever nonintervention has produced relatively stable economic outcomes, the general argument from the pro-interventionists has been that we could do even better if we added a dollop (or several dollops) of central direction to the policy mix. Whatever has been the result, the statists in our midst are capable of interpreting it as being a rationale for the extension of the role of government in macroeconomic affairs.

The thrust of what we say here is to raise the possibility that the United States, at the beginning of the decade of the 1990s, is standing on the threshold of a new era of macroeconomic intervention, despite the historical experience that tells us that such interventionism is doomed to failure, and despite the fact that throughout the twentieth century the invisible hand of the unfettered market mechanism has consistently outperformed efforts of the highly visible hand of the state in providing economic stability. In this respect, we are echoing, to a certain extent, the thesis of Arthur Schlesinger, Jr., that "at some point, shortly before or after the year 1990, there should come a sharp change in the national mind and direction . . . ."[8] If that is the case, the coming decade will almost certainly add one more example to the already vast collection of incidents that validate George Santayana's dictum, "Those who cannot remember the past are condemned to repeat it."

NOTES

1. Friedrich A. Hayek, *The Road to Serfdom* (London: George Routledge, 1944), p. 90. (Emphasis added.)

2. These data are from Milton Friedman and Anna J. Schwartz, *A Monetary History of the United States, 1867–1960* (Princeton, N.J.: Princeton University Press for the National Bureau of Economic Research, 1963), Table A-1, 708–9.

3. Beginning with 1915, the money supply measure corresponds to the conventional definition of M1. Prior to 1915, it is somewhat broader. However, the dominant factor in the pre-1915 data is the M1 component.

4. Hoover's views are quite well described in Murray Rothbard, *America's Great Depression* (Kansas City: Sheed and Ward, 1963), chap. 8.

5. For a discussion of the impact of World War I on the attitudes of influential business and political leaders during the Great Depression, see William E. Leuchtenberg, "The New Deal and the Analogue of War," in *Change and Continuity in Twentieth Century America*, ed. John Braeman, Robert E. Bremner, and Everett Walters (Columbus: Ohio State University Press, 1964), pp. 81–143.

6. We observe in passing that significant empirical evidence that contradicted the Keynesian paradigm was ignored. For example, in the *General Theory*, Keynes offered the opinion that money and real wages moved in opposite directions. When confronted with evidence that indicated that they moved together, he argued that there was no relationship between them. See John Dunlop, "The Movement of Real and Money Wage Rates," *Economic Journal* 48 (1938): 413–34; Lorie Tarshis, "Changes in Real and Money Wages," ibid., 49 (1939): 150–54; and Keynes's response, "Relative Movements of Real Wages and Output," ibid, pp. 34–51. By the end of World War II, Keynesianism was sufficiently in the ascendant to permit economists completely to disregard the Dunlop and Tarshis evidence. Lawrence Klein, *The Keynesian Revolution* (New York: Macmillan, 1947) reacted to this interchange by commenting (p. 107), "Our main concern . . . is not with the empirical problem but with the theoretical relation of wage cuts to unemployment."

7. A very recent paper has come to our attention that finds evidence consistent with our approach. Applying vector-autoregression analysis techniques to the data, Tony Caporale, "The Role of Real and Monetary Shocks in Explaining Business Cycle Fluctuations," Department of Economics, George Mason University, 1992, finds that both forms of shocks, monetary and real, have significant effects on unemployment.

8. Arthur M. Schlesinger, Jr., *The Cycles of American History* (Boston: Houghton Mifflin, 1986), p. 47.

16

Afterword

Two-thirds of the way through the 1990s, it appears that this century's last decade rates fairly poorly in terms of its unemployment experience, continuing the generally high unemployment rates observed in the era since 1970. To be sure, the average unemployment rate was lower than in the 1980s. Yet, even in good years unemployment has been high by historical standards. For example, 1996 is the twenty-third consecutive year in which the annual unemployment rate exceeded 5 percent, a rate above the typical (median) rate in six of the century's decades. The best years in the 1990s (as in the 1970s and 1980s) had higher rates of unemployment than in typical years in all decades before 1970, excepting the Depression decade of the 1930s. This reflects a continuing high natural rate of unemployment.

For the first seven years of the 1990s, the average annual unemployment rate was 6.23 percent, the median rate was 6.10 percent, and the standard deviation was 0.75 percentage points. (For a comparison of these figures with those of other decades, see table 1.1). The average and median annual rates exceed those of all decades except the 1930s and 1980s, although the numbers are only slightly higher than in the 1970s. At the same time, the deviation around the average has been smaller than in any other decade in the century, primarily because, as of late 1996, the one recession during the decade was not severe.

Unemployment and Public Policy

What were the dynamics of the recession of the early 1990s? It began in 1990. By the third quarter of that year, economic growth had turned negative and the unemployment rate had begun to rise. Consistent with the basic theoretical and statistical model that is the centerpiece of this book, the productivity-adjusted real-wage rate had begun to increase in mid-1989. Starting with the third quarter of 1989, it rose for six consecutive quarters, reaching a cyclical peak in the fourth quarter of 1990. Why did this happen? At the onset of the recession, some economists blamed the run-up in petroleum spot prices associated with Iraq's invasion of Kuwait on August 2, 1990. Although we do not deny the possibility of occasional supply-side shocks in explaining downturns, the 1990 recession was beginning well before Saddam Hussein sent his troops into Kuwait. Indeed, the initial cause was a moderate negative-productivity shock. A decline in output per hour began in the first quarter of 1989 and continued for four consecutive quarters. This contributed to a slight rise in the adjusted real wage for the year, leading to a softening of the labor market and a slowdown in the growth of output.[1]

The 1990 downturn, however, was not predominantly the result of continued productivity shocks. Indeed, output per hour rose considerably in the first half of the year and declined only very slightly for the year as a whole. Moreover, there was no unanticipated disinflation in prices; consumer prices rose more in 1990 than in the previous year and the Gross Domestic Product (GDP) price deflator increased by nearly as much.

Rather, the 1990 recession, like many that preceded it, resulted in large part from policy-induced wage shocks. Compensation per hour in the business sector grew *twice* as fast in 1990 as in the previous year. It rose at an 8 percent annual rate in the second quarter—the largest quarterly increase since the first quarter of 1982. President George Bush had signed legislation approving the first minimum-wage increase in nine years, which took place on the first day of the second quarter. It raised the minimum wage by 13.4 percent, to $3.80 per hour. Given the magnitude of aggregate compensation increases, it appears that employers raised the wages not only of those they were required to by law, but also the wages of other low-skilled workers earning a bit above the minimum. Presumably, this was to maintain some skill-based wage differential between workers.

The impact was predictable. The employment-population ratio for teenagers fell 5.4 percentage points between 1989 and 1991, the largest recorded two-year decline in that statistic since World War II. It fell more than 4 percentage points (from 47.6 percent to 43.5 percent) from March 1990 to August 1990 alone.[2] The adjusted real wage, which had risen modestly in the last half

of 1989, increased in every quarter in 1990 (since some wage increases in the
first quarter were induced by the required minimum-wage increase beginning
April 1).[3]

In early 1991, it appeared that market forces were working to correct the
disequilibrium caused by the government-induced wage shock. The adjusted
real wage fell significantly in the first quarter as real wages fell. Yet, once more,
misguided government policies thwarted a market-induced recovery. Real
wages rose sharply in the second quarter, as the minimum wage increased
again, by 11.8 percent, to $4.25 per hour. The market adjustment process was
interrupted and the adjusted real wage changed very little over the last three
quarters of the year. As a consequence, unemployment continued to rise in a
lagged response to the increase in the adjusted real wage that began in late
1989 and continued through 1990 and most of 1991. The unemployment rate,
which averaged less than 5.3 percent in the first half of 1990, reached 6 percent
before the end of that year and was averaging nearly 7 percent by the last
quarter of 1991.

The rate of wage increases fell throughout 1992. Ironically, the biggest decrease in the adjusted real wage came in the fourth quarter, when the voters
rejected incumbent President Bush. Recovery was too little and too late to
save Bush, who paid the political price of compromising on the minimum
wage (as he also had on taxes). The unemployment rate actually started falling
in the last quarter, beginning a decline that continued for two years. A moderation in wage gains—in no quarter in 1993 or 1994 did compensation rise at
an annual rate of as much as 3.5 percent—was a major factor in the unemployment and output recovery.

Although the unemployment rate fell below 6 percent in the third quarter
of 1994, where it has stayed for more than two years, the recovery in many
ways was less satisfactory than earlier ones. The lowest quarterly recorded unemployment rate, 5.2 percent in the third quarter of 1996, was slightly higher
than observed at the peak of the long prosperity of the late 1980s.

This may appear to be a rather complex and speculative scenario. However,
it is validated by estimating the extended version of our statistical model, using
quarterly data beginning with the first quarter of 1959 and concluding with
the second quarter of 1996. The results are reported in tables B.2 and B.3 of
Appendix B. Overall, the statistical model does an excellent job of explaining
the variations in unemployment in the post-1988 period, as is shown in figure
16.1.[4]

The Best of Times, the Worst of Times

The prosperity of the mid-1990s seems somewhat tentative. Polls show an
increasing percentage of Americans who think the nation is "not on the right

FIGURE 16.1

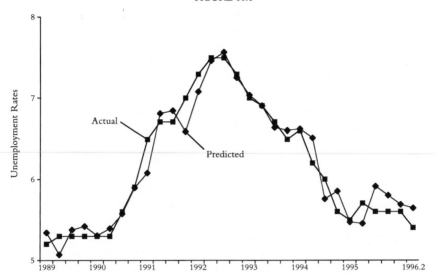

track." On the left, President Clinton's labor secretary, Robert Reich, complained almost incessantly about the deteriorating condition of American workers, as reflected in falling real wages.[5] A remarkably similar complaint has come from the right, in the form of Patrick Buchanan's unsuccessful appeal for workers' votes in the 1992 and especially the 1996 presidential primary elections.

Yet, there are several conventional measures of economic well-being that suggest the economy is performing adequately, although not spectacularly. A conventionally defined "misery index"—the inflation rate plus the unemployment rate—is at or near lows for the present generation. The stock market has boomed during the early and mid-1990s, creating literally trillions of dollars of new wealth. Per capita real consumption continues to rise, although, as we will shortly point out, at a significantly slower pace than during the 1980s. And, toward the bottom of the income distribution, a larger proportion of families classified as poor have washing machines, dryers, dishwashers, microwaves, and air conditioners than the public as a whole did in 1970.[6]

Still, by other measures, the first two-thirds of the 1990s have not been a positive experience when evaluated in terms of the long sweep of American economic history. Figure 16.2 shows an augmented misery index for six periods of prosperity during the twentieth century. The index is constructed by subtracting the rate of growth in real output from the conventionally defined misery index. Three-year periods are used to smooth out the impact of unusual performance in single years.

Note that in periods of prosperity during the era of relative laissez-faire in the first three decades of the century, the augmented misery index was either negative or negligibly positive. The 1930s brought the New Deal, the beginnings of the welfare state, and the Keynesian Revolution. By mid-century, the augmented misery index had risen, not fallen, from its earlier levels. After the vast expansion of the welfare state and vigorous application of deficit-financed fiscal policies featuring government spending, the augmented misery index rose to extraordinary levels, even during the best years of the late 1970s. During the Reagan administration, some modest retreat from the welfare state and repressive regulations and labor laws occurred (e.g., the real minimum wage rate decreased), and with that the augmented misery index fell significantly. However, that decline ceased during the Bush-Clinton era, as the data for 1994–96 indicate. It is no coincidence, in our judgment, that the modest but real retreat from governmental economic intervention observed in the 1980s also was essentially halted during the Bush-Clinton era.[7]

To pursue this point further, consider that within recent history it is possible to identify specific time periods that embrace quite different economic policies and philosophies. Thus, we may conduct something in the way of a controlled experiment by comparing the performance of the American economy during these different policy regimes. Of course, what we have in mind here is the distinction between supply-side and non-supply-side economic policy. The specific dates associated with supply-side and non-supply-side approaches to

FIGURE 16.2

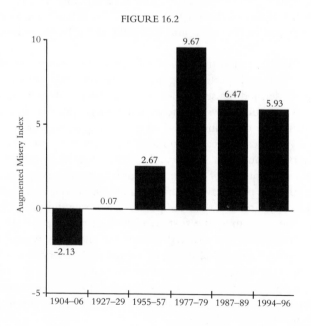

economic policy are quite straightforward. The interval 1981–89 is clearly supply-side in character, beginning with the 1981 income-tax cuts. Conveniently, 1981 contains a National Bureau of Economic Research business-cycle peak and 1989 is the last year before the recession began in 1990.[8] Thus, comparing changes in economic variables between these two years is not distorted by business-cycle considerations. Prior to 1981, another eight-year period also begins with a business-cycle peak in 1973. We treat it as a non-supply-side era. Finally, there is the interval between 1989 and the present, another non-supply-side interlude.

Independent of the dating of these periods, on what basis do we call one supply-side and the other non-supply-side? Basically, we ask whether economic policies increased or decreased the incentives to produce goods and services, either through explicit taxes and subsidies or hidden levies in the form of federal government regulations and mandates. The record on taxes is very clear in this respect. From 1973 through 1981, increases in federal government revenues claimed 22.2 percent of the rise in GDP. Between 1981 and 1989, only 18.5 percent of additional GDP found its way to the coffers of the federal government. Since 1989, that figure has reverted almost exactly to its 1973–81 level, standing at 22.3 percent.[9]

On the regulatory side, the picture is the same. In the four years 1977–81, federal regulatory costs are estimated to have risen by 36.5 percent. This is more than the 23.1 percent increase recorded in the *eight* years 1981–89, but less than the 53.9 percent rise between 1989 and 1994.[10]

Finally, there is the matter of transfers and social spending, which have been shown to have substantial disincentive effects on people's labor-market behavior.[11] Between 1973 and 1981, additional income transfers to persons amounted to 10.9 percent of the increase in GDP. From 1981 to 1989, that figure was only 7.7 percent, while over the interval 1989–95 it soared to 13.4 percent. If the focus is all social spending—defined as the sum of outlays for health, income security, and social security—the respective percentages are 12.1, 8.5, and 18.1.[12]

These various indicators of the nature of economic policy since 1973 are summarized in table 16.1. They clearly show that the interval 1981–89 was one in which greater emphasis was placed on economic strategies that encourage productive activity by the entrepreneurial sector of American society. Of course, the major legislative actions of this era were the 1981 and 1986 initiatives that reduced maximum marginal income tax rates. This is in contrast to the post-1989 period with its very substantial rounds of tax increases (1990 and 1993), which drove the marginal tax rate at the top of the income distribution up from 28 to 39.6 percent.

TABLE 16.1.

INDICATORS OF NATURE OF ECONOMIC POLICY, DIFFERENT POLICY REGIMES,
UNITED STATES, 1973–1995

	Economic Policy Indicator			
Economic Policy Regime	Ratio Increase in Revenue to Increase in GDP (x 100)	Percent Increase in Federal Regulatory Costs	Ratio Increase in Transfers to Increase in GDP (x 100)	Ratio Increase in Social Spending to Increase in GDP (x 100)
Pre-Supply-Side (1973–1981)	22.2	36.5 (Period 1977–1981)	10.9	12.1
Supply-Side (1981–1989)	18.5	23.1	7.7	8.5
Post-Supply-Side (1989–1995)	22.3	53.9	13.4	18.1

Source: National Income and Product Accounts and authors' calculations.

THE ECONOMY DURING THE PRE-SUPPLY-SIDE ERA

Given the distinctly contrasting approaches to economic policy that mark the three periods under consideration, it is interesting to compare their economic performance. Let us begin with what we call the pre-supply-side interval, 1973–81. A few very familiar economic measures will suffice. Gross Domestic Product, the estimate of the total value of goods and services produced, adjusted for price changes, grew at an average annual rate of 2.15 percentage points in the eight years following 1973. In per capita terms, real GDP rose by 11.6 percent and per capita real consumption was up by 10.8 percent. What about the employment side? Looking only at the number of jobs created can be misleading. What is important is the increase in employment compared to the growth in the working-age population.[13] Between 1973 and 1981, civilian employment rose by 15,323,000 and the working-age population increased by 23,034,000.[14] Thus, 0.67 jobs were created for every person added to the working-age population. Finally, the average output of labor, a key factor in explaining the level of real wage rates, rose by 5.0 percent, about 0.6 percent a year.

THE ECONOMY DURING THE SUPPLY-SIDE ERA

How does this performance compare with that of the supply-side years, 1981–89? As to overall economic growth, the average annual increase in real GDP in the eight years subsequent to 1981 was 3.2 percent, more than a full percentage point greater than for 1973–81. In turn, this produced a 19.3 percent increase in real per capita GDP and a 19.4 percent growth in real per capita consumption spending. As to jobs, total civilian employment increased by *more* than the rise in the working-age population, providing 1.04 jobs per person added to the working-age group.[15] In addition, worker productivity increased about twice as fast during these years, by a total of 9.8 percent, about 1.2 percent a year. Clearly, as measured by all five of these indicators of economic performance, the supply-side era outperformed the pre–supply-side period.[16]

POST-SUPPLY-SIDE ECONOMIC PERFORMANCE

What about the post–supply-side interval, the six years from 1989 to 1995 that were punctuated by two major rounds of tax increases? During this span real GDP grew at an average annual rate of 1.8 percent; real per capita GDP increased by 4.6 percent; real per capita consumption spending was up by 5.9 percent; 0.62 jobs were created for every person added to the working-age population; and the average productivity of labor climbed by 4.4 percent, about 0.7 percent a year. Not only are these measures of economic performance below those for the supply-side years, but they fail to match even those of the pre–supply-side interval.

LONGER-RUN CONSEQUENCES

The superiority of the supply-side years is obvious. Income, employment, and productivity levels improved more dramatically than in either the pre- or post-supply-side times. The magnitude of the differences in economic performance has profound implications in the longer run. To illustrate this, we have projected levels of economic performance that would result assuming the patterns of economic growth that accompanied the supply-side time period.

It is a simple exercise. The particular economic measure we focus on is real per capita GDP. Using its 1989 level as a base, we then extrapolate through 1995, employing the average annual growth rate in real per capita GDP over the period 1981–89. We then compare this "supply-side growth path"[17] to the actual levels of real per capita GDP over this six-year period. The results are startling. By 1995, the American economy had fallen 8.3 percent below the supply-side growth path.

THE GREAT SLOWDOWN

A few additional remarks will put these numbers in perspective. The upswing in the business cycle is the first sustained economic reco more than one hundred years for which reliable data are available in which the GDP did not rise by more than 3.5 percent in at least one year.[18] The median annual rate of growth in real GDP for 1990–95 was 2.1 percent, down from 3.2 percent in the 1980s, and down from more than 4 percent in the three decades prior to that.

Although there are no doubt multiple factors involved in explaining the slowdown in employment and output growth in the 1990s, some of our own recent work suggests that government expenditure growth beyond some optimal point tends to reduce the rate of economic growth.[19] The positive impact of government on economic growth when the public sector is small—for example, the gains from maintaining property rights, law and order, and, perhaps, infrastructure—are offset as government expands. Government spending crowds out private activity that, dollar for dollar, is more economically productive, which, we suspect, reflects the incentives that markets provide in the private sector to maximize efficiency. In addition, the growth in regulatory activity, which had been slowed in the 1980s, accelerated in the 1990s. There is strong evidence that this form of government involvement has a particularly debilitating impact on productivity growth, possibly explaining half or more of the observed slowdown since the 1960s.[20]

Detailed examples of the resurgence of the regulatory impulse in the 1990s are abundant. New legislative departures in the Bush-Clinton years, including the Americans with Disabilities Act, a parental-leave law, health-insurance legislation (although the potentially far more devastating major revamping of the health-care system proposed by the Clinton administration was rejected by the Congress), two major tax increases, and two minimum-wage bills that will have the effect of raising the minimum wage in four of the first eight years of the 1990s, are cases in point. All had and have the potential of raising labor costs and reducing the attractiveness of hiring labor.

The New Stagnation

As just suggested, the overall economic record of the 1990s is rather disappointing. This is especially true when viewed from a long-term perspective. Take the case of job growth. Figure 16.3 shows that the employment-population ratio rose throughout the four decades prior to the 1990s, with the most substantial increase occurring in the 1980s. Yet, in a sharp departure from the pattern of steady growth, this ratio actually fell between 1989 and 1995. This was the first decline since the 1930s. The impact of this is reflected in figure 16.4, which shows the ratio of new civilian jobs created in a decade to the growth in the working-age population. In the 1960s, 1970s, and 1980s, this statistic rose. Again, however, the early 1990s brought a reversal in this pattern.

FIGURE 16.3

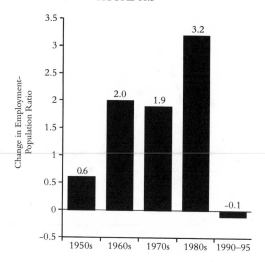

The same story emerges when patterns of growth in GDP are examined. Figure 16.5 illustrates the nature of the problem in the contemporary United States. It shows the five-year moving average of the rate of growth in GDP across the post–World War II era. The pattern is clear. Up to 1970, growth often exceeds 4 percent per year over five-year periods and only occasionally falls below 3 percent. However, after that, with the exception of the burst of

FIGURE 16.4

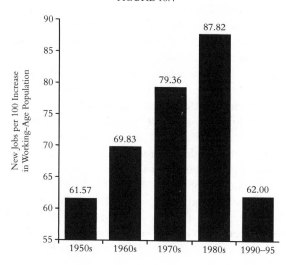

FIGURE 16.5

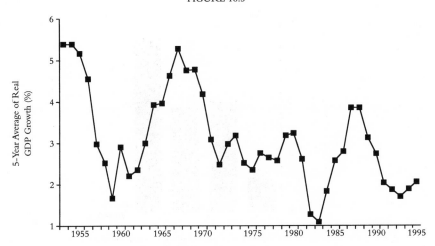

growth in the 1980s that we have already documented, the five-year averages are infrequently greater than 3 percent and often fall below 2 percent. Of special note is the almost total inability to detect a cyclical peak during the most recent economic "recovery."

All of this confirms that the 1990s can fairly be described as an era of economic stagnation. Not surprisingly, this theme has been articulated by those with an interventionist bent. As the 1990–92 recession unfolded, the call went out for government, meaning the federal government, to do something. The intellectuals and the tax-and-spend politicians rallied to the cause. For many of the leading intellectuals, it was something of a crusade. They had told us, circa 1980, that the supply-side view of the world was fatally flawed. Consequently, the economic transformation that took place in the 1980s was an affront to them and their adherents.

Almost predictably, the same savants who pronounced the American economy dead-in-the-water as the decade of the 1980s opened provided more of the same counsel as the 1990s began. For example, in their January 1992 testimony before the Joint Economic Committee, Paul Samuelson and James Tobin exude the stagnationist view.[21] Tobin speaks of maladies and malaise, stagnating real wages, and the like. Samuelson sees the long-run problem as a lack of thriftiness, too little saving and too much consumption by the American people.[22] The widely proposed solution to these alleged problems is an increase in public investment, that is, government spending.

The fascinating dimension of this new round of stagnationist thinking is the extent to which it differs from earlier versions of the same basic argument, in particular the stagnationism of the late 1930s we described earlier. Then, the problem was alleged to be that people were saving *too much,* producing a dearth of consumption spending. Interestingly, though, the mainstream intellectual solution to economic stagnation was exactly the same sixty years ago as it is today—expand government spending.

In addition, it should be recognized that the sequence of events over the course of this most recent business cycle provides a powerful confirmation of one of our primary theses, namely, that the negative consequences of one set of government policies on the American economy become the rationale for further interventions. The wage, tax, and regulatory cost shocks arising out of government policies in 1990–91 raised unemployment and slowed economic growth, creating the very real appearance of economic stagnation. The solution? For those beguiled by the siren song of planning, it is very simple—more federal government incursions into the economy.

We do not question the basic thrust of the evidence of stagnation. That might seem to be something of a contradiction. After all, following the recession that began in 1990 and peaked in mid-1992, unemployment rates have returned to levels that are low by the standards of the past quarter century. Shouldn't that mean something in terms of economic growth? The answer is yes, if the emphasis is on cyclical variations in changes in GDP. In Appendix B we demonstrate a systematic negative link between movements in the adjusted real wage and the percentage rate of growth in GDP. However, while this link is statistically significant, it is not as robust as the unemployment relationship. Also, while it tells us something about cyclical patterns, it may say little about trend growth.

That last point is important. On theoretical grounds, we would expect labor markets to adjust to any real labor cost-increasing or productivity-decreasing shocks partly through reductions in wage rates and partly through declines in employment.[23] Once such adjustments have been made, the adjusted real wage will be within its normal range of variation, moving in a cyclical pattern around its underlying economic value. Thus, if the shocks to the adjusted real wage are productivity reducing, the simple real wage (the money wage rate deflated by an appropriate price index) will adjust downward to reflect the productivity change, leaving the adjusted real wage at its equilibrium level. The upshot of this is that shocks to labor markets can have several effects, including cyclical swings in unemployment and output growth and variations in the trend values of real wages and output.

The New Stagnationism in Perspective

If we accept the thesis of economic stagnation in the United States, how do we differ from, say, James Tobin's position that there is "malaise" in America?

The answer is that we differ, not on the reality of the stagnation in economic growth, but on the question of its implications. The Tobin-style variant of the stagnationist argument is designed to make a case for new federal government initiatives that, allegedly, will "get the economy going," or stimulate wage growth, or help the poor. The basic philosophical position of such arguments is that we need more federal government, not less.

It is here that we disagree. At this stage of American history, we see the federal government as too large. Its size, relative to the overall economy, is such that it is generating the economic outcomes that give rise to the idea that we live in an age of economic stagnation. We are not unique in this view,[24] nor is it confined to just the contemporary age. Thirty-five years ago, Wilhelm Ropke wrote, "There is no likelihood that the indispensable minimum of government organized security will be lacking in this era. . . . On the other hand, it is very likely that the minimum may be dangerously exceeded, to the detriment of the people, the health of our society, and the strength of our economy."[25] How prophetic!

NOTES

1.   In the early 1990s, the government reported that the Gross National Product rose 2.5 percent in 1989, well below normal growth for the era. In the latest revisions, however, Gross Domestic Product is estimated to have risen 3.4 percent in 1989, down modestly from the 3.8 percent of the previous year. See *The Economic Report of the President,* various years, for the changing data on economic conditions during this period.

2.   *The Economic Report of the President, 1992* (Washington, D.C.: Government Printing Office, 1992), p. 337.

3.   The question of the impact of minimum wages has recently become a controversial one. David Card and Alan Krueger have been the primary contributors to an attempt to discredit the conventional wisdom that increasing minimum wages has negative effects on employment. See their *Myth and Measurement: The New Economics of the Minimum Wage* (Princeton, N.J.: Princeton University Press, 1995), and "Minimum Wages and Employment: A Case Study of the Fast-Food Industry in New Jersey and Pennsylvania," *American Economic Review* 84 (1994): 172–93. A number of studies contradict the Card-Krueger position, and serious questions have been raised about the reliability of some of their data sources. See, among others, David Neumark and William Wachser (responding to an earlier Card-Krueger paper), "Employment Effects of Minimum and Subminimum Wage Panel Data on State Minimum Wage Laws," *Industrial and Labor Relations Review,* October 1992, pp. 55–81. We do not accept the Card-Krueger view. Our own position on this matter is spelled out in Richard Vedder and Lowell Gallaway, *Minimum Wage Costs Jobs* (London: Adam Smith Institute, 1995).

4.   It might be asked why we did not estimate the model for only the interval

1989 I through 1996 II. In its full version, with some twenty-five independent variables, there are an insufficient number of degrees of freedom to permit this. The full justification for our proceeding in this fashion is provided in Appendix B.

5.   An analysis of the validity of the notion that real wages are falling is presented in Lowell Gallaway and Richard Vedder, *The Impact of the Welfare State on Workers* (Washington, D.C.: Joint Economic Committee of Congress, 1996). Its basic conclusion is that the case for declining real wages is badly overstated, although it is clear that the growth of real wages has slowed significantly since 1973.

6.   See Employment Policy Foundation, *The American Workplace: 1996 Labor Day Report* (Washington, D.C.: Employment Policy Foundation, 1996), p. 39.

7.   Some specific evidence of a shift in the overall economic environment for small business is presented in Lowell Gallaway and Gary Anderson, "The Impact of Recent Regulations on Small Business Job Creation," *Journal of Regulation and Social Costs* 3 (1993): 27–61.

8.   After 1981, the next National Bureau of Economic Research cycle peak occurs in early 1990. Therefore, 1989 unambiguously reflects the end of the prosperity of the 1980s.

9.   The source of these figures is the National Income and Product Accounts data reported in *Economic Report of the President, 1996* (Washington, D.C.: Government Printing Office, 1996).

10.   These data are primarily from Thomas Hopkins, *Regulatory Costs in Profile* (St. Louis: Center for the Study of American Business, 1996).

11.   See the sources cited in chapter 13, note 20. See also M. Anne Hill and June O'Neill, *Underclass Behavior in the United States: Measurement and Analysis of Determinants* (New York: City University of New York, Baruch College, 1993).

12.   These comparisons use fiscal-year data for social spending and calendar-year data for GDP. This should not produce any significant distortion.

13.   The working-age population is defined as the civilian, noninstitutional population age 16 and over.

14.   For this and similar calculations, the Current Population Survey employment data are used rather than the establishment survey information.

15.   Between 1981 and 1989, the working-age population increased by 16,263,000 while civilian employment rose by 16,945,000.

16.   Other comparisons of the 1973–81 and 1981–89 periods are presented in Lowell Gallaway and Richard Vedder, "The Distributional Impact of the 1980s," *Critical Review,* Spring–Summer 1993, pp. 61–79.

17.   It is interesting to note that the average annual growth rate in real per capita GDP during the years 1981–89 is quite similar to that for the period 1949–73.

18.   Data before 1929 are for Gross National Product. There have been some short-lived recoveries with economic growth, but the recovery beginning in mid-1991 is notable for the tepidness of income growth. For details see *Historical Statistics,* op. cit., pp. 224–27, *Economic Report of the President, 1995* (Washington, D.C.: Government Printing Office, 1995), p. 406; and *Economic Report of the President, 1996* (Washington, D.C.: Government Printing Office, 1996), p. 283.

19.   This work is a series of five studies for the Joint Economic Committee of Congress, beginning with Lowell Gallaway and Richard Vedder, *The Impact of the Wel-*

fare State on the American Economy (Washington, D.C.: Joint Economic Committee of Congress, 1995).

20.   See Richard Vedder, *Federal Regulation's Impact on the Productivity Slowdown: A Trillion Dollar Drag,* Policy Study No. 131 (St. Louis: Center for the Study of American Business, 1996).

21.   U.S. Congress, *The 1992 Economic Report of the President,* Hearings before the Joint Economic Committee, Congress of the United States, 102nd Congress, January 9, 10, 13, and 31, 1992 (Washington, D.C.: Government Printing Office, 1992), pp. 9–17 for Samuelson and 18–27 for Tobin.

22.   Apparently, Samuelson has abandoned the notion of "the paradox of thrift" that generations of economics students have been taught using his textbook. The argument holds that attempting to save more, that is, being more thrifty, may have deleterious effects on the economy and result in people's total saving being less. In a more general sense, the paradox of thrift implies that the savings rate is not only irrelevant in terms of its effect on economic performance, but that a high rate of saving is a drag on the economy as it makes for greater "leakages" out of the expenditure stream.

23.   A not uncommon estimate of the extent to which labor cost increases arising out of government mandates or regulations would be passed through to workers in the form of wage decreases holds that 85 percent of such costs would be reflected in lower wage rates.

24.   See Dick Armey, *The Freedom Revolution* (Washington, D.C.: Regnery Publishing Company, 1995), pp. 91–93; and Gerald Scully, *What Is the Optimal Size of Government in the United States?* NCPA Report No. 188 (Dallas: National Center for Policy Analysis, 1994). Scully focuses on taxes, rather than spending, and considers all government activity, not just federal. In a similar vein, Charles L. Ballard, John B. Shoven, and John Whalley, "General Equilibrium Computations of the Marginal-Welfare Costs of Taxes in the United States," *American Economic Review* 75 (1985), identify deadweight efficiency losses from taxation that are quite consistent with this view.

25.   Wilhelm Ropke, "Welfare State and Chronic Inflation," in *Crisis of the Modern Welfare State* (Washington, D.C.: Joint Economic Committee of Congress, 1994), excerpted and reprinted from Wilhelm Ropke, *A Humane Economy: The Social Framework of the Free Market,* translated and with an introduction by Marianne Cowan (Washington, D.C.: Regnery Publishing Company, 1962), p. 2.

Appendix A

The Extended
Theoretical Model

The basic estimating equation employed in chapter 3 is derived from the following labor-market-oriented model. Consider an economy in which the demand for labor (D_L) is determined according to the familiar marginal productivity conditions:

$$(1) \qquad D_L = f(w_r)$$

where w_r denotes the real-wage rate.

Let the supply of labor (S_L) be a fixed proportion of the population, i. e., perfectly inelastic:

$$(2) \qquad S_L = S_o$$

This assumption is reasonably consistent with the facts of American society.[1] For purposes of simplifying the analysis, we will assume an invariant population over time.

Equating expressions (1) and (2) gives

$$(3) \qquad S_o = D_L = f(w_r),$$

which produces an equilibrium real-wage rate, designated hereafter as $w_r^\star$, and an equilibrium level of employment, $N^\star$. Let it be understood that, at this equilibrium, there will exist an equilibrium level of unemployment, $U^\star$, consisting partly of the frictional variety and partly of a structural kind brought about by institutional constraints (such as minimum-wage laws) that make it impossible to employ people with very low levels of marginal productivity.

Accompanying this real-wage version of the labor market is a money-wage version in which the demand schedule for labor is multiplied by the price level (P), so that at any point on the money-wage demand schedule

$$(4) \qquad w_m = w_r P$$

where w_m is the money-wage rate.

Assume an initial equilibrium at which $w_r = w_r^\star$. Now, introduce an exogenous change in the price level, induced by a change in money aggregate demand, which shifts the money-wage demand schedule for labor either to the left or to the right. In the absence of any adjustment in money-wage rates, the real-wage rate will deviate from equilibrium, a decrease in price making it greater than $w_r{}^\star$ and an increase moving it below $w_r{}^\star$. In either case, cyclical unemployment, defined as the difference between the actual and the equilibrium level of unemployment.$(U - U^\star)$, which may be either positive or negative, is created. If there is a fall in prices, real-wage rates rise, employment falls, and the unemployment level rises above $U^\star$. A rise in prices lowers real-wage rates, enabling employers to hire workers whose marginal product previously was lower than the real wage they would have commanded. Thus, unemployment falls below $U^\star$ and $(U - U^\star)$ becomes negative.

In the real-wage labor market, we assume no change in the given technological conditions of production that underlie the demand schedule for labor. Consequently, the changes in the money-wage labor market are reflected in movements along the real-wage demand schedule for labor. Thus, the market is displaced (or "shocked off") its equilibrium position.

For discussion purposes, let us assume that positive cyclical unemployment is the disequilibrium situation under consideration. A neoclassical adjustment mechanism suggests that money-wage rates will fall until the equilibrium real-wage rate, $w_r{}^\star$, is reestablished. Symbolically, the pure neoclassical adjustment mechanism would be:

$$(5) \qquad\qquad\qquad\qquad \dot{w}_m = \dot{p}.$$

where a dot over a variable indicates a rate of change.

Thus, there would be, at worst, only a temporary disequilibrium in the market. In fact, in a world of instantaneous adjustments, disequilibrium would never occur.

Contrast the neoclassical mechanism with a Keynesian adjustment response, in which there would be either no change in money-wage rates, i. e., absolute downward rigidity in wages, or, if there were some downward adjustment in money-wage rates, there would be a corresponding fall in price levels that would further shift the money-wage demand schedule for labor to the left, thus eliminating the employment effects of the wage adjustment mechanism. These two possible adjustment responses are:

$$(6) \qquad\qquad\qquad\qquad \dot{w}_m = 0, \text{ or if } \dot{w}_m < 0,$$

$$(7) \qquad\qquad\qquad\qquad \dot{p}' = \dot{w}_m$$

where $\dot{p}'$ denotes the change in the price level induced by an adjustment in money-wage rates. The end result is the same in both cases, no change in the real-wage rate once it has been shocked out of equilibrium.

The neo-Keynesian view of a situation such as that under discussion would begin by treating the real-wage rate, w_r, as being one of a range of possible equilibrium labor-market situations, which are the product of different levels of aggregate demand in the system. This implies that the real-wage rate is determined by the level of aggregate demand. In the case of a rise in unemployment induced by a negative shift in aggregate demand, prices fall more rapidly than money-wage rates, suggesting a wage adjustment mechanism of the following type:

(8) $$\dot{w}_m = a + b\dot{p}, 0 < d\dot{w}_m/d\dot{p} < 1.$$

Finally, there is the "new classical" adjustment response. Two versions may be postulated, a rational-expectations approach and what Stein calls "asymptotically rational-expectations."[2] In the former, labor-market behavior is predicated on predictions of wage and price magnitudes, where the errors in prediction are random (nonserially correlated) in character with a zero mean.[3] This implies

(9) $$\tilde{w}_m = w_m + e_m$$

and

(10) $$\tilde{p} = p + e_p$$

where the symbol $\tilde{p}$ indicates a predicted value and e represents an error term in the prediction (with appropriate subscripts). Combining (9) and (10) gives

(11) $$w_r = (w_m + e_m)/(p + e_p).$$

Now, from equations (1) through (3), we may define

(12) $$U = S_o - D_L = S_o - f(w_r),$$

where U denotes the actual level of unemployment. Keeping in mind our assumption of a fixed supply of labor, we may write

(13) $$U - U^\star = f(w_r^\star) - f(w_r) = f(w_r^\star - w_r),$$

where

(14) $$d(U - U^\star)/d(w_r^\star - w_r) < 0.$$

For convenience purposes, we redefine (12) and (13) as follows:

(15) $$U - U^\star = \phi(w_r - w_r^\star),$$
$$d(U - U^\star)/d(w_r - w_r^\star) > 0.$$

If we assume that the system oscillates about equilibrium over time,

(16) $$w_r^\star = \overline{w}_r$$

where $\overline{w}_r$ represents the mean real-wage rate over time.

With behavior being in terms of predicted wage rates,

(17) $$(U - U^\star) = f(\tilde{w}_r - \overline{w}_r)$$

and

(18) $$\tilde{w}_r - \overline{w}_r = (w_m + e_m)/(p + e_p) - \overline{w_m/p}.$$

Over time, the mean value of (11) is $\overline{w_m/p}$ and consequently,

(19) $$\overline{\tilde{w}_r - \overline{w}_r} = 0$$

and

(20) $\overline{U - U^\star} = 0,$

i.e., the mean values for $(\widetilde{w}_r - \overline{w}_r)$ and $(U - U^\star)$ are zero.

Of course, both of these magnitudes are still subject to a nonserially correlated error term with a zero mean.[4] What this produces is random variations around a stable level of unemployment. In reality, this result differs from an instantaneous neoclassical pattern of adjustment only by the random variation.

The asymptotically rational-expectations version of the new classical economics differs from rational expectations only in the sense that the error term associated with the predictions that influence behavior may be systematic in character, i. e., serially correlated. This would be the case if the predicted values of labor-market magnitudes are based on a partial response to current experience, as well as a recognition of past events. However, if the end result is to restore equilibrium in the market, the final outcome will be a gradual approach to equilibrium and, over time, equations (19) and (20) will be satisfied, subject to an error term that may be serially correlated.

The existence of several possible wage-adjustment mechanisms rather naturally leads one to wonder which best describes the American economy. To assist in answering that question, we write the following generalized short-run wage-adjustment function:

(21) $(\dot{w}_m)_t = a - b(w_r - w_r^\star)_{t-1} + c_t \dot{p}_t + c_{t-1}\dot{p}_{t-1} + \ldots$
             $+ c_{t-n}\dot{p}_{t-n} + d_t \dot{\pi}_t + d_{t-1}\dot{\pi}_{t-1} + \ldots + d_{t-n}\dot{\pi}_{t-n},$

where $\dot{\pi}$ denotes the rate of change in productivity per unit of labor.[5] The productivity measure is included at this point to adjust for changes in the demand for labor that are the result of technological progress and changes in the relative availability of the supplies of other factors of production.

The logic of the adjustment mechanism described in expression (21) is rather straightforward. The negative relationship between the rate of change in money-wage rates in the current period and the deviation, if any, of the real-wage rate from its equilibrium value in the previous period reflects an equilibrating response to the existence of any disequilibrium in the real-wage labor market. Thus, the further above equilibrium the real-wage rate lies, the less the quantity demanded of labor and the greater the pressure for a decrease in money-wage rates (or the less the pressure for increases). The other terms in (21) are designed to capture the pattern of adjustments, if any, to changes in prices and productivity in the current and past periods.

The generalized wage-adjustment mechanism embodied in (21) is capable of yielding all the possible adjustment responses that have been enumerated. For example, in the extreme case of instantaneous adjustment of the neoclassical type, the parameters c_t and d_t equal unity, all other c's and d's equal zero, and $(w_r)_{t-1}$ is always equal to $w_r^\star$. In such a case, (18) collapses into

(22) $(\dot{w}_m)_t = \dot{p}_t + \dot{\pi},$

which may be thought of as a long-run wage-adjustment function. Given that

(23) $$(w_r)_t = (w_m)_t/p_t,$$

expression (22) implies that

(24) $$(\dot{w}_r)_t = (\dot{w}_m)_t - \dot{p}_t = \dot{\pi}_t,$$

which is to say that an instantaneous neoclassical wage-adjustment mechanism yields a world in which the rate of change in the real-wage rate is equal to the rate of change in the productivity of labor.

From the previous discussion, it should be apparent that the same parametric conditions apply in the case of expression (21) if the adjustment process is of the rational-expectations type. All that is different is that rather than the relationship between changes in money-wage rates and changes in prices and productivity being one of wages adjusting to price and productivity movements, all these magnitudes are being predicted accurately except for the random error term. Thus, the causality is different, but the empirical relationship is basically the same. Therefore, hereafter, we shall regard the two processes as one, designating them an instantaneous neoclassical (RATEX) adjustment process.[6]

A modified version of the neoclassical adjustment mechanism can be constructed that incorporates some imperfections in the adjustment process. These might occur, for example, due to lags in the adjustments that must take place. Under such conditions, w_r may deviate from $w_r\star$ and c_t and d_t may be less than unity. Specifically, postulate that

(25) $$0 < b < 1,$$
$$0 < c_t < 1, \text{and}$$
$$0 < d_t < 1.$$

This modified neoclassical adjustment mechanism can become identical in the long run with the instantaneous adjustment paradigm if (1) the variations of w_r around $w_r\star$ have a mean of zero and (2) the sum of the various c's and d's are each equal to unity. Consequently, it is possible to have complete long-run adjustment of the neoclassical type, even though there is imperfect adjustment in the short run.

The deviations of w_r about $w_r\star$ in the modified neoclassical adjustment regimen do not tend to be random in character since they are the result of systematic lags in the adjustment process. Therefore, the end product is similar in nature to that generated by an asymptotically rational-expectations adjustment mechanism. In fact, again, exactly the same parametric expectations with respect to expression (21) emerge, albeit because predictions of present magnitudes based on past and current experience are systematically imperfect. Therefore, we will hereafter treat the modified neoclassical and asymptotically rational-expectations approaches as similar, using the designation "modified neoclassical" (ARE).

Turning to the Keynesian adjustment mechanism, we first consider the strict wage rigidity formulation. In it, w_r becomes unequal to $w_r\star$ as the result of an exogenous shock to aggregate demand and money wages do not adjust at all. Thus, b, as well as all the c's and d's, in expression (21) must be equal to zero. The alternative Keynesian adjustment paradigm, which emphasizes the interdependence between money wages and prices, also begins with a real-wage labor-market disequilibrium, i. e., with $w_r \neq w_r\star$. Now, however, flexible money wages are assumed, represented by the parameter b being greater than zero and less than or equal to unity. But, there is an induced price-level change that will be equal to $-b(w_r - w_r\star)$ and all the c's are equal to zero. Under these conditions, the real-wage rate remains unchanged and $(w_r - w_r\star)$ is a constant.

Finally, there is the neo-Keynesian adjustment model. Within it, w_r is viewed as the equilibrium real wage, and thus, the term $(w_r - w_r\star)$ becomes $(w_r - w_r)$, i. e., it is equal to zero and disappears from expression (21). The critical parameters are the c's, assumed to be less than one. What this yields is a variable real-wage rate that reflects only a partial adjustment of money-wage rates. In a sense, this may be thought of as a partial money illusion.

These various formulations of the money-wage rate adjustment mechanism are summarized in table A.1. The parametric conditions associated with each of these paradigms will be the basis for the conducting of empirical tests of the validity of the several alternatives.

Our empirical exploration of the money-wage adjustment mechanism in the United States will employ the same data series used in chapter 3 describing hourly

TABLE A.1

SUMMARY OF CHARACTERISTICS OF VARIOUS MONEY WAGE ADJUSTMENT
MECHANISMS

| Adjustment Mechanism | Expected Value of | | | | | |
| | Parameter | | | | | |
	$w_r - w_r^*$	b	c_t	d_t	Other c's	Other d's
Neoclassical						
Instantaneous (RATEX)	0	0	1	1	0	0
Modified (ARE)	$w_r^* \neq w_r^*$ (temporarily)	0<b<1	0<c<1	0<d<1	>0 with c_t sum to 1	>0 with d_t sum to 1
Keynesian						
Wage Rigidity	$w_r^* \neq w_r^*$	0	0	0	0	0
Interdependence	$w_r^* \neq w_r^*$	0<b≠1	0	0≠d≠1	0	0≠d≠1
Neo-Keynesian	$w_r = w_r^*$	irrelevant	0<c<1	0<d<1	may be >0: with c_t sum to <1	may be >0: with d_t sum to <1

*In Keynesian interdependence version $\dot{p}_t = -b(w_r - w_r^*)$.

compensation and productivity, as well as the price deflator series that accompanies the wage data, to estimate expression (21) for the period 1901-89. It is a simple estimate in that only current values of $\dot{p}_t$ and $\dot{\pi}_t$ are used as independent variables. [7] In order to obtain a value for the term $(w_r - w_r\star)$, we begin by expressing all wage-rate measures in index number form. Thus,

(26)
$$(w_r')_t = (w_r)_t/(w_r)_o$$

and

(27)
$$(w_r^{\star\prime})_t = (w_r^\star)_t/(w_r^\star)_o$$

where the symbols $(w_r')_t$ and $(w_r^{\star\prime})_t$ indicate the index number form of the variables. Now, we define

(28)
$$(w_r^\star)_t = (w_r^\star)_o(1 + \dot{\pi}_t),$$

which is to say that the equilibrium wage changes as productivity levels change between time 0 and t (measured by $\dot{\pi}_t$).

Combining (26) − (28) gives

(29) $(w_r - w_r^\star) = (w_r')_t - (w_r^{\star\prime})_t = (w_r')_t - (1 + \dot{\pi}_t) = [(w_r')_t - \dot{\pi}_t] - 1.$

But the term in brackets is simply the real-wage rate in time t (in index number form) adjusted for any change in productivity that occurs between times 0 and t. Consequently, we may employ that statistic (designated as $(w_r'')_t$) as a measure of $(w_r - w_r^\star)_t$. Of course, the negative one simply transfers into the constant term of expression (21), altering, in the process, any parametric expectations with respect to that constant. Actually, to preserve the sense of the equilibrating mechanism, we go further and define $(w_r - w_r^\star)$ as $[(w_r'')_t - \overline{w}_r'']$ thus expressing it as the deviation of the real-wage index, adjusted for productivity changes, from its mean value for the period under consideration.

The results of the estimation process are

(30)
$$(\dot{w}_m)_t = 2.07 - 0.11[(w_r^\star)_{t-1} - \overline{w}_r''] + 0.80\dot{p}_t + 0.39\dot{\pi}_t,$$
$$\qquad\qquad (2.37) \qquad\qquad\qquad\qquad (14.87) \quad (4.19)$$
$$R^2 = 0.74, \overline{R}^2 = 0.72, D - W = 1.98,$$

where the values in parentheses beneath the regression coefficients are t–statistics.

All the coefficients have the expected signs and are significantly different from zero at normal levels of significance. In addition, all coefficients are significantly different from unity. A comparison of the values of the parameters with the conditions established in table A.1 yields some interesting conclusions. First, there is no support for the instantaneous neoclassical (RATEX) adjustment mechanism. Not only is b < 0, but c_t and d_t are less than unity. Consequently, we may reject this form of the adjustment mechanism. Similarly, there is nothing in regression (30) to suggest consistency with the Keynesian wage rigidity formulation. It, too, may be disregarded. As to the Keynesian "interdependence" adjustment mechanism, two of the three coefficients, b and d, might be interpreted as being consistent with it, but the coefficient c_t is inconsistent.[8] Therefore, this possibility is rejected. The same can be said for the neo-Keynesian formulation. The values of the parameters c_t and d_t are consistent, but the significance of b militates against it.

Finally, there is the modified neoclassical (ARE) adjustment model. All three of the coefficients are exactly consistent with this hypothesis. However, there are other dimensions to the model that have not been explored. Some further tests are required to confirm the modified neoclassical model.

The key element in the modified neoclassical (ARE) model is the degree of permanence of the partial adjustment of money-wage rates to prices and productivity changes. In the neoclassical (ARE) model, the partial adjutment is only temporary. The most straightforward way to evaluate the permanence of the partial adjustment is to invoke expression (22), which argues that the temporary partial adjustment will disappear over time. By simply calculating the means of the rates of change in money-wage rates, prices, and productivity over the period under consideration, we can determine whether the rate of change in money-wage rates is equal to the sum of the rates of change in prices and productivity. The actual data reveal that the mean rate of change in money-wage rates conforms very closely to the sum of the rates of changes in productivity and prices, as suggested by expression (22). This is supportive of the modified neoclassical (ARE) response mechanism.

Acceptance of the modified neoclassical (ARE) money-wage adjustment mechanism has implications with respect to explaining the behavior of the level of unemployment in the American economy. Specifically, in line with our earlier discussion, deviations of the adjusted real-wage rate from its equilibrium level should produce deviations in the same direction away from the equilibrium level of unemployment, $U^\star$. At this point, to simplify the notation, let $(U - U^\star)$ be indicated by the symbol $\hat{U}$ and $(w_r{}^\star - \overline{w}_r{}'')$ by $\hat{w}_r$.

Within the context of the modified neoclassical (ARE) view of the world, the critical magnitude in explaining variations in unemployment is the portion of any change in the money-wage rate that may be considered to be exogenous, i. e., not determined by the other variables that affect the real-wage rate. Thus, we may write

(31) $$\hat{U} = f(\hat{w}_r)$$

and

(32) $$\hat{w}_r = f([\dot{w}_m]_x),$$

where the subscript x denotes exogenous. Now, we may define

(33) $$(\dot{w}_m)_x = (\dot{w}_m)_a - (\dot{w}_m)_n,$$

where the subscripts a and n represent, respectively, actual and endogenous.

Clearly, the endogenous changes in money-wage rates are defined by (21). Let us state (31), (32), and (21) in linear form, as follows:

(34) $$\hat{U}_t = a_1 + b_1(w_r)_t,$$

(35) $$(\hat{w}_r)_t = a_2 + b_2(\dot{w}_m)_{xt},$$

and

(36) $$(\dot{w}_m)_{nt} = a_3 - b_3(\hat{w}_r)_{t-1} + c_3\dot{p}_t + d_3\dot{\pi}_t.$$

Combining (34), (35), and (36) with (33) yields

(37)$\hat{U}t = a_1 + a_2b_1 - b_1b_2a_3 + b_1b_2(\dot{w}_m)_{at} + b_1b_2b_3\,(\hat{\dot{w}}_r)_{t-1} - b_1b_2c_3\dot{p}_t - b_1b_2d_3\dot{\pi}_t,$

which may be simplified to

(38) $\hat{U}_t = \alpha + \beta(\hat{\dot{w}}_r)_{t-1} + \delta(\dot{w}_m)_{at} - \mu\dot{p}_t - \sigma\dot{\pi}_t.$

The signs assigned to the parameters of expression (38) follow from the attribution of signs in equations (34) through (36). Interestingly, from (37), we infer that unless b_3, c_3, and d_3 equal unity, $\beta \neq \delta$, $\beta \neq \mu$, $\beta \neq \sigma$, $\delta \neq \mu$, and $\delta \neq \sigma$. Also, if $c_3 \neq d_3$, $\mu \neq \sigma$.

Expression (38) is the basis for the empirical explorations of chapter 3, once a minor problem is resolved, namely, the fact that the unemployment measure is defined as a deviation from the equilibrium level of unemployment, a magnitude that we do not know with precision. Until now, our assumption of an invariant population has implied, within the framework of a modified neoclassical (ARE) adjustment mechanism, a constant equilibrium level of unemployment, measured in absolute numbers. Under such conditions, that constant equilibrium would be captured in the constant term of any empirical relationship of a linear kind. Realistically, though, some adjustment must be made to take into account the changes in population and labor force that occur over time, changes that alter the equilibrium level of unemployment. This can be accomplished within the context of our basic assumption of a constant labor force participation rate, which implies that

(39) $S_t = S_0(1 + \dot{q})^t$

where $\dot{q}$ is the rate of growth in population. If we assume further that the equilibrium level of unemployment expands proportionately to the growth in population,

(40) $U_t^\star = U_t^\star(1 + \dot{q})^t.$

Expression (40) may be rearranged as

(41) $(U_t - U_t^\star) = U_t - U_0^\star(1 + \dot{q})^t.$

Dividing both sides of (41) by S_t and substituting from (39) gives

(42) $(U_t - U_t^\star)/S_t = [U_t - U_0^\star(1 + \dot{q})^t]S_t = U_t/S_t - U_0^\star/S_0.$

Since $U_0^\star/S_0$ is a constant, the ratio U_t/S_t, which is simply the unemployment rate in time t, can be employed as a measure of $\hat{U}_t$. Thus, the measured unemployment rate may be employed as the independent variable in expression (38), which then becomes the estimating equation employed in chapter 3.

NOTES

1.   Our assumption of labor force participation in the aggregate is generally consistent with Clarence D. Long, *The Labor Force Under Changing Income and Employment* (Princeton,

N.J.: 1958), who argues that the aggregate labor-force participation rate tends to be stable in a developed industrial economy.

2. Jerome Stein, "Monetarist, Keynesian, and New Classical Economics," *American Economic Review* 71 (1981): 139–44.

3. See Thomas Sargent, "Monetarist, Keynesian, and New Classical Economics," *Journal of Political Economy* 89 (1976): 207–37.

4. We assume that the respective error terms in the predictions of money wage rates are not correlated with the error terms in the prediction of prices.

5. The use of the average, rather than the marginal, productivity of labor, may seem inappropriate. We are assuming that the two are proportional to one another, i.e., that the output elasticity with respect to labor is a constant. If this is the case, the use of the average productivity of labor in our model is not a source of error.

6. We realize that purists might object to such a grouping. However, since we cannot discriminate between the two possibilities empirically, we feel justified in grouping them in this fashion.

7. Inclusion of a succession of lagged price and productivity terms in the estimating equation introduces severe problems of multicolinearity.

8. Almost any value for the estimate of the parameter d_t may be interpreted as being consistent with the Keynesian "interdependence" adjustment process.

Appendix B

The Technical Aspects
of the Statistical Analysis

Appendix A provides a model of the phenomenon of unemployment that is founded on the standard notions of the demand for and supply of labor.[1] That model generates a reduced form equation that is the basis for the estimating equations that have been reported. Beyond that model and those estimating equations, we have provided little in the way of discussion of the more technical dimensions of the statistical analysis. This was a deliberate decision on our part. We had a story to tell and did not wish to detract from it with too much technical discussion. We anticipated that this would be a problem for some readers but were willing to run that risk. However, we may have erred too much in the direction of avoiding what some would consider to be the arcane minutiae of econometric analysis. Rather than injecting such analysis directly into our narrative of America's twentieth-century employment experience, we have decided to provide a second appendix to treat technical matters.

The Issue of Replicability

Any valid analysis should be replicable by other scholars.[2] In order to facilitate such validation, we are providing here a set of basic data (see table B.1) as well as a full report of some of the regression equations estimated using these data (tables B.2 and B.3, to begin).[3] The data are quarterly, beginning with the first quarter of 1959 (1959.1) and concluding with the second quarter of 1996 (1996.2).

The regression equations reported in tables B.2 and B.3 are of the ordinary-least-squares variety, and an ARIMA adjustment scheme (of the 1,2 variety) is included in table B.3. Some adjustment for serial correlation is necessary. In the absence of such an adjustment, the regression results shown in table B.2 decisively fail the standard tests for the presence of serial correlation.[4] The introduction of the ARIMA terms increases the robustness of the statistical results, raising the

TABLE B.1.

UNEMPLOYMENT, HOURLY COMPENSATION OF WORKERS, AVERAGE OUTPUT PER
HOUR WORKED, GROSS DOMESTIC PRODUCT PRICE DEFLATOR, AND PRODUCTIVITY
ADJUSTED REAL WAGE RATE, UNITED STATES, FIRST QUARTER, 1959, THROUGH
SECOND QUARTER, 1996

Year and Quarter	Unemployment Rate (Percent)	Compensation per Hour (1992 = 100)	Average Output per Hour (1992 = 100)	GDP Price Deflator (1992 = 100)	Productivity Adjusted Real Wage (1992 = 100)
1959.1	5.8	13.24	57.35	23.11	99.92
1959.2	5.1	13.24	57.26	23.33	99.14
1959.3	5.3	13.44	56.82	23.48	100.78
1959.4	5.6	13.64	57.35	23.55	101.01
1960.1	5.1	13.97	58.59	23.77	100.34
1960.2	5.2	13.91	57.88	23.77	101.08
1960.3	5.5	13.91	57.70	23.84	101.08
1960.4	6.3	14.04	58.32	23.69	101.59
1961.1	6.8	14.17	58.68	23.69	101.92
1961.2	7.0	14.50	60.36	23.84	100.78
1961.3	6.8	14.57	60.62	23.99	100.18
1961.4	6.2	14.77	61.51	24.06	99.78
1962.1	5.6	14.97	61.51	24.28	100.22
1962.2	5.5	15.10	61.86	24.28	100.52
1962.3	5.6	15.23	62.66	24.42	99.52
1962.4	5.5	15.43	63.54	24.50	99.12
1963.1	5.8	15.56	63.90	24.42	99.71
1963.2	5.7	15.63	64.70	24.42	98.90
1963.3	5.5	15.83	65.31	24.57	98.62
1963.4	5.6	16.02	65.85	24.72	98.47
1964.1	5.5	16.36	67.35	24.64	98.55
1964.2	5.2	16.49	67.35	24.79	98.76
1964.3	5.0	16.69	68.15	24.86	98.49
1964.4	5.0	16.82	68.24	25.01	98.57
1965.1	4.9	16.95	68.68	25.30	97.57
1965.2	4.7	17.08	68.86	25.37	97.79
1965.3	4.4	17.35	69.92	25.52	97.24
1965.4	4.1	17.48	70.98	25.59	96.24
1966.1	3.9	17.95	71.51	25.88	96.96
1966.2	3.8	18.28	71.33	26.17	97.89
1966.3	3.8	18.54	71.69	26.32	98.27
1966.4	3.7	18.87	71.95	26.68	98.29
1967.1	3.8	19.07	72.13	26.83	98.55
1967.2	3.8	19.40	73.46	26.76	98.71
1967.3	3.8	19.60	73.81	27.05	98.18
1967.4	3.9	19.87	74.25	27.34	97.85
1968.1	3.7	20.46	74.96	27.78	98.27
1968.2	3.6	20.86	75.58	28.07	98.32
1968.3	3.5	21.26	75.76	28.36	98.93
1968.4	3.4	21.65	76.11	28.73	99.04
1969.1	3.4	21.72	75.49	29.02	99.15

Year and Quarter	Unemployment Rate (Percent)	Compensation per Hour (1992 = 100)	Average Output per Hour (1992 = 100)	GDP Price Deflator (1992 = 100)	Productivity Adjusted Real Wage (1992 = 100)
1969.2	3.5	22.32	75.85	29.38	100.14
1969.3	3.6	22.85	75.94	29.75	101.14
1969.4	3.6	23.31	76.47	30.04	101.48
1970.1	4.2	23.77	76.11	30.33	102.98
1970.2	4.8	24.04	76.29	30.91	101.93
1970.3	5.2	24.57	77.97	30.99	101.69
1970.4	5.8	24.90	77.88	31.35	101.97
1971.1	5.9	25.36	79.21	31.79	100.73
1971.2	5.9	25.63	79.03	32.23	100.62
1971.3	6.0	26.16	80.01	32.66	100.09
1971.4	5.9	26.29	80.27	32.81	99.82
1972.1	5.8	26.88	80.54	33.17	100.63
1972.2	5.7	27.28	81.51	33.46	100.02
1972.3	5.6	27.61	82.22	33.76	99.49
1972.4	5.4	28.21	83.72	34.27	98.33
1973.1	4.9	29.07	84.70	34.63	99.11
1973.2	4.9	29.53	83.90	35.29	99.76
1973.3	4.8	30.13	83.64	36.02	100.02
1973.4	4.8	30.79	84.34	36.89	98.96
1974.1	5.1	31.32	82.93	37.55	100.59
1974.2	5.2	32.38	82.40	38.42	102.28
1974.3	5.6	33.37	82.13	39.73	102.27
1974.4	6.6	34.10	82.48	40.76	101.45
1975.1	8.3	35.16	82.48	41.99	101.51
1975.2	8.9	35.82	84.25	42.51	100.03
1975.3	8.5	36.35	85.58	43.45	97.76
1975.4	8.3	37.15	85.67	44.04	98.47
1976.1	7.7	38.14	86.82	44.55	98.62
1976.2	7.6	38.94	86.91	45.13	99.27
1976.3	7.7	39.80	87.00	45.86	99.75
1976.4	7.8	40.66	87.18	46.51	100.27
1977.1	7.5	41.39	88.15	47.10	99.69
1977.2	7.1	42.05	88.06	48.05	99.38
1977.3	6.9	42.98	89.21	48.92	98.47
1977.4	6.5	43.77	88.50	49.72	99.47
1978.1	6.3	44.90	88.50	50.38	100.69
1978.2	6.0	45.76	89.21	51.84	98.95
1978.3	6.0	46.68	89.03	52.93	99.06
1978.4	5.9	47.88	89.03	54.10	99.40
1979.1	5.9	49.07	88.50	55.19	100.46
1979.2	5.7	50.26	88.15	56.50	100.91
1979.3	5.9	51.39	87.53	57.82	101.54
1979.4	6.0	52.58	87.62	58.84	101.99
1980.1	6.3	54.10	87.71	60.29	102.30
1980.2	7.7	55.62	86.29	61.90	104.14
1980.3	7.7	57.01	86.91	63.36	103.54

TABLE B.1. (continued)

Year and Quarter	Unemployment Rate (Percent)	Compensation per Hour (1992 = 100)	Average Output per Hour (1992 = 100)	GDP Price Deflator (1992 = 100)	Productivity Adjusted Real Wage (1992 = 100)
1980.4	7.4	58.27	88.06	64.89	101.98
1981.1	7.4	59.86	88.59	66.86	101.07
1981.2	7.4	60.92	88.50	68.02	101.20
1981.3	7.4	62.25	89.03	69.70	100.31
1981.4	8.3	63.24	87.62	71.16	101.43
1982.1	8.8	64.76	87.62	71.81	102.93
1982.2	9.4	65.76	88.24	72.76	102.42
1982.3	10.0	66.81	88.77	73.34	102.62
1982.4	10.6	67.61	89.48	73.71	102.51
1983.1	10.4	68.07	89.48	74.58	101.91
1983.2	10.2	68.47	90.98	74.95	100.41
1983.3	9.3	68.74	90.54	75.68	100.32
1983.4	8.5	69.66	91.16	76.41	100.02
1984.1	7.9	70.59	92.04	77.43	99.05
1984.2	7.5	71.25	92.66	78.16	98.38
1984.3	7.5	72.05	92.57	79.03	98.47
1984.4	7.2	72.64	93.10	79.47	98.18
1985.1	7.2	73.37	92.93	80.27	98.36
1985.2	7.1	74.23	93.72	80.78	98.04
1985.3	7.1	75.22	94.52	81.22	97.99
1985.4	6.9	76.42	94.61	81.95	98.56
1986.1	6.9	77.28	95.94	82.24	97.95
1986.2	7.0	78.07	96.11	82.46	98.51
1986.3	6.8	78.80	95.76	83.04	99.09
1986.4	6.7	79.86	95.58	83.55	100.00
1987.1	6.6	80.19	95.67	84.21	99.54
1987.2	6.2	80.52	96.64	84.65	98.43
1987.3	6.0	81.45	97.26	85.23	98.25
1987.4	5.9	82.97	97.62	85.96	98.88
1988.1	5.7	83.17	97.88	86.54	98.18
1988.2	5.4	84.23	97.44	87.56	98.72
1988.3	5.5	85.55	97.80	88.66	98.68
1988.4	5.4	86.22	97.80	89.53	98.47
1989.1	5.2	86.88	97.26	90.55	98.64
1989.2	5.3	87.34	97.09	91.57	98.24
1989.3	5.3	88.00	96.82	92.16	98.63
1989.4	5.3	88.87	96.73	93.03	98.75
1990.1	5.3	90.12	96.91	93.90	99.03
1990.2	5.3	92.11	97.62	94.93	99.40
1990.3	5.6	93.70	97.44	95.95	100.22
1990.4	5.9	94.76	97.26	96.60	100.85
1991.1	6.5	95.36	97.26	97.70	100.35
1991.2	6.7	96.48	97.80	98.43	100.23
1991.3	6.7	97.34	98.24	98.86	100.23

Year and Quarter	Unemployment Rate (Percent)	Compensation per Hour (1992 = 100)	Average Output per Hour (1992 = 100)	GDP Price Deflator (1992 = 100)	Productivity Adjusted Real Wage (1992 = 100)
1991.4	7.0	98.00	98.68	99.08	100.24
1992.1	7.3	98.60	99.30	99.66	99.63
1992.2	7.5	99.50	99.90	99.70	99.90
1992.3	7.5	100.70	99.70	100.10	100.90
1992.4	7.3	101.20	101.10	100.90	99.21
1993.1	7.0	101.60	100.20	101.70	99.70
1993.2	6.9	102.50	99.80	102.30	100.40
1993.3	6.7	103.00	100.10	102.70	100.19
1993.4	6.5	103.30	100.80	103.30	99.21
1994.1	6.6	104.00	100.40	103.90	99.70
1994.2	6.2	104.20	100.50	104.50	99.22
1994.3	6.0	104.70	101.10	105.30	98.35
1994.4	5.6	105.60	101.20	105.70	98.72
1995.1	5.5	106.60	100.70	106.50	99.40
1995.2	5.7	107.80	101.20	107.10	99.46
1995.3	5.6	108.80	101.60	107.50	99.62
1995.4	5.6	110.00	101.50	107.80	100.53
1996.1	5.6	110.80	102.00	108.10	100.49
1996.2	5.4	111.90	102.30	108.70	100.63

Source: U.S. Department of Labor, U.S. Department of Commerce, and authors' calculations.

adjusted R^2 from 0.7037 to 0.9695, while changing all insignificant coefficients to being significant with the anticipated sign.[5] Also, the equation now passes the various serial correlation tests.

The Causality Question

The basic statistical model we have presented demonstrates that variations in real wages, adjusted to reflect productivity change, are positively related to movements in unemployment. Our interpretation is that adjusted real wage movements produce the unemployment changes. However, could it be that the direction of the relationship is just the reverse, that unemployment movements generate the variation in the adjusted real wage? For example, assume negative aggregate demand variations that produce negative price shocks. If money wages are rigid downward, unemployment will be generated and the adjusted real wage will rise. Which produces which? To explore this question, we have conducted pairwise Granger causality tests for our unemployment and adjusted real wage variables for lags of from one to eight quarters (table B.4). With a one-period lag, two-way causality is

TABLE B.2.

REGRESSION RESULTS, UNEMPLOYMENT RATE AS DEPENDENT VARIABLE,
UNITED STATES, QUARTERLY DATA, FIRST QUARTER, 1959,
THROUGH SECOND QUARTER, 1996

Independent Variable	Regression Coefficient	t-Statistic
Constant Term	-47.3396	6.1274
Adjusted Real Wage (-8)	0.5408	6.9326
% Change, Money Wage	-0.7130	4.3660
% Change, Money Wage (-1)	-0.2430	1.5293
% Change, Money Wage (-2)	-0.1441	0.9047
% Change, Money Wage (-3)	0.1816	1.1422
% Change, Money Wage (-4)	0.1097	0.6928
% Change, Money Wage (-5)	0.1841	1.1473
% Change, Money Wage (-6)	0.2397	1.4278
% Change, Money Wage (-7)	0.1628	0.9730
% Change, Output per Hour	0.1216	1.0643
% Change, Output per Hour (-1)	-0.0690	0.6154
% Change, Output per Hour (-2)	0.0035	0.0297
% Change, Output per Hour (-3)	-0.2970	2.5693
% Change, Output per Hour (-4)	-0.3977	3.3870
% Change, Output per Hour (-5)	-0.2735	2.2452
% Change, Output per Hour (-6)	-0.2986	2.4044
% Change, Output per Hour (-7)	-0.3824	3.1173
% Change, GDP Price Deflator	0.0784	0.3893
% Change, GDP Price Deflator (-1)	0.1305	0.6501
% Change, GDP Price Deflator (-2)	-0.1445	0.7249
% Change, GDP Price Deflator (-3)	-0.2969	1.5010
% Change, GDP Price Deflator (-4)	-0.1983	1.0231
% Change, GDP Price Deflator (-5)	0.1421	0.7298
% Change, GDP Price Deflator (-6)	0.2479	1.2863
% Change, GDP Price Deflator (-7)	0.4987	2.5343

Other regression statistics: Adjusted R^2 = 0.7037; D-W = 0.4854.

found, but with lags of from two to eight quarters, the results support unambiguously the idea that the direction of the adjusted real wage–unemployment relationship runs from the wage measure to unemployment.

Model Specification Issues

Another potential problem is the quality of the model specification. To explore this characteristic of our analysis, we invoke a variety of tests, beginning with the Ramsey RESET test of the non-ARIMA adjusted equation reported in table B.2. The necessary calculations have been made using one-, two-, and three-fitted

TABLE B.3

REGRESSION RESULTS, WITH ARIMA ADJUSTMENTS, UNEMPLOYMENT RATE AS
DEPENDENT VARIABLE, UNITED STATES, QUARTERLY DATA, FIRST QUARTER, 1959,
THROUGH SECOND QUARTER, 1996

Independent Variable	Regression Coefficient	t-Statistic
Constant Term	-69.8362	5.7734
Adjusted Real Wage (-8)	0.7566	6.2375
% Change, Money Wage	0.0895	1.6638
% Change, Money Wage (-1)	0.2724	3.9974
% Change, Money Wage (-2)	0.4053	5.0255
% Change, Money Wage (-3)	0.5906	6.4994
% Change, Money Wage (-4)	0.6323	6.3947
% Change, Money Wage (-5)	0.6425	6.1752
% Change, Money Wage (-6)	0.6368	5.7370
% Change, Money Wage (-7)	0.6646	5.7407
% Change, Output per Hour	-0.1253	3.3790
% Change, Output per Hour (-1)	-0.2128	4.1545
% Change, Output per Hour (-2)	-0.3229	4.9923
% Change, Output per Hour (-3)	-0.5153	6.9611
% Change, Output per Hour (-4)	-0.6151	7.4882
% Change, Output per Hour (-5)	-0.6150	6.6974
% Change, Output per Hour (-6)	-0.6724	6.4457
% Change, Output per Hour (-7)	-0.7147	6.3633
% Change, GDP Price Deflator	-0.1504	2.2952
% Change, GDP Price Deflator (-1)	-0.2781	3.3777
% Change, GDP Price Deflator (-2)	-0.5174	5.7434
% Change, GDP Price Deflator (-3)	-0.5864	6.1266
% Change, GDP Price Deflator (-4)	-0.5716	5.5988
% Change, GDP Price Deflator (5)	-0.4673	4.2064
% Change, GDP Price Deflator (-6)	-0.4776	3.9986
% Change, GDP Price Deflator (-7)	-0.5532	4.4773
MA(1) Adjustment	0.4516	4.5108
MA(2) Adjustment	0.1571	1.5124
MA(3) Adjustment	0.9425	36.0462

Other regression statistics: Adjusted R^2 = 0.9695; D-W = 1.9630.

terms. The equation fails the test with two fitted terms, but it passes with one and three fitted terms. In addition, we conducted recursive residuals, CUSUM, and CUSUMSQ tests. The results for the recursive residuals and CUSUMSQ tests show that the test statistic is almost always within the region that warrants accepting the null hypothesis that there is no model specification problem. However, in the case of the CUSUM test, there is an extensive range in which the test statistic lies outside the null hypothesis range. Graphic depictions of these test statistics are shown in figure B.1.

The results of these tests can be viewed as something of a mixed bag, although

TABLE B.4.

RESULTS OF GRANGER PAIRWISE CAUSALITY TESTS, ADJUSTED REAL WAGE (ARW)
VERSUS UNEMPLOYMENT RATE (U)

Lag	Null Hypothesis	Probability
1	ARW not caused by U	0.0413
	U not caused by ARW	0.0000
2	ARW not caused by U	0.2915
	U not caused by ARW	0.0032
3	ARW not caused by U	0.1066
	U not caused by ARW	0.0043
4	ARW not caused by U	0.3962
	U not caused by ARW	0.0006
5	ARW not caused by U	0.5389
	U not caused by ARW	0.0024
6	ARW not caused by U	0.5136
	U not caused by ARW	0.0004
7	ARW not caused by U	0.7374
	U not caused by ARW	0.0031
8	ARW not caused by U	0.5925
	U not caused by ARW	0.0025

more often than not the test statistics are consistent with the absence of a model
specification problem. To provide further insight into the model specification issue, we estimated a first difference version of the basic estimating equation reported in table B.2. The results are shown in table B.5. In the first difference form,
the equation still fails the serial correlation tests. Thus, a first difference form of

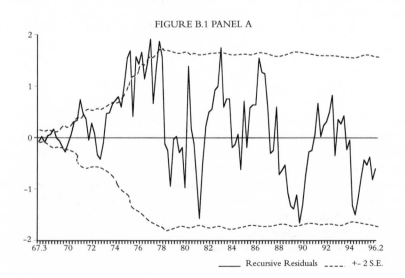

FIGURE B.1 PANEL A

Recursive Residuals ____ +- 2 S.E.

FIGURE B.1 PANEL B

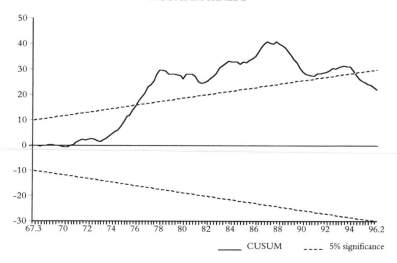

_____ CUSUM   _ _ _ _ 5% significance

FIGURE B.1 PANEL C

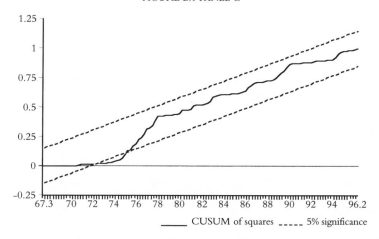

_____ CUSUM of squares _ _ _ _ _ 5% significance

the equation that includes the same ARIMA adjustment scheme (1,2) used in table B.3 is also reported. The same battery of model specification tests were conducted on the non-ARIMA version of the first difference model. In the case of the Ramsey RESET test, the equation passes with one-, two-, and three-fitted terms. It also passes the recursive residuals and CUSUMSQ tests. Most important, the CUSUM test statistic never strays from the null hypothesis range. See figure B.2 for the graphic version of the behavior of these test statistics. The first difference form of the model passes all four model specification tests.

TABLE B.5.

REGRESSION RESULTS, FIRST DIFFERENCE FORMAT, CHANGE IN UNEMPLOYMENT
RATE AS DEPENDENT VARIABLE, UNITED STATES, WITH AND WITHOUT ARIMA
ADJUSTMENT, QUARTERLY DATA, FIRST QUARTER, 1959, THROUGH SECOND
QUARTER, 1996

Independent Variable	Without ARIMA Adjustment		With ARIMA Adjustment	
	Regression Coefficient	t–Statistic	Regression Coefficient	t–Statistic
Constant Term	-0.0032	0.1330	-0.0065	0.2046
Change in Adjusted Real Wage (-8)	0.7632	6.2068	0.7738	5.1769
Change in % Change, Money Wage	0.0561	1.0124	0.1005	1.9465
Change in % Change, Money Wage (-1)	0.2578	3.7169	0.2842	3.7696
Change in % Change, Money Wage (-2)	0.4050	5.0144	0.4301	4.6036
Change in % Change, Money Wage (-3)	0.6096	6.7151	0.6193	5.8665
Change in % Change, Money Wage (-4)	0.6344	6.4236	0.6712	5.7999
Change in % Change, Money Wage (-5)	0.6348	6.1269	0.6838	5.5349
Change in % Change, Money Wage (-6)	0.6538	5.9182	0.6828	5.1923
Change in % Change, Money Wage (-7)	0.6741	5.8036	0.7053	5.0555
Change in % Change, Output per Hour	-0.1011	2.6048	-0.1326	3.4945
Change in % Change, Output per Hour (-1)	-0.1954	3.6101	-0.2229	3.6185
Change in % Change, Output per Hour (-2)	-0.3112	4.5877	-0.3406	4.2278
Change in % Change, Output per Hour (-3)	-0.5115	6.6226	-0.5307	5.7234
Change in % Change, Output per Hour (-4)	-0.6105	7.1402	-0.6307	6.1358
Change in % Change, Output per Hour (-5)	-0.6091	6.4181	-0.6361	5.5528
Change in % Change, Output per Hour (-6)	-0.6789	6.3610	-0.6955	5.3704
Change in % Change, Output per Hour (-7)	-0.7224	6.3196	-0.7348	5.2604
Change in % Change in GDP Price Deflator	-0.2243	3.3377	-0.1554	2.3273
Change in % Change in GDP Price Deflator (-1)	-0.3398	3.9556	-0.2832	2.9412
Change in % Change in GDP Price Deflator (-2)	-0.5408	5.6574	-0.5162	4.6917

Independent Variable	Without ARIMA Adjustment		With ARIMA Adjustment	
	Regression Coefficient	t–Statistic	Regression Coefficient	t–Statistic
Change in % Change in GDP Price Deflator (-3)	-0.6021	5.9450	-0.6046	5.1130
Change in % Change in GDP Price Deflator (-4)	-0.5885	5.4525	-0.6113	4.8080
Change in % Change in GDP Price Deflator (5)	-0.4758	4.0635	-0.5265	3.8227
Change in % Change in GDP Price Deflator (-6)	-0.5016	4.0090	-0.5491	3.7458
Change in % Change in GDP Price Deflator (-7)	-0.5659	4.4311	-0.6226	4.1843
MA(1) Adjustment	N. A.	N. A.	0.1804	3.8227
MA(2) Adjustment	N. A.	N. A.	0.0430	0.1915
AR(1) Adjustment	N. A.	N. A.	0.2929	0.8409

Other regression statistics: (1) Without ARIMA Adjustment: Adjusted R^2 = 0.3323; D–W = 1.2627. (2) With ARIMA Adjustment: Adjusted R^2 = 0.4324; D–W = 1.9852.

The first difference version of the estimating equation also permits exploring the quality of the model specification by comparing the coefficients and their probability limits in the original and the first difference estimating equations. This comparison is presented in table B.6 for the ARIMA adjusted form of the differenced equation. The comparison is striking. Both the coefficients and their standard errors are very similar. The importance of this has been shown by Plosser, Schwert, and White, among others.[6] As Maddala puts it, "If the model is correctly

FIGURE B.2 PANEL A

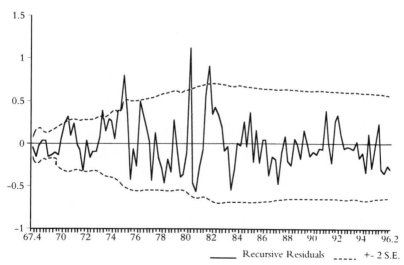

_____ Recursive Residuals   _ _ _ _   +– 2 S.E.

FIGURE B.2 PANEL B

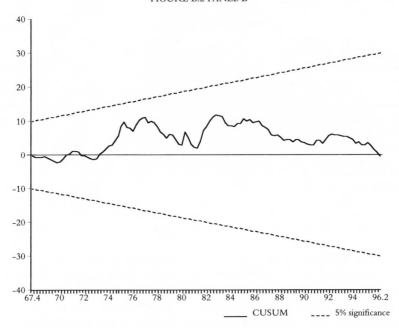

CUSUM   ---- 5% significance

FIGURE B.2 PANEL C

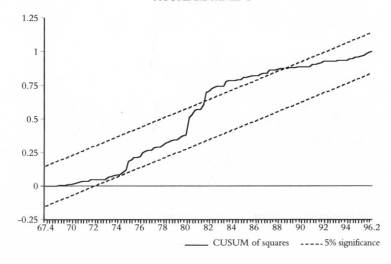

CUSUM of squares   ----- 5% significance

TABLE B.6.

COMPARISON OF REGRESSION COEFFICIENTS AND STANDARD ERRORS OF
COEFFICIENTS, UNDIFFERENCED AND DIFFERENCED REGRESSION EQUATION
EXPLANATIONS OF UNEMPLOYMENT RATE, UNITED STATES, QUARTERLY DATA, FIRST
QUARTER, 1959, THROUGH SECOND QUARTER, 1996

Independent Variable	Coefficient Value		Standard Error	
	Undifferenced	Differenced	Undifferenced	Differenced
Constant	-69.94	-0.01	12.10	0.03
Adjusted Real Wage (-8)	0.76	0.77	0.12	0.15
% Change, Money Wage	0.09	0.10	0.05	0.05
% Change, Money Wage (-1)	0.27	0.28	0.07	0.08
% Change, Money Wage (-2)	0.41	0.43	0.08	0.09
% Change, Money Wage (-3)	0.59	0.62	0.09	0.11
% Change, Money Wage (-4)	0.63	0.67	0.10	0.12
% Change, Money Wage (-5)	0.64	0.68	0.10	0.12
% Change, Money Wage (-6)	0.64	0.68	0.11	0.13
% Change, Money Wage (-7)	0.66	0.70	0.12	0.14
% Change, Productivity	-0.13	-0.13	0.04	0.04
% Change, Productivity (-1)	-0.21	-0.22	0.05	0.06
% Change, Productivity (-2)	-0.32	-0.34	0.06	0.08
% Change, Productivity (-3)	-0.52	-0.53	0.07	0.09
% Change, Productivity (-4)	-0.62	-0.63	0.08	0.10
% Change, Productivity (-5)	-0.61	-0.64	0.09	0.11
% Change, Productivity (-6)	-0.67	-0.70	0.10	0.13
% Change, Productivity (-7)	-0.71	-0.73	0.11	0.14
% Change, Price Deflator	-0.15	-0.16	0.07	0.07
% Change, Price Deflator (-1)	-0.28	-0.28	0.08	0.10
% Change, Price Deflator (-2)	-0.52	-0.52	0.09	0.11
% Change, Price Deflator (-3)	-0.59	-0.60	0.10	0.12
% Change, Price Deflator (-4)	-0.57	-0.61	0.10	0.13
% Change, Price Deflator (-5)	-0.47	-0.53	0.11	0.15
% Change, Price Deflator (-6)	-0.48	-0.55	0.12	0.15
% Change, Price Deflator (-7)	-0.55	-0.62	0.12	0.15

specified, the estimators from the differenced and undifferenced models have the same probability limits and hence the results should corroborate one another."[7] When the Plosser–Schwert–White test is conducted, the results indicate an absence of model specification problems.

Some Additional Tests

The first difference version of the estimating equation also provides insight into another potential statistical problem, heteroskedasticity. The undifferenced, non–ARIMA adjusted equation passes the White test for heteroskedasticity. However, the ARIMA adjusted version does not. In the case of the differenced equation, though, both versions of the estimating equation pass the White test. Finally, wherever possible, we also have conducted a recursive coefficients test of the coefficient associated with the adjusted real wage variable (lagged eight quarters). In every instance, the test statistic lies within the null hypothesis range.

Summary of Equation Evaluation Tests

The equation evaluation test results, especially those associated with the first difference version of the statistical model, indicate that, in general, the basic statistical estimating equations we report are not troubled by any serious model specification or other statistical problems. Combined with the results of the pairwise Granger causality tests, a strong case can be made that the estimates we have provided and the interpretations we have given them have a sound econometric foundation.

A Comparison of Predicted and Actual Levels of Unemployment

On pages 35–37 we present a graphic comparison of the predicted and actual values of the unemployment rate based on our basic estimating equation using annual data for the period 1900–1989. The results are visually striking. We do the same here for the quarterly data embracing the period 1959.1–1996.2 for both the unadjusted and adjusted for serial correlation regressions. See figures B.3 and B.4.

FIGURE B.3

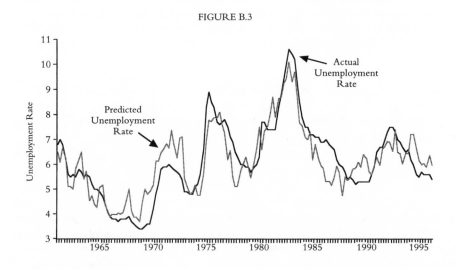

FIGURE B.4

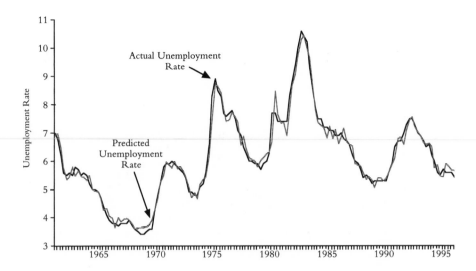

The World since 1989

How well has our basic model of the relationship between the adjusted real wage rate and the unemployment rate worked since 1989? In chapter 16 we indicate that it has done quite well, but now we will fill in the technical details. Figure 16.1, which describes the predicted and actual values of the unemployment rate over the interval 1989.1–1996.2 is based on the regression results reported earlier in this appendix. Degrees of freedom limitations do not permit us the luxury of estimating a regression model with twenty-five independent variables and three ARIMA terms for just the thirty-quarter interval in question. The alternative is to use the regression coefficients reported in table B.3 to construct the predicted (or fitted) values shown in figure 16.1. This raises the question of whether the regression results for the full data set are representative of those for the time period commencing in 1989.1.

The answer to that question appears to be yes. This is based on the results of conducting Chow break-point tests of both the undifferenced and differenced forms of the regression model, with the break-point set at 1989.1. In both cases, we accept the null hypothesis that the before the break-point and after the break-point results are similar. On the basis of this analysis, we feel secure in using the fitted observations from the overall regression to assess the model's performance beginning with 1989.1.[8]

FIGURE B.5

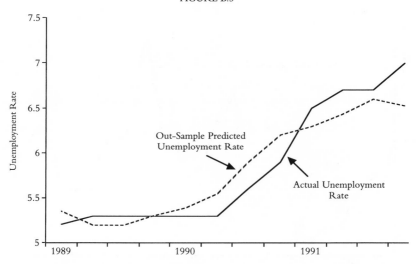

FIGURE B.5

To further confirm this conclusion, we performed one additional test. The basic model was estimated for the period 1959.1 through 1988.4. The resulting regression equation was then used to make out-sample predictions of the unemployment rate beginning with 1989.1 and extending through 1995.3. The results for the first twelve quarters (through 1991.4) are displayed in figure B.5. Clearly, the out-sample predictions conform quite closely to the actual unemployment rates. The zero-order correlation coefficient between them is 0.95. These findings are consistent with the results of the Chow break-point test. Beyond twelve quarters, the correspondence between the out-sample predictions and the actual values weaken as the model underpredicts unemployment rates at the trough of this most recent business cycle. The correlation between the entire set of out-sample predictions and the actual unemployment rate is 0.78.

Rational Expectations and Slutsky Cycles

An intriguing characteristic of the data we have used is found in the period-to-period behavior of the productivity-adjusted real wage measure. Figure B.6 describes the quarter-by-quarter percentage changes. The visual impression one gets from this graphic is that they are simply "white noise," that is, a series of random shocks. This is confirmed by the zero-order correlation between this period's and the previous period's changes, which is 0.06, not significantly different from zero.

FIGURE B.6

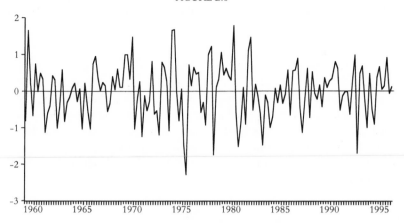

Further, the mean of the percentage changes is not significantly different from zero.[9]

How should this phenomenon be interpreted? We begin by noting that any observation (y) in a time series data set can be described by the simple linear difference equation

(1) $y_t = y_{t-1} + (dy)_t.$

By itself, this tells us little. What is critical is the nature of the process(es) that determine the value of dy_t. In this discussion, we will deal with one particular subset of the broad range of possibilities implicit in (1), the case where the vector of dy_ts is derivative from a set of exogenous shocks, denoted as x_t, whose mean and first-order autocorrelation coefficient are both equal to zero, just what we observe in the behavior of the percentage changes in the adjusted real wage data series. Our focus will be on the variability of such a time series, where variability is measured by the root mean square deviation of the series from an initial value that is arbitrarily set equal to zero.

Under such a set of assumptions, any individual observation, y_{t0}, in a set of n points can be described by

(2) $$y_{t0} = \sum_{t=1}^{t_0} x_t (1-\alpha)^{t-1,} \ 1 \le t_{t0} \le n,$$

where α denotes a "decay" parameter that measures the extent to which the impact of an exogenous shock on the data series is dissipated. α may be either exogenously determined or a product of some endogenous characteristic of the economic process described by the data set.

There are two rather notable examples of time series of the type described by (2). The first emerges when α takes the value zero. In that instance, (2) becomes

$$\text{(3)} \qquad \sum_{t=1}^{t_0} x_t \, ,$$

indicating that any y_t is merely the summation of the exogenous shocks that began with $t = 1$. Such a series was constructed by Eugen Slutsky in the 1920s.[10] Slutsky concluded that this series displayed a pronounced cycle and noted that it corresponded very closely with the English trade cycle data for the period 1855–75. Slutsky's data had one particular feature not found in (3). He truncated the summation process arbitrarily after ten periods. Thus, the individual observations in Slutsky's synthetic series took the form

$$\text{(4)} \qquad y_t = \sum_{t_0-m}^{t_0} x_t \, ,$$

where m is a truncation parameter ($= 9$ in Slutsky's analysis).

At the other extreme from Slutsky's characterization of the impact of a series of random shocks on a time series is the strict rational expectations (RATEX) model suggested by Lucas, Sargent, and Wallace.[11] The model we have in mind is one in which economic agents can identify an underlying economic equilibrium in an intertemporal process, constantly forecast an equilibrium outcome, and behave accordingly. In such a world, this period's random shock (or forecast error) would be completely discounted in the next period's forecast. This implies particular parametric assumptions for expressions (2) and (4). In the case of (2), α, the decay parameter, must be set equal to one, while with (4), m, the truncation parameter, must be given the value zero. Either way, what emerges is a random series that would correspond to the deviations of the actual values of a series from the equilibrium value forecast by the economic agents in a RATEX model.[12]

RATEX versus Slutsky Outcomes

To illustrate further the nature of the differences between the Slutsky and RATEX outcomes, a series of Monte Carlo experiments were conducted. We generated 1,000 sets of random numbers from a standard normal distribution for different values of t_0 in equation (2).[13] Using these, we then performed the following operations: first, a calculation of the value of equation (2) for the 1,000 sets of numbers in those cases where $\alpha = 0$ and $\alpha = 1$; and second, a calculation of the root mean square deviation from the initial equilibrium value, set at zero, for the 1,000 sets of numbers, again for the cases $\alpha = 0$ and $\alpha = 1$. The results are shown in table B.7. Table B.7 also shows the ratio of the two cases, $\alpha = 0$ and $\alpha = 1$.

TABLE B.7.

ROOT MEAN SQUARE DEVIATION, SLUTSKY* AND RATEX ADJUSTMENT
PARAMETERS, MONTE CARLO EXPERIMENTS

Number of Periods (all k = 1000)	Parametric Description		
	$\alpha = 0$ (Slutsky)	$\alpha = 1$ (RATEX)	Ratio: Slutsky to RATEX
5	1.000	0.749	1.335
10	1.000	0.583	1.715
20	1.000	0.450	2.222
30	1.000	0.368	2.717
40	1.000	0.319	3.135
50	1.000	0.288	3.472
70	1.000	0.245	4.082
100	1.000	0.208	4.808

*Slutsky root mean square deviation set = 1.000.

As expected, the RATEX outcome exhibits less variability than the Slutsky outcome. How much less depends on the number of periods, n, employed in the experiments. The greater n, the greater the difference between the RATEX and Slutsky outcomes. The interpretation of this is quite straightforward. A larger value for n implies that random shocks to the data series in the Slutsky format exercise their impact over a more extended period, increasing the variability of the data cycle, relative to a RATEX outcome. Unless some factor intervenes to dampen the effect of an exogenous shock, such as a decay mechanism or a sudden truncation, along the lines introduced by Slutsky, cycles will tend to exhibit increasing amounts of variability over time compared to the pure RATEX view of the world.

PARTIAL DECAY PARAMETERS

Thus far, two extreme versions of the effect of random shocks on a data series have been discussed. Which of them best fits the behavior of the productivity adjusted real wage described earlier? An answer to that question can be had by examining the pattern of movements in the *level* of the adjusted real wage. If the underlying economic processes that determine it are of the pure RATEX variety, this period's adjusted real wage should not be related systematically to last period's. Figure B.7 is a graphic display of the movement of the adjusted real wage over the interval 1959.1–1996.2. Clear cycles appear, indicating that it is not a pure RATEX process. This is confirmed by the correlation between this period's and the previous period's values for the adjusted real wage, which is 0.8627, significantly different from zero. Clearly, the adjusted real wage data series displays the characteristics of a Slutsky cycle, or a Slutsky cycle modified by some decay parameter greater than zero and less than one.[14]

FIGURE B.7

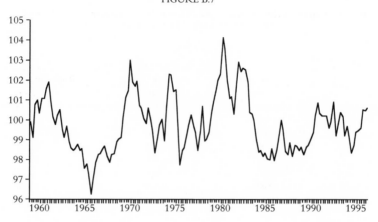

To explore this matter more fully, the experiments reported in table B.7 were extended to include consideration of intermediate values of α, ranging from 0.10 to 0.90, at 0.10 intervals. The results are shown in table B.8. Their general pattern is striking in two respects. First, they indicate that relatively small values for α produce substantial reductions in the relative variability of the synthetic data series. This can be seen by calculating the following statistic:

(5) $$DV = 100 \star (RMSD_s - RMSD_\alpha)/(RMSD_s - RMSD_R)$$

where DV denotes a measure of the decline in relative variability, RMSD indicates the root mean square deviation of the series from its initial equilibrium condition, and the subscripts s, α, and R represent the Slutsky, decay parameter, and RATEX outcomes, respectively. Values for DV are presented in table B.9. As an example, in the case of n = 5 and α = 0.10, the variability in the data series decreases by an amount equal to 31.5 percent of the difference between the Slutsky and RA-TEX models. Holding n constant, raising α to 0.20 reduces the relative variability by 54.6 percent.

This is only part of the story. The experimental results show also that the larger the value of n, the greater the reduction in the relative variability of the series. For example, with n = 100, an α of 0.10 eliminates 72.0 percent of the difference between the Slutsky and RATEX results.

DECAY PARAMETERS AS AN ADJUSTMENT MECHANISM

The decay parameter, α, may also be viewed as representing a partial adjustment mechanism, that is, an endogenous response to the disequilibrating impact of a

TABLE B.8

ROOT MEAN SQUARE DEVIATION, BY NUMBER OF PERIODS AND VALUE OF DECAY PARAMETER, MONTE CARLO EXPERIMENTS

No. of periods	Root Mean Square Deviation Decay Parameter (α)										
	0.00*	0.10	0.20	0.30	0.40	0.50	0.60	0.70	0.80	0.90	1.00
5	1.000	0.921	0.863	0.821	0.791	0.770	0.755	0.747	0.743	0.744	0.749
10	1.000	0.835	0.742	0.684	0.646	0.619	0.602	0.590	0.583	0.581	0.581
20	1.000	0.733	0.622	0.559	0.519	0.492	0.473	0.461	0.453	0.450	0.450
30	1.000	0.653	0.536	0.474	0.435	0.410	0.392	0.380	0.373	0.369	0.368
40	1.000	0.595	0.479	0.419	0.383	0.358	0.342	0.331	0.324	0.320	0.319
50	1.000	0.551	0.438	0.382	0.347	0.325	0.310	0.299	0.293	0.289	0.288
70	1.000	0.487	0.381	0.329	0.298	0.278	0.265	0.255	0.249	0.246	0.245
100	1.000	0.430	0.330	0.283	0.255	0.237	0.225	0.217	0.211	0.208	0.208

*Root mean square deviation set equal to 1.000 for $\alpha = 0.00$.

PERCENT OF VARIABILITY ABOUT INITIAL EQUILIBRIUM POSITION ELIMINATED BY ADJUSTMENT PARAMETERS, MONTE CARLO EXPERIMENTS

No. of Periods	Percent of Variability Eliminated by Adjustment Parameter (α)										
	0.00	0.10	0.20	0.30	0.40	0.50	0.60	0.70	0.80	0.90	1.00
5	0.0	31.5	54.6	71.3	83.3	91.6	97.6	100.8	102.4	102.0	100.0
10	0.0	39.6	61.9	75.8	84.9	91.4	95.4	98.3	100.0	100.5	100.0
20	0.0	48.5	68.7	80.2	87.5	92.4	95.8	98.0	99.5	100.0	100.0
30	0.0	54.9	73.4	83.2	89.4	93.4	96.2	98.1	99.2	99.8	100.0
40	0.0	59.5	76.5	85.3	90.6	94.3	96.6	98.2	99.3	99.9	100.0
50	0.0	63.1	78.9	86.8	91.7	94.8	96.9	98.5	99.3	99.9	100.0
70	0.0	67.9	82.0	88.9	93.0	95.6	97.4	98.7	99.5	99.9	100.0
100	0.0	72.0	84.6	90.5	94.1	96.3	97.9	98.7	99.6	100.0	100.0

FIGURE B.8

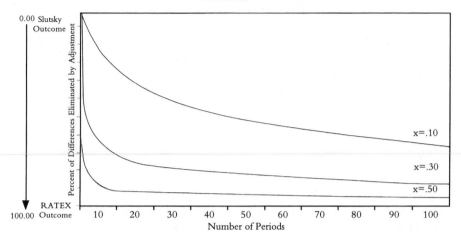

random shock, a response that attempts to return the economic process to its equilibrium state. Perceived in this manner, the simulation results shown thus far indicate that the effects of partial adjustment responses are profound. This is illustrated in figure B.8, which describes the relationship between the relative variability of a data series and the number of observations in the series for adjustment (decay) parameters of zero (the Slutsky model), 0.10, 0.30, 0.50, and 1.0 (the RATEX model). Clearly, relatively minor amounts of endogenous adjustment toward the equilibrium condition will cause a data series to move very rapidly toward the RATEX version of the world.

CONCLUSIONS

Basically, what emerges from this discussion is an image of the macroeconomic world in which there is an underlying equilibrating mechanism (the labor market) that is subject to a series of random shocks of the money wage, productivity, and price variety. Adjustment to these shocks is not instantaneous but proceeds with some lag structure. Eventually, though, the temporary disequilibria created by the random shocks are dissipated and the fundamental equilibrium reasserts itself. Thus, while the process is not, strictly speaking, of the RATEX form in the immediate term, it approaches a RATEX outcome in the longer run. This is precisely what has been suggested by Jerome Stein in his work dealing with what he describes as "asymptotically rational expectations" (ARE).[15] This is quite consistent with our analysis reported in appendix A.

Adjusted Real Wages and Economic Growth

One additional issue needs to be addressed. To this point, we have been speaking in terms of business cycles while focusing exclusively on the behavior of the unemployment rate. One critique of the first version of this book assailed us sharply on this point, complaining that we "throw numbers around without presenting a single time-series relating real wages to economic growth." This critique further asserted, "If they had bothered to, the results would stun them."[16] How valid is this complaint? To address it, we have estimated a straightforward model embodying the basic relationship

(6)   PCTCHGDP = f(ARW)

where PCTCHGDP denotes the quarter-to-quarter percentage change in Gross Domestic Product (GDP) and ARW is the productivity adjusted real wage rate. Since the critical issue here is whether cyclical variations in the adjusted real wage are associated with opposite signed swings in GDP growth, the detailed regression model is a truncated form of the expanded one used in the unemployment analysis. Its dependent variables are the adjusted real wage lagged eight quarters and a vector of percentage changes in the adjusted real wage running from the current period back through seven quarters. Of course, all of these variables are hypothesized to have a negative effect on GDP growth. The results of estimating this model (employing the same ARIMA scheme used in the unemployment analysis) are reported in table B.10.

All coefficients for the independent variables have the expected negative signs

TABLE B.10

REGRESSION RESULTS, PERCENTAGE CHANGE IN GROSS DOMESTIC PRODUCT AS DEPENDENT VARIABLE, UNITED STATES, QUARTERLY DATA, FIRST QUARTER, 1959, THROUGH SECOND QUARTER, 1996

Independent Variable	Regression Coefficient	t-Statistic
Constant Term	15.0005	5.1379
Adjusted Real Wage (-8)	-0.1431	4.8888
% Change Adjusted Real Wage	-0.7023	8.7712
% Change Adjusted Real Wage (-1)	-0.2864	2.8452
% Change Adjusted Real Wage (-2)	-0.3672	3.1024
% Change Adjusted Real Wage (-3)	-0.3178	2.5195
% Change Adjusted Real Wage (-4)	-0.1653	1.2917
% Change Adjusted Real Wage (-5)	-0.1777	1.5340
% Change Adjusted Real Wage (-6)	-0.2250	2.1945
% Change Adjusted Real Wage (-7)	-0.2231	2.8936
MA(1) Adjustment Term	0.9606	8.4664
MA(2) Adjustment Term	0.3020	3.1992
AR(1) Adjustment Term	-0.7972	6.2355

Other regression statistics: Adjusted R^2 = 0.4475; D-W = 1.9858.

and only two are not significantly different from zero at the 5 percent level, the change variables lagged four and five quarters. Even these are significant at the 10 percent level (one-tailed tests of significance). Thus, we find relationships that support, rather than undermine, our arguments. To be sure, these results are not as robust as the unemployment ones. Only about half of the variation in GDP growth is explained.[17] Nevertheless, the relationships reported here are quite in line with the unemployment analysis.

As to model specification issues, the non-ARIMA version of the model passes the Ramsey RESET test and performs well in the recursive residuals, CUSUM, and CUSUMSQ tests (see figure B.9). To explore this matter further, we also estimated a first difference version of the model. The ARIMA adjusted results are reported in table B.11. A comparison of the regression parameters of the differenced and undifferenced versions of the model reveals that they are extremely consistent, indicating a lack of model specification problems.

Spatial Variations in Unemployment Revisited

At two places in the first edition of *Out of Work* (pp. 5–7, 262–64), we examine spatial variations in unemployment. We report little empirical work, stating (p. 264) that "more work on regional unemployment differentials needs to be done." Subsequently, we have written two papers on the topic (one with Tony Caporale) that expand upon the textual evidence.[18] Some of that research is presented here.

The notion that the natural rate of unemployment may vary substantially by

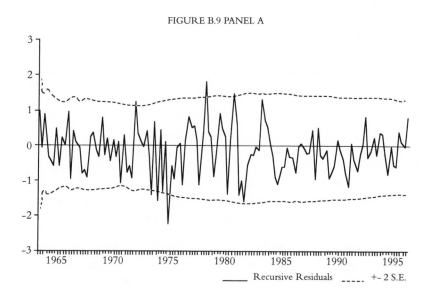

FIGURE B.9 PANEL A

Recursive Residuals _ _ _ _ +- 2 S.E.

FIGURE B.9 PANEL B

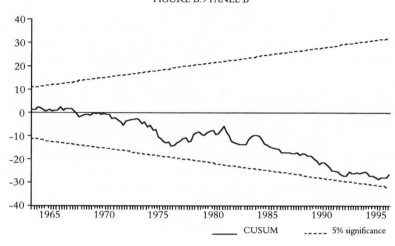

_____ CUSUM   ----- 5% significance

FIGURE B.9 PANEL C

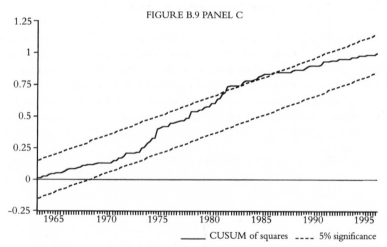

_____ CUSUM of squares ---- 5% significance

state is confirmed by examining the average unemployment rate for the fifty states based on annual data for the years 1960–91 (table B.12). Extending the data through 1995, the average annual unemployment rate in West Virginia (9.32 percent) is more than two and one-half times that of Nebraska (3.47 percent) (see figure B.10). The limited pre-1960 evidence suggests that there was some convergence in unemployment rates, but that appears largely to stop after 1960; moreover, substantial variations exist.

What explains the substantial interstate variations in the long-run average rate of unemployment? The theme of this book has been that interferences in the labor market process by governments and labor unions are important causes of

TABLE B.11

REGRESSION RESULTS, CHANGE IN PERCENTAGE CHANGE IN
GROSS DOMESTIC PRODUCT AS DEPENDENT VARIABLE, UNITED STATES,
QUARTERLY DATA, FIRST QUARTER, 1959,
THROUGH SECOND QUARTER, 1996

Independent Variable	Regression Coefficient	t-Statistic
Constant Term	0.0048	0.1068
Change in Adjusted Real Wage (-8)	-0.1054	0.4649
Change in % Change Adjusted Real Wage	-0.6941	8.0313
Change in % Change Adjusted Real Wage (-1)	-0.2936	3.0378
Change in % Change Adjusted Real Wage (-2)	-0.3620	2.9273
Change in % Change Adjusted Real Wage (-3)	-0.3488	2.5439
Change in % Change Adjusted Real Wage (-4)	-0.1470	0.9468
Change in % Change Adjusted Real Wage (-5)	-0.1926	1.1193
Change in % Change Adjusted Real Wage (-6)	-0.2072	1.0740
Change in % Change Adjusted Real Wage (-7)	-0.2447	1.1802
MA(1) Adjustment Term	-0.5271	2.5699
MA(2) Adjustment Term	-0.4219	1.8686
AR(1) Adjustment Term	-0.4395	2.3694

Other regression statistics: Adjusted R^2 = 0.5651; D–W = 1.7897.

unemployment in America. We regressed the average rate of unemployment for 1960–91 for the fifty states and the District of Columbia (UNEMPL) against variables measuring the extent of unionization (UNION), participation in welfare programs (WELFARE), and an estimate of the state and local tax burden (TAX). UNION is the percentage of the labor force belonging to labor unions in midperiod (1974); WELFARE is the average percent of the population receiving AFDC or SSI payments in five years (1962, 1971, 1976, 1981, 1990); and TAXES is the increase in state and local tax payments as a percent of personal income over the years 1960–91.

Four control variables are introduced into the analysis: BEGINUN, the unemployment rate in the first year analyzed (1960); WEST, a dummy variable denoting eleven mountain and Pacific states; SOUTH, a dummy variable denoting eight southern states; and MIDWEST, a dummy variable denoting five states in the industrial midwest.[19] These variables were introduced because of some evidence of relatively high unemployment rates in the three aforementioned regions. The numbers in parentheses are t-statistics.

The results are impressive:

(1)   UNEMPL = 1.583 + 0.023 UNION + 0.012 WELFARE + 0.104 TAXES
          (5.68)   (2.18)   (2.71)   (4.61)

          + 0.485 BEGINUN + 0.978 WEST + 0.607 SOUTH
          (10.41)   (5.89)   (2.71)

          + 0.545 MIDWEST,
          (2.13)

$\overline{R}^2$ = .858, F Statistic = 44.303.

TABLE B.12

LEVEL AND VARIATION IN UNEMPLOYMENT RATES, 50 STATES AND DISTRICT OF COLUMBIA, 1960–1991

State or Area	Average Annual Unemployment Rate (%)	Standard Deviation	Coefficient of Variation
Alabama	7.06	2.62	.37
Alaska	9.33	1.18	.13
Arizona	5.89	2.02	.34
Arkansas	6.68	1.79	.27
California	6.79	1.53	.23
Colorado	4.95	1.44	.29
Connecticut	5.49	1.75	.32
Delaware	5.46	2.08	.38
Dist. of Columbia	5.56	3.01	.54
Florida	5.63	1.99	.35
Georgia	5.43	1.49	.27
Hawaii	5.06	1.94	.39
Idaho	6.16	1.52	.25
Illinois	5.98	2.34	.39
Indiana	5.95	2.36	.40
Iowa	4.35	1.83	.40
Kansas	4.22	0.93	.22
Kentucky	6.52	2.14	.33
Louisiana	7.59	2.31	.30
Maine	6.42	1.72	.27
Maryland	5.09	1.35	.27
Massachusetts	5.83	1.86	.32
Michigan	8.08	3.03	.37
Minnesota	4.88	1.22	.25
Mississippi	7.07	2.48	.35
Missouri	5.50	1.63	.30
Montana	6.28	1.12	.18
Nebraska	3.55	1.00	.28
Nevada	6.43	1.56	.24
New Hampshire	4.21	1.70	.40
New Jersey	6.24	1.71	.27
New Mexico	6.90	1.53	.22
New York	6.23	1.78	.29
North Carolina	5.13	1.62	.32
North Dakota	4.82	0.77	.16
Ohio	6.33	2.50	.40
Oklahoma	5.18	1.56	.30
Oregon	6.87	2.06	.30
Pennsylvania	6.51	2.20	.34
Rhode Island	6.27	1.98	.32
South Carolina	5.99	1.67	.28
South Dakota	3.79	0.77	.20
Tennessee	6.14	2.15	.35
Texas	5.36	1.59	.30
Utah	5.63	1.09	.19

State or Area	Average Annual Unemployment Rate (%)	Standard Deviation	Coefficient of Variation
Vermont	5.59	1.55	.28
Virginia	4.45	1.25	.28
Washington	7.38	2.02	.27
West Virginia	9.23	3.13	.34
Wisconsin	5.28	1.90	.36
Wyoming	5.09	1.61	.32
UNITED STATES	5.84	1.03	.18

Source: U.S. Department of Labor, authors' calculations.

There is a statistically significant positive relationship between taxes, unionization, welfare incidence, and the long-run average rate of unemployment. Moreover, the coefficients indicate that these factors are moderately important determinants of unemployment. If New York, for example, had followed New Hampshire's tax lead (raising taxes slightly instead of substantially), its estimated mean unemployment rate would have been 0.44 percentage points less, or about 21 percent of the considerable New York–New Hampshire unemployment differential.

Sensitivity analysis was performed, altering the control variables introduced. In every instance, the three policy variables mentioned above maintained their positive sign. One variable of particular interest that was introduced was the average wage level. The basic proposition of this book is that, other things equal, higher wages are associated with higher unemployment. Unfortunately, it was not possible to correct completely for "other things," most importantly, productivity differentials between the states. Interestingly, however, a strong, statistically significant positive relationship was observed between wage levels and unemployment, consistent with other evidence in this book.

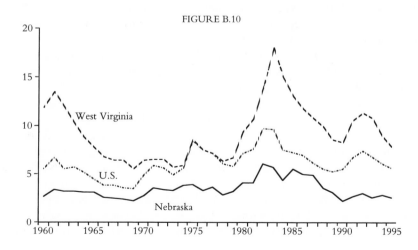

FIGURE B.10

RACE AND UNEMPLOYMENT

In chapters 12 and 13, we suggest that much of the rise in black unemployment relative to that for whites is explainable by governmental policies, particularly public assistance. We regressed the percent of the population that was black (BLACK) and some control variables against UNEMPL. Interestingly, when this is done in a model with no government policy variables, the observed relationship between BLACK and UNEMPL is positive and statistically significant at the 1 percent level: more blacks (proportionally), higher unemployment. This is not surprising since the typical unemployment rate among blacks is about double that for whites.

When, however, one introduces an additional independent variable, the percentage of population receiving public assistance (WELFARE), the observed relationship between BLACK and UNEMPL turns insignificant—and, indeed, even changes signs. This indicates that, holding welfare incidence constant between states, there is *no* relationship between race and unemployment. Race itself does not matter. What matters is welfare. Receipt of welfare raises unemployment. Since blacks receive disproportionately large amounts of welfare, they are differentially burdened with high unemployment—but not because of the color of their skin.

THE PERSISTENCE OF UNEMPLOYMENT

There is a considerable interest in the question of the *persistence* of unemployment. Using international data, Robert Barro believes that unionization and the size of government have positive effects on persistence.[20] Using the state unemployment data mentioned above (but also including observations for the years 1992 and 1993), we used a two-step procedure similar to Barro's to measure the persistence of unemployment in the United States.

In the first step, we estimate an ARMA (1,0) for the log of unemployment rates, then add enough MA terms in order to obtain a Q-statistic for generalized serial correlation of the residuals below the .05 critical value. The AR1 coefficients from these regressions provide an estimate of persistence, ranging from a low of .39 in Oklahoma to a high of .89 in the District of Columbia (see table B.13).

In the second stage, we use a weighted least squares regression approach (where the standard errors of the AR1 coefficients from the first stage are used as the weights), regressing our estimate of persistence (table B.13) against UNION and WELFARE from before, as well as four additional variables, SPENDING (average real value of each state's total state and local government spending as a percent of personal income), FORBORN (the average percent of each state's population that are immigrants), RIGHT TO WORK (a dummy variable that takes a value of

TABLE B.13

UNEMPLOYMENT REGRESSIONS FOR 50 STATES AND DISTRICT OF
COLUMBIA, 1960–1993

State	ARMA	AR1	R^2	Q(12)
Alabama	(1,1)	.81 (.09)	.77	8.21
Alaska	(1,0)	.85 (.16)	.36	8.77
Arizona	(1,1)	.87 (.18)	.31	9.27
Arkansas	(1,0)	.79 (.11)	.61	4.92
California	(1,3)	.88 (.14)	.61	2.92
Colorado	(1,0)	.63 (.14)	.39	9.98
Connecticut	(1,0)	.67 (.13)	.43	9.01
Delaware	(1,1)	.76 (.09)	.73	8.86
Dist. of Columbia	(1,1)	.89 (.06)	.88	9.83
Florida	(1,1)	.68 (.11)	.65	3.52
Georgia	(1,0)	.75 (.12)	.55	6.42
Hawaii	(1,1)	.84 (.09)	.72	7.63
Idaho	(1,1)	.62 (.12)	.59	4.48
Illinois	(1,0)	.88 (.08)	.78	5.50
Indiana	(1,0)	.81 (.10)	.65	5.50
Iowa	(1,1)	.83 (.07)	.84	6.46
Kansas	(1,1)	.42 (.16)	.37	4.84
Kentucky	(1,3)	.78 (.12)	.70	6.34
Louisiana	(1,1)	.74 (.09)	.76	6.58
Maine	(1,1)	.57 (.15)	.47	7.43
Maryland	(1,1)	.67 (.10)	.71	4.73
Massachusetts	(1,1)	.59 (.12)	.59	5.15
Michigan	(1,0)	.77 (.11)	.58	2.89

TABLE B.13 (continued)

State	ARMA	AR1	R^2	Q(12)
Minnesota	(1,0)	.72 (.12)	.51	6.87
Mississippi	(1,1)	.84 (.09)	.71	6.69
Missouri	(1,1)	.69 (.12)	.62	5.98
Montana	(1,0)	.78 (.11)	.60	9.74
Nebraska	(1,0)	.76 (.11)	.57	7.97
Nevada	(1,1)	.42 (.13)	.50	7.55
New Hampshire	(1,0)	.65 (.14)	.38	5.32
New Jersey	(1,1)	.79 (.10)	.66	9.43
New Mexico	(1,1)	.57 (.15)	.47	5.98
New York	(1,1)	.67 (.08)	.78	3.99
North Carolina	(1,1)	.53 (.17)	.42	2.82
North Dakota	(1,0)	.51 (.16)	.44	7.91
Ohio	(1,1)	.68 (.10)	.67	3.79
Oklahoma	(1,1)	.39 (.12)	.51	12.8
Oregon	(1,1)	.66 (.09)	.75	5.62
Pennsylvania	(1,1)	.70 (.09)	.75	5.59
Rhode Island	(1,0)	.72 (.13)	.51	6.97
South Carolina	(1,1)	.55 (.14)	.52	4.04
South Dakota	(1,0)	.77 (.11)	.61	2.57
Tennessee	(1,1)	.72 (.11)	.66	2.80
Texas	(1,1)	.69 (.09)	.73	6.31
Utah	(1,1)	.48 (.16)	.42	4.98
Vermont	(1,1)	.45 (.11)	.61	4.94

State	ARMA	AR1	R^2	Q(12)
Virginia	(1,1)	.59	.69	11.9
		(.10)		
Washington	(1,8)	.78	.77	11.5
		(.08)		
West Virginia	(1,1)	.73	.77	6.96
		(.08)		
Wisconsin	(1,0)	.79	.63	4.14
		(.10)		
Wyoming	(1,0)	.78	.60	4.53
		(.11)		

The dependent variable for each of the 51 regressions above is the log of the state's unemployment rate. The R^2 statistic is the adjusted R-squared for each ARMA model. AR1 is the coefficient on the autoregressive parameter for each model. The numbers in parenthesis are the standard errors of the autoregressive parameters. Q(12) represents the Ljung-Box Q-statistics for each ARMA model. The critical value at the .05 level is 21.03.

TABLE B.14

EXPLAINING THE PERSISTENCE OF UNEMPLOYMENT WEIGHTED
LEAST SQUARES REGRESSIONS
(T-STATISTICS IN PARENTHESES)

Independent Variables	Eq. 1	Eq. 2	Eq. 3	Eq. 4	Eq. 5
Constant	.37	.23	.42	.37	.40
	(4.90)	(2.58)	(3.39)	(2.68)	(2.83)
State	.009	.01	.009	.009	.008
Spending	(2.70)	(3.20)	(2.73)	(2.74)	(2.67)
Union	.0057	.004	.005	.006	.006
	(2.68)	(2.18)	(2.47)	(2.41)	(2.12)
Welfare		.031	.032	.033	.033
		(2.82)	(2.95)	(3.02)	(3.01)
Economic			-.0001	-.0001	-.0001
Diversity			(2.13)	(2.12)	(2.42)
Right to				.035	.042
Work				(0.79)	(0.96)
Foreign-					.007
Born Pop.					(1.25)
Weighted -R^2	.47	.54	.57	.57	.57
f-statistic	23.1	20.3	17.5	14.0	12.1

The dependent variable for the above cross-sectional regressions is constructed by using the AR1 coefficients from the ARMA(1,k) representation for the log of state unemployment rates. The standard errors of the AR1 coefficients are used as the weighting series in the regressions. *State Spending* is the average real value of each state's total state and local spending as a percentage of personal income over the sample period. *Union* is the average percentage of labor union membership in the labor force by state. *Welfare* is the average percentage of each state's population receiving public aid as defined by the Census Bureau. *Economic Diversity* is a Herfindahl index such as that used by Simon and Nardinelli (1992). *Right to Work* is a dummy variable equal to 1 for any state that had legislated right-to-work laws during any part of the sample period. *Foreign-Born Pop.* is the average percentage of each state's population that are not native born.

one for states with a legislated right-to-work law for all or part of the period), and DIVERSITY, a measure of concentration of economic activity. The last variable is a Herfindahl index similar to that used by Simon and Nardinelli.[21] A value of zero indicates perfect diversification.

The expectation is that large governmental or union presence (as measured by UNION, WELFARE, SPENDING) should lead to greater unemployment persistence, as rigidities prevent labor resources from responding to market stimuli in a manner that would ease persistence. Right-to-work laws might be expected to lower persistence. We have no a priori expectations regarding DIVERSITY or FORBORN, as there is reasoning or literature consistent with these factors both raising and lowering persistence.

The results (table B.14) of five different weighted least squares regressions suggest that there is a strong positive relationship between WELFARE, UNION, SPENDING and persistence, consistent with our hypothesis. Governmental and union presence aggravates the persistence of unemployment. Although the right-to-work variable has the expected sign, it is not statistically significant. There is some evidence that increases in economic diversity are associated with greater persistence of unemployment. Immigration is not a significant factor.

CONCLUSIONS

The evidence with respect to both the levels and the persistence of state-specific unemployment rates reinforces the basic conclusion reached in the main body of the text. The presence of institutional forces that encroach on private market activity tends, other things equal, to lead to both higher and more persistent rates of unemployment. Factors such as unions and non-market-determined governmental spending lead to an environment where necessary changes in the adjusted real wage to sustain high employment are difficult to implement.

Concluding Remarks

In this appendix we have explored a number of technical questions in an effort to fill in what some have perceived to be blank spots in the first edition of this book. In the process, we feel that an even more compelling case for our basic thesis has emerged. Wage rates are important in the American economy from the macroeconomic perspective. To argue otherwise is to reject a substantial body of sound empirical evidence.

NOTES

1. Portions of this appendix were coauthored by our Ohio University colleagues Chuhlo Jung and Tony Caporale.

2. We have received some complaints from scholars that they have been unable to reproduce our model. These include Robert Barro and Herbert Stein.

3. These regressions were estimated using the TSP 7.0 software. They have been cross-checked and validated using the EVIEWS software.

4. These include the Durbin-Watson, Box-Pierce Q-test, and the LM test for serial correlation.

5. One-tailed tests of significance are appropriate because the signs of all independent variables are hypothesized to be in a particular direction. The critical level of significance is the 5 percent level.

6. C. I. Plosser, G. W. Schwert, and Halbert White, "Differencing as a Test of Specification," *International Economic Review*, October 1982, pp. 535–52.

7. G. S. Maddala, *Introduction to Econometrics*, 2d ed. (Englewood Cliffs, N.J.: Prentice-Hall, 1992), p. 513.

8. We also dealt with the degrees of freedom problem by estimating a truncated version of the basic model for just the quarters 1989.1–1996.2. The truncation is accomplished by combining the percentage change in money wage, productivity, and prices variables into a single percentage change in the productivity adjusted real wage variable. The results of this procedure are almost identical with what we obtained using the fitted terms for this interval obtained from the extended version of the model.

9. The mean value of the percentage changes in the productivity adjusted real wage is 0.0075 with a standard deviation of 0.7427.

10. Eugen Slutsky, "The Summation of Random Causes as the Source of Cyclic Processes," *Problems of Economic Conditions* (Moscow, ed. Conjuncture Institute) 3, no. 1 (1927), reprinted under the same title in *Econometrica* 5 (1937): 105–46.

11. See Robert E. Lucas, Jr., "Real Wages, Employment, and Inflation," in *Microfoundations of Employment and Inflation Theory*, ed. Edmund S. Phelps (New York: W. W. Norton, 1970), pp. 257–305; and Thomas Sargent and Neil Wallace, "Rational Expectations, the Optimal Monetary Instrument, and the Optimal Money Supply Rule," *Journal of Political Economy* 83 (1975): 241–54.

12. It is worth noting that a series of naive forecasts (i.e., predicting that next period's value will equal this period's value) would yield a data series identical to Slutsky's.

13. The values for t_0 are 5, 10, 20, 30, 40, 50, 70, and 100.

14. It also could be argued that it is a RATEX process with a propagation mechanism that causes the shocks to be transformed into business cycles.

15. Jerome L. Stein, *Monetarist, Keynesian, and New Classical Economics* (New York: New York University Press, 1982).

16. David Goldman, "'Cheaper Jobs' and Cheap-Shot Economics," *Political and Economic Communications* (Newsletter of Polyconomics, Inc., Morristown, N.J., November 12, 1992).

17. The adjusted R^2 for the unemployment regression is 0.9695, more than twice the 0.4475 for the GDP growth regression.

18. Richard Vedder and Lowell Gallaway, "Spatial Variations in U.S. Unemployment," *Journal of Labor Research* 17 (1996): 445–61; Tony Caporale, Lowell Gallaway, and Richard Vedder, "The Persistence of Unemployment," unpublished paper, Ohio University Department of Economics, 1996.

19. WEST includes Arizona, California, Colorado, Idaho, Montana, Nevada, New Mexico, Oregon, Utah, Washington, and Wyoming; SOUTH includes Alabama, Florida, Georgia, Louisiana, Mississippi, North Carolina, and South Carolina; MID-WEST includes Illinois, Indiana, Michigan, Ohio, and Wisconsin.

20. Robert J. Barro, "The Persistence of Unemployment," *American Economic Review* 78 (1988): 32–37.

21. Curtis J. Simon and Clark Nardinelli, "Does Industrial Diversity Always Reduce Unemployment? Evidence from the Great Depression and After," *Economic Inquiry* 30 (1992): 384–97.

Bibliography

Books

Adie, Douglas K. *An Evaluation of Postal Service Wage Rates.* Washington, D.C.: American Enterprise Institute, 1977.

Aldcroft, Derek H. *The Inter-War Economy: Britain, 1919–1939.* New York: Columbia University Press, 1970.

American Assembly. *The Economy and the President: 1980 and Beyond.* Englewood Cliffs, N.J.: Prentice-Hall, 1980.

Anderson, Benjamin. *Economics and the Public Welfare.* Princeton, N.J.: Van Nostrand, 1949.

Armey, Richard. *The Freedom Revolution.* Washington, D.C.: Regnery Publishing Company, 1995.

Baran, Paul A., and Paul M. Sweezy. *Monopoly Capital: An Essay on the American Economic and Social Order.* New York: Monthly Review Press, 1966.

Barber, William J. *From New Era to New Deal.* Cambridge: Cambridge University Press, 1985.

Barger, Harold. *Outlay and Income in the United States, 1912–1938.* New York: National Bureau of Economic Research, 1942.

Becker, Gary. *The Economics of Discrimination.* 2d ed. Chicago: University of Chicago Press, 1971.

Bernstein, Irving. *The Lean Years: A History of the American Worker, 1920–1933.* Boston: Houghton Mifflin, 1960.

Bernstein, Michael A. *The Great Depression.* New York: Cambridge University Press, 1987.

Beveridge, William H. *Causes and Cures of Unemployment.* London: Longman, Green and Co., 1930.

———. *Unemployment: A Problem of Industry.* London: Longman, Green and Co., 1930.

Black, Fischer. *Business Cycles and Equilibrium.* New York: Basil Blackwell, 1987.

Bremer, C. D. *American Bank Failures.* New York: Columbia University Press, 1935.

Brookes, Warren. *The Economy in Mind*. New York: Universe Books, 1982.

Brown, E. H. Phelps, and Margaret Browne. *A Century of Pay*. London: Macmillan, 1968.

Brunner, Karl, ed. *The Great Depression Revisited*. Boston: Martinus Nijhoff, 1981.

Card, David, and Alan Krueger. *Myth and Measurement: The New Economics of the Minimum Wage*. Princeton, N.J. Princeton University Press, 1995.

Carver, Thomas Nixon. *Principles of National Economy*. Boston: Ginn and Co., 1921.

Casson, Mark. *The Economics of Unemployment*. Cambridge, Mass.: MIT Press, 1983.

Chandler, Lester V. *America's Greatest Depression, 1929–1941*. New York: Harper and Row, 1970.

Chase, Stuart. *The Tragedy of Waste*. New York: Macmillan, 1925.

Clay, Henry. *The Post-war Unemployment Problem*. London: Macmillan, 1929.

Cushman, Robert, ed. *Leading Constitutional Decisions*. New York: Appleton-Century Crofts, 1958.

Davis, J. Ronnie. *The New Economics and the Old Economists*. Ames: Iowa State University Press, 1971.

Dornbush, Rudiger, and Stanley Fischer. *Macroeconomics*. 5th ed. New York: McGraw-Hill, 1990.

Dorfman, Joseph. *The Economic Mind in American Civilization*, vol. 4. New York: The Viking Press, 1959.

Douglas, C. H. *Credit-Power and Democracy*. London: C. Palmer, 1920.

Douglas, Paul H. *Real Wages in the United States*. New York: Houghton Mifflin Co., 1930.

Edie, Lionel D., ed. *The Stabilization of Business*. New York: Macmillan, 1923.

Eichengreen, Barry, and Timothy J. Hatton. *Interwar Unemployment in International Perspective*. Norwell, Mass.: Kluwer Academic Publishers, 1988.

Eisner, Robert. *How Real is the Federal Deficit?* New York: Free Press, 1986.

Employment Policy Foundation. *The American Workplace: 1996 Labor Day Report*. Washington, D.C.: Employment Policy Foundation, 1996.

Epstein, Richard A. *Forbidden Grounds: The Case Against Employment Discrimination Laws*. Cambridge, Mass.: Harvard University Press, 1992.

Fairchild, Fred R., Edgar S. Furniss, and Norman S. Buck. *Elementary Economics*. New York: Macmillan, 1927.

Faulkner, Harold U. *The Decline of Laissez Faire, 1897–1917*. New York: Rinehart & Co., Inc., 1951.

———. *American Economic History*. 7th ed. New York: Harper, 1954.

Feinstein, C. H. *National Income, Expenditures and Output of the United Kingdom, 1855–1965*. Cambridge: Cambridge University Press, 1972.

Fisher, Irving. *Elementary Principles of Economics*. New York: Macmillan, 1923.

————. *The Stock Market Crash—and After.* New York: Macmillan, 1930.

————. *Booms and Depressions: Some First Principles.* New York: Adelphi, 1932.

Foster, W. T., and W. Catchings. *Profits.* Boston: Houghton Mifflin, 1925.

————. *Business Without A Buyer.* Boston: Houghton Mifflin, 1927.

————. *The Road to Plenty.* Boston: Houghton Mifflin, 1928).

Freeman, Richard B. *Employment and Earnings of Disadvantaged Young Men in a Labor Shortage Economy.* National Bureau of Economic Research, Working Paper no. 3444, 1990.

————, and James L. Medhoff. *What Do Unions Do?* New York: Basic Books, 1984.

Frenze, Christopher. *The Mellon and Kennedy Tax Cuts: A Review and Analysis.* Joint Economic Committee, Staff Study, Ninety-seventh Congress, Second Session. Washington, D.C.: Government Printing Office, 1982.

Friedman, Milton, and Anna J. Schwartz. *A Monetary History of the United States, 1867–1960.* Princeton, N.J.: Princeton University Press for the National Bureau of Economic Research, 1963.

————. *Monetary Trends in the United States and the United Kingdom and Their Relation to Income, Prices, and Interest Rates, 1867–1975.* Chicago: University of Chicago Press for the National Bureau of Economic Research, 1982.

Froyen, Richard T. *Macroeconomics, Theories and Policies.* New York: Macmillan, 1990.

Galbraith, John Kenneth. *The Great Crash, 1929.* Boston: Houghton Mifflin, 1955.

Gallaway, Lowell, and Richard Vedder. *The "Natural" Rate of Unemployment.* Joint Economic Committee, Staff Study, Ninety-seventh Congress, Second Session. Washington, D.C.: Government Printing Office, 1982.

————, and Richard Vedder. *Poverty, Income Distribution, the Family and Public Policy.* Study for the Subcommittee on Trade, Productivity, and Economic Growth, Joint Economic Committee of Congress. Washington, D.C.: Government Printing Office, 1986.

Goldman, David. " 'Cheaper Jobs' and Cheap-Shot Economics." *Political and Economic Communications.* Newsletter of Polyconomics, Inc., Morristown, N.J., November 12, 1992.

Goldsmith, Raymond W. *Studies in the National Balance Sheet of the United States.* Vol. 2. Princeton, N.J.: Princeton University Press for the National Bureau of Economic Research, 1963.

Gordon, Robert A. *Business Fluctuations.* 2d. ed. New York: Harper and Row, 1961.

————. *Economic Instability and Growth: The American Record.* New York: Harper and Row, 1974.

Gordon, Robert J. *Macroeconomics.* 3d ed. Boston: Little, Brown and Company, 1984.

Gwartney, James, and Richard Stroup. *Macroeconomics.* 5th ed. San Diego: Harcourt Brace Jovanovich, 1990.

Haberler, Gottfried. *Consumer Installment Credit and Economic Fluctuations.* New York: National Bureau of Economic Research, 1942.

Hansen, Alvin H. *Full Recovery or Stagnation?* New York: W. W. Norton, 1938.

———. *After the War, Full Employment.* Washington, D.C.: United States National Resources Planning Board, 1943.

———. *The American Economy.* New York: McGraw-Hill, 1957.

———. *The Postwar American Economy: Performance and Problems.* New York: W. W. Norton, 1967.

Harris, Seymour, ed. *The New Economics.* New York: Knopf, 1947.

Hayek, F. A. *The Road to Serfdom.* London: George Routledge and Sons, 1944.

———. *Monetary Theory and the Trade Cycle.* New York: Augustus Kelley, 1966.

Higgs, Robert. *Crisis and Leviathan: Critical Episodes in the Growth of American Government.* New York: Oxford University Press, 1987.

———. *Competition and Coercion: Blacks in the American Economy, 1865–1914.* Cambridge: Cambridge University Press, 1992.

Hill, M. Anne, and June O'Neill. *Underclass Behavior in the United States: Measurement and Analysis of Determinants.* New York: City University of New York, Baruch College, 1993.

Hobson, John A. *The Economics of Unemployment.* London: Allen & Unwin, 1922.

Hoover, Herbert C. *The Memoirs of Herbert Hoover, 1929–1941.* New York: Macmillan, 1952.

Hopkins, Thomas. *Regulatory Costs in Profile.* St. Louis: Center for the Study of American Business, 1996.

Hughes, Jonathan R. T. *American Economic History.* 3d ed. Glenview, Ill.: Scott Foresman, 1990.

Hutt, William H. *The Keynesian Episode: A Reassessment.* Indianapolis: Liberty Press, 1979.

Johnston, J. *Econometric Methods.* 2d ed. New York: McGraw-Hill, 1972.

Jones, Joseph M., Jr. *Tariff Retaliation, Repercussions of the Smoot-Hawley Bill.* Philadelphia: University of Pennsylvania Press, 1934.

Kalachek, Edward. *Higher Unemployment Rates, 1957–1960: Structural Transformation or Inadequate Demand.* Study for Subcommittee on Economic Statistics of the Joint Economic Committee of the Congress. Washington, D.C.: Government Printing Office, 1961.

Kendrick, John W. *Productivity Trends in the United States.* Princeton, N.J.:

Princeton University Press for the National Bureau of Economic Research, 1961.

Keynes, John Maynard. *The General Theory of Employment, Interest and Money.* New York: Harcourt Brace, 1936.

Killingsworth, Mark R. *Labor Supply.* Cambridge: Cambridge University Press, 1983.

Kindleberger, Charles P. *The World in Depression, 1929–1939.* Berkeley: University of California Press, 1973.

King, Willford I. *The Causes of Economic Fluctuations.* New York: Ronald Press, 1938.

———. *Employment, Hours and Earnings in Prosperity and Depression.* New York: National Bureau of Economic Research, 1923.

Klamer, Arjo. *The New Classical Macroeconomists: Conversations with the New Classical Economists and Their Opponents.* Totowa, N.J.: Rowman and Allanheld, 1983.

Lebergott, Stanley. *Manpower in Economic Growth: The American Record Since 1800.* New York: McGraw-Hill, 1964.

Lerner, Abba P., and Frank D. Graham, eds. *Planning and Paying for Full Employment.* Princeton, N.J.: Princeton University Press, 1946.

Lewis, H. Gregg. *Unionism and Relative Wages in the United States.* Chicago: University of Chicago Press, 1963.

———. *Union Relative Wage Effects.* Chicago: University of Chicago Press, 1986.

Lewis, Wilfred, Jr. *Federal Fiscal Policy in the Postwar Recessions.* Washington, D.C.: The Brookings Institution, 1962.

Lindsey, Lawrence. *The Growth Experiment: How the New Tax Policy is Transforming the American Economy.* New York: Basic Books, 1990.

McCloskey, Donald. *The Rhetoric of Economics.* Madison: University of Wisconsin Press, 1985.

Maddala, G. S. *Introduction to Econometrics,* 2d ed. Englewood Cliffs, N.J.: Prentice-Hall, 1992.

Malinvaud, Edmond. *The Theory of Unemployment Reconsidered.* Oxford: Basil Blackwell, 1977.

Marshall, Alfred. *Principles of Economics.* 8th ed. London: Macmillan, 1920.

Miller, Glenn W. *American Labor and the Government.* New York: Prentice-Hall, 1948.

Mises, Ludwig von. *The Theory of Money and Credit.* New ed. New Haven: Yale University Press, 1953.

———. *Human Action.* 3d rev. ed. Chicago: Henry Regnery Company, 1966.

Mitchell, Brian R. *Abstract of British Historical Statistics.* Cambridge: Cambridge University Press, 1976.

———. *European National Statistics, 1750–1970.* London: Macmillan, 1975.

Mitchell, Broadus. *Depression Decade: From New Era through New Deal, 1929–1941.* New York: Rinehart, 1947.

Moore, Geoffrey, ed. *Business Cycle Indicators.* Princeton, N.J.: Princeton University Press for the National Bureau of Economic Research, 1961.

Murray, Robert K. *The Harding Era: Warren G. Harding and His Administration.* Minneapolis: University of Minnesota Press, 1969.

Neumark, David, and William Wascher. *Evidence on Employment Effects of Minimum Wage Provisions from Panel Data on State Minimum Wage Laws.* Cambridge, Mass.: National Bureau of Economic Research, Working Paper no. 3859, 1992.

Nishiyama, Clark, and Kurt R. Leube, eds. *The Essence of Hayek.* Stanford: Hoover Institution Press, 1984.

Nixon, Richard M. *The Memoirs of Richard Nixon.* New York: Grosset and Dunlap, 1978.

Norton, Hugh S. *The Employment Act and the Council of Economic Advisers, 1946–1976.* Columbia, S.C.: University of South Carolina Press, 1977.

Okun, Arthur M., ed. *The Battle Against Unemployment.* New York: W. W. Norton, 1965.

Ozanne, Robert. *Wages in Practice and Theory: McCormick and International Harvester.* Madison: University of Wisconsin Press, 1968.

Perlman, Selig. *A Theory of the Labor Movement.* New York, 1928.

Peterson, John M., and Charles T. Stewart. *Employment Effects of Minimum Wage Rates.* Washington, D.C.: American Enterprise Institute, 1969.

Phelps, Edmund S. *Microeconomic Foundations of Employment and Inflation Theory.* New York: Norton, 1970.

Pigou, A. C. *Industrial Fluctuations.* London: Macmillan, 1927.

———. *Theory of Unemployment.* London: Macmillan, 1933.

Popple, Charles. *Development of Two Bank Groups in the Central Northwest.* Cambridge, Mass.: Harvard University Press, 1944.

Puth, Robert C. *American Economic History.* 2d ed. Chicago: The Dryden Press, 1988.

Rees, Albert. *New Measures of Wage-Earner Compensation in Manufacturing, 1914–1957.* Occasional Paper no. 75. Princeton, N.J.: Princeton University Press for the National Bureau of Economic Research, 1960.

Robbins, Lionel. *The Great Depression.* London: Macmillan, 1934.

Rockoff, Hugh. *Drastic Measures: A History of Wage and Price Controls in the United States.* Cambridge: Cambridge University Press, 1984.

Roose, Kenneth D. *The Economics of Recession and Revival: An Interpretation of 1937–38.* New Haven, Conn.: Yale University Press, 1954.

Rostow, Walt W. *The Stages of Economic Growth.* Cambridge: Cambridge University Press, 1959.

Rothbard, Murray. *America's Great Depression*. Kansas City: Sheed and Ward, 1963.

Saint-Etienne, Christian. *The Great Depression, 1929–1938*. Stanford: Hoover Institution Press, 1984.

Schlesinger, Arthur M., Jr. *The Crisis of the Old Order*. Boston: Houghton Mifflin, 1957.

———. *The Cycles of American History*. Boston: Houghton Mifflin, 1986.

Schumpeter, Joseph A. *Business Cycles*, 2 vols. New York: McGraw Hill, 1939.

———. *The Theory of Economic Development*. Cambridge, Mass.: Harvard University Press, 1949.

Scully, Gerald. *What Is the Optimal Size of Government in the United States?* NCPA Report No. 188. Dallas, Texas: National Center for Policy Analysis, 1994.

Smith, Adam. *An Inquiry into the Nature and Causes of the Wealth of Nations*. Oxford: Clarendon Press, 1976.

Sowell, Thomas. *Say's Law: An Historical Analysis*. Princeton, N.J.: Princeton University Press, 1972.

Stein, Jerome L. *Monetarist, Keynesian and New Classical Economics*. New York: New York University Press, 1982.

Stone, Richard, et. al. *The Measurement of Consumers' Expenditures and Behaviour in the United Kingdom, 1920–1938*. 2 vols. Cambridge: Cambridge University Press, 1954.

Taft, Philip. *The AF of L from the Death of Gompers to the Merger*. New York: Harper and Brothers, 1959.

———. *Organized Labor in American History*. New York: Harper and Row, 1964.

Taussig, Frank W. *Principles of Economics*. 3d ed. 2 vols. New York: Macmillan, 1923.

Temin, Peter. *Did Monetary Forces Cause the Great Depression?* New York: W. W. Norton, 1976.

———. *Lessons from the Great Depression*. Cambridge, Mass.: MIT Press, 1989.

Thurow, Lester. *The Zero-Sum Society*. New York: Basic Books, 1980.

Truman, Harry S. *Memoirs,* vol. 1: *Years of Decision*. Garden City, N.Y.: Doubleday, 1955.

Tugwell, Rexford G. *Industry's Coming of Age*. New York: Harcourt, Brace, 1927.

Van der Wee, Herman. *Prosperity and Upheaval: The World Economy 1945–1980*. Berkeley: University of California Press, 1987.

Vedder, Richard K. *The American Economy in Historical Perspective*. Belmont, Calif.: Wadsworth Publishing Co., 1976.

————. *Federal Regulation's Impact on the Productivity Slowdown: A Trillion Dollar Drag.* Policy Study No. 131. St. Louis: Center for the Study of American Business, 1996.

————, and Lowell Gallaway. *Minimum Wage Costs Jobs.* London: Adam Smith Institute, 1995.

Viner, Jacob. *Balanced Deflation, Inflation, or More Depression.* Minneapolis: University of Minnesota Press, 1933.

Wanniski, Jude. *The Way the World Works.* Rev. ed. New York: Simon and Schuster, 1983.

Weinstein, Michael. *Recovery and Redistribution under the NIRA.* Amsterdam: North Holland, 1980.

White, Eugene N. *The Regulation and Reform of the American Banking System, 1900–1929.* Princeton, N.J.: Princeton University Press, 1983.

Whittlesey, Charles R., Arthur M. Freedman, and Edward S. Herman. *Money and Banking: Analysis and Policy.* New York: Macmillan, 1963.

Williamson, Harold F., ed. *The Growth of the American Economy.* Englewood Cliffs, N.J.: Prentice-Hall, 1954.

Wolman, Leo. *Wages in Relation to Economic Recovery.* Chicago: University of Chicago, 1931.

————. *Ebb and Flow in Trade Unionism.* New York: National Bureau of Economic Research, 1936.

Articles

Adie, Douglas K. "Teenage Unemployment and Real Federal Minimum Wages." *Journal of Political Economy* 81 (1973): 435–41.

Akerloff, George, and Janet Yellen. "A Near-Rational Model of the Business Cycle, with Wage and Price Inertia." *Quarterly Journal of Economics* 100 (1985): 823–38.

Allen, Steven. "Changes in the Cyclical Sensitivity of Wages in the United States, 1891–1987." *American Economic Review* 82 (1992): 122–40.

Anderson, Gary M., William F. Shugart, and Robert Tollison. "A Public Choice Theory of the Great Contraction." *Public Choice* 59 (1988): 2–23.

Ando, Albert, and Franco Modigliani. "The 'Life Cycle' Hypothesis of Saving: Aggregate Implications and Tests." *American Economic Review* 53 (1963): 55–84.

Bairoch, Paul. "Europe's Gross National Product: 1800–1975." *Journal of European Economic History* 5 (1975): 273–340.

Ball, Laurence N., Gregory Mankiw, and David Romer. "The New Keynesian Economics and the Output-Inflation Tradeoff." *Brookings Papers on Economic Activity* 1 (1988): 1–65.

Ballard, Charles L., John B. Shoven, and John Whalley. "General Equilibrium Computations of the Marginal-Welfare Costs of Taxes in the United States." *American Economic Review* 75 (1985): 128–38.

Barro, Robert J. "Are Government Bonds Net Wealth?" *Journal of Political Economy* 82 (1974): 1095–1117.

———. "Second Thoughts on Keynesian Economics." *American Economic Review* 69 (1979): 54–59.

———. "The Persistence of Unemployment." *American Economic Review* 78 (1988): 32–37.

Bator, Francis M. "Prepared Statement." *Hearings, The Unemployment Crisis and Policies for Economic Recovery,* Joint Economic Committee, Ninety-Seventh Congress, Second Session, October 20, 1982, pp. 92–110. Washington, D.C.: Government Printing Office, 1983.

Beenstock, Michael, and Peter Warburton. "Wages and Unemployment in Interwar Britain." *Explorations in Economic History* 23 (1986): 153–72.

Benjamin, Daniel K., and Levis A. Kochin. "Searching for an Explanation of Unemployment in Interwar Britain." *Journal of Political Economy* 87 (1979): 441–78.

Bernanke, Ben S. "Nonmonetary Effects of the Financial Crisis in the Propagation of the Great Depression." *American Economic Review* 73 (1983): 257–76.

———. "Employment, Hours and Earnings in the Depression: An Analysis of Eight Manufacturing Industries." *American Economic Review* 76 (1986): 82–109.

———, and Martin Parkinson. "Unemployment, Inflation and Wages in the American Depression: Are There Lessons for Europe?" *American Economic Review* 79 (1989): 210–14.

Blackley, Paul R. "The Measurement and Determination of State Equilibrium Unemployment Rates." *Southern Economic Journal* 56 (1989): 440–56.

Boskin, Michael J. "Taxation, Saving, and the Rate of Interest." *Journal of Political Economy* 86 (1978): 3–27.

Boughton, James M., and Elmus Wicker. "The Behavior of the Currency-Deposit Ratio During the Great Depression." *Journal of Money, Credit, and Banking* 11 (1979): 408–18.

Brehm, C. T., and T. R. Saving. "The Demand for General Assistance Payments." *American Economic Review* 54 (1964): 1002–18.

Brockie, Martin D. "Theories of the 1937–38 Crisis and Depression." *Economic Journal* 60 (1950): 291–310.

Brown, Charles, Curtis Gilroy, and Andrew Kohen. "The Effect of the Minimum Wage on Employment and Unemployment." *Journal of Economic Literature* 20 (1982): 487–528.

Brown, E. Cary. "Fiscal Policy in the 'Thirties: A Reappraisal." *American Economic Review* 46 (1956): 857–79.

Burns, Arthur F. "Monetary Policy and the Threat of Inflation." In *United States Monetary Policy,* edited by Neil H. Jacoby, pp. 207–18. 1st ed. New York: The American Assembly, Columbia University, 1958.

Cannan, Edwin. "The Problem of Unemployment." *Economic Journal* 40 (1930): 45–55.

Caporale, Tony. "The Role of Real and Monetary Shocks in Explaining Business Cycle Fluctuations." Department of Economics, George Mason University (1992).

————, Lowell Gallaway, and Richard Vedder. "The Persistence of Unemployment." Unpublished paper, Ohio University Department of Economics, 1996.

Card, David, and Alan Krueger. "Minimum Wages and Unemployment: A Case Study of the Fast-Food Industry in New Jersey and Pennsylvania." *American Economic Review* 84 (1994): 172–93.

Carlson, Keith M. "How Much Lower Can the Unemployment Rate Go?" *Review, Federal Reserve Bank of St. Louis* 70 (1988): 44–57.

Cecchetti, Stephen. "Prices During the Great Depression: Was the Deflation of 1930–32 Really Unanticipated?" *American Economic Review* 82 (1992): 141–56.

Chapin, Gene L. "Unemployment Insurance, Job Search, and the Demand for Leisure," *Western Economic Journal* 9 (1971): 102–7.

Clark, Lindley H. "Speaking of Business." *Wall Street Journal,* November 13, 1979, p. 28.

Coelho, Philip R. P., and G. J. Santoni. "Regulatory Capture and the Monetary Contraction of 1932: A Comment on Epstein and Ferguson," *Journal of Economic History* 51 (1991): 182–89.

Coen, Robert M. "Labor Force and Unemployment in the 1920's and 1930's: A Re-Examination Based on Postwar Experience." *Review of Economics and Statistics* 55 (1973): 46–55.

Cogan, John. "The Decline in Black Teenage Employment: 1950–70." *American Economic Review* 72 (1982): 621–38.

Cowen, Tyler. "Why Keynesianism Triumphed Or, Could So Many Keynesians Have Been Wrong?" *Critical Review* 3 (1989): 518–30.

Dalio, Raymond T. "Prepared Statement." *Hearings, The Unemployment Crisis and Policies for Economic Recovery,* Joint Economic Committee, Ninety-seventh Congress, Second Session, October 20, 1982, pp. 111–65. Washington, D.C.: Government Printing Office, 1983.

Danziger, Sheldon, Robert H. Haveman, and Robert Plotnick. "How Income Transfer Programs Affect Work, Savings and the Income Distribution: A Critical Review." *Journal of Economic Literature* 19 (1981): 975–1028.

Darby, Michael. "Three-and-a-Half Million U.S. Employees Have Been Mislaid: Or, an Explanation of Unemployment, 1934–41." *Journal of Political Economy* 84 (1976); 1–15.

———. "The U.S. Productivity Slowdown: A Case of Statistical Myopia." *American Economic Review* 74 (1984): 301–22.

David, Paul A., and Peter Solar. "A Bicentenary Contribution to the History of the Cost of Living in America." In *Research in Economic History,* edited by Paul Uselding, 2:1–80. Greenwich, Conn.: JAI Press, 1977.

De Long, J. Bradford, and Lawrence H. Summers. "Is Increased Price Flexibility Stabilizing?" *American Economic Review* 76 (1986): 1031–44.

Donovan, Robert J. "The Formation of Fiscal Policy: 1953–54." In *The Battle Against Unemployment,* edited by Arthur Okun, pp. 126–34. New York: W. W. Norton, 1965.

Douglas, Paul H. "The Movement of Real Wages and Its Economic Significance." *American Economic Review* 16 (1926): 17–53.

Dumenil, Gerard, Mark Glick, and Jose Rangel. "Theories of the Great Depression: Why Did Profitability Matter?" *Review of Radical Political Economy* 19 (1987): 16–42.

Dunlop, John. "The Movement of Real and Money Wage Rates." *Economic Journal* 48 (1938): 413–34.

Eberts, Randall, and Joe A. Stone. "Teacher Unions and the Cost of Public Education." *Economic Inquiry* 24 (1986): 631–43.

Eckstein, Otto. "Choices for the Eighties." In *The Economy and the President: 1980 and Beyond,* edited by Walter E. Hoadley, pp. 74–98. Englewood Cliffs, N.J.: Prentice-Hall, 1980.

Eichengreen, Barry. "Unemployment in Interwar Britain: Dole or Doldrums?" *Oxford Economic Papers* 39 (1987): 597–623.

Eisner, Robert. "Prepared Statement." *Hearings, The Unemployment Crisis and Policies for Economic Recovery,* Joint Economic Committee, Ninety-seventh Congress, Second Session, October 15, 1982, pp. 4–20. Washington, D.C.: Government Printing Office, 1983.

———. "Which Budget Deficit? Some Issues of Measurement and Their Implications." *American Economic Review* 74 (1984): 138–43.

———, and Paul J. Piper. "A New View of the Federal Debt and Budget Deficits." *American Economic Review* 74 (1984): 11–29.

Epstein, Gerald, and Thomas Ferguson. "Monetary Policy, Loan Liquidation and Industrial Conflict: The Federal Reserve and the Open Market Operations of 1932." *Journal of Economic History* 44 (1984): 957–83.

Evans, Michael K. "Prepared Statement." *Hearings, The Unemployment Crisis and Policies for Economic Recovery,* Joint Economic Committee, Ninety-seventh Congress, Second Session, October 20, 1982, pp. 166–201. Washington, D.C.: Government Printing Office, 1983.

Evans, Paul. "Do Large Deficits Produce High Interest Rates?" *American Economic Review* 75 (1985): 68–87.

———. "Do Budget Deficits Raise Nominal Interest Rates? Evidence from Six Countries." *Journal of Monetary Economics* 20 (1987): 281–300.

Feldstein, Martin. "Social Security, Induced Retirement, and Aggregate Capital Accumulation." *Journal of Political Economy* 82 (1974): 905–26.

———. "Unemployment Compensation: Adverse Incentives and Distributional Anomalies." *National Tax Journal* 27 (1974): 231–44.

———. "Social Security and Saving: The Extended Life Cycle Theory." *American Economic Review* 66 (1976): 77–86.

———. "Does the United States Save Too Little?" *American Economic Review* 67 (1977): 116–21.

Fels, Rendig. "The U.S. Downturn of 1948." *American Economic Review* 55 (1965): 59–76.

Field, Alexander J. "Asset Exchanges and the Transactions Demand for Money, 1919–1929." *American Economic Review* 74 (1984): 43–59.

———. "A New Interpretation of the Onset of the Great Depression." *Journal of Economic History* 44 (1984): 484–98.

Filene, Edward A. "The Minimum Wage and Efficiency." *American Economic Review* 13 (1923): 411–15.

Fischer, Stanley. "Long-Term Contracts, Rational Expectations, and the Optimal Money Supply Rule." *Journal of Political Economy* 85 (1977): 191–205.

Fishback, Price. "Can Competition among Employers Reduce Governmental Discrimination? Coal Companies and Segregated Schools in West Virginia in the Early 1900s." *Journal of Law and Economics* 32 (1989): 311–28.

Fisher, Irving. " 'The Equation of Exchange,' 1896–1910." *American Economic Review* 1 (1911): 296–305.

Fremling, Gertrud M. "Did the United States Transmit the Great Depression to the Rest of the World?" *American Economic Review* 75 (1985): 1181–85.

Friedman, Milton. "The Role of Monetary Policy." *American Economic Review* 58 (1968): 1–17.

———, and Anna J. Schwartz. "Alternative Approaches to Analyzing Economic Data." *American Economic Review* 81 (1991): 39–49.

Galbraith, John Kenneth. "Statement." *Hearings, The Unemployment Crisis and Policies for Economic Recovery,* Joint Economic Committee, Ninety-seventh Congress, Second Session, October 15, 1982, pp. 21–24. Washington, D.C.: Government Printing Office, 1983.

Gallaway, Lowell E. "Labor Mobility, Resource Allocation, and Structural Unemployment." *American Economic Review* 53 (1963): 694–716.

———. "Trade Unionism, Inflation, and Unemployment." In *Monetary Process and Policy: A Symposium,* edited by George Horwich, pp. 60–66. Homewood, Ill.: Richard D. Irwin, 1967.

———. "Labor Supply Responses at Work: The Case of Early Retirement." *War on Poverty—Victory or Defeat?,* Hearing before Subcommittee on Monetary and Fiscal Policy, Joint Economic Committee, Congress of the United States, Ninety-ninth Congress, First Session, June 20, 1985, pp. 140–50. Washington, D.C.: Government Printing Office, 1986.

———, and Gary Anderson. "The Impact of Recent Regulations on Small Business Job Creation." *Journal of Regulation and Social Costs* 3 (1993): 27–61.

———, and Richard Vedder. "Wages, Prices, and Employment: von Mises and the 'Progressives'." *Review of Austrian Economics* 1 (1987): 32–80.

———, and Richard Vedder. "The Distributional Impact of the 1980s." *Critical Review,* Spring-Summer 1993, pp. 61–79.

———, and Richard Vedder. *The Impact of the Welfare State on the American Economy.* Washington, D.C.: Joint Economic Committee of Congress, 1995.

———, and Richard Vedder. *The Impact of the Welfare State on Workers.* Washington, D.C.: Joint Economic Committee of Congress, March 1996.

———, Richard Vedder, and Robert Lawson. "Why People Work: An Examination of Interstate Variations in Labor Force Participation." *Journal of Labor Research* 12 (1991): 47–59.

Gandolfi, A. E., and J. R. Lothian. Review of *Did Monetary Forces Cause the Great Depression? Journal of Money, Credit, and Banking* 9 (1977): 679–91.

Goodrich, Carter. "The Business Depression of Nineteen Hundred Thirty: Discussion." *American Economic Review* 21 (1931): 183–201.

Gordon, Robert A. "Business Cycles in the Interwar Period: The 'Quantitative-Historical' Approach." *American Economic Review* 39 (1949): 47–63.

Gordon, Robert J. "What is the New-Keynesian Economics?" *Journal of Economic Literature* 28 (1990): 1115–71.

Green, George D. "The Ideological Origins of the Revolution in American Financial Policies." In *The Great Depression Revisited,* edited by Karl Brunner, pp. 220–52. Boston: Martinus Nijhoff, 1981.

Hamilton, James D. "Was the Deflation During the Great Depression Anticipated? Evidence from the Commodity Futures Market." *American Economic Review* 82 (1992): 157–78.

Hansen, Alvin H. "The Outlook for Wages and Employment." *American Economic Review* 13 (1923): 27–44.

———. "Factors Affecting the Trend of Real Wages." *American Economic Review* 15 (1925): 27–42.

————. "Economic Progress and Declining Population Growth." *American Economic Review* 29 (1939): 1–15.

————. "The Case for High Pressure Economics." In *The Battle Against Unemployment,* edited by Arthur M. Okun, pp. 53–60. New York: W. W. Norton, 1965.

Hardy, Charles O. "An Appraisal of the Factors ('Natural' and 'Artificial') Which Stopped Short the Recovery Development in the United States." *American Economic Review* 29 (1939): 170–82.

Hatton, T. J. "A Quarterly Model of the Labour Market in Interwar Britain." *Oxford Bulletin of Economics and Statistics* 50 (1988): 1–23.

Hausman, Jerry. "Taxes and Labor Supply." In *Handbook of Public Economics,* edited by Alan Auerbach and Martin Feldstein, pp. 213–63. New York: Elsevier Science, 1985.

Heller, Walter. "The Kemp-Roth-Laffer Free Lunch." *Wall Street Journal,* July 12, 1978, p. 20.

————. "The Carter Program: Can It Work?" *Wall Street Journal,* July 18, 1978, p. 20.

————. "Statement." *Hearings, The Unemployment Crisis and Policies for Economic Recovery,* Joint Economic Committee, Ninety-seventh Congress, Second Session, October 15, 1982, pp. 24–31. Washington, D.C.: Government Printing Office, 1983.

Hicks, John R. "A Sceptical Follower." *The Economist,* June 18, 1983, p. 18.

Higgs, Robert. "Wartime Prosperity? A Reassessment of the U.S. Economy in the 1940s." *Journal of Economic History* 52 (1992): 41–60.

Holt, Charles F. "Who Benefited from the Prosperity of the Twenties?" *Explorations in Economic History* 14 (1977): 277–89.

Jaynes, Gerald D. "The Labor Market Status of Black Americans: 1939–1985." *Journal of Economic Perspectives* 4 (1990): 9–24.

Jensen, Richard J. "The Causes and Cures of Unemployment in the Great Depression." *Journal of Interdisciplinary History* 19 (1989): 553–83.

Kades, Eric. "New Classical and New Keynesian Models of Business Cycles." *Economic Review, Federal Reserve Bank of Cleveland* 4 (1985): 20–35.

Kalecki, Michael. "The Maintenance of Full Employment after the Transition Period." *International Labour Review* 75 (1945) 449–64.

Kennedy, John F. "Mythology and Economic Knowledge." In *The Battle Against Unemployment,* edited by Arthur M. Okun, pp. 1–5. New York: W. W. Norton, 1965.

Keynes, John M. "Relative Movements of Real Wages and Output." *Economic Journal* 49 (1939): 34–51.

Killingsworth, Charles. "Testimony." *The Nation's Manpower Revolution,* Subcommitte on Employment and Manpower of the Committe on Labor and Public Welfare, United States Senate, *Hearings,* part 5. Eighty-eighth

Congress, First Session, pp. 1461–83. Washington, D.C.: Government Printing Office, 1965.

Klein, Lawrence. "Comment on Sapir." *Studies in Income and Wealth,* 9:352–57. New York: National Bureau of Economic Research, 1949.

Klingaman, David C., and Rajindar Koshal. "A Model of United States Inflation, 1959–1980." *Atlantic Economic Journal* 10 (1982): 100.

Kniesner, Thomas J., and Arthur Goldsmith. "A Survey of Alternative Models of the Aggregate U.S. Labor Market." *Journal of Economic Literature* 25 (1987): 1241–80.

Lange, Oskar. "Is the American Economy Contracting?" *American Economic Review* 29 (1939): 503–13.

Leamer, Lawrence. "Let's Take the Con Out of Econometrics." *American Economic Review* 73 (1983): 31–43.

Leonard, Jonathan S. "The Impact of Affirmative Action Regulation and Equal Employment Law on Black Employment." *Journal of Economic Perspectives* 4 (1990): 47–64.

Lerner, Abba P. "An Integrated Full Employment Policy." In *Planning and Paying for Full Employment,* edited by Abba P. Lerner and Frank D. Graham, pp. 163–220. Princeton, N.J.: Princeton University Press, 1946.

Leschohier, Don. "Working Conditions." In *History of Labor in the United States, 1896–1932,* edited by John R. Commons, et al., 3:1–396. 4 vols. New York: Macmillan, 1918–35.

Leuchtenberg, William E. "The New Deal and the Analogue of War." In *Change and Continuity in Twentieth-Century America,* edited by John Braeman, Robert E. Bremner, and Everett Walters, pp. 81–143. Columbus: Ohio State University Press, 1964.

Lipsey, Richard G. "The Relation Between Unemployment and the Rate of Change of Money Wage Rates in the United Kingdom, 1862–1957: A Further Analysis." *Economica* 27 (1960): 1–31.

Long, John B., Jr., and Charles I. Plosser. "Real Business Cycles." *Journal of Political Economy* 91 (1983): 39–69.

Lucas, Robert E., Jr., and Leonard Rapping. "Real Wages, Prices, and Inflation." *Journal of Political Economy* 77 (1969): 721–54.

———. "Real Wages, Employment, and Inflation." In *Microfoundations of Employment and Inflation Theory,* edited by Edmund S. Phelps, pp. 257–305. New York: W. W. Norton, 1970.

———. "Unemployment in the Great Depression: Is There a Full Explanation?" *Journal of Political Economy* 808 (1972): 186–91.

MacCurdy, Thomas E. "Interpreting Empirical Models of Labor Supply in an Intertemporal Framework with Uncertainty." In *Longitudinal Analysis of Labor Market Data,* edited by James J. Heckman and Burton Singer, pp. 111–55. Cambridge: Cambridge University Press, 1985.

Marshall, Ray. "Prepared Statement." *Hearings, The Unemployment Crisis and Policies for Economic Recovery,* Ninety-seventh Congress, Second Session, October 15, 1982, pp. 32–61. Washington, D.C.: Government Printing Office, 1983.

McCallum, Bennett T. "Rational Expectations and Macroeconomic Stabilization Policy: An Overview." *Journal of Money, Credit, and Banking* 12 (1980): 716–46.

McCloskey, Donald N. "The Rhetoric of Economics." *Journal of Economic Literature* 21 (1983): 481–517.

Mankiw, N. Gregory. "A Quick Refresher Course in Macroeconomics." *Journal of Economic Literature* 28 (1990): 1645–60.

Mayer, Thomas. "Consumption in the Great Depression." *Journal of Political Economy* 86 (1978): 139–45.

Mercer, Lloyd J., and W. Douglas Morgan. "The American Automobile Industry, Investment Demand, Capacity and Capacity Utilization, 1921–1940." *Journal of Political Economy* 80 (1972): 1214–31.

———. "Housing Surplus in the 1920s? Another Evaluation." *Explorations in Economic History* 10 (1973): 295–303.

Minsky, Hyman P. "Banking and Industry Between the Two Wars: The United States." *Journal of European Economic History* 13 (1984): 235–72.

Mishkin, Frederic S. "The Household Balance Sheet and the Great Depression." *Journal of Economic History* 38 (1978): 918–37.

Modigliani, Franco. "The Monetarist Controversy, or Should We Foresake Stabilization Policies?" *American Economic Review* 67 (1977): 1–19.

Moffitt, Robert. "Incentive Effects of the U.S. Welfare System: A Review." *Journal of Economic Literature* 30 (1992): 1–61.

Moulton, Brent R. "A Reexamination of the Federal-Private Wage Differential in the United States." *Journal of Labor Economics* 8 (1990): 270–93.

Myatt, Anthony, and David Murrell. "The Female/Male Unemployment Rate Differential." *Canadian Journal of Economics* 23 (1990): 312–22.

Neumark, David, and William Wachser. "Employment Effects of Minimum and Subminimum Wage Panel Data on State Minimum Wage Laws." *Industrial and Labor Relations Review,* October 1992, 55–81.

Nickell, Stephen F., and James Symons. "The Real Wage-Employment Relationship in the United States." *Journal of Labor Economics* 8 (1990): 1–15.

Noyes, C. Reinhold. "The Prospect for Economic Growth." *American Economic Review* 37 (1947): 13–33.

O'Brien, Anthony P. "A Behavioral Explanation for Nominal Wage Rigidity During the Great Depression." *Quarterly Journal of Economics* 104 (1989): 719–35.

Okun, Arthur M. "Potential GNP: Its Measurement and Significance." *Pro-*

ceedings, Business and Economics Section, American Statistical Association (1962): 98–104.

Parkin, Michael. "The Output-Inflation Tradeoff When Prices Are Costly to Change." *Journal of Political Economy* 94 (1986): 200–24.

Parsley, C. J. "Labor Union Effects on Wage Gains: A Survey of Recent Literature." *Journal of Economic Literature* 18 (1980): 1–31.

Pencavel, John. "Labor Supply of Men: A Survey." In *Handbook of Labor Economics,* edited by Orley Ashenfelter and Richard Layard, 1:3–102. Amsterdam: North Holland, 1986.

Peppers, Larry C. "Full-Employment Surplus Analysis and Structural Change: The 1930s." *Explorations in Economic History* 10 (1973): 197–210.

Phillips, A. W. "The Relation Between Unemployment and the Rate of Change of Money Wage Rates in the United Kingdom, 1861–1957." *Economica* 25 (1958): 283–99.

Pigou, Arthur C. "Wage Policy and Unemployment." *Economic Journal* 37 (1927): 355–68.

———. "Real and Money Wage Rates in Relation to Unemployment." *Economic Journal* 47 (1937): 405–22.

———. "Money Wages in Relation to Unemployment." *Economic Journal* 48 (1938): 134–38.

Plosser, C. I., G. W. Schwert, and Halbert White. "Differencing as a Test of Specification." *International Economic Review,* October 1982, 535–52.

Prescott, Edward C. "Theory Ahead of Business Cycle Measurement." *Carnegie-Rochester Conference Series on Public Policy* 25 (1986): 11–44.

Ratajczak, Donald. "Prepared Statement." *Hearings, The Unemployment Crisis and Policies for Economic Recovery,* Joint Economic Committee, Ninety-seventh Congress, Second Session, October 20, 1982, pp. 202–18. Washington, D.C.: Government Printing Office, 1983.

Rees, Albert. "Dimensions of the Unemployment Problem." In *The Battle Against Unemployment,* edited by Arthur M. Okun, pp. 23–31. New York: W. W. Norton, 1965.

Reuss, Henry. "Democratic Response to President's Radio Address." October 9, 1982, mimeograph. Circulated within Joint Economic Committee of Congress, October 1982.

Roberts, Paul Craig. "The Economic Case for Kemp-Roth." *Wall Street Journal,* August 1, 1978, p. 16.

Romer, Christina. "Spurious Volatility in Historical Unemployment Data." *Journal of Political Economy* 94 (1986): 1–37.

———. "Is the Stabilization of the Postwar Economy a Figment of the Data?" *American Economic Review* 76 (1986): 314–34.

———"New Estimates of Prewar Gross National Product and Unemployment." *Journal of Economic History* 46 (1986): 341–52.

Ropke, Wilhelm. "Welfare State and Chronic Inflation," in *Crisis of the Modern Welfare State.* Washington, D.C.: Joint Economic Committee of Congress, 1994. Excerpted and reprinted from Wilhelm Ropke, *A Humane Economy: The Social Framework of the Free Market,* translated and with an introduction by Marianne Cowan. Washington, D.C.: Regnery Publishing Company, 1962.

Roth, William. "Letter to the Editor." *Wall Street Journal,* July 17, 1978, p. 11.

Samuelson, Paul A. "The General Theory." In *The New Economics,* edited by Seymour Harris, pp. 145–60. New York: Knopf, 1947.

———. "Stability, Growth and Stagnation." In *Stability and Growth in the American Economy,* pp. 23–60. Stockholm: The Wicksell Lecture Society, 1963.

———. "Outlook for the '80s." *Newsweek,* December 15, 1980, p. 88.

———, and Robert M. Solow. "Analytical Aspects of Anti-Inflation Policy." *American Economic Review* 50 (1960): 177–94.

———, and Robert M. Solow. "Our Menu of Policy Choices." In *The Battle Against Unemployment,* edited by Arthur M. Okun. New York: W. W. Norton, 1965.

Sapir, Michael. "Review of Economic Forecasts for the Transition Period." In *Studies in Income and Wealth,* 11:275–351. New York: National Bureau of Economic Research, 1949.

Sargent, Thomas. "A Classical Macroeconomic Model." *Journal of Political Economy* 84 (1976): 207–37.

———, and Neil Wallace. "Rational Expectations, the Optimal Monetary Instrument, and the Optimal Money Supply Rule." *Journal of Political Economy* 83 (1975): 241–54.

Sawhill, Isabel. "Poverty in the U.S.: Why Is It So Persistent?" *Journal of Economic Literature* 26 (1988): 1073–1119.

Schlesinger, Arthur, Jr. "Statement." *Hearings, Political Economy and Constitutional Reform,* Joint Economic Committee, Ninety-seventh Congress, Second Session, Part I, November 17, 1982, pp. 221–30. Washington, D.C.: Government Printing Office, 1983.

Schumpeter, Joseph. "The Present World Depression: A Tentative Diagnosis." *American Economic Review* 21 (1931): 179–82.

Schwartz, Anna J. "Understanding 1929–1933." In *The Great Depression Revisited,* edited by Karl Brunner, pp. 5–48. Boston: Martinus Nijhoff, 1981.

Simler, Norman J. "Long-Term Unemployment, the Structural Hypothesis, and Public Policy." *American Economic Review* 54 (1964): 985–1001.

Simon, Curtis J., and Clark Nardinelli. "Does Industrial Diversity Always Reduce Unemployment? Evidence from the Great Depression and After." *Economic Inquiry* 30 (1992): 384–97.

Sinai, Allen. "Prepared Statement." *Hearings, The Unemployment Crisis and Poli-*

cies for Economic Recovery, Joint Economic Committee, Ninety-seventh Congress, Second Session, October 20, 1982, pp. 219–262. Washington, D.C.: Government Printing Office, 1983.

Slichter, Sumner A. "The Downturn of 1937." *Review of Economics and Statistics* 20 (1938): 97–110.

Slutsky, Eugen. "The Summation of Random Causes as the Source of Cyclic Processes." *Problems of Economic Conditions* (Moscow, ed. Conjuncture Institute) 3, no. 1 (1927). Reprinted in *Econometrica* 5 (1937): 105–46.

Smiley, Gene. "Recent Unemployment Rate Estimates for the 1920s and 1930s." *Journal of Economic History* 43 (1983): 487–93.

———. "Did Incomes for Most of the Population Fall From 1923 to 1929?" *Journal of Economic History* 43 (1983): 209–16.

———. "Some Austrian Perspectives on Keynesian Fiscal Policy and the Recovery in the Thirties." *Review of Austrian Economics* 1 (1987): 145–80.

———. "Does Keynesianism Explain the 1930s?" *Critical Review* 5 (1991): 81–114.

Smith, Margaret J. "Market Recognition of Changes in Financial Condition of Large Banks." *Comptroller of the Currency Staff Papers,* 1983–1.

Stein, Herbert. "The Real Reasons for a Tax Cut." *Wall Street Journal,* July 18, 1978, p. 20.

Stein, Jerome L. "Monetarist, Keynesian, and New Classical Economics." *American Economic Review* 71 (1981): 139–44.

Stiglitz, Joseph. "Theories of Wage Rigidity." In *Keynes' Economic Legacy: Contemporary Economic Theories,* edited by James L. Butkiewicz, Kenneth J. Koford, and Jeffrey B. Miller, pp. 153–206. New York: Praeger, 1986.

Sundstrom, William A. "Was There a Golden Age of Flexible Wages? Evidence from Ohio Manufacturing, 1892–1910." *Journal of Economic History* 50 (1990): 309–20.

Symons, Jim, and Andrew Newell. "The Macroeconomics of the Interwar Years: International Comparisons." In *Interwar Unemployment in International Perspective,* edited by Barry Eichengreen and Tim Hatton. Norwell, Mass.: Kluwer Academic Publishers, 1988.

Tarshis, Lorie. "Changes in Real and Money Wages." *Economic Journal* 49 (1939): 150–54.

Taylor, John B. "Aggregate Dynamics and Staggered Contracts." *Journal of Political Economy* 88 (1980): 1–23.

Temin, Peter. "Socialism and Wages in the Recovery from the Great Depression in the United States and Germany." *Journal of Economic History* 50 (1990): 297–307.

———, and Barrie A. Wigmore. "The End of One Big Deflation." *Explorations in Economic History* 27 (1990): 483–502.

Vedder, Richard K. "The Economic Status of U.S. Teachers, 1870–1987."

Ohio University Department of Economics Research Paper Series, no. 89-06.

————, and Lowell Gallaway. "What Caused the Great Depression? A Half Century Reassessment." Ohio University Department of Economics Research Paper Series, no. 85-19.

————. "The Great Depression of 1946." *Review of Austrian Economics* 5 (1991): 3–31.

————. "Racial Dimensions of the Davis–Bacon Act." Ohio University Department of Economics (1990).

————. "Racial Differences in Unemployment in the U.S., 1890–1990." *Journal of Economic History* 52 (1992).

————, and Lowell Gallway. "Spatial Variations in U.S. Unemployment." *Journal of Labor Research* 17 (1996): 445–61.

Volcker, Paul. "Statement." *Hearings, The Unemployment Crisis and Policies for Economic Recovery,* Joint Economic Committee, Ninety-seventh Congress, Second Session, November 24, 1982, pp. 289–97. Washington, D.C.: Government Printing Office, 1983.

Wallich, Henry C. "Postwar United States Monetary Policy Appraised" in American Assembly, *United States Monetary Policy,* edited by Neil H. Jacoby, pp. 91–117. 1st ed. New York: The American Assembly, Columbia University, 1958.

Wallis, John J. "Employment in the Great Depression: New Data and Hypotheses." *Explorations in Economic History* 26 (1989): 45–72.

Warburton, Clark. "The Volume of Money and the Price Level Between the World Wars." *Journal of Political Economy* 53 (1945): 150–63.

————. "The Misplaced Emphasis in Contemporary Business-Fluctuation Theory." *Journal of Business* 19 (1946): 199–220.

Weiner, Stuart E. "The Natural Rate of Unemployment: Concepts and Issues." *Economic Review, Federal Reserve Bank of Kansas City* (1986): 11–23.

Weinstein, Michael M. "Some Macroeconomic Impacts of the National Industrial Recovery Act, 1933–1935." In *The Great Depression Revisited,* edited by Karl Brunner, pp. 262–81. Boston: Kluwer Nijhoff, 1981.

Weir, David R. "The Reliability of Historical Macroeconomic Data for Comparing Cyclical Stability." *Journal of Economic History* 46 (1986): 353–65.

Wheelock, David C. "The Strategy Effectiveness and Consistency of Federal Reserve Monetary Policy, 1924–1933." *Explorations in Economic History* 26 (1989): 451–76.

White, Eugene N. "A Reinterpretation of the Banking Crisis of 1930." *Journal of Economic History* 44 (1984): 119–38.

Wicker, Elmus. "A Reconsideration of the Causes of the Banking Panic of 1930." *Journal of Economic History* 40 (1980): 571–83.

————. "Interest Rate and Expenditure Effects of the Banking Panic of 1930." *Explorations in Economic History* 19 (1982): 435–45.

Wirtz, Willard, "Prepared Statement." *Hearings, The Unemployment Crisis and Policies for Economic Recovery,* Joint Economic Committee, Ninety-seventh Congress, Second Session, October 15, 1982, pp. 62–74. Washington, D.C.: Government Printing Office, 1983.

Woytinsky, W. S. "The Maintenance of Full Employment After the Transition Period: Notes on Mr. Kalecki's Models." *American Economic Review* 36 (1946): 641–45.

————. "What Was Wrong in Forecasts of Postwar Depression?" *Journal of Political Economy* 55 (1947): 142–51.

Government Documents

U.S. Congress. *The 1992 Economic Report of the President.* Hearings before the Joint Economic Committee, Congress of the United States, 102nd Congress, January 9, 10, 13, and 31, 1992. Washington, D.C.: Government Printing Office, 1992.

U.S. Department of Commerce. *Survey of Current Business.* Washington, D.C.: Government Printing Office, various issues.

————, Bureau of the Census. *Biennial Census of Manufactures, 1931.* Washington, D.C.: Government Printing Office, 1935.

————. *Fifteenth Census of the United Sates: 1930, Unemployment,* vol. 2. Washington, D.C.: Government Printing Office, 1932.

————. *Fifteenth Census of the United States: 1930, Population,* vol. 4, *Occupations by States.* Washington, D.C.: Government Printing Office, 1933.

————. *Sixteenth Census of the United States: 1940, Population,* vol. 3, *The Labor Force.* Washington, D.C.: Government Printing Office, 1943.

————. *Historical Statistics of the United States, Colonial Times to 1957.* Washington, D.C.: Government Printing Office, 1960.

————. *Historical Statistics of the United States, Colonial Times to 1970.* Washington, D.C.: Government Printing Office, 1975.

————. *National Income and Product Accounts of the United States, 1929–1976.* Washington, D.C.: Government Printing Office, 1981.

————. *Statistical Abstract of the United States.* Washington, D.C.: Government Printing Office, various years.

U.S., Department of Commerce and Labor. *Occupations at the Twelfth Census.* Washington, D.C.: Government Printing Office, 1904.

U.S., Department of the Interior, Census Office. *Report on Population of the*

United States at the Eleventh Census: 1890, Part II. Washington, D.C.: Government Printing Office, 1897.

U.S., Federal Reserve System. *Federal Reserve Bulletin.* Washington, D.C.: Government Printing Office, various issues.

U.S., Office of the President. *Economic Report of the President 1947.* Washington, D.C.: Government Printing Office, 1947.

———. *Economic Report of the President 1962.* Washington, D.C.: Government Printing Office, 1962.

———. *The Mid-Year Economic Report of the President 1949.* Washington, D.C.: Government Printing Office, 1949.

——— *Economic Report of the President 1970.* Washington, D.C.: Government Printing Office, 1970.

———. *Economic Report of the President 1973.* Washington, D.C.: Government Printing Office, 1973.

———. *Economic Report of the President 1985.* Washington, D.C.: Government Printing Office, 1985.

———. *Economic Report of the President 1990.* Washington, D.C.: Government Printing Office, 1990.

———. *Economic Report of the President 1991.* Washington, D.C.: Government Printing Office, 1991.

———. *Economic Report of the President, 1995.* Washington, D.C.: Government Printing Office, 1995.

———. *Economic Report of the President, 1996.* Washington, D.C.: Government Printing Office, 1996.

———. *Report of the President's Conference on Unemployment.* Washington, D.C.: Government Printing Office, 1921.

U.S. Congress, Committee on Labor and Welfare, Subcommittee on Employment and Manpower. *The Nation's Manpower Revolution.* Washington, D.C.: Government Printing Office, 1965.

———, *Hearings, Political Economy and Constitutional Reform.* Washington, D.C.: Government Printing Office, 1983.

———, Joint Economic Committee, *Hearings, The Unemployment Crisis and Policies for Economic Recovery.* Washington, D.C.: Government Printing Office, 1983.

———, Joint Economic Committee, Subcommittee of Monetary and Fiscal Policy. *The War on Poverty—Victory or Defeat?* Washington, D.C.: Government Printing Office, 1986.

Index

ABOUT THE AUTHORS

Lowell E. Gallaway is research fellow at the Independent Institute and distinguished professor of economics, Ohio University. He received his Ph.D. in economics from Ohio State University. He has been staff economist, Joint Economic Committee of the Congress of the U.S.; chief, Analytic Studies Section, Social Security Administration; and has taught at Colorado State University, Lund University, University of Minnesota, University of New South Wales, University of North Carolina, University of Pennsylvania, and University of Texas. He is the author of *The Retirement Decision, Interindustry Labor Mobility in the United States, Geographic Labor Mobility in the United States, Manpower Economics,* and *Poverty in America.* His articles have appeared in such journals as *American Economic Review, American Journal of Agricultural Economics, Business History Review, Economy and History, Explorations in Economic History, Growth and Change, Industrial and Labor Relations Review, Journal of Business, Journal of Economic History, Journal of Human Resources, Journal of Political Economy, Labor History, National Tax Journal, Public Choice, Quarterly Journal of Economics, Review of Economics and Statistics, Southern Economic Journal, Swedish Journal of Economics,* and *Social Security Bulletin.*

Richard K. Vedder is research fellow at the Independent Institute and distinguished professor of economics and faculty associate, Contemporary History Institute, Ohio University. He received his Ph.D. in economics from the University of Illinois. He has taught at the University of Colorado, Claremont Men's College, MARA Institute of Technology, and was a John M. Olin Visiting Professor of Labor Economics and Public Policy at the Center for the Study of American Business, Washington University in St. Louis. He is the author of *The American Economy in Historical Perspective* and *Poverty, Income Distribution, the Family and Public Policy* (with L. Gallaway), and co-editor of *Essays in Nineteenth Century Economic History, Essays in the Economy of the Old Northwest,* and *Variations in Business and Economic History.* A contributor to numerous scholarly volumes, his articles and reviews have appeared in such journals as *Agricultural History, Business History Review, Canadian Journal of Economics, Economic Inquiry, Economy and History, Explorations in Economic History, Growth and Change, Journal of Economic History, Journal of Labor Research, Journal of Regional Science, South African Journal of Economics, Public Choice,* and *Research in Economic History.*

389

331.1379 VED 1997
Vedder, Richard K.
Out of work

$19.50

DATE		
MAR 2 0 2000		
MAR 2 6 2001		

DETROIT COLLEGE OF BUSINESS
4801 OAKMAN BLVD.
DEARBORN, MI 48126

BAKER & TAYLOR